THE THRONE OF WISDOM

ILENE H. FORSYTH

The THRONE OF WISDOM

WOOD SCULPTURES OF THE MADONNA IN ROMANESQUE FRANCE

PRINCETON UNIVERSITY PRESS

PRINCETON, NEW JERSEY

This book has been composed in Linotype Janson
Printed in the United States of America
by Princeton University Press, Princeton, New Jersey
Illustrations by the Meriden Gravure Company
Meriden, Connecticut

Frontispiece. New York, Metropolitan Museum of Art,
Morgan Madonna (Gift of
J. Pierpont Morgan, 1916), Reg. 1

To G. H. F.

Contents

LIST OF ILLUSTRATIONS   ix

PREFACE   xvii

INTRODUCTION   1

CHAPTER I. The Character of the Sculptures   8

Materials and Technique   10

"Black Virgins"   20

Iconography   22

CHAPTER II. Function   31

The Throne of Wisdom as a Reliquary   31

Location of the Statue in the Church   38

Processions   40

Secular Practices and Popular Attitudes   45

Devotional Practices and Miraculous Immunities   48

Liturgical Drama   49

Conclusion   60

CHAPTER III. Origins: The Throne of Wisdom
Statue and the Revival of Freestanding Sculpture   61

Pagan Mother Goddesses   62

The Christian Iconographic Tradition   65

The Revival of Freestanding Sculpture and the Cult of Relics   67

The Throne   86

Conclusion   90

CHAPTER IV. Statues of the Throne of Wisdom
Prior to 1100   92

Literary Evidence   92

Extant Examples   112

Conclusion   133

CHAPTER V. The Twelfth Century   134

Regional Styles   134

Conclusion   152

REGISTER OF PRINCIPAL EXAMPLES   156

APPENDIX I   205

APPENDIX II   207

SELECTED BIBLIOGRAPHY   209

INDEX   219

ILLUSTRATIONS   227

List of Illustrations

Frontispiece. New York, Metropolitan Museum of Art, Morgan Madonna (Gift of J. Pierpont Morgan, 1916), Reg. 1
Photo: Metropolitan Museum of Art

Map, facing p. 4, Romanesque Statues of the Throne of Wisdom in France

1. Arezzo, Sta Maria della Pieve, Adoration of the Magi
Photo: Alinari

2. Beaucaire (Gard), Museum, Madonna enthroned as the Throne of Wisdom
Photo: Marburg

3. Clermont-Ferrand (Puy-de-Dôme), Bibl. Municipale, MS 145, fol. 130v, Golden Majesty of Clermont-Ferrand
Photo: Clermont-Ferrand, Bibl. Municipale

4. Antwerp, Plantin-Moretus Museum, M.17.4, fol. 15v, Adoration of the Magi
Photo: Photo 't Felt

5. Clermont-Ferrand (Puy-de-Dôme), Notre-Dame-du-Port, south portal, lintel, Adoration of the Magi
Photo: Marburg

6. Tournus (Saône-et-Loire), Saint-Philibert, *Notre-Dame la Brune* from Saint-Pourçain-sur-Sioule (Allier), Reg. 30
Photo: Archives Photographiques

7. Pompierre (Vosges), tympanum, Adoration of the Magi
Photo: author

8. Mont-devant-Sassey (Meuse), Madonna (before restoration), Reg. 96
Photo: Archives Photographiques

9. Frankfurt-am-Main, Liebieghaus, Madonna from Schillingskapellen
Photo: Gabriele Busch-Hauck, courtesy Städtische Galerie, Frankfurt-am-Main

10. Oberpleis, Adoration of the Magi, retable
Photo: Marburg

11. Bernard (Vendée), mother goddess
Photo: after Saillens

12. Saint-Germain-en-Laye, Musée des Antiquités Nationales, cast after a lost original from Prunay-le-Gillon (Eure-et-Loir), mother and child
Photo: Belzeaux-Zodiaque

13. Conques (Aveyron), St. Foy
Photo: Archives Photographiques

14. Conques (Aveyron), St. Foy, detail of the head
Photo: Archives Photographiques

15. Conques (Aveyron), St. Foy, detail
Photo: Archives Photographiques

16. Le Monastier (Haute-Loire), St. Chaffre
Photo: Archives Photographiques

17. Le Monastier (Haute-Loire), St. Chaffre with metal sheath removed
Photo: Archives Photographiques

18. Paris, Bibl. Nationale, MS lat. 17558, fol. 28r, drawing by Peiresc of the reliquary head of St. Maurice, 879-887
Photo: Bibl. Nationale

19. Paris, Bibl. Nationale, MS lat. 17558, fol. 28v, drawing by Peiresc of the reliquary head of St. Maurice, 879-887, with the crown of Hugh of Arles, 926-947
Photo: Bibl. Nationale

20. Paris, Bibl. Nationale, MS gr. 510, fol. 355, *Homilies of Gregory Nazianzus*, 867-886, the Emperor and dignitaries before the throne
Photo: Bibl. Nationale

21. Venice, San Marco, *Sedia*
Photo: Alinari

22. Aachen, Palace Chapel, Throne of Charlemagne
Photo: Ann Münchow, Aachen

23. Bern, Bürgerbibliothek, Codex 120, fol. 147, Peter of Eboli, *Liber ad Honorem Augusti*, late twelfth century, Henry VI seated on the *sedes sapientiae*
Photo: Bürgerbibliothek, Bern

24. *Notre-Dame du Puy*, engraving from B. Faujas de Saint-Fond, 1778
Photo: after Faujas de Saint-Fond

25. *Notre-Dame de Chartres*, drawing by Chanoine Etienne in 1682
Photo: Yves Delaporte

26. *Notre-Dame de Chartres*, seventeenth-century engraving by Leroux
Photo: Yves Delaporte

27. *Notre-Dame de Chartres* carried on a litter, engraving of a pilgrim's badge or *signum*
Photo: after Forgeais

28-31. Essen, Minster, Golden Madonna
Photos: Marburg

32. Essen, Minster, Golden Madonna, detail of the underside of the throne
Photo: Marburg

33. Essen, Minster Treasury, detail of the First Mathilda Cross, 974-982
Photo: Marburg

34. Cologne, Cathedral, Gero Cross
Photo: Rheinisches Bildarchiv

35. Dublin, Trinity College, *Book of Kells*, Madonna and Child
Photo: Board of Trinity College, Dublin; The Green Studio Ltd.

36. Essen, Minster Treasury, Theophanu Book Cover, ca. 1039-1056, detail of the Madonna enthroned
Photo: Marburg

37, 38. Hildesheim, Cathedral Treasury, Golden Madonna with gold sheath removed
Photos: Photo-Wehmeyer, Hildesheim

39. Hildesheim, Cathedral Treasury, Golden Madonna with gold sheath removed; back view showing removable panel
Photo: Rheinisches Bildarchiv

40, 41. Hildesheim, Cathedral Treasury, fragments of the gold sheath of the Madonna
Photos: Hans Nölter, Hannover

42. Hildesheim, Bronze Doors of Bernward, 1015, detail of the Madonna from the Adoration of the Magi
Photo: Photo-Wehmeyer, Hildesheim

43. Mainz, Altertumsmuseum, Ivory Madonna
Photo: Rheinisches Bildarchiv

44. Paderborn, Diözesan Museum, Imad Madonna, 1051-1076, the back before recent restoration
Photo: Rheinisches Bildarchiv

45, 46. Paderborn, Diözesan Museum, Imad Madonna, 1051-1076
Photos: Landesdenkmalamt, Westfalen

47a,b. Essen-Werden, Abbey Church, stone reliefs with enthroned figures
Photos: Marburg

48. Cologne, Schnütgen Museum, Madonna
Photo: Rheinisches Bildarchiv

49. Frankfurt-am-Main, Liebieghaus, Madonna
Photo: Gabriele Busch-Hauck, courtesy Städtische Galerie, Frankfurt-am-Main

50, 51. Walcourt, Saint-Materne, *Notre-Dame de Walcourt*
Photos: A.C.L., Brussels

52. Brussels, Musées Royaux d'Art et d'Histoire, Madonna from Hermalle-sous-Huy
Photo: A.C.L., Brussels

53. Liège, Musée Diocésain, Madonna from Evegnée
Photo: A.C.L., Brussels

54, 55. New York, Metropolitan Museum of Art, Morgan Madonna (Gift of J. Pierpont Morgan, 1916), Reg. 1
Photos: Metropolitan Museum of Art

56. New York, Metropolitan Museum of Art, Morgan Madonna (Gift of J. Pierpont Morgan, 1916), detail of the head, Reg. 1
Photo: Metropolitan Museum of Art

57. Moussages (Cantal), Saint-Barthélémy, *Notre-Dame de Claviers*, detail of the head, Reg. 2
Photo: Archives Photographiques

58, 59. Moussages (Cantal), Saint-Barthélémy, *Notre-Dame de Claviers*, Reg. 2
Photos: Archives Photographiques

60, 61. Private Collection, *Notre-Dame de Montvianeix*, Reg. 3
Photos: private collection

62. Private Collection, *Notre-Dame de Montvianeix*, detail of the head, Reg. 3
Photo: after Bréhier, "Vierges romanes"

63. Private Collection, *Notre-Dame de Montvianeix*, Reg. 3
Photo: after Bréhier, "Vierges romanes"

64a. Heume l'Eglise (Puy-de-Dôme), before restoration, Reg. 4
Photo: Bernard Craplet

64b. Heume l'Eglise (Puy-de-Dôme), after restoration, Reg. 4
Photo: author

65. Aubusson (Puy-de-Dôme), *Notre-Dame d'Aubusson*, Reg. 5
Photo: after Bréhier, "Vierges romanes"

66. Parentignat (Puy-de-Dôme), Château de Lastic, Reg. 6
Photo: Archives Photographiques

67. Molompize (Cantal), Vauclair Chapel, *Notre-Dame de Vauclair*, Reg. 7
Photo: Archives Photographiques

68. Cologne, Burg Collection (formerly), Reg. 8
Photo: Marburg

69. Saint-Gervazy (Puy-de-Dôme), *Notre-Dame de Saint-Gervazy*, Reg. 9
Photo: Archives Photographiques

70. Nancy (Meurthe-et-Moselle), Private Collection I, Reg. 10
Photo: Archives Photographiques

71. Geneva, Musée d'Art et d'Histoire, Reg. 11
Photo: Marburg

72. Rouen (Seine-Maritime), Musée Départemental des Antiquités de la Seine-Maritime, Reg. 12
Photo: Ellebé, Rouen

73. Rochelambert (Haute-Loire), Château, Reg. 13
Photo: Velay-Photo

74. Paris, Musée de Cluny, Reg. 14
Photo: Réunion des Musées Nationaux

75. Saint-Nectaire (Puy-de-Dôme), *Notre-Dame du Mont-Cornadore*, Reg. 15
Photo: Archives Photographiques

76. Saint-Rémy-de-Chargnat (Puy-de-Dôme), *Notre-Dame de Saint-Rémy*, before restoration, Reg. 16
Photo: after Bréhier, "Vierges romanes"

77. Saint-Laurent-Chabreuges (Haute-Loire), Entremont Chapel, *Notre-Dame d'Entremont*, Reg. 17
Photo: author

78. Chanaleilles (Haute-Loire), *Notre-Dame du Villeret d'Apchier*, Reg. 18
Photo: Monuments Historiques

79. Mailhat, near Lamontgie (Puy-de-Dôme), *Notre-Dame de Mailhat*, Reg. 19
Photo: author

80. Washington, D.C., Collection of Mr. and Mrs. Robert Sargent Shriver, Jr., Reg. 20
Photo: French and Co.

81. Geneva, Giraud Collection, Reg. 21
Photo: Giraud

82. Zurich, Bührle Collection, Reg. 22
Photo: E. G. Bührle Collection

83. Durham, North Carolina, Duke University Museum, Reg. 23
Photo: Duke University

84. Raleigh, The North Carolina Museum of Art, Reg. 24
Photo: North Carolina Museum of Art

85. Bredons (Cantal) I, formerly in the church at Albepierre-Bredons, Reg. 25
Photo: Archives Photographiques

86. Thiers (Puy-de-Dôme), Private Collection, *Notre-Dame de Montpeyroux*, Reg. 26
Photo: author

87. Chauriat (Puy-de-Dôme), Reg. 27
Photo: author

88. Echlache (Puy-de-Dôme), Reg. 29
Photo: author

89. Tournus (Saône-et-Loire), Saint-Philibert, *Notre-Dame la Brune* from Saint-Pourçain-sur-Sioule (Allier), Reg. 30
Photo: Archives Photographiques

90, 91. Orcival (Puy-de-Dôme), *Notre-Dame d'Orcival*, Reg. 31
Photos: Archives Photographiques

92, 93. Orcival (Puy-de-Dôme), *Notre-Dame d'Orcival* during restoration, with metal sheath removed, Reg. 31
Photos: Archives Photographiques

94. Orcival (Puy-de-Dôme), *Notre-Dame d'Orcival*, detail, Reg. 31
Photo: Archives Photographiques

95. New York, Metropolitan Museum of Art, loaned by Mr. and Mrs. A. B. Martin (Guennol Collection), Reg. 32
Photo: Metropolitan Museum of Art

96. New York, Metropolitan Museum of Art, loaned by Mr. and Mrs. A. B. Martin (Guennol Collection), detail of the head, Reg. 32
Photo: Metropolitan Museum of Art

97a. Lyon (Rhône), Musée des Beaux-Arts, *Notre-Dame de Saint-Flour*, Reg. 33
Photo: J. Camponogara, Lyon

97b. Lyon (Rhône), Musée des Beaux-Arts, *Notre-Dame de Saint-Flour*, Reg. 33
Photo: Cliché Photothèque Cantalienne, G. Francheschi

98-100. Paris, Louvre, Reg. 34
Photos: Archives Photographiques

101. Marsat (Puy-de-Dôme), *Notre-Dame de Marsat*, Reg. 35
Photo: Marburg

102. Chalus-Lembron (Puy-de-Dôme), Reg. 36
Photo: author

103. Clermont-Ferrand (Puy-de-Dôme), Musée Bargoin I, Reg. 37
Photo: Arriat, Clermont-Ferrand

104. New York, Metropolitan Museum of Art (Bequest of Michael Dreicer, 1921), Reg. 38
Photo: Metropolitan Museum of Art

105. Chassignoles (Haute-Loire), *Notre-Dame de Chassignoles*, Reg. 39
Photo: after Bréhier, "Vierges romanes"

106. Vergheas (Puy-de-Dôme), *Notre-Dame de l'Assomption*, Reg. 40
Photo: Archives Photographiques

107. Tourzel-Ronzières (Puy-de-Dôme), *Notre-Dame de Ronzières*, Reg. 41
Photo: Belzeaux-Zodiaque

108. Nancy (Meurthe-et-Moselle), Private Collection II, *Sainte-Marie de Verdun*, Reg. 43
Photo: Lott, Nancy

109. Mailhat, near Lamontgie (Puy-de-Dôme), Private Collection, *Notre-Dame de Mailhat*, Reg. 44
Photo: Archives Photographiques

110. Clermont-Ferrand (Puy-de-Dôme), Notre-Dame-du-Port, south portal, lintel, detail of the Madonna from the Adoration of the Magi
Photo: Marburg

111. Espalion-Perse (Aveyron), Madonna, stone relief
Photo: Yan-Zodiaque

112. Saugues (Haute-Loire), *Notre-Dame de Saugues*, Reg. 45
Photo: Buffière

113. Monistrol d'Allier (Haute-Loire), Champels Chapel, *Notre-Dame d'Estours*, Reg. 46
Photo: Antoine Mappus, Le Puy

114. Monistrol d'Allier (Haute-Loire), Champels Chapel, *Notre-Dame d'Estours*, detail of the head before restoration, Reg. 46
Photo: after Bréhier, "Vierges romanes"

115. La Chomette (Haute-Loire), Reg. 47
Photo: author

116. Bredons (Cantal) II, from Albepierre-Bredons, Reg. 49
Photo: Archives Photographiques

117. Cologne, Seligmann Collection (formerly), Reg. 50
Photo: Rheinisches Bildarchiv

118. Clermont-Ferrand (Puy-de-Dôme), Musée Bargoin II, *Notre-Dame de Vernols*, Reg. 51
Photo: Marburg

119. Rome, Private Collection, Reg. 52
Photo: Fondazione Artistica Poldi-Pezzoli, Milan

120. Zurich, Kunsthaus, Reg. 53
Photo: Kunsthaus, Zurich

121. Paris, Musée des Arts Décoratifs, Reg. 54
Photo: Musée des Arts Décoratifs

122. Laurie (Cantal), *Notre-Dame de Laurie*, Reg. 55
Photo: Archives Photographiques

123. Philadelphia, Museum of Art I, Reg. 56
Photo: Philadelphia Museum of Art

124. Thuir (Pyrénées-Orientales), *Notre-Dame-de-la-Victoire*, Reg. 57
Photo: Archives Photographiques

125. Châteauneuf-les-Bains (Puy-de-Dôme), Reg. 58
Photo: Archives Photographiques

126. Prunières (Lozère), Reg. 59
Photo: Archives Photographiques

127. Corneilla-de-Conflent (Pyrénées-Orientales), Reg. 60
Photo: Monuments Historiques

128. Odeillo (Pyrénées-Orientales), *Notre-Dame de Font-Romeu*, Reg. 61
Photo: Monuments Historiques

129. Err (Pyrénées-Orientales), Reg. 62
Photo: Archives Photographiques

130. Prats-Balaguer (Pyrénées-Orientales), Reg. 63
Photo: Monuments Historiques

131. Montbolo (Pyrénées-Orientales),
Reg. 64
Photo: Archives Photographiques

132. Planès (Pyrénées-Orientales), *Notre-Dame de Planès*, Reg. 65
Photo: Archives Photographiques

133. Cazarilh-Laspènes (Haute-Garonne),
Reg. 66
Photo: Archives Photographiques

134. Saint-Savin (Hautes-Pyrénées),
Museum, Reg. 67
Photo: Archives Photographiques

135. Saint-Savin (Hautes-Pyrénées), *La Vierge de Castère*, Reg. 68
Photo: Archives Photographiques

136. Luz (Hautes-Pyrénées), Saint-Sauveur,
Reg. 69
Photo: Archives Photographiques

137. Aragnouet (Hautes-Pyrénées), Le Plan Chapel, *Notre-Dame d'Aragnouet*,
Reg. 70
Photo: Archives Photographiques

138. Hix (Pyrénées-Orientales), Bourg-Madame, *Notre-Dame de la Cerdagne*,
Reg. 71
Photo: Archives Photographiques

139. Manosque (Basses-Alpes), *Notre-Dame de Romigier*, Reg. 72
Photo: Monuments Historiques

140. Dorres (Pyrénées-Orientales), Reg. 73
Photo: after Duby

141. Targasonne (Pyrénées-Orientales),
Reg. 74
Photo: Monuments Historiques

142. Frankfurt-am-Main, Private Collection (formerly), Reg. 77
Photo: after Schmitt and Swarzenski

143. Rocamadour (Lot), *Notre-Dame de Rocamadour*, Reg. 78
Photo: J. Vertuel, Saint-Céré

144. Monteignet (Allier), Reg. 79
Photo: author

145. Vernouillet (Allier), Musée Communal de Bourbon l'Archambault, *Notre-Dame de Vernouillet*, Reg. 80
Photo: after Bréhier, "Vierges romanes"

146. Souvigny (Allier), Saint-Pierre, sacristy, Reg. 81
Photo: Archives Photographiques

147. Nancy (Meurthe-et-Moselle), Private Collection III, Reg. 82
Photo: Lott, Nancy

148. Nancy (Meurthe-et-Moselle), Private Collection IV, Reg. 83
Photo: Lott, Nancy

149. Nancy (Meurthe-et-Moselle), Private Collection V, Reg. 84
Photo: Lott, Nancy

150. Nancy (Meurthe-et-Moselle), Private Collection VI, Reg. 85
Photo: Lott, Nancy

151. Meillers (Allier), Reg. 86
Photo: Archives Photographiques

152, 153. New York, Metropolitan Museum of Art, The Cloisters (Purchase 1947),
Reg. 87
Photos: Metropolitan Museum of Art

154. Dijon (Côte-d'Or), Notre-Dame, *Notre-Dame de Bon Espoir*, engraving after V. Petit, Reg. 88
Photo: after Caumont

155. Dijon (Côte-d'Or), Notre-Dame, *Notre-Dame de Bon Espoir*, Reg. 88
Photo: Archives Photographiques

156, 157. Saint-Denis (Seine-Saint-Denis, formerly Seine), destroyed sculptures from west facade, drawings by B. Montfaucon
Photos: Bibl. Nationale

158. Etampes (Yvelines, formerly Seine-et-Oise), south portal, left embrasure, a queen
Photo: Archives Photographiques

159. Chartres (Eure-et-Loir), Royal Portal, left portal, left embrasure, Old Testament figure
Photo: Marburg

160. Chartres (Eure-et-Loir), Royal Portal, right portal, right embrasure, Old Testament queen
Photo: Marburg

161. Chartres (Eure-et-Loir), Royal Portal, central portal, left embrasure, Old Testament queen
Photo: Marburg

162. Vievy (Côte-d'Or), Reg. 89
Photo: author

163. Thoisy-le-Désert (Côte-d'Or), Reg. 90
Photo: Archives Photographiques

164. Worcester, Massachusetts, Worcester Art Museum, Reg. 92
Photo: Worcester Art Museum

165. Collegeville, Minnesota, St. John's Abbey, Reg. 93
Photo: Taylor and Dull

166. Billy-Chevannes (Nièvre), Reg. 94
Photo: Archives Photographiques

167. Nevers (Nièvre), Musée Lapidaire de la Porte du Croux, Reg. 95
Photo: Marburg

168. Mont-devant-Sassey (Meuse), detail, Reg. 96
Photo: Kunsthistorisches Institut der Universität des Saarlandes, Saarbrücken

169. Mont-devant-Sassey (Meuse), Reg. 96
Photo: Kunsthistorisches Institut der Universität des Saarlandes, Saarbrücken

170. Vic (Moselle), *Notre-Dame d'Allyn*, Reg. 97
Photo: Archives de la Moselle

171. Jouhe (Jura), *Notre-Dame de Montroland*, Reg. 98
Photo: Monuments Historiques

172. Mouziey-Teulet (Tarn), Reg. 99
Photo: Archives Photographiques

173. Poitiers (Vienne), Abbey of Sainte-Croix, *Notre-Dame de Grâce*, Reg. 100
Photo: author

174. Beaulieu (Corrèze), Reg. 101
Photo: Archives Photographiques

175. Beaulieu (Corrèze), detail, Reg. 101
Photo: Archives Photographiques

176. Beaulieu (Corrèze), Reg. 101
Photo: Archives Photographiques

177. Paris, Louvre, retable from Carrières-Saint-Denis
Photo: Marburg

178. Cambridge, Massachusetts, Fogg Art Museum (Gift of Friends of the Fogg), Reg. 102
Photo: Fogg Art Museum

179. Cambridge, Massachusetts, Fogg Art Museum (Gift of Friends of the Fogg), detail of the head, Reg. 102
Photo: Fogg Art Museum

180, 181. Cambridge, Massachusetts, Fogg Art Museum (Gift of Friends of the Fogg), Reg. 102
Photos: Fogg Art Museum

182. Senlis (Oise), Notre-Dame, detail of the tympanum
Photo: Marburg

183. Jouy-en-Josas (Yvelines, formerly Seine-et-Oise), *La Diège*, Reg. 103
Photo: author

184. Limay (Yvelines, formerly Seine-et-Oise), Reg. 104
Photo: Archives Photographiques

185. Saint-Denis (Seine-Saint-Denis, formerly Seine), *Notre-Dame de Saint-Denis*, from Saint-Martin-des-Champs, Paris, Reg. 105
Photo: Archives Photographiques

186. Baltimore, The Walters Art Gallery, Reg. 106
Photo: Walters Art Gallery

187. Philadelphia, Museum of Art II, loaned by Raymond Pitcairn, Reg. 107
Photo: Demotte Photo Collection

188a,b. New Haven, Connecticut, Yale University Art Gallery, stone sculpture of the Madonna and Child from the church of Saint-Martin at Angers (Gift of Maitland F. Griggs)
Photos: Yale University Art Galley

189. Saumur (Maine-et-Loire), *Notre-Dame de Nantilly*, Reg. 108
Photo: author

190. Soissons (Aisne), from Presles-et-Thierry, Reg. 109
Photo: Carl F. Barnes, Jr.

Preface

THIS BOOK has grown out of an interest in the enigmatic rebirth of monumental sculpture in the Middle Ages. My fascination with the subject began when I was a graduate student and it led me to study wood statues of the Throne of Wisdom type in a doctoral dissertation at Columbia University in 1960. It was entitled "Cult Statues of the Madonna in the Early Middle Ages," and included discussion of examples of the type from most of Western Europe. The present work expands the investigation of the revival of sculpture and then concentrates on the history of the Throne of Wisdom statue in France down through the twelfth century. Research on these matters has been as continuous as academic life allows, first at Columbia University and then at The University of Michigan. It was given particular impetus in 1965 when a leave of absence from teaching duties and a Horace H. Rackham Travel Grant and Fellowship enabled me to make intensive field studies in France. The freedom of a sabbatical leave in 1969-1970 made it possible to prepare the text for the press.

In the course of these undertakings friendly assistance was provided by numerous persons. It is a special pleasure to acknowledge the help of scholars in France, particularly officials in the Monuments Historiques who authorized me to examine their archives and helped arrange inspection of sculptures in locations often remote and sometimes difficult of access. Among these learned government officials M. Jacques Dupont, M. Jean Taralon and M. François Enaud deserve my particular thanks, also M. Raymond Oursel, M. Pierre Fournier, M. Bruno Tournilhac and M. Paul Jourdan. Professor Louis Grodecki, Professor Pierre Quarré and Mme Marie-Madeleine Gauthier gave generous assistance. I owe much to the efficient aid of Mlle Maître-Devallon and Mlle Vinsot at the Monuments Historiques. The many curés who responded so courteously to my interest in "their" statues are gratefully remembered.

In Germany distinguished scholars who gave me essential advice in the early phases of my study include Professors Alois Fuchs, Harald Keller, Otto Lehmann-Brockhaus, Florentine Mütherich, Hermann Schnitzler, Drs. Wilhelm and Rosemarie Messerer and Dr. Karl-August Wirth. To my friends, Drs. Hilde Claussen, Dorothea Kluge and Ruth Meyer, I owe a debt of professional and personal gratitude.

In America officials of the Metropolitan Museum rendered every courtesy and particular thanks are due to Dr. Thomas P. F. Hoving, Dr. Florens Deuchler, Thomas Pelham Miller, Miss Carmen Gómez-Moreno and Mrs. Vera Ostoia. To William H. Forsyth, whose own work has illumined many of my research problems, I owe most

xvii

sincere appreciation for continuing interest in the present study and invaluable advice concerning it. In New England, my particular debts are to Professors John Coolidge and Agnes Mongan at the Fogg Art Museum, Dr. Hanns Swarzenski at the Institute of Fine Arts, Boston, and to Miss Louise Dresser in the Worcester Museum. I am also grateful to Professors Harry Bober, Ernst Kitzinger and Gerhart Ladner, who made most helpful suggestions, and to Professor Julius Held and Professor Mojmir Frinta, who provided expert counsel on connoisseurship problems.

To those who aided my doctoral research at Columbia, the bond of gratitude and respect remains strong. Professors Marion Lawrence and Robert Branner provided excellent guidance and Professor Rudolf Wittkower lent his encouragement and interest. Professors Otto Brendel, W.T.H. Jackson and John Mundy were most generous of their time and gave helpful criticism. To Professor Meyer Schapiro, who directed my doctoral dissertation, I feel a particular obligation for the example of his scholarly breadth, probity and insight, which are an enduring inspiration to all his students. While at Columbia my graduate study was underwritten by various University Fellowships and my doctoral research was supported by a grant from the Fels Foundation. I should like to express my thanks to those whose confidence in my work provided these indispensable aids to its success.

Among my colleagues at The University of Michigan who have offered helpful comments along with the stimulus of scholarly discussion, Professors Marvin Eisenberg, Oleg Grabar and Clifton Olds deserve special mention. In particular I am indebted to Professor Roger Pack who kindly reviewed the Latin translations. For bibliographical assistance I am grateful to the efficient Inter-Library Loan Service of the University Library and particularly to Miss Mary E. Rollman who brought treasures from afar for me to consult. To the late Mary Chamberlin, formerly librarian of the Art History Library at Columbia University, who took an early interest in my work, I should like to pay special tribute. Of the many officials who rendered courtesies in various other libraries and archives, those in the Widener Library at Harvard and in the Marburg photo archive are especially remembered and appreciated. Grateful thanks are also extended to the following scholars who took pains to make important photographs available to me: Carl F. Barnes, Jr., Justus Bier, Hilde Claussen, Robert C. Moeller, André Muzac, Raymond Oursel, Richard H. Randall, Jr., and Johanna Winkler. Many other people and institutions helped with the procurement of photographs and kindly allowed them to be reproduced. Their names will be found in the List of Illustrations.

I should also like to express gratitude to my own graduate students whose enthusiasm for the Middle Ages, freshly acquired, constantly refreshes my own. To Lois Drewer I owe an immense debt for research assistance of such a high order as to make our enterprise a true collaboration in scholarly discovery.

Finally I wish to acknowledge the good-natured patience of my husband, who willingly served as a sounding board for my ideas about medieval Virgins and who heard, I am sure, more about them than he really cared to know.

ILENE H. FORSYTH

June 1, 1970   Ann Arbor, Michigan

Introduction

owever grandly the French cathedral conjures up the medieval vision of Christian divinity, the revelation is diffuse, while the Romanesque wood statue of the Madonna in Majesty focuses it in a concise expression of the Incarnation dogma. The statue presents an enthroned Mother and Child. It is normally small, somewhat under life-size, yet monumental in portraying the *sedes sapientiae*, the Throne of Wisdom, a complex concept wherein the Virgin is seen in majesty, hence called *Maiestas*, and is understood as both the Mother of God and the *cathedra* or seat of the Logos incarnate.[1]

[1] *Sedes sapientiae* is often translated, quite properly, as "Seat of Wisdom," in preference to "Throne of Wisdom," thereby stressing the meaning of "seat" as a center or dwelling-place. However, such implications are subsumed in the meaning of the word "throne," which indicates a seat endowed with sovereign power and dignity. Although either "seat" or "throne" is correct for general usage (in French, however, the phrase *Trône de Sagesse* is customary), the art-historical term for the *sedes sapientiae* iconography is "Throne of Wisdom," an expression appropriate to the complexity of the concept and to our enthroned figures with their emphasis upon majesty.

Curiously, the statues under review were not named in any consistent manner in medieval literature, a fact which seriously complicates their study. *Maiestas* commonly refers to sculptures of the type under discussion, but it is not used exclusively for Madonnas and it does not necessarily connote three-dimensional sculpture; a two-dimensional image could also be intended. It is primarily a title of honor, indicating an image enthroned in majesty, as in the following: Christ in Majesty (*Maiestas Domini*), the Madonna in Majesty (*Maiestas Sanctae Mariae*), a saint enthroned such as the Majesty of St. Foy at Conques (*Maiestas Sanctae Fidis*) and the Majesty of St. Privatus at Mende (see below, Chapter II, note 33 and Chapter I, note 18). Of course it may also be used in connection with a secular sovereign; Suger so refers to Louis VI in his life of the king (Chapter IV, note 64 below). Despite these additional meanings it is a peculiarly appropriate term for the freestanding statues which are the object of this study. Medieval documents may use *statua* when three-dimensional statuary is intended. The ninth-century statues of Solomon and Ragenarius, and the Crucifix at Le Mans from the same period, are all referred to by that term (Chapter III, notes 79-80, 69). Bernard of Angers uses *statua* to describe reliquary statues in general (Chapter III, note 118) or to refer to the specific reliquaries of St. Foy and St. Geraldus (Chapter I, note 11). In the same passages he uses the term *imago* for those works, however, and he also uses the word *Maiestas* repeatedly, with particular reference to the St. Foy. *Effigies* is another possibility. It is used by Bernard of Angers and it also appears in the tenth-century description of the portrait statue of King Lothar (Chapter I, note 11; Chapter III, note 81). *Icona* is another commonly encountered term, which can pertain either to an icon, i.e. a two-dimensional picture on a

As a mother, she supports her son in her lap, yet as the Mother of God she serves as a throne for the incarnation of Divine Wisdom. Thus Christ's humanity and divinity are equally apparent in the image so that it expresses clearly and simply the profound meaning of the Incarnation. The theme impinges upon related subjects such as Mary the Virgin Mother, Mary as the *Theotokos*, and Mary as the Throne of Solomon. Translated into pictorial imagery in Early Christian times, the concept had an old iconography. What was new in the early medieval West was its portrayal in fully plastic, freestanding form. Sculpture as the most representational of the arts was capable of rendering the Incarnation with particular immediacy. In an age when sculpture in the round was still in a nascent stage, such an image was understandably potent.

The Majesties which expressed this concept have often retained their charisma down to the present day. Intimate in their relationship to the observer, yet hieratically aloof in style, these rigidly majestic figures have always commanded respect and veneration. Inspiring the devotion of worshipers, they were, and often still are, true cult statues. With an air of monumental calm they receive the petitions of the faithful; they are credited with countless miracles; they are subjected to cult practices such as the

---

panel, or a sculpture in the round. The latter is clearly the intention at Limoges with respect to the statue of St. Martial and at Châtillon-sur-Loire for the statue of the Virgin (Chapter II, notes 15 and 20, Chapter III, note 102 and Chapter IV, note 25). The Châtillon-sur-Loire statue is also described by the word *idea* (Chapter IV, note 25). The most common term for a statue in the literary sources is *imago*. The statue of the Madonna at Vézelay is so described (Chapter II, note 7), likewise the silver reliquary statue of St. Peter at Cluny (Chapter II, notes 15, 17), the statues of St. Foy at Conques, St. Gerald at Aurillac (Chapter I, note 11) and St. Privatus at Mende (Chapter I, note 18), as well as the statues of the Virgin at Chartres (Chapter IV, note 50), at Le Puy (Chapter IV, note 48), Ely (Chapter IV, note 22), Rodez (Chapter IV, note 19), Coventry (Chapter IV, note 28), Avallon (Chapter IV, note 27), Abingdon (Chapter II, note 10), Ghent (Chapter II, note 9) and Essen (Chapter IV, note 87). The chief text we have for the Clermont-Ferrand Majesty of Mary includes descriptive references to this statue as both *imago* and *Maiestas* used interchangeably (Chapter IV, notes 5, 7, 8). Consequently no single term employed by medieval chroniclers refers to statuary as distinct from relief sculpture or other media of representation, and one can determine their meaning only from a careful study of the context. If relics are mentioned within the image, one can usually be sure of a three-dimensional form. Indeed, this fact may have contributed to the theory which finds the origin of freestanding sculpture in reliquaries. There are undoubtedly many other sculptures mentioned in the literature which remain unrecognized because the term *imago* is ambiguous.

The inevitable conclusion is that no exclusive expression exists for our particular type of statue in the Middle Ages even though this genre seems very distinctive to us. Such a situation, reminiscent of ambiguous literary references to cult statues in Classical antiquity, compounds difficulties for the art historian who must rely upon literary evidence to piece out an otherwise incomplete history. Every effort has been made here to limit discussion to texts in which the descriptions of images clearly mean sculpture in the round. For the use of *imago* with *tabula*, see Chapter III, note 52.

Cf. Webster Smith, "Definition of *Statua*," *The Art Bulletin*, L (1968), 263-267, for the use of this term during the Renaissance and antiquity.

offering of lighted tapers, votive plaques and other gifts, or are adorned with flowers, jewelry and rich costumes. Some are still carried in annual processions, attract throngs of pilgrims and have been honored in solemn coronation ceremonies.

Considered the Christian "idols" of the Early Middle Ages, they have been thought more pertinent to a study of religion than to a serious history of sculpture. It has been difficult for art historians to realize that sculptures endowed by the boundless medieval imagination with the power to speak, to weep, to fly out of windows, to bring rain in time of drought, to deter invaders in time of war, or simply to box the ears of the naughty,[2] might also have aesthetic merit. Also their true physical character has often been obscured. Those sheathed with precious metal have for the most part disappeared or have been robbed of their gold and silver revetment and are seen in a reduced state. Others have suffered at the hands of those who treasured them most. In attempts at refurbishing, they have been disfigured by repainting with layers of indifferent polychromy, mutilated by cuttings which provided reliquary niches, or, even worse, modernized by recarving.

Now that a number of the great early masterpieces of the *Maiestas* type have been cleaned and restored, a serious and objective appraisal is possible, although still beset

[2] Countless miracles, of relatively modern date, are commemorated by votive plaques in the sanctuaries of the Massif Central, each of them telling a story of healing and rescue through intervention of the Madonna enthroned, but they have little bearing on the Middle Ages. Legends of uncertain date, attributing incredible origins to the statues, are also common, e.g. reporting their discovery by shepherds (Tourzel-Ronzières, no. 41; Thuir, no. 57), or through the agency of bulls (Manosque, no. 72), or in a forest (Odeillo, no. 61), or claiming importation from the Holy Land (Bredons I, no. 25; Saint-Savin, no. 67; Mende, no. 110).

Caesarius von Heisterbach (1180-1240) gives accounts of startling behavior by Madonna and Child statues in the early thirteenth century. These are stories which have more relevance for medieval history. In one tale, the sculptured Christ Child is said to have stood up in Mary's lap during Mass, removing her crown and placing it on his own head at the reading of the Gospel, then returning it to Mary and sitting down again at the *credo* (Caesarius Heisterbacensis Monachi, *Dialogus Miraculorum*, ed. J. Strange, Cologne, Bonn and Brussels, 1851, VII, 46; E. Beitz, *Caesarius von Heisterbach und die bildende Kunst*, Augsburg, 1926, p. 40). In another of Caesarius' tales, Mary is said to have given a resounding box on the ears to a sinful woman (VII, 33; Beitz, *op. cit.*, p. 40); and in still another, to have been forced to free from prison a mother who had "kidnapped" the Christ Child from Mary's own lap in order that the divine Mother would have to ransom in this way her own Child (III, 82; Beitz, *op. cit.*, p. 42). In another, which is a typically medieval story, a woman rudely addressed the statue as *vetus haec rumbula* ("this old trash"), but Mary deigned to speak aloud to the woman in reply before inflicting on this medieval skeptic the punishment of being perpetually unfortunate (*semper misera*), a sentence duly fulfilled. The pious conclusion to this cautionary tale is an interesting contemporary opinion of our statues: "If those who despise sacred images incur such great punishment, I think that those who venerate them are greatly deserving of Divine Grace"—"Si sacras imagines contemnentes tantam incurrunt poenam, puto quod venerantes illas magnam mereantur gratiam" (VII, 44; Beitz, *op. cit.*, p. 42).

For tales of miraculous immunities, particularly to fire, see Chapter II below. Rescues of entire cities and towns from war, flood and plague are also common (e.g. Dijon, no. 88; Thuir, no. 57; Jouhe, no. 98).

3

with difficulties. Medieval texts give all too little attention to the figures which, like many other facts of contemporary life, were simply taken for granted so that documentation is apt to be vague or lacking. A firm date is rare, and, owing to their portability, place of origin is often uncertain. In many cases we know nothing more than what can be learned from examination of the statues themselves. Fortunately this has yielded an amazing amount of information, and what emerges is a fascinating class of objects. Wood sculpture is so little known before A.D. 1200 that these works fill a serious gap in our knowledge. They also afford a new appreciation of the sophistication of Romanesque wood carving, revealing techniques which were often masterful and follow regional distinctions. Since the iconographic range is very narrow and the statues are numerous, stylistic variations become clear. This allows a classification of types which can be related to stone sculpture and can demonstrate the dissemination of stone atelier styles, helping to document them when preservation in stone is poor.

In addition to their contribution to art history, a number of the sculptures are works of art with particular elegance and power in their own right and significant individual interest. Taken as a group, they express graphically the desire in the early medieval West to embody in plastic form an elusive, religious concept and at the same time, to endow the carved form with the depth of human feeling and vitality so characteristic of the Middle Ages. Parallel to the divine Incarnation, which is the subject of the statues, is the aesthetic incarnation of human experience in visual art.

The purpose of the present work is to study the wood Throne of Wisdom sculptures from their beginnings to ca. 1200 in France. This terminal date has been chosen because, except for a few works of retarded style, later statues of the Madonna and Child are not only countless in number but different in kind. By 1200 the Romanesque *Maiestas Sanctae Mariae* had had its day and was replaced in Gothic art by a gentle, queenly Mother having little relation to our present subject.[3]

The statues were an international phenomenon, not limited to Auvergne, as is commonly thought, but actually extending to all areas of France, and to Germany, Belgium, Switzerland, Scandinavia, England, Spain, Italy and even into Hungary and Poland. This geographic spread reveals interesting patterns of artistic dissemination, and it would seem ideal to include discussion here of all statues extant in Western Europe, but this is an impossibility. The presentation of many hundreds of examples would be unwieldy, and it is premature to hope that such an international compendium could be exhaustive, for the corpus is continually growing. Previously unheeded statues are being cleaned and "discovered" with astonishing frequency, while others long thought Romanesque in date have, upon examination, revealed themselves as later copies. Therefore, the Register of Principal Examples is not intended as a definitive, comprehensive catalogue. It includes restored figures and replicas when they contribute significant additional data. Its coverage is limited to the most important of the extant statues, those made in France in the twelfth century, because the French Majesties

[3] A number of *retardataire* examples which date after 1200 have been included in the Register and in the discussion below because of their interest and usefulness in documenting twelfth-century style.

4

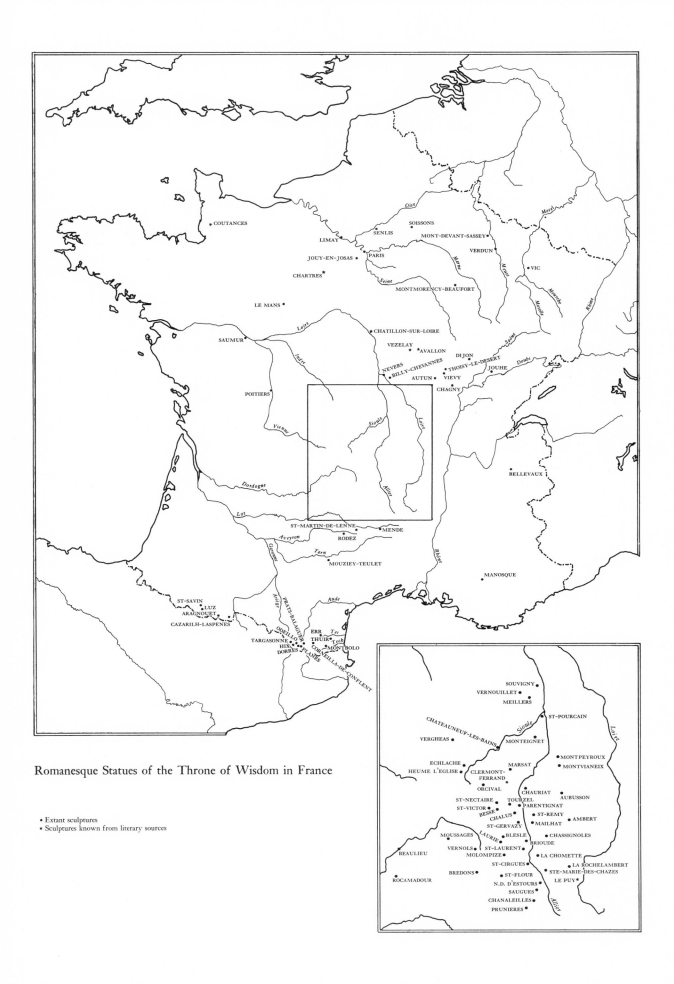

Romanesque Statues of the Throne of Wisdom in France

• Extant sculptures
∗ Sculptures known from literary sources

comprise the outstanding and central members of the international group. They reveal the character and scope of this genre of sculpture most clearly. Statues from other countries will be referred to in the text when pertinent, and a tentative list of non-French examples may be found in Appendix II.

The Register provides information on the history of individual statues along with technical data and references to further bibliography. It notes the extent of restoration insofar as that can be determined[4] but does not pretend to "authenticate" the sculptures, which would be an extremely problematic undertaking. All have been altered in some way, but even those which have been completely recarved, or even replicated, can hardly be called forgeries in the usual sense. Most were remade without fraudulent intent simply because it was necessary to renew an image deteriorated by natural decay or devotional zeal. Often the original Romanesque manner has been faithfully copied; hence some replicas are included in the Register when they have value for the general outline of our subject as, for example, when they help to explain the spread of a style. When such is the case, some cautionary remarks are included.

In Chapter I the statues are studied as a generic type identified by their physical character and their distinctive iconography. Their function is discussed in Chapter II; and the questions of their remote origins and early development are considered in Chapters III and IV. Of particular interest is the fact that their genesis was inextricably bound up with the enigmatic emergence of sculpture in the round in the Early Middle Ages. Consequently their relation to the cult of relics and to crucifixes, statues of saints and secular sculpture in wood is emphasized. Information from literary sources is particularly helpful here and is drawn upon extensively for additional documentation. The sculptures are then studied in Chapter V according to distinguishable types, allowing a broad classification of regional styles. The role of the Madonna in Majesty within the broader context of Romanesque art is also considered, and the artistic merit of the sculptures is discussed. The writer takes pleasure in presenting a number of the statues to the scholarly public for the first time.

Louis Bréhier made the first attempt at a systematic study of Throne of Wisdom statues in 1912, adding subsequent articles in 1924 and 1943.[5] He can be credited with

---

[4] Use of the sign § in the Register indicates that the author has personally examined the sculpture.

[5] L. Bréhier, "Les Origines de la sculpture romane," *Revue des deux mondes*, LXXXII (1912), 870-901; L. Bréhier, "La Cathédrale de Clermont au Xe siècle et sa statue d'or de la Vierge," *La Renaissance de l'art français*, VII (1924), 205-210; L. Bréhier, "Vierges romanes d'Auvergne," *Le Point, revue artistique et littéraire*, XXV (1943), 12-33. Cf. the studies of R. de Fleury, *La Sainte Vierge, études archéologiques et iconographiques*, Paris, 1878; P. Olivier, *L'ancienne Statue romane de Notre-Dame du Puy, Vierge noire miraculeuse, essai d'iconographie critique*, Le Puy-en-Velay, 1921: C. Pourreyron, *Le Culte de Notre-Dame au diocèse de Clermont en Auvergne*, Nancy, 1936. For a recent photographic record, see: *Vierges romanes*, La Pierre-qui-vire, 1961. Related sculptures in Belgium have recently been discussed by Comte Borchgrave d'Altena, "Madones en Majesté, à propos de Notre-Dame d'Eprave," *Revue belge d'archéologie et d'histoire de l'art*, XXX (1961), 3-114.

recognition of the importance of the Majesties, which he called *Vierges reliquaires*, with the creation of the first lists of examples and with the first attempt to relate the Madonnas to the origins of Romanesque sculpture in general. In 1927 Richard Hamann collected a number of later versions, including many from outside of France, in his important essay on the Salzwedel Madonna.[6] Other writers have been especially concerned with the role the statues had to play in the revival of sculpture in the West. In 1925 Deschamps presented his view that sculpture had developed from the minor arts, chiefly metalwork,[7] but Harald Keller insisted later, as Bréhier had done, upon the influence of the cult of relics as a motivating factor in the emergence of Ottonian sculpture in the round, and considered wood crucifixes as well as Madonnas in his explanation of the early history of sculpture.[8] This theory was seriously questioned by Hubert Schrade, who attempted in 1957 to refute the contentions of Keller and cited some additional material bearing on the difficult question of the origins of medieval statuary.[9] More recently, Christian Beutler has maintained that monumental sculpture existed in Carolingian times and that Romanesque statuary derived directly from it rather than being induced either by the cult of relics or the minor arts.[10] My own researches have convinced me that none of these conclusions provides a complete answer.[11]

The origins of the sculptural representation of the enthroned Madonna and Child are complex and elusive. It is clear that the type was not evoked by a single catalytic agent, but resulted from a curious conjunction of forces. Although the cult of relics, the Carolingian tradition in metalwork and the survival of pagan mother-goddess figures in the medieval West all contributed to its development, these stimuli could hardly have sufficed to produce the new sculptural phenomenon. Other factors must be considered. Among them the vitality of the Majesty concept in Carolingian times is important. As applied to sovereigns—whose thrones were sometimes identified with Solomon's—or to Christ in Majesty in the *Maiestas Domini* iconography, or to the Madonna in Majesty, in the *sedes sapientiae* iconography, it meant an authoritative figure enthroned. The throne itself carried strong and ancient meaning, both religious and secular. The fact that Carolingian theologians ascribed to Mary the character of a sovereign, developing this subject as a favorite theme in their literature, and that such an ascription involved a transfer to her of the regalia of imperial office including the royal

---

[6] R. Hamann, "Die Salzwedeler Madonna," *Marburger Jahrbuch für Kunstwissenschaft*, III (1927), 77-144.

[7] P. Deschamps, "Etude sur la renaissance de la sculpture en France à l'époque romane," *Bulletin monumental*, LXXXIV (1925), 6-98. This view is also taken by J. Hubert, *L'Art pré-roman*, Paris, 1938.

[8] H. Keller, "Zur Entstehung der sakralen Vollskulptur in der Ottonischen Zeit," *Festschrift für Hans Jantzen*, Berlin, 1951, 71-90.

[9] H. Schrade, "Zur Frühgeschichte der mittelalterlichen Monumentalplastik," *Westfalen*, XXXV (1957), 33-64.

[10] C. Beutler, *Bildwerke zwischen Antike und Mittelalter*, Düsseldorf, 1964.

[11] Certain of the earlier thoughts expressed in my "Cult Statues," 31-66, are superseded by the present study.

6

insignia, particularly the throne and the orb, so that they referred to her as *regina nostri orbis* or Queen of Heaven,[12] indicates a frame of mind receptive to a more vivid representation of Mary enthroned than had theretofore been provided by painting. Enhanced vividness through the tangibility of sculpture was just becoming possible, after long neglect of that art. The Carolingian revival of monumental sculpture, which was a natural concomitant of Charlemagne's Classical renascence, induced a climate of tolerance and provided the technical competence for the rendering of the enthroned Mary in plastic form. The eventual adoption in the West of the image doctrine basic to the decisions of the Second Nicene Council removed further obstacles. That Council had declared that the honor rendered an image is passed on to that which the image represents. The defenders of images had further argued that imperial images were venerated with reverential ceremonies and that, therefore, religious images should be revered in like manner.[13] Such veneration was at first resisted by Charlemagne's court, as the *Libri Carolini* attest, but as the fear of idolatry abated, religious representations took over the function which had been allotted to secular images. Reverence of the latter was never considered idolatrous; for these "portraits" were simply intended to represent absent sovereigns or rulers, to stand in their stead as proxies. Gradually religious images assumed this surrogate function as well. The image was not to be venerated in and for itself, as a material object. Rather, honor simply passed through it to the prototype, which had been the doctrine of the Council. As a substitute for the person represented, the image became a true representative and took on a transcendental role. It thus mediated between two worlds, that of experienced reality and the sacred realm beyond. As an intermediary between them it could serve as a channel of communication to the sacred realm, and it could also assure the vicarious presence of the sacred figures in the real world. This belief was an essential part of the background which provided a suitable climate for the genesis of the *sedes sapientiae* statue. The desire to render such figures as Mary and Christ in freestanding form was induced by the desire to make them experiential, an almost essential precondition for the realization of their beneficence. A similar motivation accounts for the making of crucifixes and statues of saints. By the late Carolingian period such sculpture was possible. The sources were available, the incentive was strong and proscriptions were relaxed. By at least the mid-tenth century—the earliest, well-documented Throne of Wisdom statue known to us is dated ca. 946—the birth of the sculptured Madonna in Majesty had been accomplished. Its development can be charted sketchily in the late tenth century and there is more ample information on its status in the eleventh. The brilliant culmination to its history in the twelfth century in France is illustrated by the many examples which survive and are discussed in the following pages.

[12] L. Scheffczyk, *Das Mariengeheimnis im Frömmigkeit und Lehre der Karolingerzeit*, Leipzig, 1959, pp. 477ff.

[13] See Chapter III, note 129 below.

CHAPTER I. The Character of the Sculptures

ROMANESQUE Madonnas in Majesty have two irreducible features: their Throne of Wisdom, or *sedes sapientiae*, iconography and their mobility. In turn these two requisites account for and condition a host of other characteristics. Since for iconographic reasons Mary and the Christ Child had to be represented as majestically enthroned, stately poses were required. This determined the position of the figures and allowed little variation. The resultant design is formal and symmetrical, and the ensuing frontality and rigidity convey an effect of grim fixity. The majestic connotation thus imposed a rectilinear rather than a free form upon the composition of the work and a hieratic rather than a human character upon its expression. Attributes, costumes and gestures followed accordingly.

Since mobility was also essential, the sculpture had to be light in weight. It was thus under life-size and made of wood. In its early history it was adorned with a gold or silver sheath. As such it must have been limited to indoor use and only taken out-of-doors under special circumstances. As a mobile form it was unlike the normal stone Romanesque sculpture done in high relief, for it had to be carved on all sides including the back for presentation to every point of view. It must also have been independent of other art forms in the church, its mobility precluding any permanent arrangement with them and freeing it from any role in an iconographic program. It would not even have had to conform to the aesthetic demand an architectural setting normally makes with respect to a sculptural adjunct.

On the other hand its impermanent location allowed it a flexible function. It need not be limited to didactic, ornamental or devotional uses. It might thus have a part in church ritual, where liturgical requirements might entail moving the image. It could figure in the celebrations of the feasts of the church calendar and it could participate more broadly in the life of the religious community. Indeed, a portable image could even have a role in the civil rites and ceremonies of the locale according to need.

Clearly the Throne of Wisdom statues were no ordinary sculptures. They might resemble the kings and queens of Chartres's Royal Portal but they did not function like them. If portability were not of prime importance, these Majesties might better have been made in a more permanent material, such as limestone or marble, and done on a grander scale. The lack of comparable freestanding sculpture in stone, and the fact that the wood Majesties were made even for churches where expense was no consideration

8

and where lavish stone sculptures were also commissioned, convinces us that wood was not used for purposes of economy.[1] The amazing preservation, for France alone, of more than a hundred such figures in this fragile and highly perishable medium, indicates that the wood images had a considerable and independent importance which guaranteed their survival. Their importance derived from their purpose. Not intended merely as representations—verisimilitudes—they could serve in the eyes of the faithful as representatives or proxies for Mary and Christ. As such the statues were truly iconic.

Peculiar to all the Romanesque Majesties is the look of an idol, albeit a "Christian idol." In the literature which skims over them, one is likely to find them described as "buddha-like" or *idolhaft*. What occasions this is extremely difficult to isolate. Yet their history as cult objects suggests that such a quality has been widely recognized in them. Certainly the hieratic, transcendental impact of the figures,[2] particularly marked when the wood was sheathed with a luminous covering of precious metal, is an appropriate catalyst to the imagination. In their stiffness and stillness they are closer to an abstract religious ideal than the pretty, swaying princesses which follow them in Gothic times. The image of the Madonna in Majesty, more than any other type of sculpture, was *the* cult statue of the Middle Ages, because in it divine presence seemed more fully concentrated. The mystery of the Incarnation, with its implicit fusion of God and Man, was made manifestly visible.

All of the functions for the statues which are revealed by available evidence presuppose a belief in this particular image as a medium. The carved Mother and Child are mediators or aids for communion and communication with Mary and Christ themselves. As isolated effigies within the church, close to the worshiper, like him in size, sharing his own environmental space, yet both human *and* god-like in form, the austere figures must have provided an excellent bridge for the transition from reality to abstrac-

---

[1] E.g. Chartres, Cluny, Vézelay, etc. Statues might also be made of stucco according to Bernard of Angers who wrote in the early eleventh century ("gypseam vel ligneam eneamque formari statuam," in A. Bouillet, *Liber miraculorum Sancte Fidis*, Paris, 1897, I, xiii, p. 47). The lines of the *Libri Carolini*, "imagine in gypso vel testa formata," indicate that stucco images were common in the late eighth century as well (*Libri Carolini*, I, 2; *Monumenta Germaniae Historica*, *Legum*, III, *Concilia*, vol. 2, suppl., ed. H. Bastgen, 1924, pp. 13, 41; Migne, *PL*, XCVIII, 1011). The story of the fall of a *Maiestas* from the altar of a church in Cambrai in ca. 1168, reducing it to a powder, suggests that stucco images continued to exist even in the twelfth century alongside the grander wood and metal-covered statues although none of these has survived (O. Lehmann-Brockhaus, *Schriftquellen zur Kunstgeschichte des 11. und 12. Jahrhunderts für Deutschland, Lothringen und Italien*, Berlin, 1938, no. 1692). These stucco figures would have satisfied the need for an inexpensive material in sculpture.

Occasionally wood sculptures were sheathed with copper, lead or tin, which could be gilded in simulation of gold (nos. 57-59).

[2] Such a quality does not account for the careers of those statues which became *Vierges miraculeuses*. The miraculous power attributed to such Majesties varied from place to place and grew or waned as centuries wore on. Often statues of almost identical form had very different destinies: one became the object of a fervent cult, the other was the center of only local devotion. Such religious phenomena are clearly beyond the scope of this study.

tion. For the medieval mind, there was doubtless a negligible distance between the Virgin known throughout Christendom and the wood Virgin in Majesty, representing the Throne of Wisdom, known in the local church.

Materials and Technique

The earliest examples of the *sedes sapientiae* statue were completely covered with precious metal.[3] The richest of these were customarily sheathed with sheets of silver or of fine gold just as Majesties representing saints were. The gold had been beaten to the thinness of tissue, chased into fine delineations of folds and features, and carefully fastened to a wood core (Fig. 28). Costly gems, including antique intaglios and cameos, edged the hems of garments and studded thrones. Bernard of Angers describes precious stones in a flashing shimmer of gold and color for the early Majesties of Auvergne.[4] Carried through the fields in the sun to the pavilions of the Rodez synod in the early eleventh century, a magnificent collection of "shrines and reliquaries in the form of golden statues" must have presented an awe-inspiring sight.[5] Judging from the vision of Robert, Abbot of Mozat, the tenth-century golden Madonna of Clermont-Ferrand was ornamented with dozens of precious stones, set into the gold which covered her form.[6]

The importance of precious materials is a well-known feature of early medieval art and accounts in part at least for the leading role assumed by goldsmith work in

[3] Wessex, Rome, Clermont-Ferrand, Ely and Rodez recorded gold and silver Madonnas from the eighth through the eleventh centuries (see Chapter III below). It is likely that the others we know of prior to 1100 were similarly refined with metal sheaths but our information is incomplete. Extant gold and silver sculptures are at Essen, from ca. 980; Hildesheim, ca. 1000-1015; Paderborn, ca. 1051-1076; Walcourt, eleventh century; Orcival (no. 31), ca. 1160 and Beaulieu (no. 101), second half of the twelfth century.

[4] Bouillet, *Liber miraculorum*, p. 50. As a cleric trained by Bishop Fulbert of Chartres, Bernard of Angers initially had what he called a rational attitude toward sculpture, approving the use of three-dimensional form only for images of the crucified Christ. Nevertheless he was fascinated by tales of curious reliquary statues common in Auvergne. In 1013 he traveled thither to see the statues and to witness personally the superstitious behavior which, he had heard, surrounded them. At first he and his companion railed against the golden figures of St. Foy in Conques and St. Gerald in Aurillac, scorning them as pagan idols. Soon, however, the effectiveness of the St. Foy statue as a wonder worker and its undeniable sacredness, owing to the presence of the saint's relics within it, converted him to the opposite point of view. He became a zealous devotee of the saint, recording her numerous miracles in the book which has come down to us as the *Liber miraculorum Sancte Fidis*. Its firsthand description of religious gatherings and various devotional practices make it an invaluable account of contemporary attitudes. See the discussion of Bernard's later visits to Conques below in Chapter IV. For his statement regarding his conversion, see Chapter III, note 13.

[5] *Ibid.*, pp. 71-72.

[6] R. Rigodon, "Vision de Robert, abbé de Mozat, au sujet de la basilique de la Mère de Dieu edifiée dans la Ville des Arvernes, relation par le diacre Arnaud (Ms. de Clermont 145, fols. 130-134)," *Bulletin historique et scientifique de l'Auvergne*, LXX (1950), 22-55; Bréhier, "Clermont," 205-210. See the discussion below, pp. 31ff., 95-100.

Carolingian and Ottonian times. Early medieval inventories and other accounts of lost treasures stress the weight and costliness of the materials.[7] On the other hand, these descriptions also exhibit a seeming indifference to artistic merit. That this could not be a true reflection of the situation is shown by the superb pieces of chased gold work still to be seen in such treasuries as those at Conques, Aachen or Essen. The slender, fluid form of the crucified Christ on the First Mathilda Cross in Essen or the attenuated elegance of the figures on the famous Lindau Book Cover in New York is testimony to the wondrous skill of early medieval goldsmiths. The beauty of these works implies the existence of appreciative and critical patrons.

The golden Madonna in Essen (Figs. 28-31) best exemplifies the aesthetic force such material and technique could have when applied to a work in the round. The goldsmith of this celebrated piece has conjured up the Mother of God, but, unexpectedly, he has also created an illusion of warm and delicate femininity, though using leaves of gold, material which would normally seem intractable and unsuited for this purpose. This is particularly apparent in the rendering of the protective gesture of the Virgin (Fig. 31), where the metallic sheath suggests the limpness of silk, finely pleated about a soft body and twisted around the head like the thinnest of stuffs. The solidity of the metal casing seems to dissolve in the draftsmanlike flow of line and the continual flicker of light over the surface. Albert Boeckler has called this lively play of gold glints an indispensable enhancement of the plastic form.[8] For Köhn, the bright reflections create an appearance "woven of sheen and shimmer, far removed from tangible form in a mysterious and powerful display of majesty."[9]

Gold is an obvious vehicle for symbolic values. Secular wealth and power have always been appropriately associated with it. One only need think of the varied sorts of imperial insignia. For the West, the arrival of a beautiful Byzantine letter with a famous golden seal was just cause to marvel.[10] In addition to its aura of imperial authority, however, the unique aesthetic properties of gold make it a carrier of religious meaning as well. Its success in portraying a metaphysical ambience which obtains beyond conditions of time and space, can be seen in Early Byzantine mosaics whose *tituli* indicate that this quality was appreciated by observers as well as patrons. Even when used for small objects rather than monumental wall areas, the golden surface suggests an extension beyond the object itself. The contours of the metal seem changing and fluid. Tiny ridges and pockets of sensitively worked foil collect the light and reflect it in a

---

[7] Keller, "Vollskulptur," 76; A. Freeman, "Theodulph of Orléans and the Libri Carolini," *Speculum*, XXXII (1957), 696; L. Duchesne, *Liber Pontificalis*, Paris, 1886-1892, *passim*; A. Bénet, "Le trésor de Cluny," *Revue de l'art chrétien*, 3, VI (1888), 195-205; U. Chevalier, *Cartulaire de l'abbaye de St. Chaffre du Monastier*, Paris, 1884, p. 43; A. Courson, *Cartulaire de l'abbaye de St. Sauveur de Redon*, Paris, 1863, pp. 67, 190, 420.

[8] Munich, Bayerische Staatsbibliothek, *Ars Sacra, Kunst des frühen Mittelalters*, ed. A. Boeckler, 1950, no. 395.

[9] H. Köhn, *Der Essener Münsterschatz*, Essen, 1955, p. 18.

[10] Lehmann-Brockhaus, *Schriftquellen für Deutschland*, no. 2738. See also: J. Lejeune, "Genèse de l'art Mosan," *Wallraf-Richartz Jahrbuch*, XV (1953), 64.

swiftly shifting display of shadow and brightness. The result is an intensification of the intrinsic properties of the material. In a dimly lit interior the luminosity suggests an intangible, mystical presence. Hence the many medieval interpretations of the magical "lustre" of the metal as a metaphor of divinity.

The response of the worshiper is clear. We could imagine the impact of gold-sheathed statues of Madonnas and saints upon the peasants of Auvergne even without the descriptions of Bernard of Angers. In Aurillac where Bernard saw the Majesty representing St. Gerald "of purest gold and costly gems gleaming," the statue looked so deceptively similar to the human form, that the peasants in prayer before it believed that it saw and encouraged them through its expressive look. It listened to their petitions and the rustics even imagined that the figure nodded to them in answer.[11] In Conques, Bernard pressed forward through the crowd of worshipers and addressed its Majesty (Figs. 13-15), in this case representing the local saint: "St. Foy, of whom a part rests in this image, help me on the Day of Judgment."[12] In both of these cases the mystical presence of the saint was not only conjured up by a judicious use of materials, it was confirmed by the relics of the martyr actually inside the statue. In the St. Foy the relics were carefully wrapped in oriental textiles and placed within a reliquary cavity.[13]

One might be inclined to think of these statues as Western counterparts to the Byzantine icon. The rustics of Auvergne, however, communicated with God, his Mother and his saints in a much less abstract manner than their Byzantine cousins. The likeness of the saint or the Virgin stood before the Western believer not as an image on a painted surface, but as a statue. Three-dimensional and massive, it shared his own environment. If it were also a reliquary, inhabited by fragments of the very body whose human form it fashioned, it partook of the nature of the sacred person in an identification which could not be equalled even by the "reality" of the icon.[14] No wonder that the statues fired the imagination so that they seemed to assume life and to nod to worshipers. Before the golden statue of the Madonna which contained the prize relics of the Virgin owned by Bishop Stephen II of Clermont-Ferrand, the faithful could have felt themselves before the very person of the Mother of God.

The technique of the early medieval goldsmith as it was applied to these images is described by Theophilus in his twelfth-century treatise *De Diversis Artibus*.[15] Theophilus devotes an entire book to metalwork and gives this section of his manual his

---

[11] Bouillet, *Liber miraculorum*, I, xiii, p. 47.   [12] *Ibid.*, p. 48.

[13] A. Bouillet, *L'Église et le trésor de Conques*, Mâcon, 1892, pp. 53f. The importance of gold and precious stones for the decoration of reliquaries persisted into the twelfth century when Abbot Thiofrid of Echternach explained at length their symbolism. He also stressed the magical aspect of gold and gems, considered important for the appropriate veneration of relics (Migne, *PL*, CLVII, 318f.; W. Lampen, *Thiofried von Echternach*, 1920, pp. 19ff., cited by Schrade, "Monumental-plastik," 61).

[14] E. Kitzinger, "The Cult of Images in the Age Before Iconoclasm," *Dumbarton Oaks Papers*, VIII (1954), 83-150; G. Ladner, "The Concept of the Image in the Greek Fathers and the Byzantine Iconoclastic Controversy," *Dumbarton Oaks Papers*, VII (1953), 1-34.

[15] Theophilus, *The Various Arts*, trans. C. R. Dodwell, London, 1961.

greatest care and concern. He instructs the artist in the chasing of metal for relief work, a technique which we now call repoussé. He cautions that the gold or silver must be evenly thinned out everywhere. It should be so finely thinned that the impression of a fingernail just appears on the other side. After drawing the figures lightly, the artist works from the back of the metal whence the main forms of the bodies are to be extruded by pressure. He says: "Then, to begin with, you gently rub the head, which should be in the highest relief, with a rounded, well-polished [chasing] tool, and, turning the plate on the right side, you rub around the head with the smooth, polished tool so that the ground sinks and the head stands out." After patient beatings with hammers of many different sizes, turning the metal in the process, the details are then engraved with a tracer. The artist may thus delineate the features of faces and even control the shadows of the draperies. The concave forms are then to be filled with a red wax. "When these gold and silver plates have been brought to full relief and burnished and you want to attach them, take some wax . . . and mix with it finely ground tile, or sand. . . . With this fill up all the figures, or whatever relief work there is. . . . When it is cold, attach it where you wish." The gold thus beaten and backed with wax or mastic was attached with nails to a wood core.[16] The plates covering an entire statue must have been executed in a similar manner as indicated by the Essen, Hildesheim, Orcival and Beaulieu Madonnas (Figs. 28-31, 40 and 41, 90-94, 174-176).

A graphic demonstration of this repoussé technique and its potentialities as applied to monumental sculpture became available when the gold sheath of the Hildesheim Madonna was removed in the course of its recent restoration. Herr Nölter's extraordinary photographs (Figs. 40 and 41) reveal the subtle delicacy with which the drapery patterns are worked in the gold foil and indicate the different degree of completeness which obtains for the gold chasing in relation to its wood core. The goldsmith exercised relative freedom in adding fine details to the metal sheath, such as the deft strokes, almost like those of a pen, which delineate a gossamer fabric falling in nearly imperceptible folds over Mary's knees and her back and convey the effect of finely pulled and crumpled silk in her sleeves. Only the bare outlines of these formal ideas are carved in the wood sculpture, while the full statement of them is executed in the precious metal sheath.

A similar relationship between the sheath and its wood foundation exists for the Orcival Madonna (Fig. 93). The metal reveals a fleuron motif in the nap of the fabric and an exquisitely worked border design for the sleeve, which is merely roughed out in the wood carving. The resemblance between this Romanesque technique and that of the Ottonian period suggests a continuity of craft tradition linking the two eras. Since most of the once numerous statues of this type have been lost, the Hildesheim and Orcival Madonnas allow rare glimpses of a medieval practice which felicitously

---

[16] *Ibid.*, III, lxxiv, pp. 132-135. A bone tool was used for delineating details in the gilded silver of Notre-Dame d'Orcival (no. 31), F. Enaud, "Remise en état de la statue de la Vierge à l'Enfant d'Orcival," *Les Monuments historiques de la France*, VII (1961), 79-88. See also H. Swarzenski, *Monuments of Romanesque Art*, London, 1954, fig. 92. For studies of the Hildesheim Madonna, see Chapter IV, note 97 below.

blended the qualities of the minor arts and monumental sculpture by applying the inspired skill of the early medieval goldsmith to sculpture in the round.

Despite its sacred purpose, the gold was, of course, still gold. It had monetary value, particularly inasmuch as it was normally of high quality. Nor did the fashioning of it reduce its negotiable worth. Inevitably the golden statues were easy prey for those who saw in them readily accessible cash reserves, and who were, perhaps, faint in spirit. An inventory of 1098 listing the treasures at Monastier tells us that plaques of gold and silver which had surrounded the image of the martyr Theofrid—now known in France as St. Chaffre—were removed and given to "some persons" going to Jerusalem, presumably Crusaders, in exchange for their worldly possessions. Restitution was to be made in silver from the income of their properties.[17]

In another instance, gold was taken to underwrite a less noble enterprise. From the book of the *Miracles of St. Privatus*, where events of the second quarter of the eleventh century are related, the following tale is told: two noblemen, each named Guido, went stealthily by night to the crypt of the church at Mende where the golden Majesty of St. Privatus was located; quietly they removed both the head and the right arm of the saint, in addition to gold and gems from the surface of the statue, leaving the rest in confusion; apprehended and excommunicated by the bishop, they repented, but their conversion was too late for them to escape retribution; one lost his mind, the other his property and his health.[18]

The purloining of gold from the Conques Majesty of St. Foy (Fig. 13) was more discreet, as Jean Taralon has shown.[19] Through the course of centuries sections of gold leaves were snipped away and the gaps in the surface concealed by splendid-looking gems of lesser value. The great carbuncles at the saint's knees which appear to be embellishments to the present work are thus in reality impoverishments which mask the pilferings of the past.

Monasteries and cathedrals in straitened circumstances sometimes sacrificed their treasures to satisfy the demand of invaders or simply to meet the needs of a meager existence. Revolutionary iconoclasm also took its toll. Particularly susceptible were the gold Madonnas. Their metal plates were removed, melted down and sold. The denuded statues disappeared. Such was the fate of the Clermont-Ferrand Majesty in 1793.[20] Notre-Dame d'Orcival (no. 31) suffered repeated removals of gilded silver at unknown periods. Some of the silver leaves were replaced in 1769, but further patching was done in copper in the nineteenth century.[21] Gilded copper plates covering the throne of the Essen Madonna appear in like manner to be a substitute for a more valuable, original

---

[17] Chevalier, *Cartulaire*, no. xlvii, p. 42.

[18] C. Brunel, *Les Miracles de Saint Privat*, Collections de textes pour servir à l'étude et à l'enseignement de l'histoire, Paris, 1912, no. 9, pp. 16-18.

[19] J. Taralon, "La nouvelle Présentation du trésor de Conques," *Les Monuments historiques de la France*, n.s., 1 (1955), 121-141; J. Taralon, "Majesté de Sainte Foy," *Les Trésors des églises de France*, Paris, Musée des Arts Décoratifs, 1965, 289-294, no. 534.

[20] See note 6 above.

[21] See note 16 above.

facing in gold.[22] The gold revetment of the Hildesheim Madonna has suffered various vicissitudes[23] and the pieces of silver now making up the sheath of the Walcourt Majesty are alterations which form an archaeological puzzle.[24] Of all the gold and silver Madonnas which once adorned medieval churches, only six of the twelfth century or earlier are preserved more or less intact: at Essen, Hildesheim, Walcourt, Orcival, Beaulieu and Paderborn. Something of the original revetment in gold or gilded silver remains for the first five, but the last, the Paderborn Madonna, was stripped of its gold in 1762.[25]

This range of evidence indicting the past suggests more than the usual vandalism of history and is not simply explained by the hostile tastes of other eras. Even in the time of its creation, the precious metal revetment provided the statues with an economic dimension. Like the Athena Parthenos, these Majesties were literal treasures, storehouses of negotiable currency. Investment in them could mean security against the unknown travails of the future. The gold and silver leaves were readily available as convertible capital for worthwhile enterprises—to finance Crusades or to ransom lives. The statues were thus equipped with a formidable array of powers. Should the aesthetic and symbolic impact of the work begin to seem hollow, the image lose its credibility as an intercessor, or the relics within prove ineffectual, there was always something of practical value left in hand.

Fortunately not all Madonnas in Majesty were encased in precious metal or there would be few of their number left to concern us today. The majority of surviving examples date from the twelfth century.[26] A handful of statues and literary descriptions provide information for earlier periods, chiefly the tenth and eleventh centuries. This evidence indicates that the earliest ones we know were regularly made of gold and silver.[27] By the second quarter of the eleventh century, however, simple wood sculptures were common as well, and in the twelfth century they far outnumbered their metal counterparts. Evidently once firmly established as a sculptural form, the glistening sheath was no longer absolutely essential. Without the expense and refinement of a metal casing, the type proliferated rapidly. Although less pretentious in form, the bare statue was similar in size and the wood was worked very much as it had been before. Variations in size and in treatment are related to regional preferences rather than to date.

The size of French Madonnas and their forerunners varies from 35 cm. for the smallest at Cazarilh-Laspenes to 142 cm. for the tallest at Saint-Denis. The norm is about 73 cm., but there is no canonical measure for the group. Height is an aspect of style which varies according to regional type. For the Majesties made in the Tournus

[22] See Chapter IV, note 77 below and Fig. 32.

[23] See Chapter IV, note 97 below and Figs. 40 and 41.

[24] See Chapter IV, note 116 below and Figs. 50 and 51.

[25] See Chapter IV, note 103 below; A. Fuchs, *Von Kreuzen, Madonnen und Altären*, Paderborn, 1940, p. 9.

[26] Some have been erroneously dated in the eleventh century, e.g. Notre-Dame de Bon Espoir (no. 88). Cf. the Madonna from Chur in Zurich (see Appendix II). Many are *retardataire* works from the thirteenth century and some are later renewals or replicas (see Register).

[27] See note 3 above.

manner of the Puy-de-Dôme, it ranges from about 71-74 cm., and for those of the Saugues style known in the Haute-Loire it is almost the same, about 70-73 cm. For the Morgan type found in the Puy-de-Dôme, however, the range is about 74-82 cm., while for Burgundian examples it is about 98-102 cm. Figures from the Ile-de-France area can be even taller, about 94-142 cm. In the Hautes-Pyrénées Majesties are likely to be 79-82 cm. while in the Pyrénées-Orientales they are smaller, commonly 66-72 cm. There are exceptions, of course, in each of these categories, but the differences seem substantial enough to indicate a pattern of meaningful distinctions.

Choice of material also shows interesting regional preferences. Although data are extremely difficult to procure on this count, and it is dangerous to generalize from a small number of samples, tendencies seem clear enough to merit discussion. Walnut is favored in the south of France (the Morgan Madonna, Montvianeix, Orcival, nos. 1, 3, 31), while oak (Saint-Denis, Mont-devant-Sassey, nos. 96, 105) and birch (Autun, no. 87) are used further north. Lindenwood is most common in Germany and Switzerland (Hildesheim, Paderborn, Hannover, Chur, Raron, Wil, etc.). This conforms to the analysis by Jacqueline Marette in her technical study of medieval wood panels.[28] For these walnut is commonly used in southern France, particularly Provence, and almost exclusively in Navarre, whereas it is absent to the north. There, oak and lindenwood are usual. Since walnut was not available in large, natural supply in Auvergne, where resinous woods abound in the forests, the preference for walnut in sculpture is interesting.

Although wood is readily carved, it does present hazards for the sculptor. Warping and splitting are serious problems, particularly the latter. The perimeter of a billet of wood seasons more quickly than the core and the difference in rate of shrinkage can cause the outer surface to crack. In a completed sculpture such cracks would seriously disrupt the carving and polychromy. Even if a fully seasoned billet is used, changes of temperature and humidity can produce similar effects. Many medieval sculptures show the results of such damage due to cracking.[29] As a precaution against this danger the sculptor ordinarily avoided the inner core of the tree trunk and used only the wood from the more stable perimeter. This explains why so many medieval sculptures done from a single block of wood are hollowed out in back, which allows removal of the center of the log. Since the Romanesque demand was for a mobile Majesty, complete on all sides, however, this was hardly ideal.

Two solutions to the problem can be seen in the Throne of Wisdom sculptures. The first is common to Auvergne, where wood technicians were able to simulate a solid form yet minimize the danger of cracking through careful joinery techniques akin to the usual medieval method of preparing panels for paintings. Such panels are composed of separate boards juxtaposed on a system of alternating grain of the wood from one board to the next.[30] Splitting is less likely in such composites, since the joints allow some

---

[28] J. Marette, *Connaissance des primitifs par l'étude du bois*, Paris, 1961.

[29] For an illustration of this, see L. Birchler, "Vom ältesten Einsidler Gnadenbild," *Formositas Romanica, Beiträge zur Erforschung der Romanischen Kunst, Joseph Gantner zugeeignet*, Frauenfeld, 1958, 95; cf. H. Wilm, *Die Gotische Holzfigur*, Leipzig, 1923, pp. 47-50.

[30] The grain of each board is determined by the manner in which it was sawed longitudinally

16

contraction and expansion, particularly if the pieces are arranged so that these forces neutralize one another. Two works by the same master will illustrate a similar procedure in sculpture: the Morgan Madonna and Notre-Dame de Montvianeix (Figs. 54, 60, nos. 1, 3). Both appear to be solid, three-dimensional statues fashioned from single billets of wood. Actually the former is made up of at least twenty-two individually worked pieces of walnut and the latter of at least eighteen. Particularly visible now are the seams where the heads of both Mary and the Christ Child join their bodies. Carving them separately allowed the sculptor greater ease in execution and, a more important consideration, the choice of finer pieces of material for these expressive forms.[31] It was also safer. In like manner, the hands and feet of the Child, and the elaborate colonnettes of the throne with their plinths and imposts, were all worked separately. Wood dowels, up to several inches in length, joined them to the rest of the sculpture. In some cases these dowels were pinned in place by smaller dowels, as can be seen near the lower edge of the Child's tunic in the Montvianeix work. The base is another composite.

Thus, finely detailed carving of the statue was done with small pieces of wood which could be handled easily, and the larger forms, with their broader manner, were fashioned from bigger blocks. These are solid, and presumably taken from the outer edge of a sizable billet. The result is a fairly secure work which more than compensates for the complication of the joinery. The procedure must have had economic advantages as well since small bits of walnut were efficiently put to use. The method must have imposed a limit on the size of the statue, however, since the torsos, as solids, could be no greater than the sound pieces of wood available. This would explain why larger works tended to be done in a different type of wood and in a second technique.

This second method consisted of shaping the entire figure of Mary, head and all, from a single block, but hollowing the reverse from just below the shoulders to the base. The interior of the billet was thus removed, minimizing the danger of damage and

---

from the log. The boards are juxtaposed with an alternation of their grain so that any tendency for a board to warp around its longitudinal axis will be compensated by the opposite warping in its neighbors. At worst these counter curvatures will produce a slightly undulant surface and no joints will yawn widely; also the bending forces, being distributed, do not tend to split any board longitudinally. This system could be used in our Madonna figures by juxtaposing sections of the sculpture on the same principle of alternating grains. As to panels, see Marette, *Connaissance*, pp. 95-110.

[31] The reasonable suggestion that this practice was due to workshop procedure—several artists working on one statue and specialists being assigned the more difficult head, hands, etc.—has not been borne out by examination of the statues, for one can trace the same artist's hand in both heads and torsos in most examples.

Gybal's thought that the head was detached and kept in a "secure place" must derive from popular legend and folk custom, A. Gybal, *L'Auvergne, berceau de l'art roman*, Clermont-Ferrand, 1957, pp. 89-92. I know of only one such instance where the head of the Child was stored away because of its extremely fragile state. The notion that the detachable heads give access to relic compartments is clearly untenable since, when the head is carved separately, the torso is not hollow and vice versa.

lightening the weight of the statue. The thinner the shell, the less the work was subject to cracking. The opening in the back was then closed with a separate panel. It was so carved and fitted into place with pegs that, when finished, the seams were almost invisible and the sculpture appeared as a complete three-dimensional form. The Majesties from Autun (Fig. 152, no. 87) and Hildesheim (Fig. 39)[32] illustrate this manner clearly. In many other examples, traces of pegs can be discerned so that, even when such a panel is presently lacking, it may be presumed to have existed originally. A variant of this procedure was the placing of the hollowed Madonna in a high-backed chair rather than upon a low throne. The back of the chair abutted the figure and concealed the opening (Figs. 183 and 184, nos. 103 and 104). The Child was usually carved from a second piece of wood and doweled into Mary's lap. Understandably, this smaller figure has sometimes disappeared.

Since joinery was used particularly in Auvergne for smaller statues, and, as far as can be discerned, chiefly with walnut, and since the method of hollowing the sculpture was more common further north and used normally with oak and poplar in larger sizes, the properties of the woods may be linked to these two techniques. The homogeneous grain and uniform vessels of walnut made it less likely to split as contrasted with the heterogeneous character of oak grain.[33] This may account in part for the remarkable preservation of Auvergne statues. The tendency for works of art to withstand time better in provincial areas than in urban centers, however, certainly cannot be overlooked. There seems to be no question but that the simpler second method—that of hollowing the figures—was more common in other countries, regardless of the wood employed, and it is clearly the procedure which became the rule in the later Middle Ages.

Medieval documentation for both techniques may be found in Etienne de Boileau's *Livre de métiers*.[34] The guild regulations recounted there were in operation in Paris in 1268, and pertain in part to wood sculptors. Their work was regulated with respect to the material employed, the manner of gilding, the use of the sculptures produced, etc. There was an organization of specialists, e.g. carvers of crucifixes were accorded special distinction. Moreover, it was decreed that figures must be made of one piece of wood, excluding the crown, and might not be joined together again if damaged in carving. Crucifixes, however, might be made of three pieces (for the trunk and two arms). The decree was enacted, it is explained, because sculptures were formerly made out of several pieces and were not "solid, good and lawful."

The regulations confirm that it was indeed common for late Romanesque and early Gothic sculptors to make statues from adjoined sections of wood. The *Livre* also indicates that by this date the technique had deteriorated and was improperly practiced in

---

[32] See Chapter IV, note 97 below.   [33] Marette, *Connaissance*, p. 27.
[34] R. de Lespinasse and F. de Bonnardot, *Les Métiers et corporations de la ville de Paris, XIIIᵉ siècle, Le Livre de métiers d'Etienne Boileau*, Paris, 1879, Titre LXI, viii, ix; cf. M. Blindheim, *Main Trends of East-Norwegian Wooden Figure Sculpture in the Second Half of the Thirteenth Century*, Oslo, 1952, p. 93.

thirteenth-century Paris. Romanesque sculptors of the twelfth century in Auvergne were so proficient with the practice that the largest number of surviving *sedes sapientiae* statues we have come from this area.[35] They were clearly "solid and good." Parisian sculptors, on the other hand, were already carving Madonnas from single blocks in the twelfth century, as was to be required later in the thirteenth.

According to Martin Blindheim the full procedure for carving sculptures by the hollowed-out method would be first to rough-hew the figure, then to hollow the back, to plane or chisel the inside, to drill holes for securing the figure to the bench,[36] and finally to carve the front. Tools in Romanesque times were very simple and included the small, cross-cutting axe for rough-hewing in addition to chisels, knives, awls, augers, hammers and wooden mauls.[37] Close examination of the Majesties reveals the marks of narrow chisels used for broad folds and indications of the knife, which was normally used alone for faces and other delicate features.

After the carving and joinery were complete, thin linen was normally affixed to the surface, followed by layers of gesso and polychromy.[38] The fine mesh of the fabric helped to bind the superimposed gesso and paint to the wood surface. Ornamental details were occasionally worked in slight relief in the gesso, e.g. bejeweled borders, but the chief decorative strength of the Throne of Wisdom statue resides in the linear elegance of the carving itself. This was in no way obscured by the minuscule strata of linen, gesso and polychromy.

The final enhancement for simple wood Majesties was, of course, the polychromy. Knowledge of original color schemes is limited, since preservation of Romanesque paint is fragmentary at best. Many of the statues have been repeatedly repainted so that the twelfth-century conception is totally obscured. In some cases thick overlays conceal sculptural qualities as well. Others have been stripped bare so that the early color can never be ascertained. From personal examination of dozens of statues with fairly ven-

---

[35] Note the references to the joinery of the early twelfth-century Madonna in Abingdon, England (see Chapter II, note 10 below).

[36] For illustration of benching in late medieval woodcuts, see Blindheim, *Figure Sculpture*, p. 95. Small holes drilled in a statue's base to secure the work to the bench can normally be seen with careful examination. Benching holes drilled in the crowns of heads were usually closed with a plug after the work was completed. Several Throne of Wisdom statues demonstrate these procedures. Similar but larger circular cavities, usually a few centimenters in diameter, can be found in the backs of several Madonnas and also at the tops of heads. Blindheim explains that these would have provided protection against cracking and would also have been concealed in the final finishing by fitted plugs. They are found only in solid sculptures. Flaws such as knots were the cause of openings which were plugged in a corresponding fashion. These abound. Cavities of all of these types have been mistaken for relic niches and some of them were no doubt appropriated as such.

[37] Blindheim, *Figure Sculpture*, pp. 99f.

[38] Traces of linen are particularly visible in the Morgan Madonna and Notre-Dame de Montvianeix (nos. 1, 3). French scholars refer to such a statue as "marouflé." It is not an index to specific date but was widespread throughout the twelfth century (see Register). Cf. Theophilus, *The Various Arts*, I, xvii, p. 17.

erable polychromy, I have found the following pattern to be characteristic: natural flesh tints for hands and faces, a red tunic for Mary covered by a blue mantle, cope or paenula, sometimes trimmed with gilt borders and vermilion linings; a separate white veil might be seen in the north; Christ's tunic was blue, blue-green or red, with or without gilt borders, in combination with a red or blue mantle. The book was often gilded. A few sculptures were entirely gilded, except for faces, in imitation of metal Majesties (e.g. Figs. 89, 101, nos. 30, 35).

Mary and Christ must have seemed much less remote and "thaumaturgic" dressed in blue and red garments than when they were enveloped by the luminosity of metal. The greater degree of lifelikeness corresponds to their later period and its developing taste for more natural forms in art. However, the formal style and iconography still insured a hieratic distance sufficient for the function of the figures, to be discussed in Chapter II.

"Black Virgins"

Romanesque Madonnas were not intended to be "Black Virgins" despite the tenacity with which that view is held. Many of these so-called *Vierges noires* do indeed have dark faces today (e.g. Madonnas at Avioth, Chastreix, Cusset, Dorres, Moulins, Marsat, etc.), and the general assumption is that they must have been conceived that way. Curious explanations have been advanced to account for the blackness. Most commonly, the poetry of the Songs of Songs has been adduced: "I am black, but comely, O ye daughters of Jerusalem, as the tents of Kedar, as the curtains of Solomon. Look not upon me, because I am black, because the sun hath looked upon me" (Song of Sol. 1:5-6). It would be difficult to understand why the Christ Child should also have been blackened if this passage were of significant inspiration for the idea.

Swarthy Byzantine icons have also been credited as a possible source for Black Virgins,[39] along with vaguely envisioned oriental models, e.g. Isis figures brought by Syrian merchants, Crusaders or even St. Louis, and converted into Christian Madonnas.[40]

[39] L. Bréhier, "Communication à propos de l'origine des vierges noires," *Académie des Inscriptions et Belles-Lettres, Comptes rendus des séances, 1935*, Paris, 1935, 379-386; Bréhier, "Vierges romanes," 18ff.

[40] Representations of the ancient Isis-Horus group have been confused with Christian images of Mary and Christ. According to an old legend recounted by B. Faujas de Saint-Fond in the eighteenth century, the Le Puy Virgin was a statue of Isis brought from Egypt and then "Christianized" or transformed into a Mother of God (cf. E. Mâle, *L'Art religieux du XIIe siècle en France*, Paris, 1922, pp. 287-288, ". . . et permettent de penser qu'elle pouvait être une statue d'Isis, rapportée d'Égypte par des legionnaires, puis christianisée, transformée en Mère de Dieu, ainsi que le furent à la fin du paganisme beaucoup de Déesses Mères"). A variant of this legend calls the statue the gift of St. Louis who brought it from the Sudan to the cathedral of Le Puy. This impossible explanation is echoed in Faujas de Saint-Fond's description of the statue. He examined the work shortly before its destruction in 1794 and called its attitude "celle des divinités égyptiennes assises." See B. Faujas de Saint-Fond, *Recherches sur les volcans éteints du Vivarais et du Velay*, Paris and Grenoble, 1778, pp. 417-428, ill. p. 428, and Olivier, *L'ancienne Statue*, pp. 22ff.

Vincent Sablon explained the black or "Moorish" color of the Virgin at Chartres by conflating several of these theories. He referred to the Virgin's origins in a country where exposure to the sun darkened the skin, to the color which could be imagined from Solomon's Song, and to Nicephoras' description of the paintings of the Virgin by St. Luke in which the color of Mary's skin was the "chestnut" color of ripened wheat.[41]

An ingenious theory was put forward by Rohault de Fleury.[42] He thought that the darkness of the silver which was used to ornament Byzantine icons representing Mary, and which had blackened through oxidation, was misunderstood in the West as original. It was imitated there, introducing Black Virgins into Europe. The more sober view of Olivier is that the dark look was caused by a build-up of smoke and grime, or a natural darkening of the wood, then thought intentional and reproduced.[43] He realized, however, that such blackness for images of the Virgin cannot be traced beyond the sixteenth century.[44] No documentation known to me indicates an earlier occurrence of the phenomenon.

Indeed the Black Virgins cited above are archaicizing, post-Romanesque works or are known to have been blackened long after the twelfth century. The Majesties at Avioth, Cusset and Moulins are sculptures of relative modernity as is the Madonna at Chastreix, about whom parishioners complained in the last century that their Virgin had been made a negress.[45] Notre-Dame de Marsat (Fig. 101, no. 35) is known to have

---

According to Habicht and Messerer, a statue of Isis was venerated as an image of the Virgin and Child at Saint-Germain-des-Prés in Paris until 1514; V. Habicht, *Maria*, Oldenburg, 1926, p. 62; R. Messerer, *Ottonische Goldschmiedewerke im Essener Münsterschatz*, doctoral dissertation, Munich, 1950, pp. 12f. In connection with the studies of Boll, Weber and Norden, who claim that Isis-Horus legends induced representations of Mary with the Christ Child, see also the work of Saillens and Durand-Lefébvre on Black Virgins (F. Boll, *Aus der Offenbarung Johannis*, Berlin, 1914, pp. 108f.; W. Weber, *Die aegyptisch-griechische Terrakotten*, Berlin, 1914; E. Norden, *Die Geburt des Kindes*, Leipzig, 1924, pp. 113f.; E. Saillens, *Nos Vierges noires*, Paris, 1945; M. Durand-Lefébvre, *Etude sur l'origine des Vierges noires*, Paris, 1937). Also of interest are: M. de la Faye de l'Hospital, *Etudes sur les Vierges noires*, Clermont-Ferrand, 1882; M. Degert, "Origine de la Vierge noire de la Daurade," *Bulletin de la société archéologique du midi de la France*, XXXI (1903), 355-358. For the St. Louis legend, see A. Jacotin and L. Pascal, *Bibliographie du Velay et de la Haute-Loire*, published under the auspices of the Société agricole et scientifique de la Haute-Loire, I, Le Puy, 1903, pp. 50-52. For a recent interpretation of the theory that the Madonnas derive from Isis statues, see P. Bloch, "Überlegungen zum Typus der Essener Madonna," *Kolloquium über frühmittelalterliche Skulptur*, 1968, 65-69.

[41] Vincent Sablon, *Histoire de l'auguste et vénérable église de Chartres*, Chartres, [1671], trans. by R. Branner, *Chartres Cathedral*, New York, 1969, p. 110. For the full passage, see Chapter IV below, pp. 107-108.

[42] Fleury, *Vierge*; Olivier, *L'ancienne Statue*, p. 13.   [43] Olivier, *L'ancienne Statue*, p. 13.

[44] Saillens, *Nos Vierges noires*, p. 20. The association of the dark beauty of the Queen of Sheba with the passage from the Song of Songs quoted above (Song of Sol. 1:5-6) was made in the Romanesque period, and it may have contributed to the later development of a swarthy Virgin Mary in popular tradition. See note 67 below.

[45] B. Craplet, "Vierges romanes," *Richesses de la France, Le Puy-de-Dôme*, XLIV (1960), 66-68.

been blackened in 1830 and again recently.[46] Notre-Dame de Montvianeix (Fig. 60, no. 3) was black until the cleaning of 1931 revealed the original, natural flesh tints beneath the dark paint.[47] Notre-Dame de Bon Espoir (Fig. 155, no. 88) has had a similar but more complicated history.[48] A cleaning in 1945 uncovered a fair-skinned face, but out of respect for tradition, it was again blackened. Now that tastes have changed, the face has been re-cleaned and is today seen as it was originally intended, in natural color. The reasons for these alterations have to do with religious customs of the communities in which the Majesties are honored and their analysis is obviously beyond the scope of the present study. The evidence we have indicates that such customs were not common to the Romanesque world which saw in the Madonna an equally complex but very different form of the Mother of God.

Iconography

Variables in the iconography of the Throne of Wisdom statue are few. The subject is rich and complex in its meaning, but simple in its composition which consists of a distinctive type of double enthronement. Poses rather than attributes are particularly telling. Mary is represented as a mature, regal figure. She is normally imperious in bearing, clearly a queen rather than a princess. She wears a simple tunic, usually covered by a full overgarment which may be intricately pleated and draped, but which normally has the form of a paenula. This is sometimes pulled up over her head as a mantle. A pallium may or may not be worn over it. A cope, a separate veil for the head and a crown are common in northern France.[49] She supports the Child with her hands and usually holds no attributes.[50]

The Christ Child is also portrayed as a mature figure. Despite his smaller size and his position in his mother's lap which indicates that he is the son of Mary, he is not represented as an infant but as a miniature adult, a child-man. Were he shown as a small child suckling at the breast or reclining helplessly, all conviction of majesty would disappear.

---

[46] *Ibid.*

[47] L. Bréhier, "Notes sur les statues de Vierges romanes, Notre-Dame de Montvianeix et la question des Vierges noires," *Revue d'Auvergne*, XLVII (1933), 193-198; Bréhier, "Communication," 383-384.

[48] P. Quarré, "La Statue de Notre-Dame de Bon Espoir à Dijon et son ancienne polychromie," *Mémoires de la commission des antiquités de la Côte-d'Or*, XXIII (1947-1953), 190-197. For a reference to the blackness of the statue in 1591: H. Drouot, "La Ligue et le règne d'Henri IV en Bourgogne, études et documents, VI, Dijon à l'automne de 1589," *Mémoires de l'académie des sciences, arts et belles-lettres de Dijon* (1932), 12-13. See the discussion in the Register (no. 88).

[49] The presence of a crown is not an indication of date, as is sometimes supposed, but of regional preference. It is common in the Hautes-Pyrénées but not in the Pyrénées-Orientales. Cf. M. Lawrence, "Maria Regina," *The Art Bulletin*, VII (1924-1925), 150-161.

[50] Orbs, apples, lily-like sceptres and the like rarely appear in twelfth-century examples. See Lawrence, "Maria Regina," 161.

Christ may be seated on Mary's left knee or placed somewhat obliquely in her lap in accordance with regional styles, but normally he is strictly centered and frontal. As in the hieratic, Byzantine *nikopoia* iconography, the Romanesque Christ is the center of the main axes of the composition.[51] This arrangement is understandably most common since it perfectly balances his relation to Mary. It enhances her role as a frame of reference for him and allows a many-faceted interpretation of his own character. His costume, though simply made up of a tunic and mantle (*himation*), is as rigidly ordered as his pose.[52] In his imperious aloofness he recalls the vivid description which Ammianus Marcellinus applied to the attitude affected by the emperor Constantius in procession at the time of his triumphal entry into Rome: "and looking straight before him as though he had had his neck in a vice he turned his eyes neither to the right nor to the left, as if he had been a statue."[53]

Thus Christ's maturity and his stiffness are pertinent to his portrayal as a sovereign who assumes his high majesty in ascending the throne, which is in this case the figure of Mary. As a throne she is subordinate to him, yet as his mother she embodies the lineage of the house of David whence the Savior, who is son of Man as well as son of God, inherits the rights of an earthly king.[54]

Upon this throne, the royal Christ holds a book with one hand and makes the gesture of benediction with the other, an attitude which reflects his priestly character, related again to Mary as symbol of the Church.[55] He is head of the institution which

[51] This similarity has been cited in support of the theory that the Majesties derive from Eastern sources: J. Baum, "Romanische Marienbilder im schweizerische Landesmuseum," *Anzeiger für schweizerische Altertumskunde*, xxvii (1925), 215-227. This view is taken up by I. Baier-Futterer, *Kataloge des schweizerisches Landesmuseums in Zurich, Die Bildwerke der Romanik und Gotik*, Zurich, 1936, *passim*.

[52] A crown for the Christ Child is rare, but it is known in northern France.

[53] *The Roman History of Ammianus Marcellinus*, trans. C. Yonge, London, 1902, xvi, 10, p. 101.

[54] The genealogy of Christ linking him with David is traced in the Gospel of Matthew through Joseph. Medieval theologians also spell out the lineage of Christ from David to the Virgin through the kings of Judah in the famous Tree of Jesse.

[55] A. Katzenellenbogen, *The Sculptural Programs of Chartres Cathedral*, Baltimore, 1959, pp. 59ff., provides an excellent exegesis of the history and meaning of the Mary-Ecclesia concept. Particularly pertinent are the parallels which figure in the liturgy, e.g. the *Glossa Ordinaria*, which indicate that Psalm 44 (Vulg.; AV Ps. 45) is sung on the Virgin's day because its reference to the Church may be specifically related to her ("Cantatur hic psalmus de festo beatae Mariae Virginis, quia quae de Ecclesia generaliter hic dicuntur, ad Mariam specialiter referri possunt"; Migne, *PL*, cxiii, 911), and the *Rationale divinorum officiorum* of John Belethus, ca. 1160, which relates the Church and the Virgin (Migne, *PL*, ccii, 150; Katzenellenbogen, *Chartres*, pp. 60, 128 nn. 27-28). Katzenellenbogen (*ibid.*, pp. 127-128 n. 26) also draws attention to the commentaries on the Song of Songs by Alan of Lille and the chancellor of the School of Chartres, probably Peter of Roissy (1208-1213), who interpret the Song of Solomon as a spiritual reference to the Church and the Virgin in an interchangeable manner. Cf. H. Coathalem, S.J., *Le Parallélisme entre la Sainte Vierge et l'église dans la tradition latine jusqu'à la fin du XIIe siècle*, Analecta Gregoriana, lxxiv, Sectio B, no. 27, Rome, 1954; Scheffczyk, *Mariengeheimnis*, pp. 390-428.

she personifies. Her sacerdotal nature is often accented in turn by her garb, the priestly chasuble and pallium which she wears in many examples (Figs. 112-121, nos. 45-54).

Christ must also be understood as the Logos incarnate on his mother's lap. The Virgin is not simply the mother of a child, she is the god-bearer or *Theotokos*. Her maternity is human and divine at one and the same time. Adam of St. Victor (d. 1180) expresses this with economy and elegance in Romanesque times: "O Maria, Redemptoris/ Creatura, Creatoris."[56] As Christ himself made his divinity manifest in human form, Mary was human by nature but the *Theotokos* by divine will, a view authorized by the Councils of Ephesus (431) and Chalcedon (451). Christ's humanity and divinity formed an indissoluble unity of distinct but indivisible parts, for Divine Wisdom had become mortal flesh. The Word of God was incarnated in man. Mary was the agency through which the mystery of the Incarnation was realized and, therefore, as the bearer of that Wisdom, to be regarded as *sedes sapientiae*, the Seat of Wisdom.[57]

She was likened to a throne continually in writings from Early Christian times through the Romanesque period. Athanasius (296-373) had written that Mary represents the throne of God,[58] and Andrew of Crete (660-740) had referred to Mary in a homily in which, basing himself on Isaiah's vision of "the Lord sitting upon a throne, high and lifted up" (Isa. 6:1), he speaks of her in the same terms.[59] Most pointed are the words of John of Damascus (675-749) in which he likewise recalls the passage in Isaiah and addresses her: "Hail, throne lifted up on high in glory, living throne, representing in thyself the throne of God."[60]

In Romanesque times, allusions to Mary as the Throne of Solomon are frequent. Particularly pertinent is Guibert of Nogent's (d. 1125) explanation of Solomon's famous throne which is described in 1 Kings 10:18-20: "Moreover the king made a

[56] D. S. Wrangham, *The Liturgical Poetry of Adam of St. Victor*, London, 1881, III, xcii, p. 100, gives the following translation, "Mary, our Redeemer's Creature!/ Mother of thine own Creator!" I am indebted to Professor Harry Bober for pointing out this passage.

[57] Katzenellenbogen investigates the sources of the *sedes sapientiae* iconography (*Chartres*, pp. 9-10, 15, 109 nn. 40-42). Bede had referred to the "wisdom of the Lord who assumed flesh" ("ipsa Dei sapientia carnem in qua videri posset, induta est . . ."), Migne, *PL*, XCIV, 40. Of particular note are the homilies of Bede, cited by Katzenellenbogen, present in the twelfth-century Lectionary of Chartres which stress the union of Christ's Godhead and manhood (*Chartres*, pp. 11-12, 108 n. 17). Jean Meyendorff, "L'Iconographie de la sagesse divine dans la tradition Byzantine," *Cahiers archéologiques*, x (1959), 259-277, presents an analysis of the Byzantine interpretation of Divine Wisdom in relation to the Old Testament passage in Proverbs: "Wisdom hath builded her house, she hath hewn out her seven pillars . . ." (Prov. 9:1-6).

[58] "Thronus autem Dei per Virginem Mariam figurebatur," H. Marraccii, *Polyanthea Mariana*, Cologne, 1710, p. 724. For other examples, see *ibid.*, pp. 724-731.

[59] "Thronus excelsus et elevatus in quo sedens Dominus Sabaoth visus est," *ibid.*, p. 724. Cf. Migne, *PG*, XCVII, 879.

[60] *Ibid.*, pp. 724-731, N.B. p. 725; Migne, *PG*, XCVI, 690, "Ave, thronus in sublime elatus in gloria, animata sedes, Dei in se sessionem designans." These words are part of a lengthy and elaborate panegyric on the Virgin.

great throne of ivory, and overlaid it with the best gold. The throne had six steps, and the top of the throne was round behind: and there were stays on either side on the place of the seat, and two lions stood beside the stays. And twelve lions stood there on the one side and on the other upon the six steps: there was not the like made in any kingdom." Guibert likens the lions to the prelates of the Church and Mary to the Church itself ("ecclesia illustratur Maria"). He further praises her as the ivory throne of Solomon and goes on to identify the Wisdom of the Father as Solomon himself.[61]

His interpretations parallel a long excursus on the Throne of Solomon in a sermon on the Nativity of Mary, which has been attributed to Peter Damian (d. 1072): "Today she is born through whom we are all born again, whose honor the Almighty greatly desired, and in whom God established his throne (Vulg. Ps. 44; AV Ps. 45). She herself is that glorious throne concerning which in the Book of Kings it is written in these words: 'King Solomon made a great throne of ivory and overlaid it with the best gold beyond measure. . . .'" Damian delineates the pacific, hortatory and glorious character of Solomon's wisdom and elaborates on the justice and benevolence of his throne which is seen as the seat or tribunal for the Wisdom of God. Damian says further that the Virgin's womb is the image of the seat of this majesty: "Our Solomon [i.e. Christ], not only wise but indeed the Wisdom of the Father, not only pacific but indeed our peace, who unified both, has prepared a throne, manifestly the womb of the chaste Virgin, in which sat that Majesty which shakes the world with a nod." He adds that the ivory of Solomon's throne is an image of the virginity of Mary and, after describing the glowing gold with which the throne was sheathed, he concludes with the elaborate simile that "in like manner God sheathed the Virgin and was sheathed in the Virgin."[62]

[61] "Ecclesia illustratur Maria.—Et terra splendebat a majestate ejus (Ezek. XLVIII:2)" (*De laude Sanctae Mariae*, Migne, *PL*, CLVI, 543). "Thronus est eburneus Salomonis.—Haec est thronus quem fecit Salomen de ebore grandem et vestivit eum auro fulvo nimis (III Reg. X:19). Sapientia Dei Patris primum, juxta apostolum, pacifica (Jac. III:17), ipsa est Salomon, quae thronum de ebore sibi facit, dum sedem in Virgine, qua nil unquam fuit castius, sibi ponit. Elephas enim, cujus ossa sunt ebur, continentis ac mundae naturae est. Porro grandem, nimirum ex Filio coelis, terris, et inferis praesidentem. Hunc auro fulvo nimis vestit, cum eam non virtutum scintillis ut alios, sed ipsa substantialiter propria divinitate interius exteriusque infercit" (*ibid.*, 541-542).

[62] "Hodie nata est illa, per quam omnes renascimur, cujus speciem concupivit Omnipotens, et in qua Deus posuit thronum suum (Psal. XLIV). Ipsa est thronus ille mirabilis, de quo in Regnorum historia legitur in haec verba: 'Fecit rex Salomon thronum de ebore grandem, et vestivit eum auro fulvo nimis. . . .' Salomon noster, non solum sapiens, sed et sapientia Patris; non solum pacificus, sed et pax nostra, qui fecit utraque unum, fecit thronum, uterum videlicet intemeratae Virginis, in quo sedit illa majestas, quae nutu concutit orbem. . . . Hoc est aurum fulvum nimis, quo thronus est vestitus, quia tali modo Deus Virginem induit et in Virgine indutus est, ut meliori non posset" (*In nativitate Beatissimae Virginis Mariae*, Migne, *PL*, CXLIV, 736-740). The last passage is particularly interesting in relation to the early wood Majesties noted above which were adorned with a gold repoussé sheath. See note 3 above, and particularly the Essen Madonna (Figs. 28-31).

Damian goes on to interpret the twelve lions of Solomon's throne as the twelve apostles, and the stays of the throne as Gabriel and John the Evangelist.

Francis Wormald ascribes the sermon to Nicholas of Clairvaux in "The Throne of Solomon

Adam of St. Victor's (d. 1180) hymn to the Virgin which begins "Salve Mater Salvatoris" gives additional emphasis to the idea:

Tu thronus es Salomonis
Cui nullus par in thronis
Arte vel materia:
Ebur candens castitatis,
Aurum fulvum charitatis
Praesignant mysteria.[63]

According to the hymn Solomon's ivory and gold throne, fairest of all thrones ever, shadows forth the chastity and charity of the Virgin.[64]

Thus, for the Romanesque period Mary clearly figured the Throne of Solomon. She held in her lap the New Testament counterpart to the wise king of the Old Testament, the incarnation of Divine Wisdom, the Word become flesh, and was herself the *sedes sapientiae*. That this concept was current is further indicated by inscriptions, associated with depictions of the Throne of Wisdom in relief sculptures, such as those at Arezzo and Beaucaire (Figs. 1 and 2), where it is expressed with epigrammatic terseness: "On the lap of the Mother sits the Wisdom of the Father."[65]

---

and St. Edward's Chair," *De Artibus Opuscula XL, Essays in Honor of Erwin Panofsky*, New York, 1961, 534.

Although the Virgin is not specifically alluded to, the association of the Throne of Solomon with the Church, made in Carolingian times by Rabanus Maurus in his commentary on the Book of Kings, anticipates the concept of our period, Migne, *PL*, cix, 197. Wormald gives the following translation: "The throne is the Church in which Solomon promulgates his judgments and the soul of the righteous is the seat of wisdom. The throne was made of ivory . . ." *op. cit.*, 534.

Cf. P. Bloch, "Nachwirkungen des Alten Bundes in der christlichen Kunst," *Monumenta Judaica*, Handbuch, Eine Ausstellung im Kölnischen Stadtmuseum, 1963, Cologne, 1964, 770.

[63] Migne, *PL*, cxcvi, 1503; Wrangham, *Liturgical Poetry*, ii, lxxiii, pp. 220-223.

[64] Wrangham's translation is paraphrased here. For additional references to the Virgin as the Throne of Solomon in medieval textual sources, see F. Piper, "Maria als Thron Salomos und ihre Tugenden bei der Verkundigung," *Jahrbücher für Kunstwissenschaft*, v (1873), 116-121; N.B. 118-119 for passages from Abbot Guerricus (d. 1157), follower of Bernard of Clairvaux, and from Walter von der Vogelweide.

For the later pictorial development of the Virgin seated on Solomon's throne, which includes the steps, lions and typological accoutrements such as apostles, virtues, etc., see: A. D. McKenzie, "The Virgin Mary as the Throne of Solomon in Medieval Art," unpublished Ph.D. dissertation, New York University, 1965; C. Michna, *Maria als Thron Salomonis*, doctoral dissertation, Vienna, 1950; C. Michna, "Das Salomonische Thronsymbol auf Österreichische Denkmäler," *Alte und moderne Kunst*, vi (1961), 2-5, 43; Wormald, "Throne of Solomon."

[65] "IN GREMIO MATRIS: RESIDET SAPIENTIA PATRIS," G. Vezin, *L'Adoration et le cycle des Mages*, Paris, 1950, pl. xx; F. Kayser, *Werdezeit der abendländischen Kunst*, Freiburg-in-Breisgau, 1948, pp. 148-150; R. Hamann, *Die Abteikirche von St. Gilles und ihre künstlerische Nachfolge*, Berlin, 1956, pp. 190, 358-359, fig. 456; these reliefs probably represent three-dimensional Throne of Wisdom statues. Cf. the statue by the "presbiter Martinus" of 1199 with a similar inscription: "IN

26

In addition to this fundamental significance in the Throne of Wisdom iconography, the equation of Mary and the *sedes sapientiae* carried further allusive meaning. In the *Speculum humanae salvationis*, probably written in the second quarter of the fourteenth century, the traditional identification of Mary and the Throne of Solomon is maintained in the couplets consecrated, as the author says, to the oblation of the Magi:

> Thronus veri Salomonis est Beatissima Virgo Maria,
> In quo residebat Jesus Christus, vera Sophia.
> Thronus iste factus erat de nobilissimo thesauro,
> De ebore videlicet candido et fulvo nimis auro.
> Ebur propter sui candorem et frigiditatem
> Designat virginalem munditiam et castitatem . . .[66]

The text explains further that the Throne of Solomon has prefigured the Virgin as King Solomon has prefigured Christ. It says also that the Queen of Sheba, who makes an offering, has prefigured the oblation of the Magi. The miniatures accompanying the Miélot edition illustrate this as follows. Typologically, Solomon's throne—with its six steps, the lions, and the Queen of Sheba before it, presenting to Solomon in sign of homage the "things one would never have seen until then in Jerusalem"—is pictured on the page opposite the enthroned Madonna approached by the Magi with their gifts. The offerings of gold, frankincense and myrrh are interpreted symbolically in the text as is usual: the gold represents nobility, referring to the Child-King; the frankincense represents the oblation of the priest, indicating Christ as priest; the myrrh represents Christ's mortal body destined for the tomb:

> Magi igitur venientes, assumpserunt munera talia,
> Quia talia puero viderentur congrua et non alia.
> Aurum enim propter sui nobilitatem munus est regale,
> Per quod ostendebant puerum regem esse et se decere tale.
> Thus autem oblatio erat sacerdotalis,
> Et puer ille erat sacerdos cui nunquam fuit aequalis.
> Cum myrrha solebant antiqui corpora mortuorum condire
> Et Christus rex et sacerdos voluit pro salute nostra mortem subire.[67]

GREMIO MATRIS, FULGET SAPIENTIA PATRIS," H. Hager, "Die Anfänge des italienischen Altarbildes, Untersuchungen zur Entstehungsgeschichte des toskanischen Hochaltarretables," *Römische Forschungen der Bibliotheca Herziana*, XVII (1962), fig. 171.

[66] J. Lutz and P. Perdrizet, *Speculum humanae salvationis* (ed. J. Miélot, 1448), Mulhouse, 1907-1909, cap. ix, lines 53-58, p. 21. The lines can be freely translated: "The throne of the true Solomon is the Most Blessed Virgin Mary, in which sat Jesus Christ, the true Wisdom. That throne had been made of the most noble treasure, to wit dazzling white ivory and exceeding ruddy gold. Ivory, by reason of its intrinsic candescence and coolness, represents virgin purity and chastity."

[67] "Accordingly when the Magi came they chose such gifts because such would seem suitable to the Child, and not any others. Indeed gold, because of its intrinsic noble quality is a royal gift by which they indicated that the Child is King, and as such it is appropriate. Frankincense, on the

The interpretation of the gifts of the Magi, as having reference to the regal, priestly and mortal aspects of Christ, had wide currency in the Middle Ages and was understood in related contexts. Indeed, the references are all tacitly implied in our statues of the Child on the lap of the Virgin, since Christ appears as priest and king ("rex et sacerdos"), and as a mortal, being willing "to suffer death" ("mortem subire"). Although neither Magi nor gifts are represented in the wood Majesty, Christ's roles as the Child-King (i.e. enthroned), as priest (i.e. giving benediction), and as a mortal (i.e. son of Mary) are all implicit. To be sure, these three qualities are subsumed in the concept of Christ as the Divine Wisdom. The Logos has become man, in kingly and priestly manner.[68]

While the passages of the *Speculum humanae salvationis* quoted above must be dated in the fourteenth century, they are lifted almost literally from earlier sources, e.g. the Golden Legend chapter on Epiphany. Of course, the interpretation of the mystic gifts has a long history reaching back to the Early Christian period and was well established as a part of Romanesque symbolism.[69] Their implication was widely understood and described repeatedly with only minor variations, e.g. gold as greatness, frankincense as the true God, and myrrh as the sepulchre.[70] Honorius of Autun,[71] William Durandus[72] and others[73] mention them. Adam of St. Victor's twelfth-century Epiphany hymn cites them in lines of memorable beauty:

---

other hand, was a priestly offering and that Child was the Priest to whom was never an equal. Inasmuch as the ancients were accustomed to embalm the bodies of the dead with myrrh, even Christ the King and Priest was willing to endure death for our salvation," *ibid.*, cap. ix, lines 87-94, pp. 20-21, pls. 17-18; P. Perdrizet, *Etude sur le speculum humanae salvationis*, Paris, 1908, p. 65.

Illustrations of the Adoration of the Magi and the Queen of Sheba before the Throne of Solomon are also juxtaposed typologically in the enamel panels of Nicholas of Verdun's Klosterneuburg ambo of 1181; F. Röhrig, *Der Verduner Altar*, Vienna, 1955, pls. 12-13; New York, The Metropolitan Museum of Art, *The Year 1200*, 1970, no. 179. The Queen of Sheba is given a black face, whereas the Virgin's face is light in these panels.

Adam of St. Victor's hymn on the dedication of a church takes note of the Queen of Sheba's black comeliness (L. Gautier, *Oeuvres poétiques d'Adam de Saint-Victor*, Paris, 1858, I, pp. 154-167, N.B. pp. 157, 166-167, a reference I owe to the kindness of Dr. Helmut Buschhausen): "Huc venit Austri regina,/ Salomonis quam divina/ Condit sapientia./ Haec est nigra sed formosa,/ Myrrhae et thuris fumosa,/ Virga pigmentaria." Digby Wrangham gives an English translation of this strophe (*Liturgical Poetry*, I, pp. 140-141): "Hither Sheba's queen progresseth,/ She, whom Solomon impresseth/ With his wisdom all-divine:/ Black she is, but comely; blending/ Charms, as when in smoke ascending/ Myrrh and frankincense combine."

[68] John Meyendorff traces the early Byzantine tradition which associates the Divine Wisdom with the mission of the Savior, born of the Virgin: "Sagesse divine," 259-277.

[69] Perdrizet, *Etude*, p. 65. [70] Young, *Drama*, II, pp. 32ff.

[71] Migne, *PL*, CLXXII, 845.

[72] *Rationale divinorum officiorum*, Lib. VI, caps. 16, 17, Venice, 1568, p. 184v: "Tertio, quia aurum ad tributum, tus ad sacrificium, myra vero ad sepulturam pertinet. Per haec ergo tria insinuantur in Christo regia potestas, divina maiestas, et humana mortalitas." Cf. p. 186v.

[73] Perdrizet, *Etude*, p. 65.

Tria dona reges ferunt:
Stella duce Regem quaerunt,
Per quam certi semper erunt
    De superno lumine:
Auro Regem venerantes,
Thure Deum designantes,
Myrrha mortem memorantes,
    Sacro docti Flamine.

Here the gifts refer to the regal, divine and mortal character of Christ.[74] Such associations would inevitably accompany observation of the sculptures of the Madonna and Child.

A final reference, even wider than that suggested by the Magi's gifts, cannot be overlooked. The statue combines the majesty of male and female figures in one image. The Child-King, the divine ruler of the Christian world, is enthroned in the lap of the Queen of Heaven. These two figures may also be understood as the Logos of the New Dispensation with the seat of the Wisdom of Solomon from the Old, or as the Godhead with his Church. Male and female provinces interlock as do the figures. Mother-child divinities are to be found in ancient art, but they invariably stress only one or a few of the many ideas which meet and merge in the Romanesque statue. The Gallo-Roman mother goddess known as the *Magna Mater* underscores the mother or fertility aspect.[75] Isis-Horus groups also emphasize the mother-infant relationship, particularly in the suckling of the child. They add more specifically to the concept of the throne, however, since Isis means "the seat" or "the throne" and personifies the "sacred coronation stool charged with the mysterious power of kingship."[76] The Christian image goes beyond both in its multi-dimensional meaning. It is intensely religious as well as human. In claiming a seat for himself in the Virgin, Christ takes possession of her not as male possesses female, but as Christian divinity possesses the earth and his Church.

When fully developed, this iconographic form, so rich in meaning and association, dominated the stone tympana of great cathedrals in the last half of the twelfth century.[77] There Mary was portrayed in monumental form as the Throne of Divine Wisdom. For

[74] Wrangham, *Liturgical Poetry*, III, xc, p. 92; see the translation of these stanzas and the fuller discussion of them in connection with Epiphany plays below in Chapter II, p. 59.

[75] Note also the bronzes from Sardinia, Caligari, Museo Archeologico Nazionale (Zervos, *La Civilization de la Sardaigne*, pls. 455, 459, cited in E. Neumann, *The Great Mother*, trans. R. Manheim, New York, 1955, pls. 46-47), and the statue from Thebes of Demeter and Kore, Louvre (Neumann, *Mother*, pl. 147).

[76] *Ibid.*, p. 99. See also E. O. James, *The Cult of the Mother Goddess*, London, 1959, p. 241. For studies of the parallels between Isis and Mary, see Norden, *Die Geburt*, pp. 113ff.; Weber, *Terrakotten*; Boll, *Offenbarung*, pp. 108ff. Cf. note 40 above.

[77] E.g. Royal Portal at Chartres; St. Anne Portal at Notre-Dame, Paris; north transept portal at the Cathedral of Notre-Dame, Reims; west facade, left portal, Laon Cathedral; north transept portal, Bourges Cathedral.

a brief period, the iconography represented a supreme achievement in the illustration of medieval thought. On the west facade at Chartres, the Apocalyptic Vision of the central tympanum showed Christ in Majesty with the four symbols of the Evangelists, but the tympanum over the right portal, now known widely as the Incarnation Portal, pictured Christ in relation to another vast world and a broader context of meaning, Christ in relation to the Virgin.[78] The thirteenth century was to turn to other things, stressing one aspect or another of this relationship. Christ would become an infant again cuddled in the lap of his mother or would be carried on her arm as she stands, or the two would be rendered separately, Christ sharing the throne equally with the Virgin Queen in the Coronation of the Virgin theme. The Romanesque meeting of all of these statements in one image was to change with the advent of the Gothic Age.

[78] The iconography of the Chartres tympana is, of course, much more complex when considered in relation to the lintels and archivolts. See Katzenellenbogen, *Chartres*, pp. 7ff.

CHAPTER II. Function

The Throne of Wisdom as a Reliquary

IN 1924 LOUIS BRÉHIER published an account of a neglected text found in an early manuscript of Gregory of Tours.[1] The text contains information on the artistic activities of Stephen II, Bishop of Clermont-Ferrand (937-984). With the discovery of this document, Bréhier was able to show that the ancient statue of the Madonna and Child which formerly existed in the Clermont-Ferrand cathedral treasury was a golden image created for Bishop Stephen about A.D. 946. It was fashioned as a reliquary to hold and honor relics of the Virgin. A drawing accompanies the text and reproduces what would seem to be the first Throne of Wisdom statue in the medieval West (Fig. 3).[2] Inasmuch as the text explicitly states that Stephen wished to honor the relics of the Virgin in a manner very different from the gold and silver chests which were ordinarily used for the relics of saints, Bréhier concluded that this reliquary statue was an innovation. Citing the statue of St. Foy of Conques (Fig. 13) as a close follower to this golden Madonna, he claimed the lost Clermont-Ferrand Majesty to be the most ancient reliquary statue known to us and the prototype for later statues of similar form. He believed these were likewise reliquaries, and in this way the tradition of a reliquary function became established in the literature devoted to the *sedes sapientiae* statue.

Before dealing with the validity of this theory, the question of the relics themselves should be briefly considered. That Bishop Stephen had been able to acquire relics of Mary at all might seem at first difficult to equate with belief in her Assumption. But in fact the zeal of relic seekers could be rewarded with locks of hair and secondary relics, such as personal adornments. Some of the Virgin's hair was reputedly preserved at Aachen, from Charlemagne's hoard, and at Basel, Canterbury, Centula, Clermont-Ferrand, Conques, London, Mende, Paris, Senlis and Vézelay, among others.[3] The fillet

---

[1] Bréhier, "Clermont," 205-210. It is more fully studied by Rigodon, "Vision," 22-55, who dates the text in the late tenth or early eleventh century. The material has recently been reviewed by Beutler, *Bildwerke*, pp. 39-42.

[2] The drawing was published by Fleury, *Vierge*, II, p. 214. Other texts relative to this sculpture are published by Bréhier, "Deux Inventaires du trésor de la cathédrale de Clermont au Xᵉ siècle," *Etudes archéologiques, Mémoires de la société des "Amis de l'Université de Clermont-Ferrand," Supplément à la "Revue d'Auvergne,"* II, Clermont-Ferrand, 1910, 34-48. See also note 62 below.

[3] Numerous lists have been compiled, e.g. A.J.M. Hamon, *Notre-Dame de France ou histoire du culte de la Sainte Vierge en France, depuis l'origine du christianisme jusqu'à nos jours*, Paris, 1861-1866; Fleury, *Vierge*, I, pp. 288-297; J. E. Drochon, *Histoire illustrée des pèlerinages français*

which held all these locks in place was claimed at Canterbury and pieces of the veil(s) which covered them were known at Autun, Laon, Chartres, and Montecassino. Mary's various tunics, robes and chemises, sometimes in fragmentary form, were venerated at Aachen, Clermont-Ferrand, Chartres, Cologne, Schaffhausen, Senlis, Stavelot, Trier, Vézelay, etc., whereas Cluny was proud to have a sleeve. Le Puy claimed a slipper as a gift of St. Martial,[4] and girdles and other items under the simple heading of "relics of the Virgin" were scattered elsewhere, as recorded in inventories.

In the case of the Clermont-Ferrand Majesty made for Bishop Stephen, the relics of the Virgin which were enclosed within her statue included some of her hair, fragments of her clothing and drops of her milk, but such an identity of image and contents was evidently rare. Relics of Mary continued to be sheltered in shrines quite apart from the Throne of Wisdom statues long after the latter were widespread. Such was the case at Chartres where an elaborate and famous *châsse* of normal box-like form contained the Virgin's tunic.[5] At Le Puy and at Cluny the Virgin's relics were also kept apart from the statue of Mary.[6] Conventional reliquary chests and similar containers were used for *Mariana* at Aachen and Cluny and, as far as we know, elsewhere. Statues of the Madonna might contain no relics of the Virgin at all but fragments of saints and other sacred items instead, sometimes in a varied mixture.

For a statue at Vézelay we have specific information. It comes from the account of Hugh of Poitiers who records events of ca. 1161-1165 following a fire in the church of the Madeleine.[7]

---

de la très Sainte Vierge, Paris, 1890; H. Schiffers, *Der Reliquienschatz Karls des Grossen und die Anfänge der Aachenfahrt*, Aachen, 1951; cf. L. Réau, *Iconographie de l'art chrétien*, Paris, 1957, II, ii, pp. 61-63. See the references to the relics at Clermont-Ferrand, Rodez and Le Puy in Jean Savaron, *Les Origines de Clairmont*, ed. P. Durand, Paris, 1662, p. 343, which reproduces Savaron's *De sanctis ecclesiis et monasteriis Claromontii*, Paris, 1608. For the relics at Laon and Senlis, see: J. F. Benton, *Self and Society in Medieval France, The Memoirs of Abbot Guibert of Nogent*, New York, 1970, p. 191; M. Aubert, *Monographie de la cathédrale de Senlis*, Senlis, 1910, p. 162.

[4] Olivier, *L'ancienne Statue*, p. 18; Savaron, *Les Origines*, p. 343.

[5] Hamon, *Histoire*, I, pp. 181f.; E. de Lépinois, *Histoire de Chartres*, Chartres, 1854, I, pp. 36, 224 n. 3, 550-553; Drochon, *Histoire*, pp. 344-345.

[6] Olivier, *L'ancienne Statue*, p. 19; Benet, "Trésor," 195-205, N.B. no. 23, p. 196.

[7] "Accidit interea in eadem ecclesia quoddam futurae calamitatis praesagium simul et solatium. In crypta enim, quae supra B. dilectricis Mariae Magdalenae sepulcrum exstat, tantus ignis casu erupit, ut etiam tyrannos, quos Francigenae trabes vocant, qui erant in superiori parte, combusserit. Imago tamen B. Dei genitricis Mariae lignea, in ipsius pavimento cryptae posita, nullum omnino passa est incendium, sed tantummodo denigrata est. Sericum autem quod ad collum imaginis pueri Jesu pendebat phylacterium, nec odorem fumi contraxit, nec in parvo aut magno colorem mutavit. Unde liquido claruit, quod nec ipsa imago aliquantisper fumo obduceretur, nisi ut reparationis ejus occasione thesaurus inaestimabilis latens in ea per divinam dispensationem panderetur. Nam praedicta imagine ad reparatorem missa, dictum est ab ipso reparatore, quod imago, uti sibi videbatur, occultissimum ostiolum inter scapulas haberet: quo audito, Gilo prior praecepit eam portari in sacristiariam; vocansque secum Gaufredum subpriorem, et Gervasium sacristam, et Girardum conestabulum, Mauricium quoque succentorem, et ipsum Lambertum imaginis reparatorem, accepto

Meanwhile in this church there took place a certain presage of a future calamity which was simultaneously a solace. For in the crypt which rises above the tomb of the blessed, beloved Mary Magdalene, by chance so great a fire broke out that it consumed even the braces, which the French call beams, which were in the upper part. The wood statue of the blessed Mary, Mother of God, which was placed on the floor of the crypt, suffered nothing at all from the fire, but was only blackened. Moreover, the silken phylactery which hung at the neck of the image of the Child Jesus contracted no odor of smoke nor did it change color in lesser or greater degree. Whence it was crystal-clear that not even the image itself would have been coated with soot for a while were it not that, through divine dispensation, the occasion of its repair revealed an inestimable treasure lying hidden in it. For when the afore-mentioned image had been sent to the restorer, he said that the image, as it seemed to him, had a most secret little door between the shoulders. Having heard this, Giles, the prior, ordered it carried into the sacristy; and calling with him Godfrey, the sub-

---

cultello ipsemet rasit colores, lignoque retecto nullius juncturae indicium potuerunt deprehendere: demum accepit malleolum ferreum, tentavitque aure percipere quod omnes oculis nequibant investigare, audiensque quasi sonum rei concavae, spe succinctus hilari ostiolum illud propriis manibus pie audax reseravit, invenitque capillos illius intemeratae Virginis, quae nec primam similem visa est nec sequentem habere; et de tunica ejusdem genitricis Dei Mariae, et ossium unum B. Joannis Baptistae. Invenit etiam ossa BB. apostolorum Petri et Pauli et Andreae in ligatura una: unam quoque unciam pollicis B. Jacobi fratris Domini; sed et duas ligaturas de ossibus B. Bartholomaei apostoli, et quasi unum brachium de Innocentibus, atque reliquias S. Clementis, et unam massam de capellis S. Radegundis reginae; de vestimentis praeterea trium puerorum, Sidrach, Misach, et Abdenago; et de veste purpurea quam indutus est Dominus Jesus Christus in passione. Per singula autem supra dicta singulos breves invenerunt, qui singulorum docerent differentiam; et cum omnes praedicti breves adeo inveterati essent quod vix legi potuissent, inventi sunt et alii tres non legibiles; sed cujus vel quorum exstiterint soli Deo cognitum est. Quos ergo legere potuerunt, transcribi fecerunt, et vetera scripta cum novis ligaverunt in testimonium. Postquam autem omnia diligenter viderunt, loco suo, ut prius fuerant, reddiderunt, ipsamque imaginem cum praedictis sanctorum pignoribus super majus altare locaverunt: et induti omnes cappis, omnibusque signis majoribus cum campanis pulsatis, laudaverunt Creatorem omnium, qui ad illorum custodiam et loci tutelam tot et tam praeclara pignora largiri dignatus est. Tunc confluentibus populis tam peregrinis quam vicinis fit laetitia et exsultatio permaxima, tam in ecclesia quam tota villa atque in locis vicinis, ex agris et ex vicis circumquaque properantibus ad gaudii celebritatem. Denique, vix omnium clamores Gilo compescens, manu silentium imperavit, causamque laudis et gaudii sub brevitatis moderamine reddidit, omnibus flentibus prae gaudio, et dum postea sepulcri dilectricis Dei cryptae imaginem reddere niterentur, tantus factus est concursus populorum volentium eam osculari, vel etiam tangere, ut vix eam in omnium praesentia loco pristino possent restituere. Quod autem ipsam imaginem tangi non permiserunt, causa fuit ne notarentur avaritiae. Ignis ergo divinitus erumpens instantis tribulationis praesagium fuit; inventio autem sanctorum pignorum ejusdem tribulationis optimum finem edocuit." *Historia Vizeliacensis Monasterii*, IV; Migne, *PL*, CXCIV, 1659-1661. Cf. F. Salet, *La Madeleine de Vézelay*, Melun, 1948, p. 87; E. Viollet-le-Duc, *Dictionnaire raisonné de l'architecture française du XIe au XVIe siècle*, Paris, 1875, IV, pp. 460-461. Although the normal meaning of "dilectrix" ("dilectricis" above) would be "loving," in context it seems to mean "beloved."

prior, Gervase, the sacristan, Gerard, the constable, as well as Maurice the sub-cantor, and Lambert, the restorer of the image, he himself took a small knife and scraped away the colors, but they were able to discern no indication of a join in the uncovered wood. At length he took a small iron hammer, and attempted to detect by ear what all were unable to discover with their eyes. And hearing as it were the sound of something hollowed-out, he was spurred on with cheerful hope. Piously brave, he opened the little door with his own hands, and found a lock of hair of the Immaculate Virgin, the like of which has not been seen before or after, and a part of the tunic of the same Mary, Mother of God, and one of the bones of the blessed John the Baptist. He also found bones of the blessed apostles Peter and Paul and Andrew in one bundle; also a bit of the thumb of St. James, brother of the Lord; and also two bundles of the bones of the blessed apostle Bartholomew; and almost one arm of the Innocents; and relics of St. Clement; and a lock of the hair of St. Radegond the queen; besides some of the clothing of the three young men Shadrach, Meshach and Abednego; and a fragment of the scarlet robe which the Lord Jesus Christ wore at his Passion. For each of the above-mentioned, moreover, they found separate little notes, which identified each; and all of the aforesaid notes were so old that they could scarcely be read, and they found three others, illegible; but of whom or of what only God knows. Therefore, they had transcribed the notes which they were able to read, and they tied together the old writings with the new as a testimony.

Now after they had looked at everything diligently, they returned the objects to their place, as they were at first, and placed the statue with the aforesaid relics of the saints upon the high altar. And all wearing capes, and all the major bell [towers] ringing with bells, they praised the Creator of all, who deigned to grant so many and such splendid relics for their protection and for the guardianship of the place.

Then there was joy and very great exultation, with people flocking together, strangers as well as those from the neighborhood, in the church as well as in the whole town and in the vicinity, and hastening in from the fields and from the hamlets round about for the celebration of the joyful occasion. Then Giles, scarcely restraining the clamor of [them] all, ordered silence with a gesture, and briefly explained the cause for praise and joy while all wept for joy.

And when afterwards they tried to return the statue to the crypt of the sepulchre of the beloved of God, such a crowd of people gathered, wishing to kiss it, or even touch it, that they were scarcely able to restore it to its original place in the presence of all. As to the fact that they did not permit the statue to be touched, the reason was so that the people should not be reprimanded for their over-eagerness. Therefore, the fire erupting by Divine Providence was a presage of immediate tribulation; however, the finding of the relics explained the most propitious purpose of this same tribulation.

This valuable text provides much information that is pertinent to the function of the Majesty statues. A more explicit confirmation of the existence in the twelfth century of reliquaries fashioned as images of the Virgin and Child could hardly be found.

34

From the account we learn that the Vézelay Madonna was made of wood and that it preserved within it many relics in addition to the bits of the Virgin's hair and clothing, such as the Clermont-Ferrand Majesty of the tenth century enclosed. The manner in which these prizes were secured within the Clermont statue is unknown, but it is very clear that at Vézelay they were hidden in a compartment closed by a small door (*ostiolum*) between the shoulders of the Virgin. Although the long list of additional relics and their identifying notes (*breves*) make the Vézelay statue sound like an extraordinary armoire, the hollowed niche was probably only a few centimeters square, judging by the openings in extant statues of similar type (Fig. 92).[8] The treasures were no doubt most fragmentary but this would hardly have dimmed their importance. They must have constituted an impressive assemblage since they represented not only the Mother of God but also Old Testament worthies, the Princes of the Apostles among other saints, and even Christ himself, through the fragment of his Passion garment.

It is curious that the presence of relics in the Vézelay statue had been completely forgotten. Their discovery was a great surprise to all. Lambert, the restorer, alone suspected the hidden receptacle, and then only after examining the statue with a view to its repair. The authenticating inscriptions were in part aged and illegible. Evidently, despite their importance knowledge of them had not survived in the memories of the townspeople or in their traditions. With respect to many of the relics, the text says "of whom or of what only God knows." Even the drastic measures used to open the little door, first by means of an iron hammer and then with bare hands, indicate the lapse of some time and a change of custom. The practice of enclosing relics within a statue must have waned sufficiently so as to evoke surprise. Yet there was still enough enthusiasm for the arrangement to replace the relics exactly as they were found and to continue the veneration of the statue. There is no question that it was venerated before, as indicated by the tone of the account, the belief in the statue's immunity to fire, the silken phylactery hanging about it and the interest in its restoration. The discovery of the reliquary function was an event of sufficient scale to be marked by ceremony and popular celebration. The clamorous attention which followed suggests that such statues were still very potent devotional images in the 1160s.

These considerations provide some criteria for dating the creation of the statue and for assessing its later importance. They allow us to assume that it was carved and the relics installed long before the fire and the events related by Hugh (1161-1165). Since the relics had been totally forgotten, an early twelfth-century date would seem the latest possible *ante quem*. More likely several generations intervened to blot out memory of the relics, so that a date in the late eleventh century seems even more plausible.

The passage demonstrates further that in the 1160s it was not considered necessary for statues of Mary to be reliquaries. Nor can we even suppose that it was common, or the presence of some relic within this image would have been assumed as a matter of course. The text allows us to conclude that at this date in an important monastic community the reliquary function of such statues was no longer their distinguishing

[8] E.g. Notre-Dame d'Orcival, and Majesties at Mailhat, Saint-Nectaire, Tournus.

35

feature or their *raison d'être*. The function was appreciated but it was clearly regarded as accessory.

Two other literary accounts provide evidence for employment of statues of Mary as reliquaries in the twelfth century. Both come from outside of France. In Ghent relics brought from Constantinople by Walter Strumme and given to Abbot Arnould (1114-1132) at the monastery of St. Peter were enclosed in a new image of Mary ("He sunt reliquie que continentur in nova ymagine Sancte Marie").[9] They included garments of Christ, bones of John the Baptist, and relics of various apostles and saints, but none of the Virgin. About the same time in Abingdon, England, Abbot Fabritius (1100-1115) had an image of Mary made and so joined that it provided a hollow for relics of saints;[10] but the text does not indicate the saints or the character of the statue. These three accounts, from Vézelay, Ghent and Abingdon, thus refer to reliquary statues which are roughly contemporary in date. Their locations in present-day France, Belgium and England indicate a practice which must have been both current and widespread in the late eleventh and early twelfth century, half a century before the abatement of such procedure attested at Vézelay.

Surely many such reliquaries were made in the earlier eleventh century as well, but texts are imprecise. Bernard of Angers implies that the golden image of Mary from Rodez mentioned by him ca. 1013 was a reliquary and it is so interpreted by Bouillet.[11] The famous Virgin at Le Puy, Notre-Dame du Puy, probably made in the eleventh century, was certainly a reliquary at the time of her demise on June 8, 1794. The eye-witness account of Duranson describes the scene before the town hall when to the cry of "Vive la république" a soldier turned the statue in a bonfire to "roast" the other side. As he prodded it, the polychromed linen covering the wood of the statue burst into flame revealing a little door in the back. From it a ball of parchment, presumably a record of the relics, rolled out before startled onlookers.[12] It seems likely that the compartment under the linen was a part of the statue's original construction, even though its existence had been forgotten as in the case of the Vézelay Madonna. Rohault de Fleury notes that an inscribed roll of parchment referring to the Virgin's hair ("capelli Beatae Mariae Virginis") was discovered in 1857 between the shoulders of the statue of Notre-Dame de Mende, along with many relics.[13]

Other early Majesties of Mary—from ca. 725 to ca. 1114—are mentioned in medi-

[9] A. Fayen, *Liber traditionum Sancti Petri Blandiniensis, Cartulaire de la ville de Gand— Oorkondenboek der Stad Gent*, I, *Livre des donations faites à l'abbaye de Saint-Pierre de Gand*, Ghent, 1906, p. 130.

[10] O. Lehmann-Brockhaus, *Lateinische Schriftquellen zur Kunst in England, Wales und Schottland vom Jahre 901 bis zum Jahre 1307*, Munich, 1955-1960, no. 36.

[11] Bouillet, *Liber miraculorum*, I, xxviii, p. 72. Bernard explains the local custom of making reliquaries in the form of the human figure, *ibid.*, I, xiii, pp. 46-47.

[12] Olivier, *L'ancienne Statue*, p. 17; A. Jacotin, "Mémoire de Antoine-Alexis Duranson sur le département de la Haute-Loire," *Mémoires de la société agricole et scientifique de la Haute-Loire*, XII (1902-1903), 47-111, N.B. 83.

[13] Fleury, *Vierge*, II, p. 243. See Register no. 110.

eval literature, specifically in Wessex, Rome, Cologne, Ely, Chartres, Châtillon-sur-Loire, Coutances, Coventry, Avallon, Payerne and Utrecht.[14] Unhappily, the texts are absolutely silent regarding relics so that we do not know whether these early works resembled the Clermont-Ferrand Majesty in being *Vierges reliquaires* or not. It may be that the custom was so usual that no mention of it was necessary, a statue automatically being presumed a reliquary at the same time. Given the medieval pride in relics, their careful recording in inventories and the documentation of them within images of saints,[15] however, such a conjecture seems out of character under normal circumstances.

Less reliable data come from examination of extant statues. The presence of a compartment need not imply a true reliquary statue. A niche is often cut too roughly or placed too rudely for us to consider it contemporary with the original state of the sculpture. This is particularly true if the cutting disrupts elegant drapery patterns where it seems more likely an afterthought, even though the date of the revision can hardly be determined. Incisions for cabochon gems often provided space for relics, but these are usually obvious, later elaborations. The situation is also confused by the presence of small holes, presumably once plugged but now open; they were a technical precaution intended to mitigate cracking. They may have secured relics at some time even though not originally intended for this. Of course, phylacteries containing relics could have been hung about the statues at any period.

An overall view of the many Majesties studied here reveals some interesting statistics. Of the 110 French examples listed in the Register, seventy-nine show no evidence whatever of a relic compartment. Among the thirty-one which have some provision for enclosures, thirteen are archaicizing works of post-1200 date. Although they retain Romanesque style, the presence of a compartment cannot be regarded as a necessarily Romanesque feature. The other eighteen of these thirty-one seem to be authentic twelfth-century works and *may* have had a relic receptacle. The uncertainty comes from the fact that in four of the eighteen the opening looks like a much later alteration and in another four the existence of the niche, while probable, cannot be verified. Ten statues from the group of thirty-one clearly show a compartment in an indisputably twelfth-century sculpture, but of course the date of the aperture is unknown. Even if all of these possible examples are accepted as documenting Romanesque procedure, the percentage of reliquary statues is very low in the twelfth century.[16] Most significantly, thirty-eight

[14] See the discussion of these Majesties in Chapter IV.

[15] E.g. Cluny, St. Peter: *Disciplina Farfensis*, Migne, *PL*, CL, 1284; Limoges, St. Martial: H. Duplès-Agier, *Chroniques de Saint-Martial de Limoges, publiées d'après les manuscrits originaux pour la société de l'histoire de France*, Paris, 1874, pp. 6, 43; Monastier, St. Chaffre: Chevalier, *Cartulaire*, p. 42.

[16] The presence of a relic compartment is even rarer in twelfth-century sculptures of the Madonna in Majesty from Germany, Belgium and Switzerland. Except for the eleventh-century Paderborn Madonna, it is apparently non-existent in Germany.

Statuettes which represent the Madonna and Child in miniature and are made of copper and enamel, such as those collected and studied by W. Hildburgh, constitute a separate genre of liturgi-

excellent, bona fide, twelfth-century sculptures show no trace of a relic compartment. Clearly in these cases, at least, it was not essential.

As thus surveyed, the literary sources and the statues themselves present an irregular picture. Evidently, in the twelfth century the relic compartment was acceptable as an accessory feature of Majesties. It seems more likely to appear early in the development of the type, i.e. in the eleventh and early twelfth century, than later on but continued to be a possibility even in the later twelfth century. At no time was it the rule; some Majesties were reliquaries and some were not. By the middle of the twelfth century their reliquary function was becoming exceptional.

Some pertinent conclusions seem possible at this point. Returning to Bréhier's theory, outlined at the beginning of our discussion, we can concede that the Clermont-Ferrand Majesty of 946 is the earliest reliquary statue of the Madonna known to us. That it was also the prototype for later statues as Bréhier claimed is questionable. Since it is clear that later Majesties were not necessarily reliquaries, such a function cannot be presumed as the identifying feature motivating the creation of the type and determining the structure of the entire group. Consequently the term *Vierge reliquaire* can no longer be seen as generically appropriate for this class of sculptures. Other considerations also influenced the creation of the statues, contributed to their development and informed them with purpose. Among these the reliquary function had a place, but not an over-riding one as formerly supposed.

The question of the cult of relics as the catalytic agent which induced the medieval revival of sculpture in the round is another matter. The fact that very early Majesties were provided with relics cannot be overlooked in this connection and will be considered at length in the next chapter, where the origins of the Throne of Wisdom statues are discussed. Before taking up this topic, however, the subject of the function of the statues requires further clarification.

Location of the Statue in the Church

If not primarily reliquaries, then what was the chief purpose of the Throne of Wisdom statues? One significant fact is that they are particularly ill preserved and show greater deterioration than a purely devotional statue, even when made of wood, is likely to have suffered. The greatest losses are usually concentrated about the base. Thrones are often badly damaged or totally replaced, and the feet of the Madonna are often missing. Such

---

cal objects. They are known from the late twelfth century chiefly in southern France and Spain. In some examples, the throne contains a cavity, closed by a small door, which is interpreted as a relic compartment by Hildburgh or as a tabernacle for the reserved host by Gauthier. See the example in the Metropolitan Museum of Art, New York, *1200*, 1970, no. 132; W. Hildburgh, "Medieval Copper Champlevé Enamelled Images of the Virgin and Child," *Archaeologia*, xcvi (1955), 115-158; M. Gauthier, "Les Majestés de la Vierge 'limousine' et méridionales du XIIIe siècle au Metropolitan Museum of Art de New York," *Bulletin de la société nationale des antiquaires de France* (1968), 66-95.

recurrent signs of wear and tear, especially in the lower parts, support the view that the statues were meant to be mobile, not affixed to one spot. Some erosion was likely to occur as their places were changed, and they were often kept in crypts, where dampness must have taken its toll. According to Hugh of Poitiers, as related above, the Vézelay Madonna was in the crypt at the time of the fire. She was displayed afterward on the high altar of the church and then returned to the crypt. Usually the figures were placed on altars. Medieval documents, discussed in Chapter IV, attest this position for the Madonna at Châtillon-sur-Loire, also in a crypt, and for Majesties at Coutances, Cambrai and Le Puy. Later accounts note that the Virgin of Chartres was on an altar in the crypt, although moved several times to other altars as was true of the Le Puy Virgin. Although often moved about, the golden Madonna at Essen remained on the altar during the feast of the Ascension in the fourteenth century.

In like manner statues of saints were normally placed on altars, a custom which may have derived from the practice of exhibiting reliquaries there. At Cluny, William and Gunrada of England knelt before the image of St. Peter on the high altar as they paused on their way to Rome.[17] At Aurillac, Bernard of Angers saw the statue of St. Gerald over the altar, and at Conques he saw the St. Foy in the crypt, presumably on an altar.[18] She was moved later to the high altar of the church.[19] The golden figure of St. Martial of Limoges was described as "sitting" upon an altar in the tenth century,[20] and the statue of St. Privatus in the crypt at Mende was probably also on an altar.[21] Evidently it was common practice in France to locate sacred images, even rather large three-dimensional ones, upon altars where reliquaries had traditionally been placed.

The Clermont-Ferrand Majesty, on the other hand, was originally displayed in more singular fashion. She was not on the high altar of the cathedral, whose chief ornament she was intended to be, but rather on a specially prepared column of marble surmounted by a socle of jasper.[22] The column was set up behind the altar, to the east. The silver Madonna at Orcival is exhibited in similar fashion today.

An account of 1484 indicates that the Paderborn Madonna (Fig. 46), which had been made for Bishop Imad in the eleventh century, was exhibited only during special festivals and then for a limited number of days. Alois Fuchs believed that on these ceremonial occasions she was placed atop a pedestal in a procedure similar to that at Cler-

[17] R. Graham and A. W. Clapham, "The Monastery of Cluny, 910-1155," *Archaeologia*, LXXX (1930), 144; *Antiquores consuetudines Cluniacensis Monasterii*, Migne, *PL*, CXLIX, 764; cf. B. Albers, *Consuetudines monasticae*, Stuttgart, Vienna and Monte Cassino, 1900-1912, I, Lib. II, cap. l, p. 184.

[18] Bouillet, *Liber miraculorum*, I, xiii, p. 47.

[19] M. Gauthier, "Le Trésor de Conques," *Rouergue roman*, La Pierre-qui-vire, 1963, p. 109. Of course, in medieval texts the work *crypta* often referred to a chapel and such might be intended in some references which follow.

[20] "Isdem Gauzbertus iconam auream Marcialis apostoli fecit sedentem super altare . . . ," Duplès-Agier, *Chroniques*, pp. 5, 43.

[21] Brunel, *Les Miracles*, pp. 9, 16-18.

[22] Rigodon, "Vision," 54. She was moved to the high altar later, however, *ibid.*, 40.

mont and Orcival.[23] This arrangement would have allowed her to be viewed easily from all sides.

The full, massive form of the Paderborn figure is appropriate to a freestanding position. Like the Essen and Hildesheim Madonnas in Germany, the back shows carefully delineated details of drapery. The present practice in Auvergne of placing the statues on chapel altars with their backs to the wall unfortunately hides from the observer much of the interest of the drapery and the precisely modeled thrones. It is hard to imagine that these embellishments were meant to be seen only on stately occasions. Yet one can hardly argue the point; for Romanesque sculptures were usually carved with fastidious care even if they were intended for a distant corner where they could not be seen easily.

The likelihood is that there was no one system in the Romanesque period and that the Throne of Wisdom was moved about according to need. Either in a crypt or in the upper church, it was sometimes placed on an altar, which at that time would have been open to view from all sides, sometimes set up at the entrance to the sanctuary, as was the case with the gold statue of Christ at St. Peter's, and sometimes placed on a pedestal behind the high altar where the figure would be particularly visible from the ambulatory. In any case it is clear that this type of statue was not confined to a single location. Were such peripatetics not desirable, the Madonna would more likely have been made of a durable material such as stone.

Processions

Mobility helps to explain the function of the figures. The statues could not only be moved about in the church as occasion demanded, they might also be carried in processions which served a variety of purposes. The modern habit of carrying the *Maiestas* of Mary through the streets of a city, or from shrine to shrine—as is particularly common on August 15 in Auvergne—has its roots in the custom of the Early Middle Ages. Bernard of Angers describes in detail processions which must have been almost as colorful as parades. The golden statue of St. Foy (Fig. 13) was borne about repeatedly—trailed by bearers of golden crosses, Gospel books, lighted candles and censers—to the accompaniment of clashing cymbals and sounding oliphants.[24] The statue was credited with numerous miracles on these outings, including the healing of the blind and the afflicted as well as the freeing of those wrongly imprisoned. Bernard's vivid account gives an excellent idea, no doubt, of how the triumphal procession of a *Maiestas* of Mary would have appeared to a contemporary.

Bernard was well aware that the procession was an effective instrument in fundraising. He comments on the manner in which the enthusiasm of onlookers was stimulated as the cortège passed and how purse-strings were thus loosened so that numerous contributions were made.[25] This was an important source of revenue for the abbey and

[23] Fuchs, *Madonnen*, p. 9.
[24] Bouillet, *Liber miraculorum*, II, iv, p. 100.
[25] The use of relics for this purpose is well attested, e.g. the twelfth-century account of Gui-

accounts in no small way for its prosperity during the eleventh century. In other ways St. Foy gave excellent material support to the abbey, as in the incident of the golden doves described in the *Liber miraculorum*.[26] According to this account she appeared in a dream to Abbot Bernard of Beaulieu and asked him for the gift of a pair of golden doves which he possessed. The Abbot needed two further reminders from the saint, in the form of dreams, before he realized that her request was the will of heaven. Consequently he made a pilgrimage to Conques and presented there an offering—not the two doves but an equivalent weight of gold. Unabashed, St. Foy appeared to him again pressing for the golden doves themselves, rather than all of his gold. Of course the Abbot, thus badgered, gave them up to her in the end and they became ornaments for her throne. Other offerings to the saint were used to provide a new altar and additional furnishings as the monastery enriched its circumstances and elevated the grandeur of its appointments.

The statue of St. Privatus at Mende was put to similar good purpose. In 1036 at the Council of Le Puy, the golden Majesty representing St. Privatus was borne processionally by the bishop and clergy for the veneration of the people of Velay.[27] Miracles performed by the saint included one at which Odilo of Cluny was present. Many others occurred as the statue was carried before parishioners, and we may be sure that those who were assisted by the saint's intervention provided suitable thank offerings. When an avaricious seigneur made an insufficient contribution, it was thrice rejected by the statue, into whose hand it was placed in the customary way.

Processions at Cluny were numerous. They varied in length and richness in accordance with the importance of the feasts of the church year. The *Consuetudines Farfensis*, from Odilo's time and now dated ca. 1023-35, describes the impressive Palm Sunday ceremony in which the silver Majesty representing St. Peter was the chief feature.[28] Following the distribution of palm fronds, servants went forth carrying banners; then came carefully vested lay monks with gold crosses and crucifix, gold thuribles, holy water, candlesticks and reliquaries; behind them, at length, sixteen more lay monks bore the great statue of St. Peter and chests of relics. Children, more monks, the abbot, and

---

bert of Nogent, *De vita sua*, III, xii, Migne, *PL*, CLVI, 938; Benton, *Memoirs of Abbot Guibert of Nogent*, p. 191.

[26] Bouillet, *Liber miraculorum*, I, xvi, pp. 51-53.

[27] Brunel, *Les Miracles*, pp. 14-16; for a twelfth-century procession, see *ibid.*, pp. 59-60; for the rejected contribution, *ibid.*, pp. 8-11.

[28] Graham and Clapham, "Monastery of Cluny," 152; Albers, *Consuetudines*, I, Lib. I, cap. liii, pp. 43-45; cf. *ibid.*, I, Lib. II, cap. l, p. 184 and the *Disciplina Farfensis* of Guido, Migne, *PL*, CL, 1284; cf. Ulrich's *Consuetudines* of ca. 1080 in L. d'Achery, *Spicilegium*, Paris, 1728, I, p. 668 and Migne, *PL*, CXLIX, 698. For similar processions, see *Disciplina Farfensis*, Migne, *PL*, CL, 1227-1228; Albers, *Consuetudines*, I, Lib. I, caps. xxxii, lxxxv, ci, pp. 24, 87, 100; IV, pp. 43-48; V, pp. 117-118. For the recently revised chronology of the *Consuetudines Farfensis* manuscripts, see the study of J. Hourlier, "Saint-Odilon bâtisseur," *Revue Mabillon*, LI (1961), 303-324. Cf. K. J. Conant, *Cluny, les églises et la maison du chef d'ordre*, The Mediaeval Academy of America, Mâcon, 1968, pp. 42ff.; N. Hunt, *Cluny under Saint Hugh, 1049-1109*, London, 1967, pp. 33ff.

a large number of laymen made up the rest of the procession. As the bells were rung, they proceeded through the town to St. Majolus and then back through the galilee of the abbey church and on into the church itself. This was a festive observance associated with the liturgical calender rather than with the pecuniary needs of the abbey. We do not know of the Cluny *Maiestas* of St. Peter being used specifically for fund-raising processions, but we are told in the *Consuetudines* of Ulrich, ca. 1080, that in case of urgent necessity, of unspecified type, the statue of the saint might be borne out of the monastery by an elaborate retinue made up of children, laymen, vested monks and the abbot. Reliquaries were carried on an ornate litter. Also included were banners, crosses, thuribles, candles and similar accoutrements. Intermittently they sang designated psalms, antiphons and appropriate responses, the bells and the *tintinnabulum* sounded, or all were silent.[29]

These accounts, which describe the manner in which statues of saints were carried in medieval processions, enlarge our view of the situation which must have obtained with regard to the figure of the Madonna in Majesty. It is clear that images played a part within the medieval liturgy at Rome. The *Ordo Romanus XI (auctore Benedicto)*, written prior to 1143, and the *Ordo Romanus XII (auctore Cencio)*, of the late twelfth century, both mention images being carried processionally to the church of Sta Maria Maggiore on the feast of the Purification of the Virgin.[30] The character of the "images" is not described, but other service books for this feast indicate that the Virgin might have been represented as an image in the procession. The *Ordo in purificatione in S. Mariae*, in Milan, from a pontifical of the ninth-tenth century used at Mainz, refers to an image of the Blessed Virgin Mary being translated in the procession for this feast.[31] The tenth-century *Consuetudines* from Saint-Benoît-sur-Loire records that an image of Mary was carried in procession at the abbey of Fleury on the feast of the Purification ("In Purificatione portatur imago sanctae Mariae ad processionem . . .").[32] Although it is unclear in each of these instances whether the image was fully three-dimensional, it is likely considering the more specific references in the accounts of Madonnas which follow.

Bernard of Angers gives special mention to a statue of the Virgin Mary in his long account of the miracles of St. Foy. In the colorful gathering at the synod called by Bishop Arnaldus of Rodez in the early eleventh century, the golden statues of St. Foy from Conques and St. Amandus of Rodez, among others, were accompanied by the golden statue of Mary, Mother of God, from Rodez Cathedral.[33] These Majesties were all reliquaries. They were ranged about in the tents and pavilions set up on the field of Saint-Félix, near the city. As might be expected, St. Foy performed miracles while there.

---

[29] D'Achery, *Spicilegium*, I, pp. 694-695; Migne, *PL*, CL, 758-759.

[30] J. Mabillon, *Museum Italicum, seu collectio veterum scriptorum ex bibliothecis Italicis*, Paris, 1724, pp. 131, 134, 174.

[31] M. Magistretti, *Monumenta veteris liturgiae Ambrosianae, I, Pontificale in usum ecclesiae mediolanensis*, Milan, 1897, pp. xxxiv, 81.

[32] Albers, *Consuetudines*, V, p. 151.

[33] Bouillet, *Liber miraculorum*, I, xxviii, pp. 71-73.

The other statues seem to have been brought chiefly for the pomp and circumstance of the occasion. They demonstrated effectively the importance of their congregations and served to represent the patron saints, which included the Virgin, of the dioceses concerned.

At Chartres pilgrims saw the statue of the Virgin known as Notre-Dame-sous-Terre borne in procession. These processions had evidently become common enough by the late twelfth and early thirteenth centuries for pilgrim badges to be decorated with a scene illustrating the figure borne on a litter (Fig. 27).[34] Such pilgrim memorabilia proliferated in later centuries, of course, and many of these are preserved. They indicate a practice which had a long and continuous life.

At Le Puy processions including the statue Notre-Dame du Puy were frequent and attended by intense crowds. They are documented from 1254, but they were undoubtedly common earlier as well.[35]

In the Early Middle Ages processions were also a regular part of festival celebrations in Germany. We know that the women of the convents of Essen and Rellinghausen carried reliquary shrines on such occasions,[36] and the golden Madonna at Essen was among them. The *Liber Ordinarius* of the Essen convent, a service book of the fourteenth century which depends upon an earlier model, describes in detail the processional use of the golden image of Mary. On the feast of the Purification, it was carried vested, then disrobed and crowned at the height of the ceremony. It was carried on other occasions as well, such as the feast of the Assumption of the Virgin. On the octave of this day, it was replaced by the convent's modest silver statue of Mary ("parva tamen ymago fabrice beate Marie virginis"). On the feast of the Ascension the gold Madonna is said to have remained on the altar while the silver Madonna was paraded about.[37] The Hildesheim and Paderborn Madonnas seem rather large and heavy for processional use but this fact does not preclude the possibility. In the later Middle Ages, the Hildesheim Virgin was led annually through the town in a grand procession on August 1 and Beissel claimed this to have been true even earlier.[38]

Modern cult practices give ample evidence of the continuation of processions in pilgrimage festivals which probably have their source in the Early Middle Ages. In 1717

[34] A. Forgeais, *Collection de plombs historiés trouvés dans la Seine*, II, *Enseignes de pèlerinages*, Paris, 1863, pp. 28-32.

[35] Jacotin and Pascal, *Bibliographie*, p. 57.

[36] L. Potthoff, "Prozessionen im ehemaligen Stift Rellinghausen," *Das Münster am Hellweg*, VII (1954), 88-92; F. Arens, *Der Liber Ordinarius der Essener Stiftskirche*, Paderborn, 1908, pp. 182-184, where a litter is specifically mentioned; see note 87 in Chapter IV below. Cf. F. Oslender, "Die goldene Madonna," *Das Münster am Hellweg*, XI (1958), 34-56.

[37] Arens, *Liber Ordinarius*, pp. 4, 33-35, 80-89, 104-107, 168-173, 181-185; Young, *Drama*, II, p. 252.

[38] K. Algermissen, "Die Geschichte der Marienverehrung in der Diözeses Hildesheim," *Unsere Diözese, Zeitschift des Vereins für Heimatkunde im Bistum Hildesheim*, 1954, 7-8; J. Kratz, *Der Dom zu Hildesheim*, Hildesheim, 1840, II, p. 175 n. 62; S. Beissel, *Die Geschichte der Verehrung Marias in Deutschland*, Freiburg-im-Breisgau, 1890, p. 49.

Martène and Durand witnessed the festivities in Toulouse on the feast of the Assumption and saw the statue of Notre-Dame-la-Daurade being carried in a procession through the city along with candles and other accoutrements.[39] The custom persisted until 1785 and 1790, the last instances of it on record, when the Virgin was escorted by municipal officers.[40] The statue was burned in 1799 after a long history of miraculous interventions and deliverances. Notre-Dame-la-Daurade was believed to prevent public calamity, particularly drought, and was frequently carried out from the church for that purpose. Although these events and beliefs are of the type associated with Romanesque Majesties, and a twelfth-century Throne of Wisdom sculpture undoubtedly existed in Toulouse at one time, the seventeenth- and eighteenth-century accounts which describe Notre-Dame-la-Daurade seem to refer to a later replacement.[41] The descriptions of the festivals are significant, nevertheless, in acquainting us with medieval practices. A detailed record of similar festivities at Chartres involving a procession and, this time, the famous relic of the Virgin's tunic, survives from the sixteenth century.[42] The prowess of Notre-Dame de Bon Espoir, who reputedly delivered the townspeople of Dijon from invasion in 1513, as again in 1944, is depicted in a processional scene on a tapestry commemorating the sixteenth-century event.[43]

Modern celebrations resembling these practices are known in many French communities. In them Romanesque Majesties, or their replicas, are followed by long and impressive retinues which wind through the village streets. The annual festival at Orcival is an outstanding example.[44] In this case, the value and fragility of Notre-Dame d'Orcival precludes her participation at the present time and a replica is substituted. Notre-Dame-la-Brune, now at Tournus, must have been frequently honored in procession before the practice was curtailed in 1860, when the bishop of Autun ruled that the statue could be included on outings only in extraordinary circumstances.[45]

Such processions in the Middle Ages, or in later periods, were a form of public devotion, served to attract pilgrims, offered the occasion to solicit funds for the church and, in time of distress, encouraged public morale; yet such situations were too rare or too casual to explain the development of a whole type of sculpture. Thus, a search for additional reasons for portability seems in order. Clues are provided from the accounts

[39] E. Martène and U. Durand, *Voyage littéraire de deux religieux bénédictins de la Congrégation de Saint Maur*, I, Paris, 1717, bk. II, p. 49.

[40] Degert, "Vierge noire," 355-358, N.B. 355.

[41] *Ibid.* [42] Lépinois, *Histoire*, pp. 355-358.

[43] Quarré, "La Statue de Notre-Dame de Bon Espoir," 192.

[44] Drochon, *Histoire*, p. 1000, for the description of Père Branche. In his day it included soldiers, barefooted priests and 3,000-4,000 pilgrims. The modern procession which accompanies Notre-Dame de Vassivière from her summer residency in the mountains is attended by honorific bonfires, salutes of gun salvos and fireworks; see Craplet, *Richesses*, pp. 66-67. For the procession at Evron, see J. Taralon, "Le Trésor d'Evron," *Les Monuments historiques de la France*, VIII (1962), 29-40. For other accounts of modern processions, see Hamon, *Histoire*, I, pp. 53-58. Cf. the procession at Walcourt, Chapter IV, note 118 below.

[45] Henri Curé, *Saint-Philibert de Tournus*, Paris, 1905, p. 336 n. 3.

where we note that, regardless of the immediate service of the procession, the role of the Throne of Wisdom statue in it was that of a representative of Notre Dame. Just as the statue of St. Foy was identified with the saint, the statue of the Virgin was equated with Mary herself as the *sedes sapientiae*. Thus the statue might vicariously manifest the Virgin's presence and authority.

Secular Practices and Popular Attitudes

Such vicarious manifestation seems to be the principle behind the use of the Madonna in Majesty in civil ceremony. We have evidence that prior to the sixteenth century, knights swore feudal oaths in the presence of the golden Madonna at Hildesheim.[46] She also presided when homage was paid to newly elected bishops and they occasionally took their oath of office before her. In 1631 vows were made by the local aldermen to Notre-Dame d'Orcival who had been ceremoniously saluted by Louis II, Duke of Bourbon, and his knights after conquest of the English at Roche-Sardaigne.[47] A common modern ceremony involves the Majesty as a protectress for children who are presented to her.[48] The origins of this custom are unknown but may have medieval precedent.

An account from the twelfth century demonstrates more fully the vicarious authenticity possessed by the wood Majesty as a representative of the Virgin in the Romanesque period and also testifies to its portable character. The text comes from the letter written by the monks of Utrecht to Bishop Frederick in Cologne, to thank him for imprisoning the heretic Tanchelm.[49] The monks relate some of his objectionable activities in Utrecht in 1112-1114. According to them, one day Tanchelm ordered a statue of the Virgin to be brought out to him amidst a multitude of people. Approaching the Majesty, he put his hand on the hand of the Madonna and uttered sacrilegious words: "See, my friends, that I am uniting myself in marriage with the Holy Virgin: and you [should] now offer betrothal gifts and the expenses of the wedding." He encouraged the men present to compete with the women in making their offerings, "to see which of the two sexes burns with the greater charity toward me and my spouse." The women threw to him their earrings and jewels and he thus collected a vast sum.

Tanchelm's mock wedding with the Virgin would have seemed to the monks of Utrecht outrageous and sacrilegious in every way, but they appeared to be particularly incensed by the fact that he exploited the vicarious character of the statue. In the minds of Tanchelm's followers, the role of the sculpture as proxy for the Madonna was unquestioned, so that they offered their possessions as if to the Madonna in person.

The Tanchelm incident recalls the tale of Marriage to Mary which enjoyed wide currency in the Middle Ages. Paull Franklin Baum has collected medieval variants of

[46] Kratz, *Der Dom*, II, p. 175 n. 62; Beissel, *Verehrung*, p. 49.
[47] Enaud, "Vierge," 79-88.
[48] E.g. Notre-Dame-la-Brune, Tournus (no. 30); Notre-Dame du Villeret d'Apchier, Chanaleilles (no. 18).
[49] E. de Moreau, *Histoire de l'église en Belgique*, Brussels, 1945, II, pp. 417-418.

45

the theme of the young man betrothed to a statue and has demonstrated its classical roots; Venus is transformed into Mary by medieval authors. The Venus story as known about 1100 and related by William of Malmesbury is given by Baum as follows:

At Rome there was a wealthy young man of noble birth and newly married, who was accustomed to entertain his friends with frequent feasts. One day as they went out into a field to settle their dinner by playing ball he took off his marriage ring and put it on the finger of a bronze statue of Venus nearby. When the game was finished he found the statue's finger so bent that it was impossible to withdraw the ring; nor could he break the finger. He said nothing to his companions about it, but that night went back to the image with a servant; and found the finger again straight and the ring gone. Still concealing his loss, he returned to his wife, but as he got into bed he felt come between him and his wife "quiddam nebulosum et densum, quod posset sentiri, nec posset videri." Then the phantom spoke: "Lie with me, whom you have married today. I am Venus, on whose finger you placed your ring, and I will not give it back."

Some time elapsed, during which the youth was prevented by the statue from intimacy with his wife; until finally, aroused by her complaints, he related the whole affair to his parents; and they in turn laid the matter before Palumbus, a certain "presbyter suburbanus," skilled in necromancy. . . .[50]

Mary replaces Venus in the tale as related by the Benedictine monk Gauthier de Coincy.[51] This story typifies the Marriage of Mary group and was in existence by about 1200. It is told by Baum thus:

In front of a ruined church there was an image before which sinners left their offerings. One day a group of young men were playing ball near by, among them one who had a ring that his *amie* had given him. In order to avoid all risk of injuring this ring he went to the church seeking some safe place to deposit it. When he saw the statue there so fresh and beautiful, he knelt down and saluted it, and was so moved that "Lady," he cried, "I will serve you all my life. You are the fairest lady I have ever seen, a thousand times more beautiful than she who gave me this ring. I will forsake her, and love, and its joys, and give you this ring *par fine amor*." He then put the ring on her finger, and immediately she bent her finger so that none could withdraw the ring. He was frightened by this, and told the bystanders what had happened. They all advised him: *lest le siecle*, serve God all thy life and Our Lady Saint Mary. But

[50] P. F. Baum, "The Young Man Betrothed to a Statue," *Publications of the Modern Language Association of America*, XXXIV (1919), 523-579, N.B. pp. 548-574. Cf. the following related items in S. Thompson, *Motif-Index of Folk Literature*, Bloomington, Indiana, 1955-1958, C 51.2.4, D 1610. 21.1, D 1620.1.4, D 1622.2, D 1623.1, Q 558.5, T 117.11, T 376. I am grateful to Prof. George Henderson for suggesting these studies. For the tale of William of Malmesbury, see Baum, "Statue," 524-526.

[51] Baum, "Statue," 548-549.

the days came and went, and soon he forgot Our Lady, so powerful were the eyes of his *amie*; so that finally he was married to her with great ceremony. But as soon as he approached the bridal bed he forgot his desire and at once fell asleep. Our Lady lay between him and his wife, proving her right by the ring, and upbraiding him for his disloyalty. The clerk awoke in terror, but finding no trace of the image near, he supposed he had been deceived by a dream. Still he could not arise. Then Our Lady reappeared and again angrily chided him. In despair he implored the Holy Spirit to aid him; he forsook the world, and became a monk and a hermit and a servant of God and of *Ma Dame Sainte Marie*.

Many variants of the narrative survive. Closely related is the story of the Clerk of Pisa which also enjoins service to the Virgin. It had an even earlier vogue, the oldest manuscripts dating from the early twelfth century.[52] The story belongs to the type known as the Neglected Mary Image. Miélot's collection of Miracles of the Virgin includes one of this genre, in which the young man forsakes his earthly marriage for an exemplary life in service to the Virgin.[53]

The theme of these legends is seen reflected in the medieval belief in mystical marriages. One such marriage which dates close to our period, and relates to a distinguished historical personage, is that of Edmund Rich who became Archbishop of Canterbury in 1234. As a young man he had made a vow of celibacy. In order "that he might be able to keep it, he wedded himself to the mother of our Lord. He had two rings made with 'Ave Maria' engraved on each. One he placed on the finger of an image of the Virgin, which stood in a church at Oxford, and the other he wore on his own finger, considering himself espoused in this manner to the Virgin."[54]

No claim is made here that the statues of Mary-Venus which figure in the medieval tales above are to be identified with the wood sculptures of the Madonna in Majesty which are the subject of our study. The stories were told as fiction rather than as fact. In addition to being amusing fables, however, they disclose didactic intent as they express clearly the rewards of service to the Virgin. Their chief interest for us is the revealing view of medieval beliefs which they afford. The attitude toward the statue of Mary is particularly interesting. Human actions and emotions are ascribed to it, such as bending her finger to retain the ring and her subsequent retributive anger. A promise to a statue of the Virgin was regarded as an avowal to Mary herself.

Baum says: "There were many men in the Middle Ages who had no doubt the Virgin Mary had appeared to them and spoken to them; and the Church was busy teaching those who had not enjoyed this miracle that it was possible to them also if they lived devoutly and obeyed the priest. Thus, while for the practical minded these divine marriages are a childish notion, for the mystics and the religious idealists they are a consummation of exalted contemplation and denial of the flesh. They may be amusing now, but in their day and for their purpose they were genuine reflections of human

---

[52] *Ibid.*, 552-554. [53] *Ibid.*, 555.
[54] *Ibid.*, 566, from William Jones, *Finger Ring Lore*, London, 1898, p. 240.

life."[55] Were it not possible for people to believe in the statue as a representative of the Virgin, the stories would not have enjoyed such wide and lively circulation.

Devotional Practices and Miraculous Immunities

Embedded within more sober sources, chronicles, charters and the like, there are medieval accounts of attitudes toward sculptures of Mary which are very similar to those seen in the Marriage stories above. Various forms of attention could be lavished on the statues of Mary in Majesty. They were often objects of excessive religious zeal. The Vézelay Madonna discussed earlier was overwhelmed by worshipers after the celebration ordered by Giles. As the twelfth-century text says, "such a crowd of people gathered, wishing to kiss it, or even touch it, that they were scarcely able to replace it" in its original location.[56] Even before the discovery of the relics within it, the work had been honored with a silken phylactery hung at the neck of the Child Jesus, implying a cult attention. And the statue had reportedly enjoyed a miraculous immunity to the fire which devastated the wood beams of the church above it, the phylactery even escaping traces of the smell as well as the scorch of the blaze. At Châtillon-sur-Loire Andreas of Fleury reported on a similar set of circumstances in ca. A.D. 1030.[57] Burning coals fell on an altar during a fire which he described as a raging furnace. They reduced to ash the *châsse* on the altar, but did not harm a venerated statue of the Madonna and Child nearby or leave any odor of fire on the curtain hung in honor about it. One is reminded of the curious legend at Walcourt, according to which in the thirteenth century a silver-sheathed Madonna in Majesty, still the center of a fervent cult there, rescued herself from a fire by leaping out of the church, amidst the flames, into the branches of a tree and thence into the arms of Count Thierry who watched outside.[58]

The habit of honoring statues with gifts of jewelry, so common today, was also the custom in the Early Middle Ages. In addition to the episodes discussed above, there are other Romanesque references. In the eleventh century the Countess of Malmesbury hung a necklace about a Madonna in Coventry,[59] and at Avallon in ca. 1078 a statue of Mary was adorned with a golden crown and bracelets.[60]

[55] Baum, "Statue," 567. [56] See note 7 above.

[57] E. de Certain, *Les Miracles des Saint-Benoît (Miracula Sancti Benedicti)*, Paris, 1858, Lib. v, cap. xi, pp. 209-210; V. Mortet, *Recueil de textes relatifs à l'histoire de l'architecture en France, XIe-XIIe siècles*, I, Paris, 1911, pp. 7-8. See Chapter IV, note 25 below for the text.

[58] D. Thierry, *Notre-Dame de Walcourt*, Walcourt, 1938, pp. 6-7, 22. Ernst Kitzinger points out a similar story which recounts the miraculous immunity of the icon of the Virgin at Sta Francesca Romana in Rome to a devastating fire in the time of Honorious III, "Some Icons of the VII Century," *Late Classical and Medieval Studies in Honor of Albert Mathias Friend, Jr.*, Princeton, 1955, 148.

[59] Lehmann-Brockhaus, *Schriftquellen in England*, I, no. 1131; see below, Chapter IV, note 28.

[60] A. Bruel, *Recueil des chartes de l'abbaye de Cluny, formé par Auguste Bernard*, Paris, 1876-1903, IV, no. 3518, p. 640. Cf. the discussion of such gifts in E. Lesne, *Histoire de la propriété ecclésiastique en France*, III, *L'Inventaire de la propriété. Eglises et trésors des églises du commencement du VIIIe à la fin du XIe siècle*, Lille, 1936, p. 143 and *passim*.

The psychology of popular credulity, expressed vividly in these accounts, is obviously beyond the scope of art history. The texts provide guidance, however, in an assessment of the function of the Throne of Wisdom statue. The devotion seems based upon a belief in the statues as being more than mere simulacra fashioned to serve a didactic or commemorative purpose. It recalls the relationship between image and prototype assumed in the Eastern icon, as we noted in Chapter I. Evidently the statues sometimes had special powers attributed to them because they were particularly apt agencies of divinity. In sculpture in the round, which was still a novelty in the eleventh century, the three-dimensional manifestation of the supernatural would have seemed powerfully tangible. These early examples could, therefore, readily acquire an aura of peculiar sanctity and be understood as having divine personalities or as being sacred presences. As such they would have been convincing impersonators of the Virgin and her Son.

Liturgical Drama

That such associations would be effectively utilized within the rites and ceremonies of the religious community is an obvious probability. Within the liturgical drama the Majesty might be expected to find a significant place and this conjecture is fortunately supported by valid evidence.[61] A most appropriate role for the statue was that of the enthroned Madonna and Child in the *Officium Stellae*, a medieval play which was performed at the Epiphany to commemorate the Adoration of the Magi. As participants in this play the revered wood figures of Mary and the Christ Child were presiding presences, witnessing the mimetic re-enactment of the visit of the Three Kings. They received the homage and offerings of high clerics dressed as the Kings in the realistic dramatization which preceded the drama of the Mass itself at the feast of Epiphany.

Corroboration for these assertions is provided by texts of the period and by art historical evidence. For the latter a relationship between the *Maiestas* statue and a Magi iconography is suggested even in the earliest surviving record of a Madonna representing the Throne of Wisdom, the previously mentioned golden Majesty of Clermont-Ferrand. The basic text providing information as to its history is of the late tenth or early eleventh century and contains a tiny marginal drawing which purportedly illustrates the figure (Fig. 3).[62] On the basis of the description in the text and the references to the Majesty in inventories of the tenth century for the Cathedral, we can imagine the Clermont-Ferrand Virgin as a typical *Maiestas*: the statue was of gold, probably repoussé, sheathing a wood core; it represented Mary with the Christ Child in her lap; she was seated on a golden throne decorated with gems; the whole was surmounted by a ciborium and was intended to serve as a reliquary. The iconography would have been that of the *sedes sapientiae*.

Bréhier believed that the statue was faithfully reproduced in the tiny illustration

[61] See the author's preliminary article, "Magi and Majesty: A Study of Romanesque Sculpture and Liturgical Drama," *The Art Bulletin*, L (1968), 215-222.

[62] Clermont-Ferrand, Bibliothèque Municipale, MS 145, fols. 130v-134v. See notes 1-2 above and the discussion in Chapter IV below.

of the text. Although the heading which is interlarded with the drawing clearly begins the account while the making of the Majesty is described on the opposite leaf, so that drawing and text are contemporary, the value of the drawing itself in helping us to visualize the stylistic character of the early Madonna seems slight. The drawing illustrates in a general way the basic features of the work but it does not correspond closely to the textual description which accompanies it. The ciborium is omitted and there are other discrepancies. In particular, the drapery about the lower legs lacks clarity. It indicates a frontal view even though it is otherwise clear that we are being shown both figures from the side. This confusion of frontal and profile views, while inexplicable and wholly improbable in an isolated image such as the Clermont-Ferrand Majesty, is understandable in the rendering of the Virgin in a Magi iconography, for it allows Mary to maintain the frontal position of her enthronement, as in the lower part of our drawing, and at the same time turn to receive the Magi, who advance from one side.[63] The nimbi of the drawing would have been extremely unlikely in the statue. All in all, it seems highly probable that the artist of the Clermont-Ferrand rendering did not feel obliged to reproduce Stephen's statue accurately, but was content to utilize a conventional image of a seated Madonna which would serve as general illustration of his story. Apparently, to his mind an obvious model was a Madonna from an Adoration of the Magi scene.

Probably very like this supposed model is a drawing in a Sedulius manuscript made in 814 (now in the Plantin-Moretus Museum in Antwerp; Fig. 4).[64] Despite some obvious differences, such as the use of wash, the figures in it are remarkably close in their ambivalence of posture and in their style to the Clermont-Ferrand drawing, but in the Sedulius manuscript the Madonna is actually a part of a Magi scene. Thus there seems to be, even as early as the tenth century, an established association between a Majesty statue such as the one at Clermont-Ferrand and traditional Magi iconography.

Further demonstrations of an association between the wooden *Maiestas* statues

---

[63] Both frontal and profile dispositions for Mary in the Magi scene are common from the beginnings of Christian art. See Mâle, *L'Art religieux*, pp. 64-70; Vezin, *Mages, passim*; G. A. Wellen, *Theotokos, Eine ikonographische Abhandlung über das Gottesmutterbild in frühchristlicher Zeit*, Utrecht and Amsterdam, 1961, pp. 55-60.

[64] Antwerp, Plantin-Moretus Museum, M.17.4, fol. 15v, exhibited in 1965 at Aachen, *Karl der Grosse*, 1965, no. 442 and the subject of a doctoral dissertation by Carol Lewine, "The Miniatures of the Antwerp Sedulius Manuscript: the Early Christian Models and their Transformations," unpublished Ph.D. dissertation, Columbia University, 1970. Comparison of the two manuscript representations of the Madonna reveals striking similarities: in both nimbi are shown, Mary wears a short headcloth and crosses her feet and, above all, she assumes the contorted pose, partly frontal and partly three-quarter, which seems motivated by the presence of the Magi in the Sedulius manuscript, whereas a *Maiestas*, such as that described by the text of the Clermont-Ferrand manuscript, is always a frontal figure. Also interesting in the Antwerp drawing are the dark, sigma-shaped patches of color behind the heads of the Magi. Although lightly sketched, they suggest a row of round-headed openings and an architectural setting, but the indication is too summary to allow us to assume that the scene is enacted inside a church.

and Madonnas in Magi groups may be presented. The relationship is evident from a simple comparison of certain wood and stone sculptures. A pair of examples from the Clermont-Ferrand area provides an illustration. On the lintel of the south portal of the church of Notre-Dame-du-Port in Clermont-Ferrand, the Adoration of the Magi is represented in stone relief.[65] The Madonna in this group (Fig. 5) is almost identical in style with a wood Madonna, Notre-Dame-la-Brune at Tournus (Fig. 6), by tradition originally from Saint-Pourçain-sur-Sioule, not far away.[66] Formal affinities are particularly clear in the garments of both Mary and Christ, in the oblique, forward position of the Child (reversed in the relief), and in the arcaded throne.

Another wood and stone pair is found farther north in France. At Pompierre, the twelfth-century tympanum contains reliefs which include an Adoration of the Magi group (Fig. 7).[67] When the Madonna from this relief is compared with the wood statue of the Virgin (Fig. 8) venerated as a cult object in the crypt at Mont-devant-Sassey, a short distance away, the two figures show a striking resemblance in general pose and in the almost identical costume, veil, crown and type of throne.[68] The tympanum seems

[65] Unfortunately the Clermont-Ferrand portal is not dated. The record of work still in progress on the church in 1185 does not clarify the chronology of the reliefs, but the style of the tympanum and lintel is consonant with the generally accepted dating in the third quarter of the twelfth century; M. Aubert, "Notre-Dame-du-Port à Clermont-Ferrand," *Congrès archéologique de France, Clermont-Ferrand, 1924*, Paris, 1925, 35; H. du Ranquet, *Notre-Dame-du-Port*, Clermont-Ferrand, 1913. Anne Lewis Miller has recently proposed a date of ca. 1160 and posits possible Burgundian influence on the south portal sculptures; both hypotheses are compelling and merit further study ("The Sculptural Decoration of Notre-Dame-du-Port: Its Place in Romanesque Sculpture of the Auvergne," unpublished Ph.D. dissertation, Johns Hopkins University, 1964, pp. 258, 270).

[66] Register no. 30. It is one of many examples of this type, cf. Notre-Dame de Saint-Flour at Lyon (no. 33), Notre-Dame de Marsat (no. 35), Notre-Dame d'Orcival (no. 31), the Martin Madonna on loan to the Metropolitan Museum in New York (no. 32) and the Madonna at Chalus-Lembron (no. 36).

[67] The Romanesque church was demolished in the nineteenth century when the portal was incorporated in a new structure. The sculptures have been loosely dated in the second half of the twelfth century on the basis of style; G. Durand, "Portail de l'église de Pompierre," *Gazette archéologique*, IX (1884), 20-24; G. Durand, *Eglises romanes des Vosges*, Paris, 1913, pp. 266-273. N. Müller-Dietrich (*Die Romanische Skulptur in Lothringen*, Munich and Berlin, 1968, pp. 92-103, 186-190 nn. 345-382, figs. 58-60) derives the style from Metz and implies a date well after the mid-twelfth century. Comparisons with Ile-de-France sculpture of this period are also appropriately considered. Cf. J. Schmoll Gen. Eisenwerth, "Sion—Apokalyptischen Weib—Ecclesia Lactans," *Miscellanea pro arte, Hermann Schnitzler zur Vollendung des 60. Lebensjahres am 13. Januar, 1965*, Düsseldorf, 1965, 91-110, who presumes a late twelfth-century date for the tympanum.

[68] Register no. 96. The statue is still heavily marred by former restorations despite a recent cleaning. It has been dated in cursory fashion to the early thirteenth century, but the hair-style, garments, etc., and above all the affinities to the Pompierre tympanum, support a much earlier, twelfth-century date. Müller-Dietrich assigns it to ca. 1147 on the basis of comparison with the choir sculptures at Verdun (*Romanische Skulptur*, p. 84). Cf. H. Reiners and W. Ewald, *Kunst-*

to be a representation in stone of a dramatic performance wherein actors impersonating the Magi offer their gifts, not to a living mother and child who participate in the action, but to one of our wooden Majesties. Here we seem to have not merely a resemblance, implying association, but an actual substitution.

Another outstanding illustration of the affinity between a wood Majesty and the Virgin and Child in an Adoration of the Magi in stone can be seen in Germany. The statue from Schillingskapellen now in the Liebieghaus in Frankfurt-am-Main (Fig. 9) and the Madonna of the retable at Oberpleis (Fig. 10) obviously share a common style.[69] In spite of the losses to the wood statue (e.g. the Christ Child and Mary's crown, among others) the resemblance is clear: the folds and collar of Mary's dress and the high-backed, spooled, chairlike throne are so like those of the stone sculpture that the works cannot be widely divergent in time or place of origin.

The question which concerns us is whether these formal relationships imply merely a stylistic affinity between contemporary works of art, or whether we are entitled to go further, as suggested above in connection with the Pompierre tympanum, and to maintain that the Mother and Child in stone Magi scenes were like the wood statues because the latter "participated" in a Magi drama. In other words, is it not a reasonable assumption that these stone replicas of the Mother and Child resembled wood Majesties because the wooden statues, not actors, filled the principal role in Magi plays? Their cult personalities suggest such a liturgical role, to which their mobility would have been admirably suited.[70]

The texts of the plays themselves provide an answer to this question. The *Officium Stellae*[71] had its genesis during the Early Middle Ages in the West and throve during

---

denkmäler zwischen Maas und Mosel, Munich, 1921, p. 65; E. Fels, "Mont-devant-Sassey," *Congrès archéologique de France, Nancy et Verdun, 1933*, Paris, 1934, 471-487; M. Aubert, *Cathédrales et abbatiales romanes de France*, Grenoble, 1965, p. 547, fig. 178.

[69] The third quarter of the twelfth century is the most probable date for both, H. Beenken, "Die Kölner Plastik des 12. Jahrhunderts," *Jahrbuch für Kunstwissenschaft*, 1923, 125-152, N.B. 148-149; A. Wolters, "Die Madonna von Schillingskapellen," *Form und Inhalt, Kunstgeschichtliche Studien Otto Schmitt zum 60. Geburtstag*, Stuttgart, 1950, 51-66. Cf. F. Mühlberg, "Grab und Grabdenkmal der Plektrudis in St. Marien im Kapitol zu Köln," *Wallraf-Richartz Jahrbuch*, XXIV (1962), 54-56.

[70] Of course the Madonna enthroned, with or without Magi, had been represented in art since the Early Christian period and this iconographic tradition was still vital. It was tapped by the imagers of the Magi scenes in question as well as by the sculptors of the earliest wood statues of the Virgin. The important point here, however, is that the wood Majesties and Madonnas from Magi scenes are similar, not just in assuming the attitude of enthronement but in style, pose, costume, throne, etc.; and in the Pompierre tympanum and the Oberpleis retable the Magi certainly appear to be addressing themselves to an image, not a real, responding Madonna and Child.

[71] An attempt was made by Mâle to relate the *Officium Stellae* to pictorial art in "Les Rois mages et le drama liturgique," *Gazette des beaux arts*, LII (1910), 261-270; it has been contested by Vezin, *Mages*, pp. 65-66, among others. Cf. N. Wibiral, "Beiträge zur Ikonographie der früh-

the Romanesque period.[72] It developed particularly during the eleventh and twelfth centuries. Of the twenty-two texts of the play recorded by Karl Young, the majority date from the eleventh and twelfth centuries. Only a few are later: four from the thirteenth century, one from the fourteenth, and two from the fifteenth.[73] Thus the play was clearly a Romanesque phenomenon.

Curiously, the Epiphany play exhibits no particular chronological growth pattern. One might expect dramatic intricacies in an elaborate play to be an indication of a rather late date, but apparently the Adoration drama did not experience a "Darwinian evolution" at all. A more complex or a more realistic play is not necessarily later than

---

romanischen Fresken im ehemaligen Westchor der Stiftskirche von Lambach (Oberösterreich)," *Wurzburger Diözesansgeschichtsblätter*, xxv (1963), 63-91, where the frescoed Magi cycle at Lambach is studied in relation to the manuscript preserving an eleventh-century *Officium Stellae* there.

[72] The question arises here as to whether such plays were known as early as the ninth century. The beginnings of liturgical drama can be clearly traced to the tenth century, the most famous early play being Ethelwold's *Quem quaeritis* of ca. 965-975 in the *Concordia Regularis* of Winchester, which probably depended upon an earlier model from the Continent. The earliest text known to Young which records a dramatization of the Magi story, on the other hand, is the tenth- or eleventh-century fragment on the flyleaf of the famous Carolingian Psalter of Charles the Bald (Paris, Bibl. Nat., MS lat. 1152), but the *offertorium* of the Mass was clearly troped with antiphons relating to the offerings of the Kings much earlier in the Middle Ages. Such tropes are particularly numerous from the ninth century. Whether impersonation was involved is unknown, but this is implied by Chambers. See E. K. Chambers, *The Medieval Stage*, Oxford, 1903, II, pp. 13-15, 44-52, and Young, *Drama*, I, pp. 184, 210, 249-250, II, pp. 33, 53, 397, 443.

Although Hardison dwells at length upon the dramatic character of the Mass in the ninth century, he presents no further evidence for impersonation during this period (O. B. Hardison, Jr., *Christian Rite and Christian Drama in the Middle Ages, Essays in the Origin and Early History of Modern Drama*, Baltimore, 1965, p. 43). Cf. C. Heitz, *Recherches sur les rapports entre architecture et liturgie à l'époque carolingienne*, Paris, 1963.

In reviewing the origins of the drama, Donovan concludes that the Epiphany play developed approximately 100 years later than the Easter *Visitatio*, or in the eleventh century. This conservative view is based on the preservation of the ritual recorded at Nevers (ca. 1060), whereas the tenth-century record in Ripoll, cited by Anglès as evidence of an earlier history for the Three Kings play, is cautiously interpreted by Donovan. The indebtedness of the Epiphany play to the Easter *Quem quaeritis* cannot be denied, but the dramatic beginnings of both may revert to an earlier date than can yet be attested. Surely the mature form of the tenth-century plays presupposes a much earlier initial appearance. See R. Donovan, *The Liturgical Drama in Medieval Spain*, Pontifical Institute of Medieval Studies, Studies and Texts, no. 4, Toronto, 1958, pp. 17 n. 33, 94; H. Anglès, "La Musique en Catalogne aux Xe et XIe siècles, L'École de Ripoll," *La Catalogne à l'époque romane*, Paris, 1932, 157-158. Cf. Young, *Drama*, II, pp. 442-443.

[73] See Young, *Drama*, II, pp. 29-101, 432-452, for the texts of the plays. Hardison, *Drama*, p. 314, lists most of the plays in tabular form. Cf. H. Anz, *Die lateinischen Magierspiele*, Leipzig, 1905; Chambers, *Stage*, II, pp. 44-52.

a simple one.[74] In fact, one of the earliest surviving Epiphany plays presents Herod in an elaborately dramatized role.[75] Moreover, details of the presentation became fixed at an early date. The three Magi are clearly and individually distinguished in the earliest plays on record. Their names, Kaspar, Balthazar and Melchior, were in common use by the twelfth century. Their gifts, referred to as symbols of greatness (gold), the true God (frankincense), and the sepulchre (myrrh); their silken tunics of different colors; and the star (usually pulled on a string) which heralds their journey are all a part of the usual Romanesque staging of the play.[76] Also from a fairly early manuscript (eleventh-twelfth century) comes the realistic touch of nonsense syllables uttered by the oriental Kings before Herod to indicate their foreign tongues and remote origins.[77]

Although manuscripts with descriptive rubrics directing the use of these trappings are unevenly preserved, the presence or absence of stage directions seems utterly fortuitous and is clearly independent of date. When they are omitted, one is hardly more justified in assuming there was no *mise-en-scène* than in the case of Shakespeare's plays.

Given such a situation, scholars tend to consider the Epiphany plays as a group, finding that all must be studied for certainty about the slightest detail. Indeed, their communal nature is underscored by the lack of significant regional distinctions in the Romanesque period. Hardison stresses their international character, which is to be expected in the core scenes at least. The part of the Epiphany drama pertinent to the present discussion is, of course, the Adoration scene. It recurs uniformly and is conventionally treated in all the plays known.[78]

The Adoration episode in the plays took its cue from the Mass itself. The offertory provided an opportunity for a suitable digression in the form of a trope, or short dialogue, involving the Magi, whose gifts were thought of as a Biblical parallel to the offering (*oblatio*) of the Mass, in which the *oblata* were gifts of bread and wine offered by those expecting to receive communion (*oblatio populi*) or, later, by the celebrant on behalf of the people (*oblatio sacerdotalis*). At the time of the offering, a psalm or antiphon, the *offertorium*, was sung. During the Romanesque period the offertory might be farsed with a minuscule play in which a boy dressed as an angel stood behind the altar while three cantors dressed as kings entered the choir and placed their gifts on the altar; the star was strung above them. The actual oblation (*oblatio*) would then follow.[79]

After achieving an existence independent of the Mass, the play had a more liberal development. Performed after Matins but before Mass on the Epiphany, it might be a fairly lively presentation. There are many manuscripts providing texts, but only those

---

[74] Chambers, *Stage*, II, p. 45; Hardison, *Drama*, Essay I.

[75] From Freising (Munich, Staatsbibl. MS lat. 6264ª); Young, *Drama*, II, p. 92. Note that Herod's theatrics are accompanied by very scanty information on staging.

[76] Young, *Drama*, II, pp. 29ff.

[77] From Rouen (Montpellier, Bibl. de la Faculté de Médecine, MS H 304); Young, *Drama*, II, pp. 68, 70.

[78] Donovan, *Drama*, p. 4; Hardison, *Drama*, *passim*; Young, *Drama*, II, pp. 29-101, 425.

[79] Young, *Drama*, II, pp. 32f.

few which furnish information on the *mise-en-scène* of the offering scene need concern us here.

Particularly informative is an eleventh-century text from Nevers.[80] In this play three clerics dress as the Magi, as is usual. They appear before the high altar, advance toward Herod (who is probably seated near the entrance to the choir) and inquire of him regarding the Christ Child, then proceed following the star (on a string) presumably to another altar where clerics dressed as midwives ask whom they are seeking. The Magi answer that they seek the Christ Child. The rubrics then explain that the midwives point out to them an image and say: "Behold, here is the Child whom you seek" ("Ostendentibus illis Imaginem dicant: ECCE PUER ADEST QUEM QUERITIS").

Of particular interest here is the representation of Mary and the Christ Child. Clearly they are "impersonated" by an image. Moreover, the use of *imaginem* in the singular indicates that it is a combined image, Mother and Son together as they would be in the *sedes sapientiae* formula, making it likely that the "image" was a statue of Mary with the Child in her lap, presumably placed on the altar where the midwives are stationed. *Imago* is the word commonly used for such statues of the Madonna, although it might also refer to a relief, as in a retable.[81] In view of the texts cited below, however, the latter possibility seems precluded. Significant too is the casual character of the allusion, with no further explanation of the place or type of image, suggesting that this text does not announce an innovation in the staging of the play, but rather presupposes that the gesture will be readily understood as normal procedure.

Other eleventh-century Epiphany plays which have rubrics contain the customary references to the Three Kings, the star, the gifts and the midwives. They use almost identical dialogue, including the words of the midwives, "Behold, here is the Child whom you seek," but are silent as to what means of visualizing the Madonna and Child the worshiper shall have. A seeming exception is found in the fragment of a play preserved in the monastery archive at Lambach in Austria. The manuscript, which can be dated ca. 1056-1091, is so mutilated that a reconstruction of the full text is impossible, but the presence of a venerated image is clear. Also the sequence of the action is evident. The Magi announce themselves; the midwives point out the Child, before whom the Magi then prostrate themselves; they offer their gifts, the symbolic significance of which is indicated; a cleric in the guise of an angel proclaims the fulfillment of prophecies and exhorts the Magi to return home by a different route; finally, in preparation for celebration of the Mass, they advance into the choir singing (and approach?) with great veneration the image (*imaginem*) and (before it?) they place (their gifts?). Unfortunately critical losses in the three lines relevant to the image ("[. . .] vadunt in chorum cantantes [. . .] magna veneratione imaginem [. . .]im imponunt.") prevent definite conclusions about it, but it may well have been a statue of Mary and her Son, such as we have assumed for the Nevers play above. It is so interpreted by Norbert

---

[80] Paris, Bibl. Mazarine, MS 1708; Young, *Drama*, II, p. 51.

[81] See the text from Vézelay quoted above, note 7, where *imago* is used and a statue is clearly intended, and Introduction, note 1.

55

Wibiral who believes that the *imago* was such a cult statue of the Madonna and, indeed, that it is represented along with the attendant midwives and Magi in the existing eleventh-century fresco at Lambach.[82]

Another clue to the casting of Mary and her Son in the drama is provided in an eleventh/twelfth-century text of a play from Rouen, which develops in the same manner.[83] The Three Kings assemble before the high altar, follow the star through the choir, and meet the midwives at the "Presepe," which must have been represented by an altar in the nave or transept.[84] There, the Kings explain their quest and the mid-

[82] N. Wibiral, "Beiträge zur Ikonographie der frühromanischen Fresken im ehemaligen West-chor der Stiftskirche von Lambach (Oberösterreich)," *Würzburger Diözesangeschichtsblätter*, xxv (1963), 63-91, N.B. 70, pl. 4 n. 1, figs. 2 and 5. For the entire original passage, see K. Schiffmann, review of H. Anz, *Die lateinischen Magierspiele*, Leipzig, 1905, in *Anzeiger für deutsches Altertum und deutsche Litteratur*, xxxi (1907), 12-17, in *Zeitschrift für deutsches Altertum und deutsche Litteratur*, xlix (1907), Berlin, 1908. The other eleventh-century plays referred to in this paragraph are from Nevers (Paris, Bibl. Nat., MS lat. 9449, ca. 1060), Young, *Drama*, ii, p. 439; Compiègne (Paris, Bibl. Nat., MS lat. 16819), *ibid.*, p. 53; fragment of unknown origin (Paris, Bibl. Nat., MS lat. 1152), *ibid.*, p. 443; Malmédy (Rome, Bibl. Vat., MS lat. 8552), *ibid.*, p. 443; Freising (Munich, Staatsbibl., MS lat. 6264ª), *ibid.*, p. 92; Einsiedeln (Stiftsbibl., MS 366), *ibid.*, p. 447. For the Lambach text, see *ibid.*, p. 445. Dr. Helmut Buschhausen kindly called my attention to the publication by Norbert Wibiral cited above.

[83] Rouen (Montpellier, Bibl. de la Faculté de Médecine, MS H 304), Young, *Drama*, ii, p. 68; dated by Donovan in the eleventh century along with the play from Bilsen (Brussels, Bibl. Boll., MS 299), *Drama*, p. 17 n. 33; cf. Young, *Drama*, ii, p. 75. Cf. Rouen (Paris, Bibl. Nat., MS lat. 904, thirteenth century) and Saint-Benôit-sur-Loire (Orléans, MS 201, thirteenth century), where the action is very similar.

[84] In this instance the text states that the Kings proceed to the "Presepe" where the midwives reveal the Child, but the rubrics are by no means consistent on this matter. In general, there are three stations for the Kings' action in the play: the first before the high altar in the choir, where the Magi meet and exchange the kiss of peace; the second before Herod, whose throne is (probably) near the entrance to the choir; and the third before Mary and the Christ Child. Very often the location and character of this third station are not specified at all. If so, the reference is either to an altar, usually in the nave or transept, or to the "Presepe" in the same area. These are probably one and the same thing, however, for the altar represented the "Presepe" in the Christmas drama just as it symbolized the sepulchre in the Easter plays. Justification for the association of the two in medieval thought and image is amply provided in texts (particularly pertinent being the Christmas sermon of Guerricus, the Cistercian abbot [died ca. 1157]: ". . . Fratres, et vos invenietis hodie infantem pannis involutum, et positum in praesepio altaris"; cf. the *Theoria* of Germanus I, Patriarch of Constantinople [d. 733], who says, "Altare est et dicitur praesepe, et sepulchrum Domini") and in the traditional use of the relic of the *praesepe* itself. It had been brought from Bethlehem to Rome by Pope Theodore (642-649) and was used there as an altar. The Pope laid the consecrated *Corpus Christi* upon this relic or "altar" as he celebrated his annual Christmas Mass in the chapel of Santa Maria ad Praesepe. It is significant that Pope Gregory III (731-741) provided a golden figure of Mary and the Christ Child for this chapel (Duchesne, *Liber Pontificalis*, i, p. 418). For the above texts see Young, *Drama*, ii, pp. 8, 25.

The identification of altar and *praesepe* is very common in medieval art (e.g. Chartres, west

wives, "uncovering the Presepe" (which surely implies the withdrawing of a curtain, as in the Rouen text cited below), say: "Behold, here is the Child whom you seek" ("Item Obstetrices aperiendo Presepe dicant: ECCE PUER ADEST QUEM QUERITIS").

While it is theoretically possible that the curtain was drawn aside from a relief carving, such as the reredos over an altar, the unveiling at this climactic moment of flat, diminutive figures barely visible to the audience would be an almost humorous anticlimax. On the contrary, to draw back the curtain of a baldachin such as commonly sheltered the Majesty of Mary and thereby unveil the awesome cult image of the Throne of Wisdom would be an appropriate and resounding climax.[85]

The fortunate preservation of a fourteenth-century text from Rouen, in which the summary directions of the eleventh- and twelfth-century texts just discussed are combined in a very explicit statement of staging, greatly strengthens the above hypothesis. The action is very much the same. The Three Kings in their silken robes meet before the high altar, follow the star through the choir, and proceed to the nave where they meet the midwives at the Altar of the Cross. In connection with this second altar appears a highly significant reference to "the statue of Saint Mary previously placed upon the Altar of the Cross." At the appropriate moment, when the Kings have explained their quest, two men in priestly robes (apparently representing midwives) draw aside a curtain and proclaim: "Behold, here is the Child whom you seek" ("et Magi, Stellam ostendentes, ad Ymaginem Sancte Marie super Altare Crucis prius positam cantantes pergant: . . . Tunc duo dalmaticati aperientes cortinam dicant: ECCE PUER ADEST QUEM QUAERITIS"). The Kings prostrate themselves and present their gifts.[86]

---

facade and west windows, La Charité-sur-Loire, etc.) and is so interpreted by Katzenellenbogen, *Chartres*, p. 9.

Although the possibility of a temporary stand of some sort representing the *praesepe* should not be ruled out, the likelihood is that for the above-cited Epiphany plays the Magi brought their gifts to a second altar furnished with baldachin, curtains, an image of Mary and the Christ Child enthroned, and a star above, as is so often pictured in medieval art. I believe that it is to such a group that the term "Presepe," as used in the plays, is most properly applied.

It is interesting to note that in recorded examples of the offertory dramatized within the Mass (Young, *Drama*, II, pp. 32ff.) the Three Kings clearly place their gifts upon the altar (Limoges, *ibid.*, II, p. 34; Besançon, *ibid.*, pp. 37, 40, 433), just as is directed in the *Rationale divinorum officiorum* of the twelfth century (Migne, *PL*, CCII, 50).

[85] The frequency of ciboria with images of the Madonna in medieval art and the references to them in medieval literature imply that it was customary for the enthroned Mary to be sheltered by a baldachin, as is very often the practice today. The inventories of Stephen and Begon of Clermont-Ferrand (tenth century) describe a ciborium adorned with a crystal jewel for the golden Majesty there. See note 2 above. The use of curtains in medieval church ceremonies was, of course, very common. See the reference to curtains below, Chapter IV, note 25.

[86] Rouen (Paris, Bibl. Nat., MS lat. 384); Young, *Drama*, II, p. 43. Anz considered this play to follow the oldest form of the Epiphany drama, probably current in the eleventh century when Jean d'Avranches described its uses in Rouen, *Magierspiele*, p. 39. As to the probability that the two "dalmaticati" represent midwives as in the other similar plays, see Young, *Drama*, II, p. 47.

This action, including the reference to the image of Mary on the altar and the drawing of the curtain, is repeated almost verbatim in a fifteenth-century text, a fact which argues that the tradition was long-lived and continuous.[87]

On the basis of texts alone, Young concluded that plastic figures of the Madonna and Child must have been used on the altar during Epiphany plays.[88] The possibility that Mary and the Christ Child might have been impersonated by members of the clergy or the community seems out of the question.[89] A modern congregation might find such impersonations acceptable for the pageants which are the sequel to medieval Nativity and Epiphany plays, but this would have been as inconceivable to the Early Middle Ages as would the Oberammergau drama. Moreover, the texts cited here are utterly silent with regard to human representations of Mary and Christ, yet very explicit as to who shall assume all of the other roles—the Three Kings, the midwives and so forth. In addition, the documented use of wood figures in dramas played for other church festivals indicates that, even in the late Middle Ages, for particular sacred roles an image was preferred to a human being. Following the custom of the "burial of the cross," it was common for wood crucifixes to be "buried in the tomb" (the altar) on Good Friday and to be "resurrected" on Easter Sunday, or for the *Palmesel* in wood to be wheeled to the gates of a mock Jerusalem during a Palm Sunday procession.[90] The temporary arrangements for these festivals were obviously well served by wood figures which could be moved about at will. In the case of the Epiphany celebration, the Madonna might have been moved from her regular location to the altar in the nave or transept, as required by the play.

[87] Rouen (Paris, Bibl. Nat., MS lat. 1213); Young, *Drama*, II, p. 437. Further evidence of the continuity of the tradition is the withdrawing of the curtain in an identical passage from the Rouen play (Paris, Bibl. Nat., MS lat. 904, thirteenth century) mentioned in note 83 above.

[88] Young, *Drama*, II, p. 47, but Young himself never associated the figures used in the plays with the sculptures which are the object of this study.

[89] To my knowledge the earliest Epiphany play in which the human impersonation of Mary is clearly expressed (with dialogue) is the fifteenth-century vernacular Erlauer *Three Kings Play*, K. Kummer, *Erlauerspiele*, Vienna, 1882, reproduced in R. Froning, *Das Drama des Mittelalters*, Darmstadt, 1964 (reprint of orig. ed. Stuttgart, 1891-1892), p. 947. Cf. Young, *Drama*, II, pp. 27-28.

[90] Young, *Drama*, I, pp. 112-148, 149-177, N.B. 137-148; II, pp. 534, 538. For the *Palmesel* see: H. Gräf, *Palmenweihe und Palmenprozession in der lateinischen Liturgie*, Steyl, 1959; V. Ostoia, "A Palmesel at the Cloisters," *Metropolitan Museum of Art Bulletin*, XIV (1955-1956), 170-173; Schrade, "Monumentalplastik," 64; E. Wiepen, *Palmsonntagsprozession und Palmesel*, Bonn, 1903; Young, *Drama*, I, pp. 90-97. The earliest reference to the use of the *Palmesel* is in the *Vita* of St. Ulrich of Augsburg (d. 973) by Gerard (*Monumenta Germaniae Historica, Scriptores*, IV, pp. 377-378, 391). See also the censure of sixteenth-century reformers, e.g. Thomas Kirchmayer (1511-1563), translated into English by Barnabe Googe, ca. 1570, "A wooden Asse they haue, and Image great that on him rides," Young, *Drama*, II, p. 532. For other figures see *ibid.*, pp. 225-227, 337-338. Grateful thanks are here extended to Lois Drewer, who is preparing a new study on this subject, for her assistance with this and other problems. On the use of crucifixes, see also G. and J. Taubert, "Mittelalterliche Krucifixe mit schwenkbaren Armen. Ein Beitrag zur Verwendung von Bildwerken in der Liturgie," *Zeitschrift des Deutschen Vereins für Kunstwissenschaft*, XXIII (1969), 79-121.

The wood Madonna and Child would have done more than give visual completeness to the narration of the story. As a sculpture in the round, it must have served as a particularly effective equivalent for Mary and her Son, far more so than any picture or relief sculpture. If the statue already had a reputation as a performer of miracles, or if it enshrined precious relics, how convincingly like the presence of the divine Mother and Child it must have seemed in that age. Such a mimetic equivalence is surely at the very heart of the *raison d'être* of the Romanesque Majesty. As the clergy and the congregation offered their gifts to the *Maiestas*, they must have felt themselves to be in the very presence of Mary and the Christ Child, participating in a mystical equation.

This equation was enlarged by rich substrata of meaning. The Romanesque Epiphany hymn of Adam of St. Victor expresses the symbolism of the Kings' offering. The hymn begins "Virgo, mater salvatoris" and continues in the second stanza, translated by Wrangham as follows:[91]

> Threefold gifts the three kings carry;
> Sure of heaven's bright luminary,
> As, star-led, they haste nor tarry,
>   Seeking for the new-born King:
>
> Gold, the Monarch venerating;
> Incense, Godhead indicating;
> Myrrh, His death commemorating,
>   By the Spirit led, they bring.

As previously observed in the discussion of iconography, the gifts of gold, frankincense and myrrh signified the regal, divine and mortal character of Christ, as the hymn explains. The Epiphany play facilitated visual recognition of the significance implicit in the gifts, allowing the associations to be seen as well as heard.

Mary presided over the reception of the gifts as the Mother of the Savior *and* as the Throne of Solomon. Not only was she *Virgo, mater salvatoris* but, as Adam says in another hymn written for the Nativity of the Virgin, she was also the *Thronus Salomonis*.[92] In her lap was the *sapientia Patris*,[93] the wisdom of the Father, the Word or Logos become flesh. Together Mary and Christ represented the seat of wisdom and Divine Wisdom itself, allowing the pair to be further understood as Church and Godhead. The iconography of the image was a visible composite of these concepts. By combining the sculptured Majesty with human impersonators in the Epiphany drama, the ideas were given experiential immediacy. A more moving revelation could hardly be imagined.

[91] Wrangham, *Liturgical Poetry*, III, xc, pp. 92-93. For the Latin text, see above pp. 28-29.

[92] *Ibid.*, II, lxxiii, p. 220; see the discussion in Chapter I above in relation to the iconography of the sculptures.

[93] See Chapter I, note 65.

Conclusion

Thus the *Maiestas* statue allowed the worshiper to come face to face with his Christian beliefs. This experience could be extended to others. George Henderson writes that "in the twelfth and thirteenth centuries Notre-Dame de Chartres was not primarily a building or an institution but a personality."[94] The resident semblance of that personality was the wood sculpture within the Cathedral, "Notre-Dame de Chartres," or the *Virgo paritura* as she was also called. No distinction was made between the image known as Notre-Dame de Chartres and Notre-Dame in the broad sense. The same claim can be made for Notre-Dame d'Orcival, Notre-Dame de Bon Espoir and countless others. They seemed vital personalities to their congregations.

As personalities, their presences were continually needed, for they provided sanction of the highest order for the enterprises of the community. To make that sanction locally visible was the true function of the Throne of Wisdom statue. Portability only enhanced the scope and range of each Majesty's prowess. Their roles were variously interpreted according to locale and occasion. They might participate realistically in the Epiphany festival, as well as in other celebrations and ceremonies within and without the church calendar, or they might simply be honored quietly and visited privately. Some served as reliquaries as well. Doubtless, purposes beyond those discussed above were also known and elude us because of incomplete documentation. Judging by the traces of devotional practices which have survived to the present time, these customs must have been common enough to obviate the need to record them. Texts transmitting knowledge of them are therefore understandably scanty and late. They nevertheless give glimpses of the distinctive character of the Throne of Wisdom statues. What inheres in the sculptures is a mimetic function which almost transcends the bounds of plastic art. They were sculptured representatives of the Virgin and her Son which brought the *sedes sapientiae* into the local church in a most tangible way. For the medieval observer the Majesty was the embodiment of the Romanesque vision of hieratic divinity. But the image was also endowed by his imagination with a vivid, living reality. As in the Eastern icon, the link between image and prototype was close and firm. Both the icon and the Majesty were agencies of access. Both allowed immediate, personal experience of Christian godhead, but the Romanesque sculpture was massive and three-dimensional and its style curiously bridged the abyss between the visible and the invisible.

[94] G. Henderson, *Chartres*, Harmondsworth, 1968, p. 76.

CHAPTER III. Origins: The Throne of Wisdom Statue and the Revival of Freestanding Sculpture

THE ORIGINS of the Romanesque Throne of Wisdom statue, the *Maiestas Sancte Marie*, are obscure and complex. The historian's search for its sources inevitably leads him into the dark thicket of problems surrounding the study of the early medieval West. Questions regarding this period continue to bedevil scholars even though the view of the era as a time of intellectual hiatus—a notion which spawned the term "Dark Ages"—is now outmoded. As in any formative age, forms and forces are difficult to distinguish, whether they be social, political or artistic. Such is the case with the Throne of Wisdom. In the twelfth century it was a distinctive type of sculpture, represented by a large number of extant examples which can be subjected to regional classification. However, its emergence as an independent genre of sculpture was not the result of a simple linear evolution from similar antecedents. In the eleventh century its history was linked with other manifestations of the revival of the plastic arts: early stone sculpture, metalwork, and wood and metal reliquaries. In the ninth and tenth centuries, its genetic course was even more intricately interwoven with new concepts of art and its purposes. Spurred by the force of the cult of relics and, even more, by the demand for a new type of imagery—a type which could fulfill a transcendental as well as didactic function—Carolingian art groped for new goals. Driven by the accelerating power of the Church and the Empire, the impetus was great. Curiously, the Byzantine East had already articulated similar objectives in the post-Justinianic period when "attempts were made to justify images, not on the basis of their usefulness to the beholder, but on the strength of a transcendental relationship to their prototypes," as Ernst Kitzinger[1] and André Grabar[2] have already observed. The process was aborted by the Iconoclast Controversy in the Eastern world, but its reverberations in the West can be discerned,[3] where to be sure a very different set of forces was at play.

[1] The quotation is from Kitzinger, "Icons," 142.

[2] A. Grabar, "La représentation de l'intelligible dans l'art byzantine du moyen âge," *Actes du VIe congrès international d'études byzantines, Paris, 1948*, Paris, 1951, II, 134-135.

[3] See, among others: L. Bréhier, *La Querelle des images, VIIIe-IXe siècles*, Paris, 1904; W. Delius, *Die Bilderfrage im Karolingerreich*, Berlin, 1928; G. Ostrogorsky, "Rom und Byzanz im Kampfe um die Bildverehrung, Papst Hadrian I und das VII. Oekumenische Konzil von Nicaea," *Seminarium Kondakovianum*, VI (1933), 73-87; G. Haendler, *Epochen karolingischer Theologie*, Berlin, 1958.

Pagan Mother Goddesses

Statues of pagan figures were numerous and widespread in Gaul and the Rhineland prior to the Christianization of the West.[4] Female goddesses were especially plentiful: Venus, Cybele, Artemis, Astarte and matronly figures known as Epona or Fortuna, all being goddesses of fertility and abundance. Celtic-Germanic "Matronen" such as those seen on the "Three Matron" reliefs were also common.[5] The importance of the cults of these mother goddesses in the early years of the Christian era suggests that statues of pagan deities might have played a role in inducing the creation of statues of the Christian Mother. Medieval legend, in fact, sometimes attributes pagan origins to Christian cult statues in an effort to ascribe venerable, even pre-apostolic, antiquity to local cults. The most famous instance is the story told of the "pre-Christian" statue of the Virgin formerly venerated at Chartres.[6] For Emile Mâle, these stories were not all fabulous. He argued that medieval peasants must often have taken Gallo-Roman figurines to be statues of the Virgin since nothing resembles the Virgin and Child more closely than some of the mother-goddess statuettes in the museums of France.[7] In describing the Majesty of St. Foy (Fig. 13), Mâle compared her to the pagan *Magna Mater*: "Elle s'avançait avec majesté, comme jadis la Magna Mater, au temps où ces montagnes étaient paiennes."[8]

Memories of pagan traditions in Western Europe were not completely extinguished in the Early Middle Ages, particularly in France. Mother goddesses and folk idols had had a more recent history and importance there than in Rome and Byzantium. Their vogue had not been overlaid with a Christian substitution such as the cult of icons in the East. The Mother of God in the form of such a statue could take hold of the imagination easily. The confusion of Christian and pagan mother images mentioned in the *Libri Carolini* lends support to this possibility. Whoever wrote the Caroline Books, their content issued from Charlemagne's court and represented official policy.[9] The

[4] E. Espérandieu, *Recueil général des bas-reliefs, statues, et bustes de la Gaule romaine*, Paris, 1907-1955; E. Espérandieu, *Recueil général des bas-reliefs, statues et bustes de la Germanie romaine*, Paris and Brussels, 1931.

[5] Espérandieu, *Gaule romaine*, e.g. nos. 3377, 7761.

[6] Vincent Sablon's explanation of the statue is given below in Chapter IV, see note 51. Cf. M. Jusselin, "Les Traditions de l'église de Chartres," *Mémoires de la société archéologique d'Eure et Loir*, xv (1915-1922), 1-26. A similar tradition was known at Nogent in the early twelfth century; Benton, *Memoirs of Abbot Guibert of Nogent*, ii, i, p. 122. For the analogous story of the Virgin at Le Puy and its confusion with a pagan statue of Isis, see Chapter I, note 40 and the full discussion in Chapter IV below.

[7] Mâle, *L'Art religieux*, p. 281.

[8] *Ibid.*, p. 201. For Gallo-Roman figure sculpture in wood, including statues of various sorts, see R. Martin, "Sculptures en bois découvertes aux sources de la Seine," *Revue archéologique de l'Est et du Centre-Est*, xiv (1964), 1-19; and C. Vatin, "Wooden Sculpture from Gallo-Roman Auvergne," *Antiquity* (forthcoming), a study of statues found recently near Clermont-Ferrand.

[9] Freeman, "Theodulph," *passim*; Wattenbach-Levison, *Deutschlands Geschichtsquellen im Mittelalter*, Weimar, 1953, pp. 201, 226; L. Wallach, "The Unknown Author of the Libri Carolini,"

writer attacks those who adore images by offering an example where such a person, being perplexed as to the identity of two very similar statues of beautiful women, threw out both of them, only to be told that one represented the Virgin and the other, Venus. In another passage concerned with the same problem, the writer of the Books asks how we are to know that an unidentified representation of a beautiful woman with a child in her lap is an image of the Virgin and Child rather than Sarah and Isaac or Venus and Aeneas or Alcmene and Hercules.[10] These often quoted passages are important in the present discussion since they indicate the possibility of close resemblance, even of actual confusion, between Christian representations of the Virgin and pagan works similar in theme, and thus suggest these works as a possible source for the Christian representations.[11]

In the early eleventh century Bernard of Angers and his companion Bernerior expressed contempt for certain statues of Christian saints and martyrs by likening them to representations of pagan deities. This was before Bernard's acceptance of such statues. Bernerior scornfully addressed the St. Gerald statue in Aurillac as an idol to be called "Jupiter" or "Mars";[12] and Bernard at first alluded to the St. Foy at Conques (Fig. 13) disdainfully "as if it were a likeness of Venus or Diana."[13]

Didascaliae. Studies in Honor of Anselm M. Albareda, New York, 1961, 469-516; cf. H. Fichtenau, *The Carolingian Empire, The Age of Charlemagne*, Oxford, 1957, p. 30. See note 60 below.

[10] Freeman, "Theodulph," 697. The following passages of the Books are relevant: "Offeruntur cuilibet eorum, qui imagines adorant, verbi gratia duarum feminarum pulc[h]rarum imagines superscriptione carentes, quas ille parvipendens abicit abiectasque quolibet in loco iacere permittit. Dicit illi quis: 'Una illarum sanctae Mariae imago est, abici non debet; altera Veneris, quae omnino abicienda est,' vertit se ad pictorem quaerens ab eo, quia in omnibus simillimae sunt, quae illarum sanctae Mariae imago sit vel quae Veneris?" (*Libri Carolini*, IV, 16; *Monumenta Germaniae Historica, Legum*, III, Concilia, vol. 2, suppl., ed. H. Bastgen, 1924, p. 204, 18-23); "Esto, imago sanctae Dei genitricis adoranda est, unde scire possumus, quae sit eius imago aut quibus indiciis a caeteris imaginibus dirimatur . . . ? Cum ergo depictam pulchram quandam feminam puerum in ulnis tenere cernimus, si superscriptio necdum facta sit aut quondam facta casu quodam demolita, qua industria discernere valemus, utrum Sara sit Isaac tenens . . . unde scire valemus utrum Venus sit Aeneam tenens an Algmena Herculem portans . . . ?" (*Libri Carolini*, IV, 21; *ibid.*, p. 213, 24-33).

On the relationship between Venus and the Virgin in medieval literature, see Chapter II, note 50 above.

Cf. the instance of an inscription "Ave Maria gratia plena," placed around an image of Minerva by the chapter of Noyon in the thirteenth century, J. Seznec, *The Survival of the Pagan Gods*, New York, 1953, p. 105, n. 98.

[11] For further discussion of the passages, see p. 73.

[12] Bouillet, *Liber miraculorum*, I, xiii, p. 47.

[13] Later he recorded his repentance for having had such an attitude: "But that vain utterance or mean conception did not proceed from a very honest heart, when I disdainfully alluded to the sacred image, which is not consulted, like an idol, with offering of sacrifices but is regarded as honoring the highest God through commemoration of the reverend martyr—alluded to it, I say, as if it were a likeness of Venus or Diana. And afterward I sorely repented that I had behaved so foolishly toward one of God's saints." "Verum istud vaniloquium sive parva conceptio non adeo

Many monuments depicting pagan mother goddesses are preserved and can be seen in the museums at Clermont-Ferrand, Vienne, Saintes, Dijon, Reims or further north in Stuttgart, Trier, Mainz, Bonn and Cologne.[14] The monumental volumes published by Espérandieu on Roman Gaul and Roman Germany illustrate large numbers of them.[15] They may be statuettes of terracotta only a few inches high or larger stone reliefs.[16] They also assume fairly monumental proportions as stone sculptures in the round.[17] Normally the mother is seated in a frontal position on a plain chair or throne and her costume is reduced to simple, symmetrical stylizations of familiar Classical forms. Her rigid pose anticipates the stiff, hieratic manner of Romanesque statues of the Virgin. In her lap the pagan mother goddess carries a child or holds fertility symbols such as baskets of fruit, a calf or a cornucopia of abundance. The statues discovered at the bottom of wells in Bernard (Vendée) by the Abbé Baudry included one of wood representing a woman seated on a throne with a child in her lap (Fig. 11).[18] She is veiled and draped in a manner remarkably similar to the Romanesque statues of the Virgin at Tournus or Orcival (Figs. 89, 90).

The tiny statuette of a mother and child from Prunay-le-Gillon (Fig. 12) also resembles the typical Romanesque Madonna.[19] This Gallo-Roman figure is now lost but a cast is preserved in the Musée des Antiquités Nationales at Saint-Germain-en-Laye. The frontal pose with the child rigidly centered in the mother's lap, the schematic symmetry of the hands of the mother on her knees, and the parallel pleating of the drapery, all suggest features of twelfth-century Virgins centuries later.

As compelling as these comparisons may seem to be, however, they are hardly sufficient explanation of the sources of the medieval *Maiestas* of Mary. The most telling of the mother and child examples are diminutive in size. They probably escaped destruction fortuitously, being personal objects whose smallness seemed to render them harm-

---

ex bono corde procedebat, quando sacram imaginem quae non ut idolum sacrificando consulitur, sed ob memoriam reverendae martyris in honore summi Dei habetur despective tamquam Veneris vel Dianae appellaverim simulachrum. Et hoc ita stulte in sanctam Dei egisse valde me postea penituit." *Ibid.*, p. 48.

[14] Those from the Altbachtal excavations at Trier are mentioned by Keller, "Vollskulptur," 85; cf. E. Gose, *Der Tempelbezirk des Lenus Mars in Trier*, Berlin, 1955, figs. 21-23, pp. 54-55.

[15] See note 4 above.

[16] In addition to the examples cited in Espérandieu, there are a number of pieces without inventory numbers in the Musée Bargoin, Clermont-Ferrand and the Römisch-Germanisches Zentralmuseum, Mainz. See also nos. 89, 90 in the Musée Rolin, Autun and nos. 3189, 3576, 23-192, 3182, 23-35 in the Römisch-Germanisches Museum at Cologne; cf. Espérandieu, *Gaule romaine*, no. 1326.

[17] Espérandieu, *Gaule romaine*, N.B. nos. 4831, 7617, 8323.

[18] F. Baudry, *Puits funéraires gallo-romains*, La Roche-sur-Yon, 1873, p. 181.

[19] M. H. Vertet, "Terres cuites africaines trouvées en Gaule," *Actes du 86ᵉ congrès national des société savantes, Montpellier, 1961*, Paris, 1962, 41-43; *L'Art gaulois*, La Pierre-qui-vire, 1956, p. 314, fig. 16. For the Vertet reference I am indebted to Vera Ostoia.

less. Monumental examples are preserved in lesser number, evidently because they were more readily regarded as pagan idols; most of them must have been destroyed during the conversion of Europe to Christianity. A most important consideration is that these Gallo-Roman figures date from at least five to six centuries earlier than the emergence of the first medieval statues in Carolingian times.

During that 500-year interval the production of monumental statuary is generally thought to have ceased. Literary sources indicate that some statues were still produced, but we do not know whether they constituted anything more than a crude folk art. Among the Merovingian texts which allude to sculptured idols, still popular in most of Western Europe, a few descriptions give some idea of their character. For example, an eighth-century text reproducing a sixth-century account describes briefly the gods made for the Franks whose custom it was to adore idols of gold, silver, wood and stone.[20] Pope Gregory III (731-741) also speaks of folk idols fashioned of gold, gilded silver and stone.[21] That the idols were statues and generally in human form is clear.[22] That they depicted mother and child images is likely, considering the strength of the mother cults, but more than this we can only guess. Christian missionaries were busy destroying the idols wherever they found them.[23] The relentless zeal of Willibrord and Boniface are well known in the story of the conversion of pagan Europe, and the popes themselves were active in sweeping Europe clean of idolatrous statuary.[24] Burned or buried, the idols were removed and relics of saints placed in their stead. Wettinus (816-824) writes that Columban ordered the images worshiped at Bregenz to be thrown into Lake Constance. He then removed all taint of them by blessing the water of the lake and sanctifying the place through dedication to St. Aurelian. So complete was the cleansing that no trace remains of these ancient cult objects.[25]

Whether these types of pagan sculpture, the Gallo-Roman mother goddesses and the indigenous folk idols, provided specific models for Madonnas or not, they had prepared the native population of Western Europe for the ready acceptance of a Christian sculpture. This was a foundation which proselytizing missionaries were to turn to Christian advantage.

The Christian Iconographic Tradition

A rich Christian heritage in the form of an iconographic tradition was available to the first artists in the medieval West who were given the task of rendering the *sedes sapientiae* in sculptural form. The iconography was established in the Early Christian period and had developed into the *nikopoia* Madonna in the Byzantine East. In addition to the famous mosaics and wall paintings illustrating the theme in Rome, Ravenna and

[20] E. Knögel, *Schriftquellen zur Kunstgeschichte der Merovingerzeit, Bonner Jahrbücher,* cxxxx-cxxxxi (1936), 1-258, no. 738.

[21] *Ibid.*, no. 867. [22] *Ibid.*, no. 832.

[23] *Ibid.*, nos. 173, 192, 366, 472, 487, 508, 607, 643, 738, 768, 782, 832, 861, 867, 918, 940, 979.

[24] *Ibid.*, no. 940. [25] *Ibid.*, no. 598.

65

Parenzo,[26] from the period of catacomb painting on, there were portable examples in the form of ivories,[27] manuscript miniatures,[28] metalwork[29] and even icons.[30] The *Liber Pontificalis* mentions images of the Virgin and Christ in precious metal[31] and these were known in the North as well. A silver retable of the Virgin was prized at Luxeuil[32] in Carolingian times, while Hincmar had a gold altar with the Virgin in Majesty at Reims[33] and Tuotilo donated one, presumably a relief, which served as a gold altar frontal at Metz.[34] Similarly, manuscripts and ivories representing the *Maiestas* of Mary were produced in Northern ateliers.[35] The Madonna in Majesty was clearly an important part of the Carolingian artists' thematic repertory.

The related theme of the Adoration of the Magi was also prominent in early medieval art. Examples in manuscripts (Fig. 4) and ivories are well known, and the theme could also be seen in more monumental form. Einhard described a painting of it, presumably of the mid-eighth century, in the apse of the church of John the Baptist at Gravedona on Lake Como, as being in need of renewal in 823.[36] Carolingian wall painting is preserved in very fragmentary form, but it is unlikely that this was an isolated example.

[26] E.g. Sta Maria Antiqua, Rome, Sant' Apollinare, Ravenna, the Euphrasiana, Parenzo; see the study of this iconographic group in C. Ihm, *Die Programme der christlichen Apsismalerei vom vierten Jahrhundert bis zur Mitte des achten Jahrhunderts*, Wiesbaden, 1960, pp. 55-68. Other iconographic studies include: V. Lasareff, "Studies in the Iconography of the Virgin," *The Art Bulletin*, xx (1938), 26-65; N. Kondakov, *Ikonografia Bogomateri*, St. Petersburg, 1914-1915; Wellen, *Theotokos*.

[27] W. Volbach, *Elfenbeinarbeiten der Spätantike und des frühen Mittelalters*, Mainz, 1952, nos. 127, 131, 137, 142, 145, pls. 39, 41, 42, 44, 47.

[28] D. V. Ainalov, *The Hellenistic Origins of Byzantine Art*, trans. E. and S. Sobolevitch, ed. C. Mango, New Brunswick, 1961, p. 91.

[29] A. Grabar, *Ampoules de Terre Sainte*, Paris, 1958, pp. 16f., pls. I, IV, VIII, x.

[30] Kitzinger, "Icons"; G. and M. Soteriou, *Icones du Mont Sinai*, Athens, 1956, I, pl. 4; K. Weitzmann, M. Chatzidakis, K. Miatev and S. Radojčić, *Icons from South Eastern Europe and Sinai*, London, 1968, pp. ix-x, lxxix, pls. 1-3; cf. M. Chatzidakis, "An Encaustic Icon of Christ at Mount Sinai," *The Art Bulletin*, XLIX (1967), fig. 16.

[31] Duchesne, *Liber Pontificalis*, I, pp. 418-419, 453, II, pp. 9, 14-16, 61, 144; cf. J. von Schlosser, *Quellenbuch zur Kunstgeschichte des abendländischen Mittelalters*, Vienna, 1896, pp. 68ff.

[32] Deschamps, "Etude sur la renaissance," 52.

[33] *Ibid.*; Hubert, *L'Art pré-roman*, p. 131.

[34] Beissel, *Verehrung*, pp. 83, 162.

[35] E.g. the Book of Kells; cf. E. Kitzinger, "The Coffin of St. Cuthbert," *The Relics of St. Cuthbert*, ed. C. F. Battiscombe, Durham, 1956, 248-264, for the Virgin and Child on the seventh-century coffin of St. Cuthbert and its relation to the Madonna in the Book of Kells. Ivories are illustrated in Volbach, *Elfenbeinarbeiten*, no. 224, pl. 62 and A. Goldschmidt, *Die Elfenbeinskulpturen aus der Zeit der Karolingischen und sächsischen Kaiser VIII. bis XI. Jahrhunderts*, I, Berlin, 1914, figs. 14, 16. See Chapter II, note 64 above.

[36] A. Grabar, "The Virgin in a Mandorla of Light," *Late Classical and Medieval Studies in Honor of Albert Mathias Friend, Jr.*, Princeton, 1955, 308-309.

These various representations of the Virgin and Child from the Christian iconographic tradition provided a rich and vital reserve which could be utilized by early sculptors and obviated their dependence upon Classical models. Of course the great gap in our knowledge has to do with the leap from two- to three-dimensional representation of the theme rather than with the sources of the iconography. Depicting the Virgin in Majesty in painting or relief was surely no problem for early medieval artists, whereas rendering the subject in solid, three-dimensional form was quite another matter.

The Revival of Freestanding Sculpture and the Cult of Relics

An artist such as Adelelmus who was the master of the earliest Madonna in Majesty known to us, the Clermont-Ferrand figure of ca. 946,[37] would have had no difficulty in determining the stylistic or iconographic type of the Virgin which Bishop Stephen wanted him to model in gold. The antecedents were many. As a goldsmith he must have already worked altar frontals or repoussé plaques which may have included representations of the Virgin enthroned. Even for an artist well trained in the working of metal in relief, however, the handling of the massive, plastic form must have presented a more serious challenge. If he simply worked his statue as a four-sided relief, doing one side first and then the next, rather than conceiving the whole at once and visualizing its relation to its spatial environment, he would still have needed models to help inspire his arrangement of the sides and back of the figure and to give assistance with the difficulties of the head. Such models need not have been limited to the remains of ancient statuary, although pagan sculptures of seated goddesses would have illustrated poses very like that of the Virgin, for other models were at hand. Now that the revival of statuary can be seen as a Carolingian phenomenon rather than an invention of the late tenth century, we can assume that Adelelmus would have known Christian statues and might have used them as models. Among them could have been the St. Foy at Conques.

For insight into the problems which beset the first sculptors of medieval statuary in the West, the statue of St. Foy (Figs. 13-15) provides helpful clues. When stripped of its gold sheath during the recent restoration under the direction of Jean Taralon, the wood core beneath the metal could be studied.[38] It is quite unlike the other early examples we know, such as those at Hildesheim, Paderborn, Orcival and Monastier (Figs. 37-39, 44-46, 90-93, 16 and 17).[39] They too were once covered with metal. They are,

[37] See Chapter I, note 6, Chapter II, notes 1 and 2, above, and the discussion in Chapter IV below.

[38] The restoration was executed by Lucien and Jean-Claude Toulouse in 1954. See the thorough discussion by Jean Taralon, "Majesté"; cf. Taralon, "La nouvelle Présentation," 121-141. I am particularly grateful to M. Taralon for his kindness in discussing with me the unpublished photographs of his admirable work on this figure. The statue had been opened earlier for examination in 1878 when the skull of the saint, wrapped in silver foil and oriental textiles, and other small relics were revealed; Bréhier, "Les Origines," 888; Bouillet, L'Eglise, pp. 53f.

[39] In the case of the Hildesheim and Orcival Madonnas, where both the wood core and the metal sheath are preserved, the extent to which the details in the wood carving approximate those

nevertheless, fully modeled wood sculptures, obviously done by carvers already accomplished at work in the round. The surfaces to be hidden later by the metal were articulated with finely cut pleats and folds of drapery. The body masses were understood and controlled as powerful three-dimensional forms. The St. Foy, however, shows none of these later refinements. In fact, nothing could look more like a rude folk idol than this denuded statue. Made up of a cylindrical trunk and simple shafts for legs, the figure lacks any further subtlety. Completely unworked, the core is of two rough pieces of wood joined at the knees.

The coarseness of the St. Foy wood core can hardly be due to the fact that it was to be covered with metal, for the Paderborn, Hildesheim and Orcival Madonnas were also sheathed. Rather, its simplicity suggests the tentative groping of an artist commissioned to do something he had not done before, an artist without the benefit of traditions for conceiving and executing a three-dimensional figure and who was, therefore, ill at ease with his commission. The St. Foy at Conques seems to have been made when sculpture in the round was still in its initial stages of development.

For Louis Bréhier the St. Foy followed closely the Clermont-Ferrand Majesty and was, therefore, to be dated in the late tenth century, the period to which he ascribed the emergence of freestanding sculpture.[40] Since his publications, studies of medieval sculpture have tended to follow his lead and to accept the Clermont-Ferrand Madonna as the prototype for later statuary.[41] Most scholars have thus been content to place the origins of Western freestanding sculpture in the middle of the tenth century. Keller agreed to this thesis, bracketing the period of origin between ca. 950 and ca. 1000,[42] and accepting as the earliest examples the Clermont-Ferrand *Maiestas* of ca. 946 and the Conques St. Foy which he dated as ca. 984. Schrade was also satisfied with the idea of a tenth-century origin for the first statues and assigned what he called "Ottonian" dates to those of Clermont-Ferrand and Conques.[43] Although Schrade was aware of the investigations carried out in Conques by Jean Taralon, he continued to assume that a tenth-century artist was responsible for the St. Foy. Actually, examination of the figure had led Taralon to advance the hypothesis that the St. Foy is of Carolingian date, created in the ninth century, thus long before the Clermont-Ferrand Majesty and almost a hundred years earlier than any previous scholar had dated it.[44] Taralon believes that the

---

in metal can be observed. Some of the delicate ornamentation is visible in the metal alone, indicating the use of a true repoussé technique, i.e. the metal was driven into raised designs, the relief being supported on the underside by wax if necessary, rather than being beaten directly against the wood core as is sometimes erroneously supposed. See the remarks on the repoussé technique above in Chapter I.

[40] Bréhier, "Les Origines," 892ff.; *idem*, "Clermont," 209-210.

[41] Mâle, *L'Art religieux*, p. 286; Hubert, *L'Art pré-roman*, p. 137; cf. Beutler, *Bildwerke*, pp. 13, 39-40.

[42] Keller, "Vollskulptur," 81, 88.   [43] Schrade, "Monumentalplastik," 57ff.

[44] Marie-Madeleine Gauthier suggests that the earlier, ninth-century version of the statue was a head-reliquary only ("Le Trésor," 103).

core of the statue and its basic metal casing were complete in the last half of the ninth century. Since the relics of the young Foy were brought to Conques in ca. 864-875,[45] the original statue of the saint may have been made at that time.

In studying the metal sheath of the figure, Taralon noted that the tunic had been cut away near the lower hem and also at the edges of the sleeves, and that these alterations were masked by the addition of the ornamental borders which are now prominent. Since the crown and some of the details added to the head show the same gem settings and filigree patterns as these borders, he concluded that all of these embellishments, which can be dated in the tenth century, were added to the figure at the same time as the edges of the sleeves and tunic were cut away to accommodate the borders. The throne is also an addition to the original conception, for the wood core indicates that a primitive chair was formerly carved in one piece with the figure.[46]

These many alterations must have radically transformed the statue. Moreover, the changes must have been complete when Bernard of Angers saw the image at the beginning of the eleventh century, for his description accords in general with what we see today. Bernard himself called the statue a "renovated" figure: "However that which is the principal distinction of the church treasure, is the splendid image; which, having been made in antiquity, would now be regarded as a trifling thing, if it were not renovated in a better form, having been completely remodeled."[47] The renovation, probably consisting of those changes singled out by Taralon, was sufficient to alter completely the aspect of the figure. This would have taken place just after the famous miracle of Guibert L'Illuminé in 984, well before Bernard's visit in the early eleventh century.

Although the core of the statue and the dress may, therefore, be given a Carolingian date, the head is probably still older (Fig. 14). Bernard's reference to the image, as *ab antiquo fabricata*, now seems to us amazingly precise; for after a careful analysis of the head, Taralon has conjectured that it is an antique head of an emperor, possibly of fifth-century date.[48]

A major objection to the acceptance of a Carolingian date for the St. Foy statue, or for a belief in the existence of Carolingian sculpture in the round at all, is the widely accepted view that proscriptions against statuary still held firm sway in Carolingian times. Evidence for the assumed dread of plastic representation in Carolingian Europe has been found primarily in the tone of the *Libri Carolini*, along with later reports of

---

[45] Taralon, "Majesté," 290.

[46] A complete photographic record of these discoveries was made at the time of Taralon's examination of the statue. See his report on his findings in "Majesté." Cf. note 38 above.

[47] "Quod autem erat precipuum ornati, hoc est decus imaginis, que ab antiquo fabricata nunc reputaretur inter minima, nisi de integro reformata in meliorem renovaretur figuram," Bouillet, *Liber miraculorum*, I, xvii, p. 53.

[48] Taralon has compared the ornamental motifs of the tunic with the Crosses in Oviedo of 878. The body of the statue was clearly made to go with the head. For a discussion of the latter, which is of heavier gold and worked in a different manner, see "Majesté," 292.

69

attempts by the Church to combat idolatrous practices.[49] Whether these sources have been properly interpreted is a question that should now be posed.[50]

There are a number of literary references which show an interest in religious statuary in the eighth and ninth centuries. Freestanding images were known not only in Charlemagne's court. As far west as Wessex, we hear of statues of the Savior, the apostles, and of Mary, made of gold and silver for King Ine (ca. 725).[51] The *Liber Pontificalis* mentions a gold image of the enthroned Madonna made for Pope Stephen II (d. 757) along with other, gilded silver images. A gold statue of the Virgin was made for Gregory III (731-741); a number of silver statues of Christ and the apostles and a gold statue of the Savior, for Leo III (795-816); a gilded silver statue of the Virgin, for Paschal I (817-824); and a standing figure of Christ, for Benedict III (855-858).[52]

[49] E.g. the decisions of the Council of Frankfurt in 794 and the Paris Synod in 825. See note 55 below.

[50] Christian Beutler has discussed these sources in *Bildwerke*, pp. 31-33. See the review of his book by Victor Elbern, *Zeitschrift für Kunstgeschichte*, XXVIII (1965), 261-269.

[51] William of Malmesbury, *De antiquitate ecclesiae Glastoniensis* in Adami de Domerham, *Historia de rebus gestis Glastoniensibus*, I, pp. 1-22, ed. T. Hearne, Oxford, 1727, p. 55, cited by S. Pfeilstücker, *Spätantikes und germanisches Kunstgut in der frühangelsächsischen Kunst nach lateinischen und altenglischen Schriftquellen*, Berlin, 1936, p. 184.

[52] According to the *Liber Pontificalis*, further donations of images of the Madonna were made by Gregory III, one to St. Peter's (1, 417-418) and another for an unknown destination (1, 419). An effigy of Mary in gilded silver made for Paul I (757-767) is also mentioned (1, 465). These images are usually interpreted as sculptures (Schlosser, Keller, Beutler), but scholars have regarded some of them as icons (Kitzinger, Wellen). Normally icons, panels and other images on flat surfaces are referred to as *tabulae*: "tabulam honorantes" (see note 129 below); "tabulam . . . ubi imago nostri domini est depicta et genitricis eius" (Albers, *Consuetudines*, I, p. 24); "tabulas quidem cum imaginibus sanctorum . . ." (*ibid.*, pp. 54, 69, 73); "tabulam, ubi affixa est imago domini nostri jesu christi et eius genetricis . . ." (*ibid.*, p. 87); "tabulam cum imagine domine nostri jesu christi atque ipsius genitricis" (*ibid.*, p. 100). *Imago*, when used alone, normally indicates a three-dimensional image: "portent duo vel quattuor Imaginem sancti petri cum reliquiis . . ." (*ibid.*, p. 44); "In imagine sancti petri continentur he reliquiae" (*ibid.*, p. 184). It is difficult to imagine an icon weighing 150 lb. as noted in the text (1, 465) or even 50 lb. (1, 419), and it is awkward to visualize a flat panel wearing a golden crown and a pendent jeweled collar, as the text says of the image of Mary in St. Peter's (1, 417-418), though it is not beyond the bounds of medieval possibility. This donation of Gregory III was described later by Peter Manlius, papal chamberlain in the 1190s (*Acta Sanctorum*, Junii VII, pp. 39, 100). The wording of the text recounting Stephen II's donation (1, 453) of a gold, enthroned Madonna and Child seems to imply an independent statue ("Hisdem vero temporibus sanctissimus vir praelatus papa fecit in ecclesia sanctae Dei genitricis Mariae imaginem ex auro purissimo, eidem Dei genitricis in throno sedentem, gestantem super genibus vultum Salvatoris domini nostri Jesu Christi, quem et multis lapidibus pretiosis adornavit, id est hyacintis, zmaragdis, prasinis et albis; et inter alias duas eadem Dei genetricis Mariae imagines qui ab antiquo ibidem ex argento ante altare erant statuit; qui et ipsas inaurare fecit"). On the other hand, the gold Virgin made for the Praesepe Chapel of Sta Maria Maggiore (1, 418) is said to weigh only 5 lb.; if in this case the reference is to the weight of a sheath of precious metal alone, it is understandable (cf. a similar formula in the ninth-century text regarding Duke Solomon's gift, note 79 below).

The popes gave limited approval to the decisions of the Second Council of Nicaea in 787, which restored the use of icons. They were somewhat in favor of the veneration of images.[53] Charlemagne's doctrine in the Caroline Books opposed the papal stand, but it did not condemn images outright. To the contrary, the Books admitted the usefulness of images for instruction.[54] Veneration was another matter, however, for in practice when acts of homage became involved the differences between adoration and veneration appeared negligible, and it was the idolatrous character of such worship which antagonized Charlemagne and his circle.[55]

The evidence of terminology, while not conclusive, suggests that these papal donations were three-dimensional works. Duchesne, *Liber Pontificalis*, I, pp. 417-419 (Gregory III), 453 (Stephen II), 465 (Paul I); II, pp. 9, 14-16 (Leo III); 61 (Paschal I), 144 (Benedict III). Cf. Schlosser, *Quellenbuch*, pp. 68f.

[53] E. Bevan, *Holy Images*, London, 1940, p. 146; A. Harnack, *History of Dogma*, trans. N. Buchanan, New York, 1961, v, p. 306.

[54] Bevan, *Holy Images*, p. 147; Harnack, *Dogma*, v, p. 306.

[55] Harnack, *Dogma*, v, p. 306; Freeman, "Theodulph," 699; R. L. Poole, *Illustrations of the History of Medieval Thought and Learning*, 2nd ed., New York, 1960, pp. 24-26, 29-30, 35. Harnack cites from the *Libri Carolini*: ". . . having images in the ornaments of our churches and in memory of past events, and worshiping God alone, and exhibiting fit veneration to his saints, we are neither iconoclasts with the one party nor worshipers with the other." The distinction between veneration (προσκύνησις) of images and absolute adoration or worship (λατρεία), as drawn by the Seventh Oecumenical Council, was expounded by Pope Hadrian I, who agreed that the latter, adoration, was reserved to God alone (Harnack, *loc. cit.*; Poole, *Illustrations*, p. 29 n. 15). The Synod of Frankfurt (794) condemned the Nicene Council's decision, considering the reverence it had enjoined for images to be excessive, and the Paris Synod in 825 reflected the even more stringent stand taken against such attitudes in the time of Louis the Pious (Harnack, *Dogma*, v, p. 307). Agobardus wrote derisively in that year that whoever adores a picture or a statue, whether it is cast or made of beaten metal (i.e. repoussé?), does not display worship of God or honor of angels or holy men but venerates mere copies. He says that the devil is at work in this, that the pretext of honoring saints is his wily means of reintroducing idols, and that through such worship of effigies Satan will attempt to turn us away from spiritual to carnal desires. Agobardus accepts and approves the aesthetic value of art ("let the eye be refreshed by the vision"), and he recommends it for instruction, but he condemns its use for cult purposes. For him a picture is only a picture, devoid of life, sense and reason. (*Liber contra eorum superstitionem qui picturis et imaginibus sanctorum adorationis obsequium deferendum putant*, Migne, *PL*, CIV, 225; cf. Poole, *Illustrations*, p. 35.)

Even more outspoken an iconoclast was Agobardus' contemporary Claudius of Turin, who called for the destruction of all images and pictures throughout his diocese. He says that people "worship the images of saints after the fashion of demons" (that is, in the manner of the ancient gods); "they have not left idols but changed their names." He says: "You worship all wood fashioned after the manner of a cross, because for six hours Christ hung upon a cross. Worship then all virgins, because a Virgin bare him." He adds: "Why dost thou humble thyself and bow to false images? Why bend thy body a slave before vain likenesses and earthly fashions? God made thee erect . . ." (the translation is from Poole, *Illustrations*, pp. 29-30).

Both authors provide excellent evidence for the existence of sculptured images in this period as they complain of abusive religious regard for them. The insistent condemnation of acts of

In writing on the *Libri Carolini*, de Bruyne says that it would be difficult to find a more forceful affirmation of the autonomy of art.[56] The Books stress the fact that art has pedagogic and illustrative value, but they also emphasize its aesthetic validity.[57] In Book III, xxii, art is mentioned as being neither pious nor impious in itself. It has its own "autonomous value," and sculpture is no more "idolatrous" than painting. It too has its own technique and beauty. Both arts, therefore, are justified on an aesthetic basis.[58]

Thus, to assume that the content of the *Libri Carolini* precludes the existence of sculpture in Carolingian times would surely be a grave error. Moreover, the broad separation between image doctrine and image practice in the Carolingian era has already been recognized.[59] In fact, if one accepts Theodulph of Orleans as author of the Caroline Books,[60] one is faced with the ironic circumstance of the supposed condemnation of images being written by a sophisticated connoisseur of art. The author actually champions the cause of art, attacking the Eastern clerics for their disregard of the artistic aspect of images.[61] He speaks with concern for the artist's craft, his need for good models and good masters.[62] Indeed he seems uniquely acquainted with art. He mentions not only painted images, but also "figures formed of wax, stucco, stone and wood, in the round and in relief, fashioned from precious metals, engraved upon gems. . . ."[63] These

---

homage before images surely indicates that such practices were rife, from which we may infer that the images themselves were not uncommon.

Compare the more tolerant attitudes of Jonas of Orleans, who saw the crucified Christ on the Cross as an example of sculpture in gold and silver which could keep one mindful of the passion of the Lord (*De cultu imaginum*, Migne, *PL*, CVI, 340), and of Rabanus Maurus at Fulda, who attempted a definition of the plastic modeling of form and said that man would be the first example of such work, having been modeled out of mud (Beutler, *Bildwerke*, p. 33).

Passages in the Caroline Books themselves reflect some inconsistency of attitude even in the time of Charlemagne, since the term *adoratio* is used there to describe an acceptable attitude toward images (see note 10 above).

Further discussion of the difference between *adoratio* and *veneratio* and the theological concepts they reflect would take us beyond the scope of this study. In the present context the important point is that the literature of the period reveals the early existence of some sort of sculpture in the round.

[56] E. de Bruyne, *Etudes d'esthétique médiévale*, Bruges, 1946, I, p. 261.

[57] *Ibid.*, I, p. 274.   [58] *Ibid.*, II, p. 98; see Agobardus' comment, note 55 above.

[59] J. Deér, "Ein Doppelbildnis Karls des Grossen, Tugendbild und Kaiserbild," *Wandlungen christlicher Kunst im Mittelalter*, Forschungen zur Kunstgeschichte und christlichen Archäologie, II, Baden-Baden, 1953, pp. 141-142; W. Messerer, "Zur byzantinischen Frage in der ottonischen Zeit," *Byzantinische Zeitschrift*, LII (1959), 52 n. 75; H. Schade, "Die Libri Carolini und ihre Stellung zum Bild," *Zeitschrift für katholische Theologie*, LXXIX (1957), 69f., N.B. 77f.

[60] Persuasively argued by Freeman, "Theodulph," although contested by Wallach, "The Unknown Author"; cf. note 9 above. Alcuin is commonly credited with the authorship of the Books, but this view has been seriously challenged and the question remains unsettled. See the review of the problem in Wallach, *op. cit.*

[61] Freeman, "Theodulph," 695.   [62] *Ibid.* (*Libri Carolini*, III, 15).

[63] *Ibid.*, 698 (*Libri Carolini*, I, 2; II, 29; IV, 19).

references imply the common existence of some sort of sculpture in the round. More-over, he enjoys displaying his knowledge of Classical art and his ability to identify mythological figures in a manner which recalls Theodulph's admiration for Classical art in the *Ad Judices*.[64] In the latter work, Theodulph describes at length the allegorical figures from classical mythology which appear on gifts brought to the court of Charlemagne.[65] The author of the *Libri Carolini* goes so far as to note resemblances between representations of the Virgin and Venus, as we have discussed earlier.[66] In sum, these passages leave little doubt regarding the general interest in Classical art and the existence of sculptured figures in Charlemagne's time.

In addition to these treatises which evince an interest in sculpture and confirm its currency, textual documentation of specific monuments can be cited. In ninth-century Europe large, sculptured crucifixes existed in considerable numbers. Among them were the life-size crucifix placed by Theodard in the cathedral in Narbonne (ca. 890),[67] Angelelme's (813-823) gold and silver crucifix at Auxerre,[68] Aldric's crucifix in the cathedral of Le Mans (ca. 835),[69] and Duke Solomon's crucifix given to Saint-Sauveur, Redon, in 869.[70] The descriptions of these lost works suggest that the crucifixes were of grand size, often of human proportions and ordinarily made of gold or silver attached to a wood base and ornamented with gems.

The insistence of the *Libri Carolini* upon art as a secular rather than a religious phenomenon makes it possible to imagine that sculptures of profane subjects were pro-duced along with these sacred figures. Indeed, profane works of the period are known to us. They were made of bronze, gold repoussé, wood, stucco and stone.[71]

For the working of bronze, we are fairly well informed. The bronze atelier of Charlemagne which produced the splendid screens, railings and doors surviving at the Palace Chapel in Aachen has become better known recently.[72] The ancient bronze bear still preserved in Aachen, and the bronze equestrian statue of Theodoric which Charle-

---

[64] *Ibid.*, 695, 697.

[65] *Ibid.*, 695.

[66] *Ibid.*, 697 (*Libri Carolini*, IV, 16, 21), quoted above, note 10.

[67] "Ad instar humanae staturae protractam," Hubert, *L'Art pré-roman*, p. 138, n. 2; Keller, "Vollskulptur," 71f.; Beutler, *Bildwerke*, p. 28; *Acta Sanctorum*, Maii, I, p. 153F.

[68] Hubert, *L'Art pré-roman*, p. 138 n. 2; Beutler, *Bildwerke*, p. 28; *Monumenta Germaniae Historica, Scriptores*, XIII, p. 396.

[69] Hubert, *L'Art pré-roman*, p. 138 n. 3; Beutler, *Bildwerke*, p. 29; *Gesta domni Aldrici*, ed. E. Charles and L. Froger, Mamers, 1889, p. 16; *Acta Sanctorum*, Januarii I, p. 388. See Beutler, *Bildwerke*, pp. 27-29, for the further possibilities of crucifixes at Metz and Figeac, and one sent to Rome by Charles the Bald for which size is not indicated.

[70] Hubert, *L'Art pré-roman*, p. 138; Courson, *Cartulaire*, pp. 190, 420.

[71] Beutler, *Bildwerke, passim*.

[72] W. Braunfels, "Karl des Grossen Bronzewerkstatt," *Karl der Grosse*, III, *Karolingische Kunst*, Düsseldorf, 1965, 168-202; Aachen, Rathaus, *Karl der Grosse*, 1965, nos. 3, 4, 6. Cf. F. Kreusch, "Im Louvre wiedergefundene Kapitelle und Bronzebasen aus der Pfalzkirche Karls des Grossen zu Aachen," *Cahiers archéologiques*, XVIII (1968), 71-98.

magne had brought from Ravenna, could have served as models for Carolingian artists.[73] The masters who made the bronze appointments for Charlemagne's chapel were already accomplished masters, however. Whether it is true that they came from northern Italy or not, their art flourished in Aachen,[74] where an appreciation of classicizing styles obtained. The amazing naturalism of the acanthus foliage and the *rinceaux* which are seen in the screens, and the full, plastic vigor of the lion heads which adorn the doors, denote the skills of artists who were at ease with the modeling of organic forms. Although there is not yet complete agreement on the matter, the same bronze atelier probably produced human representations as well. The small equestrian statuette portraying a Carolingian emperor,[75] and the tiny corner figures representing the Rivers of Paradise at the base of the famous bronze pine cone at Aachen,[76] illustrate the casting techniques of this workshop. Although their exact dates are still in question, the results of recent studies make an attribution to the early Carolingian period seem most likely. They are diminutive figures, of course, but the lifelike qualities of the equestrian statuette and the vitality of the symbolic river figures indicate that the artists who modeled them were capable of rendering the human form and were interested in it as a subject.[77] When considered in relation to the bronze fittings for the church, one must conclude that Carolingian metalworkers were concerned with plasticity and were competent in rendering sculptural qualities in their glyptic art.[78]

Medieval texts confirm that more monumental figure sculpture representing non-religious subjects was also produced. An outstanding example was the statue of Duke Solomon of Brittany. Solomon had vowed to make a pilgrimage to Rome as a penitent, but because Norman raids required his constant vigilance in the Breton countryside, he acquitted his promise in 871 by sending to Pope Hadrian II a statue of himself in his stead. The statue was life-size, made of gold and gems and adorned with a crown of

[73] Hoffmann, "Die Aachener Theoderichstatue," *Das Erste Jahrtausend*, Textband 1, Düsseldorf, 1962, 318-335. The statue is no longer seen as evidence of the incapacity of Carolingian metalworkers but rather as a monument imported for purposes of prestige.

[74] See the comment in Einhard, *Life of Charlemagne*, ed. S. Painter, trans. S. Turner, Ann Arbor, 1960, p. 54.

[75] F. Mütherich, "Die Reiterstatuette der Metzer Kathedrale," *Studien zur Geschichte der Europäischen Plastik, Festschrift Theodor Müller*, Munich, 1965, 9-16; Aachen, *Karl der Grosse*, 1965, no. 29a-b.

[76] Aachen, *Karl der Grosse*, 1965, no. 3.

[77] Cf. the bronze figures of saints at Saint-Riquier, Hubert, *L'Art pré-roman*, p. 135; Beutler, *Bildwerke*, p. 30.

[78] An interest in the portrayal of figures which convincingly suggest the volumes of three-dimensional form has long been recognized in the more familiar examples of manuscript painting, particularly those of the Court School. The architectural scenes in such miniatures demonstrate particular sophistication in the handling of spatial qualities. These characteristics are also apparent in ivory carving and small objects, such as book covers and reliquaries, in gold repoussé, and lead us to expect a contemporary interest in depicting the human form in the round.

gold set with small precious stones.[79] In exchange for this munificent gift, he requested relics from the Pope for the benefit of the monastery he had built. Judging by the values of the gold mentioned, the statue must have been of wood sheathed with gold foil (i.e. repoussé), while the crown was of solid gold. Other valuable items, including linens, woolens, deerskins and sixty pairs of stockings were also sent. The statue was on the back of a mule—the text is unclear whether an actual animal or a representation—and the whole train journeyed across the Alps and on to Rome. The reception given by the Pope to this curious embassy, in which a wood and gold surrogate for Solomon fulfilled a serious Christian vow, can only be guessed. We know that Hadrian looked favorably on Solomon's request, however, for he sent a substantial relic in exchange for the gifts, the arm of the martyr St. Léon. As singular as this statue might seem, it was not an isolated instance of such freestanding sculpture.

According to an account of the miracles of St. Germanus, a pagan Duke of the Normans, Ragenarius, had a similar gold statue made ca. 850. Being afflicted with a tormenting illness as a punishment for his violent invasion of the monastery of Saint-Germain-des-Prés, he ordered a golden statue to be fashioned in his own likeness and to be borne by Kobbo, King Louis's legate, to the Paris monastery promising that, in the event of his recovery, he would immediately become a Christian and believe in the God of the Christians. His wish was not granted, however, and he died after most grievous sufferings. The statue, being considered unworthy of a place in the church treasure (*sacris oblationibus indigna*) was kept apart, "as if it continued to be rejected as most unclean by the most pure judge of hearts." The golden statue was considered a valid proxy by Duke Ragenarius himself, and by the king's legate who conducted it, and apparently by the monks who saw in it the evil genius of its original and refused it a place among the holy offerings.[80]

[79] ". . . hoc est, statuam auream nostrae magnitudinis tam in altitudine quam in latitudine, cum lapidibus diversi generis, et mulum cum sella et freno et chamo, valentem per omnia .CCC solidos; et coronam auream lapillis adornatam preciosis, .DCCC. solidos valentem, et .XXX camsilas . . ." Courson, *Cartulaire*, p. 67; Hubert, *L'Art pré-roman*, p. 138; Beutler, *Bildwerke*, p. 25. Colin's interpretation of the figure does not accord with the wording of the text, "La Plastique 'greco-romaine' dans l'empire carolingien," *Cahiers archéologiques*, II (1947), 87-114. Cf. the large crucifix commissioned by Solomon, note 70 above.

[80] "[Ragenarius] qui maximis per triduum tormentis ignominiose afflictus, praecepit tandem unam auream suae similitudinis statuam fieri, atque per eumdem Kobbonem Germano seni deferri, spondens se, si evaderet, Christianum deinceps futurum, Deumque Christianorum indubitanter crediturum: sed quia non erat ex ovibus Christi, idcirco quod petebat, obtinere non meruit. Ita prorsus inflatus, quemadmodum nobis idem Kobbo manifestum fecit, ac totus turgidus exstitit, ut nec auditus, nec visus, nec odoratus, vel gustus in eius corpore discerni potuerit. Sicque diffusis ad postremum visceribus medius crepuit, vitamque miserrimus mane finivit. Statua vero sacris oblationibus indigna, a quibus delegata fuerat retenta, veluti immundissima a mundissimo cordium inspectore refutata remansit." J. Mabillon, *Acta sanctorum ordinis s. Benedicti*, III, 2, Venice, 1734, p. 100. Beutler (*Bildwerke*, p. 27 n. 1) recounts the same episode from a slightly different version in the *Monumenta Germaniae Historica, Scriptores*, xv, p. 16.

The statue of King Lothar (941-986) is a later example of this type of ruler effigy. To the consternation of the monks of Saint-Médard-de-Soissons, the dean of the monastery, Fulchoinus, ordered a sumptuous reliquary shrine of St. Gildardus to be destroyed in order that its gold and silver might be used to make a life-size portrait statue of King Lothar in 954.[81] The statue was to express Fulchoinus' thanks to Lothar for the realization of his ecclesiastical ambitions.[82]

In his important study of the origins of freestanding sculpture, Harald Keller contended that the earliest fully plastic sculptures in the West were containers or vessels for liturgical purposes.[83] A reliquary function cannot be attributed to any of the examples discussed above, which obviously were not liturgical objects. Neither the image of Duke Solomon nor that of the pagan Duke Ragenarius was intended for a Carolingian altar. Nor can either of these statues be imagined as reliquaries. The bronze figures from Aachen are equally improbable in that role. Even in the case of the religious figures cited at Rome or Wessex,[84] there is nothing to make us assume that they were intended to be reliquaries. For those religious figures of Charlemagne's time the presence of relics would surely have increased reverence and homage toward the statue, thereby aggravating the contemporary dispute concerning the veneration of images.[85]

[81] "Anno dominicae Incarnationis DCCCCLIIII Fulchoinus decanus monasterii sanctorum Sebastiani, Gregorii papae et Medardi, rege Lothario regnante, Remis ordinatur episcopus. Qui sanctorum praedictorum destruens monasterii structuram auream et argenteam, sancti praevaricator juris, praedicto regi ad instar suae effigiei episcopatus causa imaginem dedit. Quare monachi praedicti loci, ira commoti, organum jubilationis in vocem flectunt tristitiae et maeroris. Praedictus etenim monachus summi et incomparabilis viri Gildardi Rothomagensis ecclesiae archiepiscopi scrinium mire opere sculptum, quod divae memoriae antiquorum dux Northmannorum, Richardus nomine, sancto dederat Gildardo ob remedium animae suae, destruxit" ("Miracula SS. Gregorii et Sebastiani Suessione in Monasterio S. Medardi," *Catalogus codicum hagiographicorum Bibliothecae regiae Bruxellensis*, Brussels, 1889, I, 2, pp. 240-241). Cf. Hubert, *L'Art pré-roman*, p. 138; Beutler, *Bildwerke*, p. 15, n. 1.

[82] In addition to these sheathed wood figures and the bronze works from Aachen discussed above, Carolingian sculpture was also produced in stucco and stone. Christian Beutler has gathered interesting and persuasive evidence for the Carolingian dating of extant carvings in these media. The Cividale stuccoes and the works related to them at Brescia are unquestionably to be dated in the eighth century. Whether all of the additional stucco and stone examples Beutler has singled out can be considered Carolingian as well, however, is still an open matter. Problematic pieces are included in the group and further discussion of them in art historical studies will necessarily precede their final acceptance as constituting a Carolingian corpus. The work of Beutler is extremely valuable in presenting conclusive evidence that such sculpture could exist. The literary sources unequivocally attest to it. They have been cited before, but never in such a comprehensive and compelling way. For example, the descriptions of gable sculptures from 848-851 at the monastery of Glanfeuil, representing Charles the Bald and Duke Nomenoi, and at Saint-Pierre, Reims, associated with Louis the Pious and Pope Stephen in ca. 816, can only be interpreted as references to monumental stone sculpture. Cf. G. Plat, *L'Art de bâtir en France des Romains à l'an 1100*, Paris, 1939, p. 175. See note 50 above.

[83] Keller, "Vollskulptur," 71.   [84] See notes 51 and 52 above.

[85] Cf. the discussion above, p. 71. For the contemporary attitude toward relics, see Bevan, *Images*, p. 147.

The earliest example cited by Keller of a reliquary in the form of a human figure in the round is the lost golden bust given by King Boso of Burgundy (879-887) to the monastery of Saint-Maurice in Vienne.[86] This head, representing St. Maurice and supposedly enshrining the relic of his skull, survived until the seventeenth century. Before its destruction a careful description and two drawings of it were made by Fabri de Peiresc in 1612 in the course of a treasury inventory. According to him the work was life-size; it was made of wood covered with a gold sheath; and the eyes were inlaid with agate and chalcedony.[87] The drawings illustrate the head wearing two different crowns. The first was presented in the late ninth century by King Boso (Fig. 18), and the second (Fig. 19) was the gift of King Hugh of Arles (926-947). Peiresc says that the head was once supported by a body ("corps qui soustenoit ladite teste") which was lost in the time of the Huguenots.[88] Both the obituary of Boso in 887 and his epitaph mention the gift of the golden head.[89] The form of the figure, beyond what is indicated in the drawings, is unclear. The little bells which, according to Peiresc, were said to have hung about it, along with a large agate, were probably later embellishments. They had disappeared before his time. It is difficult to imagine the work as much more than a bust or a half-figure, but the question is open.

Keller claimed that all extant Ottonian sculptures were simultaneously reliquaries,[90] referring specifically to the Gero Cross (ca. 970) and its followers. Considering also the Clermont-Ferrand Majesty of the Virgin (ca. 946) and the St. Foy of Conques (dated by Keller ca. 984), he concluded that the origins of reliquary statues were thus to be placed about 950-1000.[91] He based on this evidence his thesis that only through its reliquary function did sculpture find its way back into the Western Church and justify its existence there.[92] The idea is intriguing, but requires considerable qualification.

The list of Ottonian crucifixes which Keller had in mind as reliquary sculptures, when he referred to the Gero Cross (ca. 970) and its followers, can be augmented by a

[86] Keller, "Vollskulptur," 84; F. Mütherich, "Die ursprüngliche Krone des Mauritiusreliquiars in Vienne," *Kunstchronik*, VI (1953), 33-36; P. E. Schramm, *Herrschaftszeichen und Staatssymbolik*, Stuttgart, 1955-1956, pp. 398-403; Beutler, *Bildwerke*, 37-39; E. Kovács, "Le Chef de Saint Maurice de la cathédrale de Vienne," *Cahiers de civilisation médiévale*, VII (1964), 19-26. The basic text is R. Poupardin, *Le Royaume de Provence sous les carolingiens*, Paris, 1901, pp. 357-368.

[87] In the manner of the St. Foy, Conques, and the golden Madonna at Essen.

[88] Beutler, *Bildwerke*, p. 38; Kovács, "Le Chef de Saint Maurice," 21 n. 13.

[89] "III id. Jan (887) obiit Boso rex, qui caput sancti Mauricii auro et gemmis preciosissimis fabricavit et coronam auream ei imposuit," Beutler, *Bildwerke*, p. 38 n. 4, cited from Poupardin; "Sancti Mauricii capud est circumdedit auro/ Ornavit gemmis clavis super atque coronam/ Inposuit totam gemmis auroque nitentem./ (Epitaphium Bosonis regis)," *Monumenta Germaniae Historica, Poetae latini aevi carolini*, IV, p. 1028. Both are given by Beutler, Schramm and Kovács.

[90] Keller, "Vollskulptur," 85.

[91] Even though he refers to the ninth-century head of Boso in this discussion, see note 86 above.

[92] "Niemals würde die Plastik den Weg in die abendländische Kirche zurückgefunden haben, wenn sie nicht dies Bündnis mit dem Reliquienschrein geschlossen hätte. Nur als Reliquienbehälter hat sie in der ottonische Kirche ihr Daseinsrecht erringen können" (Keller, "Vollskulptur," 87). See the review by W. Messerer, "Die Kunst der vorromanischen und romanischen Zeit," *Archiv für Liturgiewissenschaft*, V, 2 (1958), 375-376.

number of crosses which have only recently been recognized as works of the period. Among them are the Gerresheim Crucifix, from the time of Archbishop Gero (d. 970),[93] the Birkenbringhausen Crucifix (ca. 1000),[94] the Ringelheim Crucifix (after ca. 1000),[95] the St. George Crucifix in Cologne (ca. 1067)[96] and the Benninghausen Crucifix (late eleventh century).[97] In Reiner Haussherr's valuable study of this group of sculptures in 1963, he writes that only seven of the seventeen known German crucifixes of the tenth and eleventh centuries actually contain receptacles for relics.[98] Certainly, such a low proportion of reliquary crucifixes among the known Ottonian examples contradicts Keller's claim that all Ottonian sculptures were simultaneously reliquaries.

Haussherr goes on to say that the monumental Carolingian crucifixes, which are known only from descriptions but which must be the antecedents of Ottonian examples, apparently did not contain relics since there is no mention to that effect.[99] In most cases, the texts are silent with respect to the question of relics, as Haussherr says, but an exception must be made for the life-size crucifix from Narbonne (ca. 890), mentioned above, which is described in a contemporary text as containing a fragment of the True Cross ("in qua particula Crucis Domini condita erat").[100] Moreover, like figures of the Madonna or saints in majesty, it was made of wood and sheathed with gold and silver ("auro argentoque adopertam . . ."). As far as crucifixes are concerned, then, we must admit that in both the Carolingian and Ottonian periods they might, or might not, contain relics.

We encounter a similar situation with regard to images of saints. It has been claimed that the relics of St. Foy were installed in her image by Stephen II (d. 984) who was Abbot of the Conques abbey in addition to being Bishop of Clermont-Ferrand.[101] According to Bernard of Angers, however, the renovation of the statue followed the famous miracle of Guibert L'Illuminé in 985. It was this incident which brought the saint's fame into a new phase and motivated the remaking of the sculpture. Consequently the renovation must have been carried out under Stephen II's successor. As dis-

[93] H. Haedecke, "Der Krucifixus der Stiftskirche zu Gerresheim," *Karolingische und Otto-nische Kunst*, Forschungen zur Kunstgeschichte und christliche Archäologie, III, Wiesbaden, 1957, 298-307.

[94] A. Kippenberger, "Der Krucifixus aus Birkenbringhausen," *Wallraf-Richartz Jahrbuch*, XIV (1952), 41-45.

[95] R. Wesenberg, "Das Holzkrucifixus von Ringelheim," *Harz-Zeitschrift*, III (1951), 67-72.

[96] H. Schnitzler, *Das Schnütgen-Museum*, Cologne, 1958, no. 19.

[97] R. Fritz, "Der Krucifixus von Benninghausen, Ein Bildwerk des 11. Jahrhunderts," *West-falen*, XXIX (1951), 141ff. See also R. Wesenberg, "Der Bronzekrucifixus des Mindener Domes," *Westfalen*, XXXVII (1959), 57-69, for a discussion of this series.

[98] R. Haussherr, *Der Tote Christus am Kreuz, Zur Ikonographie des Gerokreuzes*, doctoral dissertation, Bonn, 1963, p. 40.

[99] *Ibid.*

[100] See note 67 above; cited by Beutler, *Bildwerke*, p. 28, no. 2, and Hubert, *L'Art pré-roman*, p. 138 n. 2.

[101] Bréhier, "Clermont," 209-210; Gauthier, "Le Trésor," 117; cf. Taralon's discussion, "Ma-jesté," 293-294.

cussed above, Taralon's examination of the statue has shown that the late tenth-century alterations consisted essentially of the ornamental borders of the tunic, the crown and the throne. These were added to the earlier, ninth-century version of the statue whose basic core and sheath survive. The original Carolingian image was therefore a seated figure, essentially as it now appears, and very likely it enshrined the relics of the saint acquired by the abbey when the statue was made. There is no doubt of their presence within it in Bernard of Angers's time since he mentions them.

At Limoges, under Abbot Hugh, Gauzbert had made an image of St. Martial immediately after the fire of ca. 952.[102] It was of gold, presumably applied in the normal repoussé manner over a wooden core, and represented the saint making the gesture of benediction with the right hand and holding the book in the left hand. It was set up on the altar. When Hugh died in 973 his successor, Josfredus, deposited within the statue relics of the body of St. Martial. In this case we know from literary sources that the image was only converted into a reliquary some twenty years after its creation. Texts indicate that the statues of St. Privatus at Mende[103] and St. Peter at Cluny[104] contained relics in the early eleventh century. For the Cluny figure, the relics are listed in individual detail. The statues of St. Gerald at Aurillac, St. Amandus at Rodez, St. Marius at Vabres, all mentioned in the early eleventh century (ca. 1013) by Bernard of Angers, were reliquaries.[105] As to later works we cannot always be sure. The late eleventh-century account of the lost golden image of St. Lazarus at Avallon makes no mention of relics,[106] whereas the figure of St. Chaffre at Monastier is said to have contained them at this period.[107] Extant statues of saints which are related to these and which date from the twelfth or early thirteenth century also fall into both categories. The busts and half figures of St. Candidus at Saint-Maurice d'Agaune,[108] St. Peter at Bredons[109] and St. Césaire at Maurs[110] all have some provision for relics, whereas the St. Baudimus at Saint-Nectaire[111] has none. Moreover, the date of a relic compartment is not always certain. Thus, the heads of St. Paul, Münster,[112] and Frederick Barbarossa,

[102] Duplès-Agier, *Chroniques*, pp. 5-6, 43; cf. Gauthier, "Le Trésor," 107; O. Lehmann-Brockhaus, *Die Kunst des X. Jahrhunderts im Lichte der Schriftquellen*, Leipzig, Strasbourg and Zurich, 1935, no. 43, p. 49.

[103] Brunel, *Les Miracles*, pp. 14-16; see Chapter I, note 18 above.

[104] Albers, *Consuetudines*, I, p. 184.

[105] Bouillet, *Liber miraculorum*, I, xiii, pp. 46-48; I, xviii, p. 72.

[106] Bruel, *Recueil*, no. 3518, p. 640.

[107] Chevalier, *Cartulaire*, no. xlvii, p. 42; see Chapter I, note 17 above; Paris, Musée des arts décoratifs, *Les Trésors des églises de France*, 1965, no. 428.

[108] R. Schnyder, "Das Kopfreliquiar des Heiligen Candidus in St. Maurice," *Stil und Überlieferung in der Kunst des Abendlandes, Akten des 21. Internationalen Kongresses für Kunstgeschichte in Bonn, 1964*, Berlin, 1967, 169-171.

[109] Aurillac, Maison Consulaire, *Orfèvrerie et statuaire romane*, ed. A. Muzac, 1959, no. 44.

[110] Paris, *Trésors*, 1965, no. 417.   [111] *Ibid.*, no. 447.

[112] Münster, Landesmuseum für Kunst und Kulturgeschichte, *Westfalia Sacra*, 1951-1952, no. 62; P. Pieper, "Der goldene Pauluskopf des Domes zu Münster," *Studien zur Buchmalerei und Goldschmiedekunst des Mittelalters, Festschrift für Karl Hermann Usener zum 60. Geburtstag am 19. August, 1965*, Marburg, 1967, 33-40.

Cappenberg,[113] have relic compartments, but there is the possibility in both cases that they were converted to reliquaries after their manufacture.

From these observations we can only conclude that, despite the medievalist's desire for a straightforward answer concerning the possible influence of relics on the revival of sculpture, no simple explanation exists. Just as in the early history of the *sedes sapientiae* statue itself, some early sculptures—representing the crucified Christ or martyr saints—were reliquaries and some were not. The reliquary function was a possible adjunct in the late ninth century but not an essential feature. Haussherr expressed this clearly for the Ottonian crucifixes when he said that the relics lend accessory value to the crucifix but are not the condition essential to its creation.[114] The view that medieval sculpture in the round owes its origin solely to the reliquary statues of the ninth and tenth century is surely untenable. We have seen that non-reliquary statues existed even before those which had provision for relics. Purely secular statues of Carolingian rulers, such as those made for Duke Ragenarius (ca. 850) and Duke Solomon (871), antedate the Narbonne crucifix (ca. 890), the head of St. Maurice (879-887) and the figure of St. Foy (ca. 867-875?). Moreover, there is ample evidence that the golden statues were only a part of a general development of three-dimensional sculpture, including sculptures in stucco and stone which would not have been appropriate for relics.

Even if the relic cannot be regarded as the sole agent in the revival of three-dimensional images, its later association with such images in reliquary statues, beginning in the late ninth century, contributed to the general acceptance, especially by ecclesiastical authorities, of all sculpture in the round. The relic helped to expurgate all statuary. Acceptance of the veneration of images was important to the changing philosophy in the early Western Church regarding the role of images in general. The relic was particularly effective in establishing such veneration in areas where the fear of pagan and idolatrous overtones in freestanding sculpture was even stronger than in Charlemagne's circle. It was also useful in converting vestigial pagan cult practices to Christian purpose in provincial areas. Therefore the decisive role of the relic was less the revival of statuary as such than the acceleration of its widespread acceptance and dissemination.

In contrast to iconodule extremists at this period in the East, the Western Church stressed alternative religious incentives and cult equivalents which were less questionable in practice but equally inspiring. The relic was a physical bridge between the dead saint and the worshiper. For the West the great shrines of Christendom were far distant. There was need of tangible evidence of Christian heroism at home. In dislodging pagan beliefs and customs, stronger in the West than in the long Christianized East, the cult of relics was particularly effective. As veneration of the relic gradually gained momentum, costly shrines and appropriate statues were fashioned to enhance the attraction of these treasures. The result was a process in which the age-old devotion to pagan idols seems

[113] Münster, *Westfalia Sacra*, 1951-1952, no. 64; P. E. Schramm and F. Mütherich, *Denkmale der deutschen Könige und Kaiser*, Munich, 1962, no. 173; H. Fillitz, "Der Cappenberger Barbarossakopf," *Münchener Jahrbuch der bildenden Kunst*, Dritte Folge, xiv (1963), 39-50. The group has been studied recently by Eva Kovács, *Kopfreliquiare des Mittelalters*, Leipzig, 1964.

[114] Haussherr, *Ikonographie des Gerokreuzes*, p. 40.

to have been channeled and diverted to Christian purposes, just as pagan temples had been converted to Christian use in earlier centuries by installing relics and consecrating them to Christian saints.

In pre-Carolingian times every effort was made to wipe out idols by destroying them.[115] Bede recounts the events of ca. 675 when Willibrord destroyed pagan idols and put relics of saints in their place.[116] The next step was taken by the creators of the first reliquary statues. Combining relic with statue was a fruitful merger. The presence of the relic made the statue acceptable and the form of the statue gave visual immediacy to the relic.

The making of Christian cult statues was influenced by the sanction granted through such a process. Bernard of Angers, at first opposed to statues of divine persons, was converted to acceptance of them upon seeing the reliquary statues in Auvergne, and it was clearly the presence of the relic which caused his change of mind.[117] Moreover, he tells us that at that time the habit of constructing statues as reliquaries was well established in southern France: "And, in fact, there is an ancient custom and practice in the whole territory of Auvergne, Rouergue, Toulouse, and indeed in the rest of our territories adjoining these round about, that everyone according to his ability should set up for his saint a statue, of gold or silver or any other metal, in which the head of the saint or, if preferred, another part of the body should be reverently treasured up."[118]

Bernard's explanation is perfectly clear. The only question is how ancient the custom was at the time of his visit to Auvergne. If Taralon is correct in pushing back the date of the St. Foy statue to the second half of the ninth century—and his evidence is very persuasive—this golden sculpture would be roughly contemporary with the Narbonne crucifix and the golden head of St. Maurice, both of which contained relics. These three examples would be the earliest medieval reliquary figures known to us and would indicate the emergence of this type of sculpture in the late Carolingian period.

The veneration of religious images, so mistrusted in the Carolingian Empire of the late eighth century and still opposed at the Paris Synod (825), was gradually condoned in the broad sense in the second half of the ninth century.[119] After the eighth general synod (869) contentions over the veneration of images seem to have abated,[120] and it is significant that the reliquary sculptures we know appeared shortly afterward. It is impossible to determine at what exact point in time the type was invented and the first reliquary statue actually created in Western Europe, but it is highly probable that the last decades of the ninth century saw its emergence. The antecedents to such a mutation

---

[115] Knögel, *Schriftquellen*, nos. 173, 366, 508, 607, 643, 832, 861, 940, 979.

[116] *Ibid.*, no. 979.

[117] Bouillet, *Liber miraculorum*, I, xiii, pp. 48-49. See Chapter I, note 4 above.

[118] "Est namque vetus mos et consuetudo, ut in tota Arve[r]nica patria sive Rotenica vel Tolosana, necnon et reliquis nostris his circumquaque continuis, de auro sive argento seu quolibet alio metallo, sancto suo quisque pro posse statuam erigat, in qua caput sancti, vel potior pars corporis venerabilius condatur" (*ibid.*, pp. 46-47).

[119] Poole, *Illustrations*, p. 25 n. 1.

[120] Harnack, *Dogma*, v, p. 307. Of course some traces of hostility remained, *ibid.*, p. 308.

in the history of art can only be imagined. Before its advent, however, simple statues, both profane and religious in subject but devoid of any reliquary function, existed in Western Europe: crucifixes, statues of the Virgin and Child and of martyr saints, as well as of emperors, kings and dukes. In discussing the sources of Romanesque sculpture, these forerunners should be noted along with the influence of the cult of relics.

Therefore, the tenth century can no longer be seen as an appropriate date for the beginning of statuary in the medieval West. Statues began to assume an artistic role at least as early as the late eighth century in Western Europe (viz. *Libri Carolini* and *Liber Pontificalis*) where they may be seen in relation to the Carolingian Renaissance. While reviving so many features of Roman culture in the attempt at creating a New Rome in Aachen, Charlemagne could not have been immune to this conspicuous aspect of Roman art. His effort to make his city resemble great capitals of the past has been well studied.[121] He planned a *sacrum palatium* in imitation of the imperial palace at Constantinople, and it had a Western version of the *chrysotriclinos* or throne room of the Byzantine emperor. The structure was also conceived as an equivalent to Constantine's Lateran palace in Rome, and was even called by this name.[122] Although its great palatial hall recalls the Constantinian basilica in Trier, its courtyard displayed the equestrian statue of Theodoric following the scheme at the Lateran where the bronze equestrian, thought to be Constantine, stood in the square outside. Charlemagne had had the bronze horse and rider brought from Ravenna along with splendid marble fittings for his Palace Chapel. This church recalled the apogee of Ravenna's history during the time of Justinian, not only in its internal decoration, which was made up of the marbles used as revetment and of mosaic handled in the Byzantine manner, but also in its octagonal form, which resembled that of the church of San Vitale.[123] Its atrium, however, was adorned with a fountain in the form of a bronze pine cone, recalling the arrangements at Old St. Peter's in Rome. Many other architectural features, including baths in the Roman manner, along with the forms of the pictorial arts and of literature, music, liturgy and the pattern of court life, were modeled on paradigms from Rome. Nor were such learned references to the Roman past confined to Charlemagne's court circle. They were known throughout the empire, as the plans of Carolingian basilicas and the style

[121] R. Krautheimer, "The Carolingian Revival of Early Christian Architecture," *The Art Bulletin*, XXIV (1942), 1-38; E. Panofsky, *Renaissance and Renascences in Western Art*, Stockholm, 1965, pp. 43-54; P. Schramm, *Kaiser, Rom und Renovatio*, Darmstadt, 1957.

[122] Aachen, *Karl der Grosse*, 1965, no. 567; W. Kaemmerer, "Die Aachener Pfalz Karls des Grossen in Anlage und Überlieferung," *Karl der Grosse*, I, *Persönlichkeit und Geschichte*, Düsseldorf, 1965, 322-348; F. Kreusch, *Über Pfalzkapelle und Atrium zur Zeit Karls des Grossen*, Aachen, 1958; F. Kreusch, "Kirche, Atrium und Portikus der Aachener Pfalz," *Karl der Grosse*, III, *Karolingische Kunst*, Düsseldorf, 1965, 463-533.

[123] G. Bandmann, "Die Vorbilder der Aachener Pfalzkapelle," *Karl der Grosse*, III, *Karolingische Kunst*, Düsseldorf, 1965, 424-462; N.B. the discussion of the *chrysotriclinos* of the imperial palace at Constantinople as model for the octagonal form, an idea put forth by Fichtenau and others, 453ff.; cf. I. Lavin, "The House of the Lord: Aspects of the Role of Palace Triclinia in the Architecture of Late Antiquity and the Early Middle Ages," *The Art Bulletin*, XLIV (1962), 15-24.

of Carolingian manuscripts demonstrate. In sum, these features constitute what we call the Carolingian Renaissance.

The Carolingian revival was remarkable in that it accomplished the feat of fusing elements from various sources—Greek, Roman, Constantinian and Justinianic—with indigenous forms in the creation of a new culture, which for all its indebtedness to the past was not merely eclectic. The ingredients were smoothly and successfully blended so that the product was new, distinctive and vital. It was geared sensitively to the developing ambitions and aspirations of emergent European civilization. Charlemagne imported ideas for serious reasons, not simply for superficial prestige. His interest in identifying himself with illustrious Christian emperors is apparent in many examples of art from the period. Outstanding are the Triclinium mosaic of the Lateran Palace (ca. 800),[124] where he and Pope Leo were shown receiving Christian insignia from St. Peter himself as pendants to Constantine and St. Peter receiving their mission from Christ, and the Arch of Einhard (ca. 815-830),[125] where the form of the ancient Roman Arch of Triumph linked Constantinian and Carolingian equestrian heroes in a broad Christian context. Such an identification with the great Christian emperors of the past, particularly Constantine and Justinian, obviously lent the youthful realm the look of venerability; immediately it was vested with the authority of established Christian tradition and committed to upholding the values and extending the frontiers of Christendom. These were goals with which Charlemagne completely sympathized. Thus Charlemagne's policy of revival served his aims for the future. With the force of such prestige behind him, the conversion of Europe to the Christian cause could proceed more easily.

The potential propaganda value of art in this conversion process seems to have been gradually realized. The didactic use of imagery had long been accepted. An image was worth a thousand words of instruction, and for an illiterate population the lessons and histories of Christianity could be taught in no easier way. However, the idea that an image could also be used as a means of communication between worshiper and prototype was more recent. It had evolved in the East during the seventh and eighth centuries and was at the heart of the theological polemics in the Iconoclast Controversy.[126] In the

---

[124] Recently discussed by Peter Classen, "Karl der Grosse, das Papsttum und Byzanz," *Karl der Grosse*, I, *Persönlichkeit und Geschichte*, Düsseldorf, 1965, 537-608, N.B. 575; S. Waetzoldt, *Die Kopien des 17. Jahrhunderts nach Mosaiken und Wandmalereien in Rom*, Munich, 1964, nos. 208, 218; C. Davis-Weyer, "Eine patristische Apologie des Imperium Romanum und die Mosaiken der Aula Leonina," *Munuscula Discipulorum, Kunsthistorische Studien Hans Kauffmann zum 70. Geburtstag 1966*, Berlin, 1968, 71-83.

[125] Aachen, *Karl der Grosse*, 1965, no. 9, where the earlier literature is cited.

[126] See note 1 above; Harnack, *Dogma*, v, p. 307. Cyril Mango's discussion in *The Brazen House*, Copenhagen, 1959, p. 128 provides a summary of the related question of circumscription. The defenders of images in the East maintained that the dogma of the Incarnation had demonstrated that Christ had made it possible to apprehend the divine in human form, for Christ was the image of God. When the iconoclasts claimed that Christ was incapable of being circumscribed and hence could not be represented in pictorial form, the classic answer was that Christ's divine nature was obviously uncircumscribable, but that as a man he was "vulnerable, mortal and limited by time

West, the concept seems to have taken root as well. By considering the image as a vehicle for passage from one level of understanding to another, the didactic function of art was supplemented by a new use which allowed a transcendental relationship between viewer and prototype. This was in essence what every man believed, namely that everything in the church was a symbol which led from knowledge of the material to the immaterial. The shrewdness of Carolingian iconodules was the realization that the idolatrous inclinations of superstitious country folk and provincials could be channeled to a Christian purpose. Pagan cults did not die easily in an area long accustomed to the religious veneration of idols. They had prepared a fertile soil for the birth and growth of Christian cult statues, which converted devotion from pagan to Christian form. The stabilizing effect of this procedure in areas where pockets of paganism were troublesome would have been one happy result. The Empire could be kept more firmly unified in the interests of Christian civilization in general and of the advancement of the imperial frontiers.

In Auvergne, as Bernard says, the mountainous region of the Massif Central was particularly prone to retain its traditions. He mentions the indigenous and invincible custom of venerating statues in this area which he says stems from ancient and ignorant tradition.[127] His own writings on the miracles of St. Foy testify to the effectiveness of transforming these customs into Christian practices through the agency of statues in the form of Christian martyrs.

Just as religious figures could be accorded veneration as representatives of their prototypes, so could secular images perform a similar surrogate function. Kantorowicz discusses the solemn receptions commonly accorded imperial images in the Early Middle Ages[128] and he quotes from the *Libri Carolini* that people "meet with candles and incense the imperial representations and images sent to cities and provinces, not [as if] honoring a panel overlaid with wax [i.e. a panel painted in encaustic], but the emperor [himself]."[129] Such a conception underlies the production of the three-dimensional

---

and could therefore be represented and circumscribed." In denying this the iconoclasts were accused of rejecting the reality of the Incarnation.

[127] *Liber miraculorum*, i, xiii, p. 47.

[128] E. Kantorowicz, *Laudes Regiae, A Study in Liturgical Acclamations and Mediaeval Ruler Worship*, Berkeley and Los Angeles, 1958, p. 72 n. 25.

[129] *Ibid.*; *Libri Carolini*, iii, 15. The quotation is taken from the following passage: "Contra eos, qui dicunt: 'Si enim imperiales effigies et imagines emissas in civitates et provincias obviabunt populi cum cereis et timiamatibus, non cera perfusam tabulam honorantes, sed imperatorem, quanto magis oportet in ecclesiis Christi depingi imagines Salvatoris nostri Dei et intemerate matris eius et sanctorum omnium?'" From the same chapter: "Nam quis furor est quaeve dementia, ut hoc in exemplum adorandarum imaginum ridiculum adducatur, quod imperatorum imagines in civitatibus et in plateis adorantur, et a re inlicita res inlicita stabiliri paretur? Doctor enim gentium non nos imperatorum imitatores, sed suos, immo Christi fieri hortatur dicens: *Imitatores mei estote, sicut et ego Christi.*"

The first statement is the rubric heading one of the arguments against the decrees of the Second Nicene Council. "Against those who say: 'For if the people shall meet with candles and incense the

images we know from the later Carolingian period as well. Pope Hadrian's acceptance of Solomon's statue (871) as the Duke's legitimate representative, or the attitude of the monks at Saint-Germain-des-Prés toward Ragenarius' statue (ca. 850), indicates a willingness to accept an image as a substitute for an actual person.[130]

Therefore, in creating the Conques St. Foy, the Carolingian artist would have participated in this view. He produced an image which served as a vehicle of Christian veneration but, to judge by Bernard of Angers's early attitude, the admixture of pagan elements was strong. Medieval artists were not reluctant to profit from the actual appropriation of pagan works in the making of Christian monuments. Just as the columns of pagan temples were used in the building of Early Christian basilicas, so were antique intaglios representing pagan deities incorporated into Christian goldsmith work. The St. Foy statue was decorated with thirty-one of these antique stones. That the presence of pagan objects in a Christian work could not have been offensive to medieval taste is evidenced by many examples in metalwork, one of the most outstanding being the Herimann Cross in Cologne where the lapis-lazuli head of a Roman woman is set into the cross to represent the head of the crucified Christ.[131] Whether the head of the St. Foy statue was that of a Christian or pagan emperor of the late antique period is still uncertain. The artist was not averse to using a male head for the statue of a young female saint, however, indulging his high regard for the quality and value of ancient art. As a conception of the Carolingian period, and as the earliest reliquary statue preserved to us, the St. Foy is an extremely important document. It illustrates the intermingling of various early medieval interests: the fondness for work in the wood and gold repoussé technique; the preference for an enthroned *Maiestas* pose in the representation of honored figures; the appreciation of Classical forms including sculpture in the round and specific Classical ornaments (i.e. intaglios); and the acceptance of the image as a carrier of Christian propaganda through its role as an intermediary in the religious veneration of Christian saints. The St. Foy also illustrates the power of the third dimension in art and the effect that relics might have in enhancing that power; for despite the modest plasticity and the simple archaic form of the statue, it has had an

imperial representations sent to cities and provinces, not as if honoring a panel overlaid with wax, but the emperor himself, how much more proper it is that representations of Christ our Savior and God be depicted in churches and of his virgin Mother and all the saints?'" And further: "For what madness is it or what folly that this fact be adduced as a ridiculous precedent for the adoring of images, namely that images of emperors are adored in cities and in the open streets and that by an unlawful case an unlawful right be established. For the teacher of the Gentiles [St. Paul] does not exhort us to become imitators of emperors but his own imitators, nay more of Christ, saying, *Be ye followers of me even as I am of Christ.*" The argument leaves no doubt that imperial images were accorded extraordinary reverence in this period. See the discussion in Kitzinger, "Images," 122-123.

[130] See Bevan's account of Eastern practices in which images "informed with grace" were treated as if they were real persons, e.g. as sponsors at children's christenings, *Images*, p. 145.

[131] Essen, Villa Hügel, *Werdendes Abendland an Rhein und Ruhr*, 1956, no. 460. For the St. Foy, see Taralon, "Majesté."

illustrious history. That relics were enclosed within the statue was important, but the location of the relic receptacle in the saint's throne was also significant. In fact, the throne was an essential part of the ensemble. This feature had its own history and its own symbolic values, and it must be seen as stemming from still another tradition which contributed to the creation of the *sedes sapientiae* statue.

The Throne

The element which made a *Maiestas* of the St. Foy was the throne and it was an essential ingredient in the iconography of the Madonna in Majesty as well. The throne as a motif in Christian iconography has been well studied. The Early Christian themes of the Etimasia and of the *Maiestas Domini*, as well as the sources for both of these in imperial court ceremony and oriental ritual, have been explained by such scholars as Alföldi,[132] Nordström,[133] Stommel,[134] Van der Meer[135] and Von Bogyay.[136] The Etimasia or the throne prepared for Christ's Second Coming, is the forerunner of the Apocalyptic throne upon which Christ sits as judge in the vision of Revelation, the essence of which is the theme of Christ in Majesty. The Etimasia was not, however, an empty throne. Normally the Cross and the Book were placed upon it, symbolic of the presence of Christ. By analogy, in the Throne of Wisdom iconography Mary would parallel the throne of the Etimasia while Christ, holding the Book, is actually present.

The symbolism of the Etimasia persisted in Byzantine court ritual, as André Grabar has pointed out.[137] In the *Book of Ceremonies* from the mid-tenth century, Constantine Porphyrogenitus describes the custom of leaving the imperial throne empty in the Palm Sunday celebration in Constantinople.[138] When the emperor enters the *chrysotriclinos* or throne room of the imperial palace, the patricians, bearing candle and cross in procession, arrange themselves on the left side of the throne while the emperor sits on the right of it. The priests are nearby. The deacon then places the Gospel Book on the imperial throne while the usual litany is recited. The 880-883 manuscript in Paris of the *Homilies* of Gregory Nazianzus provides an illustration of the second Oecumenical

[132] A. Alföldi, "Insignien und Tracht der römischen Kaiser," *Mitteilungen des deutschen archaeologischen Instituts, Römische Abteilung*, L (1935), 134-139.

[133] C. O. Nordström, *Ravennastudien, Ideengeschichtliche und ikonographische Untersuchungen über die Mosaiken von Ravenna*, Stockholm, 1953, pp. 47-53.

[134] E. Stommel, "Die bischöfliche Kathedra im christlichen Altertum," *Münchener Theologische Zeitschrift*, III (1952), 21-22.

[135] F. van der Meer, *Maiestas Domini, Théophanies de l'Apocalypse dans l'art chrétien*, Rome and Paris, 1938, pp. 231-254.

[136] T. von Bogyay, "Zur Geschichte der Hetoimasie," *Akten des XI. Internationalen Byzantinisten-Kongresses, München, 1958*, Munich, 1960, 58-61; cf. P. Durand, *Etude sur l'Etimacia, symbole du jugement dernier dans l'iconographie grecque chrétienne*, Chartres, 1867.

[137] A. Grabar, "Le Trône des Martyrs," *Cahiers archéologiques*, VI (1952), 31-42; cf. A. Grabar, *L'Empereur dans l'art byzantin*, Paris, 1936, pp. 196-200.

[138] *Constantin Porphyrogénète, Le Livre des cérémonies*, ed. A. Vogt, Paris, 1935, I, p. 163; von Bogyay, "Geschichte," 60 nn. 14-15.

Council in Constantinople (381), which corresponds to this tenth-century description of the Palm Sunday event in the *Book of Ceremonies* (Fig. 20).[139] The throne with the Gospel Book upon it appears amidst the emperor and his dignitaries. At the Council of Ephesus (431) and later at the eighth Oecumenical Council in Constantinople (869-870), a similar procedure was evidently enacted; in the latter case, however, a relic of the Cross was placed next to the Book on the empty throne.[140] In all of these instances the throne recalled the spiritual presence of Christ.

In his study "Le Trône des Martyrs," André Grabar notes that the term used by the Byzantines to describe the depositing of relics in a new sanctuary was to "enthrone," and he concludes that the patron saints of these churches were being "enthroned" symbolically in this ceremony.[141] Similarly, in the early medieval West, the choir of Saint-Riquier was called the "throne of St. Riquier" ("Thronus sancti Richarii").[142] Grabar cites other texts of the period which speak of a throne when referring to the east end of a church, the apse, the chevet or the altar.[143] The traditional place for the bishop's throne in the early church was behind the altar in the depth of the apse, or in the center of the *synthronon*, and would be a source for such expressions. Thus, in tracing out the ancestry of the throne used in representations of martyrs in our period, such as the St. Foy, Grabar appropriately explains that the throne was a feature intended to show the reflection of the Majesty of Christ in the enthroned saints; for they preside in his name over the eucharistic *agape* of the liturgy.

In his later study on the "Sedia di San Marco" in Venice, Grabar demonstrates that this throne symbolizes the presence of Christ.[144] Unlike other episcopal thrones of the period, the stone *sedia* of San Marco is completely freestanding (Fig. 21). This sixth-century chair, which in the Middle Ages stood behind the high altar in San Marco, is worked on all sides with reliefs. Most significantly, it is a reliquary. As it supposedly enclosed a fragment of the wood chair of St. Mark, it was fashioned in such a form. Openings in the left side and the back allow a view of the relic cavity. The reliefs refer to Paradise and include the Tree of Life and the Rivers of Paradise, the Four Evange-

[139] H. Omont, *Miniatures des plus anciens manuscrits grecs de la Bibliothèque Naitonale, du VIe au XIVe siècle*, Paris, 1929, pl. L; S. Der Nersessian, "The Illustrations of the Homilies of Gregory of Nazianzus: Paris Gr. 510," *Dumbarton Oaks Papers*, xvi (1962), pl. 16; Grabar, "Le Trône," 40 n. 3; von Bogyay, "Geschichte," 59 n. 10. Cf. G. Galavaris, *The Illustrations of the Liturgical Homilies of Gregory Nazianzenus*, Princeton, 1969.

[140] Von Bogyay, "Geschichte," 59-60 nn. 9, 12; Grabar, "Le Trône," 40 n. 2; J. D. Mansi, *Sacrorum conciliorum nova et amplissima collectio*, xvi, Venice, 1771, 17ff. Van der Meer discusses the custom of placing the Gospel Book on a throne, as known at Ephesus, Chalcedon, Nicaea and Constantinople, and its reflection in art, *Maiestas Domini*, p. 238. According to Philip Hughes, the fifth session of the Second Nicene Council, devoted to discussion of the veneration of images, closed with "the solemn enthronement of an image" in the church of Hagia Sophia, P. Hughes, *The Church in Crisis: A History of the General Councils 325-1870*, New York, 1961, p. 155.

[141] Grabar, "Le Trône," 37; for the "enthronization" (ἐνθρονισμός) ceremony at Hagia Sophia, *ibid.*, 37 n. 3.

[142] *Ibid.*, 38.   [143] *Ibid.*, 39.

[144] A. Grabar, "La 'Sedia di San Marco' à Venise," *Cahiers archéologiques*, VII (1954), 19-34.

87

lists as symbolic beasts and in human form, with the Cross and the Lamb as symbolic counterpart to the imagined occupant of the throne; the whole suggests the Apocalyptic vision, the center of which is normally Christ enthroned in Majesty. The Classical forerunners to the San Marco *sedia* are described by Charles Picard in "Le Trône vide d'Alexandre et le culte de trône vide," a study which makes it apparent that majestic connotations from secular ceremonial custom had been appropriated by the Christian Church in the iconography of the Etimasia.[145] This heritage contributed significantly to the early medieval conception of the throne in the West.

The famous throne of Charlemagne in Aachen represents a merger of these two traditions, the Classical and the Christian. Like the *sedia* of San Marco, Charlemagne's throne was of stone. It also contained relics which were among those most prized in the Imperial Treasure (Fig. 22).[146] Yet it was the seat of the secular authority of the Empire so that secular and religious implications intermingled in its meaning. The throne's importance to German dynastic history is well known and explains in part the preservation of this work. For the German people it has effectively symbolized the power of the Empire. When the Carolingian emperor sat enthroned in it, he represented a visible analogy to Christ in Majesty whence that power came. The analogy extended to the environmental setting for the throne, the royal loge, which was the architectural counterpart in the church to the apse opposite. There Christ's presence was manifested in the altar of the Savior at the upper end of the eastern choir. Below was the altar of Mary. The relationship of these two areas in the sanctuary—dedicated to Mary below and to her Son above—was not unlike that of the Virgin and Christ in the Throne of Wisdom imagery. Inasmuch as the Carolingian king claimed that the task of maintaining peace in the earthly sphere had been entrusted to him by Christ, whose vice-regent he was and on whose behalf he ruled, the king or emperor received his administrative, judicial and military authority from the heavenly emperor.[147] The appropriation of the ritual insignia and the manner of enthronement traditionally associated with the *Maiestas Domini*, or Christ, made the relationship between the earthly and heavenly emperors clear, and the linking of them through the architectural expression of the westwork[148] made it seem locally realized. Thus, the chain of command which extended

[145] C. Picard, "Le Trône vide d'Alexandre et le culte de trone vide," *Cahiers archéologiques*, VII (1954), 1-17. For the symbolism of the chair in antiquity and its use in banquets, processions, theatres, etc., see also S. Weinstock, "The Image and the Chair of Germanicus," *Journal of Roman Studies*, XLVII (1957), 144-154.

[146] The throne of Charlemagne was approached by six stone steps, the same number as the biblical Throne of Solomon. Schramm provides the basic data in *Herrschaftszeichen*, pp. 337-344; cf. his discussion of the *cathedra* of St. Peter and related thrones, pp. 689ff. For the recent literature on the Aachen throne, see: Aachen, *Karl der Grosse*, 1965, no. 2; Kreusch, *Pfalzkapelle*, pp. 85-100; Kreusch, "Kirche, Atrium und Portikus der Aachener Pfalz," 478-479, 503-504; H. Beumann, "Grab und Thron Karls des Grossen in Aachen," *Karl der Grosse*, IV, *Das Nachleben*, Düsseldorf, 1967, 26-38. The question of the original position of the throne has given rise to considerable discussion; see in particular Beumann, *loc. cit.*, 26ff.

[147] Fichtenau, *The Carolingian Empire*, pp. 56-57.

[148] Among the many studies devoted to the westwork, see the comments by E. Baldwin Smith, *Architectural Symbolism of Imperial Rome and the Middle Ages*, Princeton, 1956, pp. 79-96.

88

from the Christian Godhead through the Carolingian emperor and on down to his subjects was expressed in a most tangible way.[149] Further, the emperor's divine right of rulership was strengthened by the actual presence of sacred relics in the Aachen throne.

The notion of a Christomimetic emperor was, of course, a Byzantinizing idea, as were the acclamations addressed to Carolingian kings and emperors. Charlemagne was hailed as the "New Constantine" by Pope Hadrian, but Carolingian lauds included references to him as the "New Moses" and the "New David," and Theodulph had acclaimed him the "New Solomon."[150] Amalar of Metz also styled Louis the Pious the "New David" and the "New Solomon."[151] According to Kantorowicz, Charlemagne's aim was to make of Aachen a *sedes davidica*, in the metaphorical sense, yet the Biblical undertone of this was certainly extended later to include reference to Solomon.[152] The metrical lauds of Sedulius Scottus written for Louis the German, Charles the Bald and Lothar exemplify this, particularly the fifth stanza of one for Lothar:

> Rex tuus mitis, sapiens, honorus,
> Pacifer ductor Salemonis instar
> Nunc venit Caesar, tuus, alma, princeps,
> Filia Sion.[153]

The Old Testament precedent of Solomon anointed king at David's command was probably in the minds of Carolingian rulers: "When David was old he made Solomon his son king over Israel" (1 Chron. 23:1); "And they made Solomon the son of David king the second time, and anointed him unto the Lord to be the chief governor, and Zadok to be priest. Then Solomon sat in the throne of the Lord as king instead of David his father, and prospered" (1 Chron. 29:22-23).[154] This Solomonic precedent, as a guarantee of royal legitimacy and wisdom, was claimed by other rulers in the Early Middle Ages. Allusions to Solomon occur in the earliest known service for an English

---

[149] Ernst Kantorowicz distinguished between the imperial and ecclesiastic relationships to God and Christ, *The King's Two Bodies*, Princeton, 1957, pp. 160-163.

[150] Kantorowicz, *Laudes Regiae*, pp. 57 n. 148, 69 n. 15. Heinrich Fichtenau, who relates Charlemagne's throne to the Throne of Solomon, gives a full discussion of the concept of Charlemagne as the "New David" and the "New Constantine" in "Byzanz und die Pfalz zu Aachen," *Mitteilungen des Instituts für Österreichische Geschichtsforschung*, LIX (1951), 25-54. He also notes Theodulph's honorific reference to Charlemagne as the "New Solomon" (*Poetae lat.* 1, 484), *op. cit.*, 27. Cf. Bloch, "Nachwirkungen des Alten Bundes," 769.

[151] Kantorowicz, *Laudes Regiae*, pp. 57 n. 148, 69 n. 15.

[152] *Ibid.*, pp. 57 n. 148, 63. Cf. the allusions made by Alcuin and Notger to the Temple of Solomon; Bloch, "Nachwirkungen des Alten Bundes," 769; Fichtenau, "Byzanz," 27.

[153] Kantorowicz, *Laudes Regiae*, p. 73 n. 28. The stanza may be translated: "Your mild king, wise, honorable,/ Pacific leader like Solomon/ Now appears as Emperor, your Prince,/ Oh propitious Daughter of Zion."

For identification of Charles the Bald with Solomon, see H. Schrade, "Studien zu der karolingischen Bilderbibel aus St. Paul von den Mauern in Rom," *Wallraf-Richartz Jahrbuch*, XXII (1960), 13ff.; Bloch, "Nachwirkungen des Alten Bundes," 769.

[154] Kantorowicz, *Laudes Regiae*, p. 93 n. 93. Cf. the passages in the *Libri Carolini* (1, 1).

Coronation. In the First and Second Coronation Orders, from manuscripts of the ninth-tenth century and prior to 1066, appears the anthem sung at the anointing of the king: "unxerunt salamonem sadoc sacerdos et nathan propheta regem in gion"—"And Zadok the priest and Nathan the prophet have anointed him [Solomon] king in Gihon" (1 Kings 1:45); and the words of consecration prior to the unction recalled Solomon's gifts of wisdom and peace.[155] These became traditional. Francis Wormald notes the representation of the Throne of Solomon in the *Hortus Deliciarum* of the last quarter of the twelfth century where Solomon is seated in the guise of a Byzantine monarch.[156] In the case of the late twelfth-century manuscript of Peter of Eboli, also cited by Wormald, the Emperor Henry VI is seated on the Throne of Solomon (Fig. 23).[157] The trappings of the Old Testament king's throne are represented, including the lions, and the seat is labeled *sedes sapientiae*. Henry III's throne for Westminster Abbey in the mid-thirteenth century and the Chair of Edward the Confessor from the late thirteenth century were also reflections of this idea.[158]

Thus, the iconography of the Throne of Solomon could be applied to secular rulers as well as to the Virgin in the early Middle Ages. This secular tradition, which lent overtones of Solomonic wisdom to royal thrones, was vital in the period which saw the emergence of the statue of the Madonna in Majesty and must have contributed to its formation as a representation of the Throne of Wisdom. The state of enthronement not only made a Majesty of the image of the Virgin and her Son, but also lent to the statue the appearance of judicial authority, for the Throne of Solomon was associated with the royal thrones of the day. The statues of Mary must have absorbed much from the strength of these associations. Just as the Etimasia indicated the presence of Christ and the Carolingian imperial throne indicated Christ's sanction for the Christian ruler who was likened to a new Solomon, the Madonna in Majesty allegorized both of these concepts.

Conclusion

When Adelelmus was called by Stephen II to fashion the golden Madonna at Clermont-Ferrand, the sources upon which he could draw were many, and they can be traced far back into the religious and secular spheres of early Western thought. His statue represented a mother and child, as pagan sculptures had represented mother goddesses. However, since it conformed to the Christian tradition with respect to its iconographic details, it represented the Mother and Son on an elaborate throne, which was an established indicator of majestic presence, often carrying overtones of divinity. The Majesty of Adelelmus also contained relics, as did the monumental thrones with relic compartments at Venice and Aachen. Mary and the Christ Child upon the throne recalled the

[155] Pointed out by Wormald, "Throne of Solomon," 539. See L.G.W. Legg, *English Coronation Records*, Westminster, 1901, pp. 5, 16-17 and *passim*.
[156] Wormald, "Throne of Solomon," 535.
[157] *Liber ad honorem Augusti* (Bern, Bürgerbibliothek, Cod. 120, fol. 147), *ibid.*, 537.
[158] *Ibid.*, 537.

90

majesty of secular rulers and more especially, of Solomon, whose Throne of Wisdom was regarded as the prototype of the divine *sedes sapientiae*, Christ enthroned upon his enthroned Mother. Moreover, Adelelmus' statue was an image in the round, made of gold repoussé and wood, as early medieval reliquaries so often were, and as were the images of secular rulers in the ninth century, e.g. Duke Solomon of Brittany and Duke Ragenarius. Like such secular sculptures and even in the manner of the empty throne, the Etimasia, the Clermont-Ferrand *Maiestas* was meant to serve as a true representative or proxy for the figures imaged, in this case, the Virgin and her Son.

The conjunction of all of these ideas produced the Madonna in Majesty as we know it, yet such a phenomenon could not have occurred were it not for the Carolingian revival of Classical and Byzantine forms of art and culture, especially sculpture, and were it not for the late Carolingian adoption of an image theory which admitted the transcendental usefulness of such images. The view of the Second Council of Nicaea (787), which stated that honor given to the image is passed on to its prototype, was eventually accepted in the West despite initial resistance in the *Libri Carolini*. Just as "portraits" were not considered idolatrous, even though acclaimed with reverential ceremony, religious figures could be accorded veneration as representatives of their prototypes, thus appropriating the surrogate function of secular images. The desire to make vividly real the idea of Christ crucified or a local saint or the enthroned Madonna and Child led men of the Early Middle Ages actually to visualize and represent these sacred figures in full three-dimensional form, and even more to attain a transcendent experience of them. By the power of sculpture in the round, the images made the presence of their prototypes vicariously manifest in the observer's reality. The acceptance of their roles as intermediaries between the observer's world and the divine realm beyond was a necessary precondition to the original conception and subsequent development of them. By the late Carolingian period such sculpture was possible. The sources were available, the incentive was strong and the proscriptions were relaxed. These factors must be considered as intrinsic in explanation of the origins of the *sedes sapientiae* statue.

Since the revival of freestanding sculpture is known from literary sources to date from the late eighth century, at the latest, and since the beginnings of reliquary statues can be documented from the late ninth century, it is most likely that there were attempts at fashioning the Madonna as a Throne of Wisdom statue in the late Carolingian period, when such sculptures would have been effective in disseminating these concepts into provinces where superstitious beliefs were rife and Christian dogma was still resisted. Whether any of the sculptured images of the Madonna mentioned in the *Liber Pontificalis* or in the Carolingian textual sources discussed above were specifically Throne of Wisdom statues is uncertain. It seems highly probable, on the basis of all available evidence, that there were in the late ninth or early tenth century such antecedents to the Clermont-Ferrand Majesty, even though it is the earliest example for which we have ample contemporary records.

CHAPTER IV. Statues of the
Throne of Wisdom Prior to 1100

Literary Evidence

IF ONE were to consider only preserved statues of the *sedes sapientiae* in tracing out its early history, a very misleading picture would emerge. Since extant works of the period before 1100 are to be seen in such cities as Essen, Hildesheim, Paderborn and Walcourt, one would probably conclude that the earliest efforts to portray the Madonna in the round were made in Northern Europe, specifically present-day Germany and Belgium. Actually, however, the statues were known at an early moment in many different parts of Europe, including England as well as France. Literary sources provide accounts of early lost Madonnas from such places as Ely, Coventry, Abingdon, Ghent, Utrecht, Châtillon-sur-Loire, Coutances and Avallon, in addition to the more famous Virgins from Chartres, Le Puy and Clermont-Ferrand. These locations indicate that the sculptures constituted a widespread phenomenon and they can thus hardly be seen as issuing only from the limited region suggested by surviving examples. All of these forerunners to the French Romanesque Throne of Wisdom statue will be considered in this chapter.

Our study of origins in Chapter III indicated that freestanding sculpture had been revived in Carolingian times—in both Northern European and Southern ateliers. The sources show that images of the Madonna were a part of this development. Their emergence as an independent genre of sculpture seems to have been slow, however, inasmuch as the early examples, for which we have specific descriptive information, are very few indeed. In addition to the one golden Madonna from the tenth century which actually survives at Essen, possibly four others are mentioned in the literature covering this early period, i.e. at Clermont-Ferrand, Rodez, Ely and Cologne. In the late eleventh century they were much more numerous, apparently developing and spreading without interruption on into the Romanesque period. They were known in all of Western Europe and a number have come down to us. Their increasing popularity ran a course parallel to that of the growing cult of the Virgin which doubtless stimulated their production.

Sabbe maintains that the eleventh century was the first great "siècle marial."[1] He

[1] Sabbe, "Le Culte marial," 101-125. Cf. the discussion in Chapter I above where eleventh-century textual sources for Marian devotion are cited. Cf. Beissel, *Verehrung*; Hamon, *Histoire*; W. Delius, *Geschichte der Marienverehrung*, Munich and Basel, 1963, pp. 156ff.

supports his arguments by noting the number of churches, monasteries and crypts dedicated to the Virgin, the hymns composed and sung in her honor and the great body of literature about her written by the leading minds of the century including such lights as Fulbert of Chartres and Anselm of Canterbury. The intiation of the Office of the Virgin as an integral part of the liturgy and the introduction of feasts of Mary in churches throughout Western Europe especially propagated the Mary cult. In her epithets, the Virgin was no longer simply the *Theotokos*, Mother of God, but also Mary the Great Intercessor, or Mary, Queen of Heaven and Earth. The growing importance of the Virgin's patronage would seem to have reached a climax when Urban II called for the First Crusade in 1095. It was to be led under the sign of the Virgin. Through her favor success in the conquests of the Holy Land might be assured.

Earlier in the century, the Synod of Arras (ca. 1025) had made decisions which must have provided a particular spur to the production of images made in Mary's honor. The Synod voiced a vigorous defense of sacred images in general. After a chapter on the veneration of the Cross, in which a typological simile of Christ as the second Adam is developed, it is recommended that representations of the Savior on the Cross be set up in church so that illiterates unable to read the Scriptures may contemplate the meaning of Christ's mortality and divinity through his image. Turning from images of Christ, the Synod calls upon us to see in an image of Mary the working of divine grace and to be moved by her example to seek the heavenly kingdom which was closed to us by the pride and disobedience of the first virgin, Eve. Following are some of the most striking parts of the Synod's eloquent and cogent statement:

While they venerate this outward appearance of Christ's ascent on the Cross, Christ suffering on the Cross, dying on the Cross, they are adoring only Christ, not the work of men's hands. For it is not a stock of wood that is adored; rather, through that visible image is awakened man's inner discernment, in which the passion and the death of Christ undertaken for us are inscribed as if on the scroll of the heart, so that each one recognizes within himself how much he owes to his Redeemer. . . . Likewise concerning images of the Saints it can be concluded that they are set up in the holy church for the following reason: not that they should be adored by men but rather that we should be inwardly moved by them to contemplate the operation of divine grace, and that we should derive from their deeds something to the advantage of our own conduct. For example, when we look upon an image of Mary the Blessed Mother of God, we do indeed through it reflect upon the benefits of divine grace which, out of the heritage of the Fall, has created anew the inheritance of Atonement. Without doubt it moves us by her zeal for obedience and her example of humility to seek the heavenly kingdom which the pride and disobedience of the first virgin [Eve] sealed off. So, accordingly, while we see through outward images the Angels standing in attendance upon the Creator, by the glory which they receive from the God of splendor we are inspired with zeal for abode among their number. While contemplating effigies of the Apostles and Blessed Martyrs, what else are we admonished through them if not that, spurning the concerns of this life and scorning

93

our bodies, being imbued with their teachings and made strong by their glorious combat, we should make ourselves worthy to be crowned among those who have triumphed over this world. Likewise observing images of Confessors and Virgins, we are reminded to reject worldly desires in imitation of them, to trample upon the incitements of the flesh, [and] to offer to God our very own selves as a sinless oblation. Likewise therefore the array of other Saints, being made visible, teaches us to emulate their virtues, just as sometimes the valiant deeds of men incite others by their glories to dare anything.[2]

In taking this official stand, the Western Church aligned itself with the doctrine promulgated earlier at the Second Nicene Council, namely that in the veneration of images, honor passes from the image to the prototype. In addition, the Arras Synod expressed a new philosophy regarding the effectiveness of images, their power to incite a mystical contemplation of the meaning of Christian grace. The stimulating effect of these pronouncements on the production of statuary in the area is attested by evidence from literary sources and by sculptures of the Madonna and Child which have survived from this period.

Of course we know that such statues were also made prior to the 1025 synod. As discussed in Chapter III, Bernard of Angers described statuary of the Virgin and of saints in Rouergue about 1013 and textual sources attest them elsewhere. As is so often the case, the Arras decree may simply have given ecclesiastical sanction to what was already an established fact in some parts of Europe. Nevertheless, the pronouncement must have encouraged incipient production substantially.

[2] "Dum hanc speciem venerantur, Christum in Cruce ascendentem, Christum in Cruce passum, in Cruce morientem, Christum solum, non opus manuum hominum adorant. Non enim truncus ligneus adoratur, sed per illam visibilem imaginem mens interior hominis excitatur, in qua Christi passio et mors pro nobis suscepta tanquam in membrana cordis inscribitur, ut in se unusquisque recognoscat quanta suo Redemptori debeat. . . . Similiter de imaginibus Sanctorum ratiocinari licet, quae ideo in sancta ecclesia fiunt, non ut ab hominibus adorari debeant, sed ut per eas interius excitemur ad contemplandam gratiae divinae operationem, atque ex eorum actibus aliquid in usum nostrae conversationis trahamus. Verbi gratia, cum imaginem beatae Dei genitricis Mariae intuemur, profecto divinae dignationis per eam beneficia recolimus, qui [sic] de massa perditionis recreavit massam reconcilationis. Quae nimirum studio obedientiae & humilitatis exemplo suadet nos supernam patriam quaerere, quam primae virginis superbia atque inobedientia clauserat. Sic itaque Angelos in ministerio conditori assistentes, dum per exteriores imagines contemplamur, per eam quam a Deo claritatis gloriam accipiunt, ad eorum numerum studio conversationis incitamur. Apostolorum atque Sanctorum Martyrum imaginatas effigies intuentes, quid aliud per eas jubemur, nisi ut calcatis curis saeculi, spretisque corporibus, eorum doctrinis imbuti, & glorioso certamine roborati, inter mundi triumphatores coronari mereamur? Simili modo Confessorum ac Virginum imagines speculantes, monemur ex eorum imitatione mundi concupiscentias declinare, lenocinia carnis calcare, immaculatam hostiam Deo nosmetipsos offerre. Sic igitur aliorum Sanctorum ordines inspecti ad aemulationem virtutum nos instruunt, sicut quondam fortia facta virorum ipsis suis laudibus ad quaeque audendum alios accendunt" (Mansi, *Consiliorum*, xix, 453-455, N.B. 455).

Cf. the discussion of Eve in relation to Mary in note 89 below.

The formation of pilgrim circuits in the eleventh century must also have affected the making of statues of the Virgin. Wealth as well as pilgrims were attracted to the great shrines of the West: Santiago, Saint-Gilles and Rome. As the pious journeyed toward these goals, the pilgrimage roads became vital streams which watered the growth of Christian sanctuaries along their ways. In practice a pilgrimage to Santiago included visits to Conques, Aurillac, Toulouse and so on. The churches at these locations flourished and their art treasures multiplied. Majesties were among objects exhibited to the faithful and they in turn became attractions for pilgrims. For those who could not venture to the distant goals across the Alps or the Pyrenees, pilgrimage zeal might take them to the tombs of local saints or to the venerated shrines of the Virgin. To Chartres and to Le Puy-en-Velay came thousands devoted to Mary.[3] At Chartres the holy tunic of the Virgin could be seen as well as the statue of Notre-Dame-sous-terre, and at Le Puy one of the Virgin's slippers along with the statue of Notre-Dame du Puy. The relics of the Virgin enshrined in the gold *Maiestas* of Mary at Clermont-Ferrand must also have drawn crowds of itinerant worshipers.

Of all the Madonnas known exclusively from textual sources, the Clermont-Ferrand Majesty stands out sharply as a key figure. The abundance of almost contemporary description of this lost statue seems unique in the documentation of early medieval art.[4] We know the name of the patron and the name of the artist. A drawing (Fig. 3) accompanies the basic text where an account full of interest and even of drama allows us to witness the circumstances of the creation of the statue. This tale is told on folios 130v-134v of a tenth-century Gregory of Tours manuscript now in the Clermont-Ferrand library.[5] The folios had been left blank and the scribe who entered the Clermont account on them wrote in a slightly later hand which may be dated in the late tenth or early eleventh century. Rigodon compares the script to that of the inventory done for Bégon at Clermont (980-1010), and considers it representative of eleventh-century paleography. Bréhier, who first made the text widely known, regarded it as a work of the tenth century. In any case, persons, buildings and events of the mid-tenth century are described, chief among them being Bishop Stephen II (937-984) and his cathedral (consecrated in 946).

The text is not the objective description of a chronicler or even of an eye-witness reporter, such as Bernard of Angers. It is the recounting of a vision. The moral implications of the story evidently gave it a certain didactic value and it was incorporated into a sermon by the priest Arnaldus, who used it to explain Stephen's creation of the statue.

[3] E. R. Labande, "Recherches sur les pèlerins dans l'Europe des XIe et XIIe siècles," *Cahiers de civilisation médiévale*, 1 (1958), 159-169, 339-347; E. R. Labande, " 'Ad limina': le pèlerin médiéval au terme de sa démarche," *Mélanges offerts à René Crozet*, Poitiers, 1966, 1, 283-291; Olivier, *L'ancienne Statue*, p. 20; C. de Couturier de Chefdubois, *Mille Pèlerinages de Notre-Dame, Region B*, Paris, 1953; Drochon, *Histoire, passim*.

[4] See above, pp. 31, 49-50.

[5] Clermont-Ferrand, Bibliothèque Municipale, MS 145, fols. 130v-134v. The text is much too long to be quoted here in full. It is given verbatim by Rigodon and summarized by Bréhier. See notes 7-8 below. Cf. Savaron, *Les Origines*, pp. 341-344.

In the text Robert, Abbot of Mozat, experiences the vision. He imagines himself visiting the workshop of Adelelmus, a renowned goldsmith of Clermont-Ferrand. While there, Robert sees his deceased predecessor, Druchbert, enter the atelier as the companion of Bishop Stephen II. The Bishop had come to observe the work of Adelelmus on the statue of the Virgin which was to enshrine Stephen's relics of Mary. These were of particular value and Stephen wished to honor them in a singular way. Stephen explains that he is placing other relics of saints in gold and silver coffers, but that he wishes to have the precious fragments of the Virgin's tunic and pallium, and some locks of her hair, placed within an image. He has ordered a Majesty to be made for them and this *Maiestas* is to be placed behind the high altar of his recently completed cathedral. He had provided the purest gold and many precious stones for its fabrication and had entrusted the commission to Adelelmus.

A cleric and a member of a noble family, Adelelmus was a goldsmith, an architect and a sculptor in stone. He had already worked for Stephen, distinguishing himself as architect of the new cathedral. The manuscript describes the way in which he had made his measures "with a reed" for this project and says that the new church was "so full of wonder that nowhere on the entire earth was one to be seen so beautiful in appearance."[6] Nor was anyone able to equal the master's stone carving or his work in gold. In the vision Adelelmus was giving advice to his younger brother Adam when his visitors arrived. He seems to have been instructing Adam in how a Majesty was to be constructed. He made a throne (*cathedra*) of gold and precious stones and an image of the Mother of God seated upon it; the image of the Child was placed upon the knees of the Mother and the relics were concealed within.[7]

As Bishop Stephen and Abbot Druchbert sat down to watch, work was suddenly interrupted by an attack on the image by a swarm of flies which could be dispersed only by exorcism. Druchbert interpreted the onslaught as the work of the devil, and called the flies the missiles of Satan. The Bishop impatiently chased them with his fan, but

[6] The cathedral plan illustrates an early example of an ambulatory with radiating chapels, parts of which survive. See M. Vieillard-Troiekouroff, "La Cathédrale de Clermont du Ve au XIIIe siècle," *Cahiers archéologiques*, IX (1960), 199-247. The quotation is from Bréhier, "Clermont."

[7] "Abebat namque penes sae quendam clericum Adelelmum vocitatum, nobilissime genitum, quem obtime idoneum omnique opere ex auro et lapide peritum cuncti nostri afines noverunt. Nam similem ei, multis retroactis temporibus, in auro et lapide omnique artificio nequimus assimilare. Ipse namque supradictam aecclesiam arundine metivit et mirifice consummavit. Supra memoratas namque reliquias cupiens venerabilis pontifex honorare, iamdicto Adelelmo fecit cathedram ex auro et lapidibus preciosissimis fabricare et instar Dei Genitricis miro opere ex auro purissimo in ea locare, Filii quoque, Domini nostri, imaginem super genua Matris sedi et in ipso ornatu predictas reliquias nobilissime recondere. Qui sagaci insistens studio benigne conplevit opere iniuncto. Etenim necdum perfectum erat opus, quando prefatus abbas Rotbertus testatur se in sompnis visionem hanc vidisse. Referebat namque se in quoddam esse palacio cum iam dicto aurifice simulque cum quoddam suo fratre Adam nucupante, qui et ipse per doctrina fratris aurifex extiterat; et ibi convenerant ut ipsam mirificam maiestatem iungi deberent . . ."; fols. 130v-131r, Rigodon, "Vision," 47. The terms *imago* and *maiestas* are used interchangeably throughout the text.

Druchbert, with the aid of holy water and the singing of the antiphon *Asperges me*, effectively made them disappear with his "Amen." The flies were followed by a battalion of three hundred bees which flew in from an east window. They circled the image and settled on the gems. Stephen forbade molesting them and explained their symbolic importance. The bees were symbols of the virginity of Mary as, he said, St. Gregory and others have told us. They had effaced the action of the flies, which had evinced the devil's displeasure at the veneration of the Virgin. The bees had then come to honor Mary by proclaiming her chastity.

The symbolic battle over, the men sat down on benches to watch as the goldsmith's work neared completion. Druchbert admired the beauty of the statue, marveling that such a thing could be the work of human hands when it seemed the creation of angels. He asked where the Majesty was to be placed. It was clearly a rhetorical question. The Bishop was surprised and answered: "Don't you know the church I have built for the Lord and his Mother the Eternal Virgin, which all of Auvergne knows?" He explained that the image would be placed in this basilica, on a column of marble, atop a cylinder of jasper, behind the high altar.[8] Druchbert and Stephen then toured the church and observed its ornaments.[9] At the end of the text Robert awakens from his dream and the account terminates as we are told that the Bishop did indeed order a statue as just described.

Under the inimitable charm of medieval fancy, the vision provides valuable factual data on the statue, which conform to our information from other sources. The drawing (Fig. 3), which is contemporary with the text of the manuscript, indicates an enthroned Madonna and Child of the *sedes sapientiae* type, and there are two inventories of the period which give further support to the reliability of the account.[10] One is from the episcopacy of Stephen himself, ca. 970, and the other dates from the period of his successor Bégon (980-1010). Both mention the Majesty of Mary as the outstanding treasure in the cathedral, while listing other precious objects which include a golden head (reminiscent of that given by King Boso to the monastery of Saint-Maurice), liturgical objects, books, vestments and the like. In both inventories the Majesty is

---

[8] "Retro autem altare videbatur columna esse ex mirifico marmore posita; et in sumitate ipsius columne videbatur in modum iaspidis quedam rotunditas esse mire magnitudinis, supra quem sessorium ipsam, quam superius narravi constuctam, imaginem obtabat venerabilis pontifex salutifere poni"; fol. 134r, *ibid.*, 55.

[9] This extremely interesting description of the basilica includes references to other images; among them are the twelve apostles and a Crucifixion group, which are described very summarily. Only the Virgin reliquary appears to have been a freestanding sculpture. The text makes it clear that it was intended as the capstone of these decorations.

[10] Bréhier, "Inventaires"; published earlier by M. Douet-d'Arcq, "Inventaire du trésor de la cathédrale de Clermont, document de la fin du Xᵉ siècle," *Revue archéologique*, x (1853), 160-174, and noted, along with an unpublished inventory of 1055-1073, by M. Cohendy, "Inventaire de toutes les chartes antérieures au XIIIᵉ siècle," *Annales scientifiques, littéraires et industrielles de l'Auvergne*, XXVII (1854), 364-366, 398; A. Tardieu, *Histoire de la ville de Clermont*, Moulins, 1870, pp. 316-317. See the discussion in Vieillard-Troiekouroff, "La Cathédrale," 214 n. 5.

described as *vestita*, that is, made of wood and sheathed with precious metal. A ciborium and a crystal cabochon are mentioned as further adornments to the work.[11]

The later history of the statue is also sketchily known. Rigodon says that it was the object of numerous pilgrimages, and Pourreyron claims that the Madonna was removed from her throne and carried through the streets for processions.[12] While neither gives a date or any documentation for these festivities, we do learn that in 1285, when the new Gothic cathedral had replaced that of Bishop Stephen and Adelelmus, Bishop Ademar de Cros had a sumptuous silver altar made for the Majesty from his own collection of silver plate.[13] A fourteenth-century martyrology contains a memorial which lists the relics Bishop Stephen had deposited in the image of Mary and Christ. Its text is mentioned by Jean Savaron in 1608 and by Pierre Audigier, who described the high altar of the cathedral in 1683 and noted thereon "a statue of the Virgin of which the head is in vermeil, surrounded by bright gems, and within which Stephen, Bishop of Auvergne, had enclosed a number of the relics said to have been brought from the Orient by St. Austremonius."[14]

Thus, subsequent centuries credited Stephen with the making of the statue, which continued to serve as a reliquary. In 1760 reference was made to new fittings being arranged for the statue on the high altar and later, on the eve of the Revolution, Dulaure described the cathedral and mentioned the statue as still being on the high altar; he called it the Majesty of Stephen II.[15] Pourreyron has pointed out the inventory of 1792 which lists works of precious metal in the cathedral at the time of its devastation. Therein the Majesty "seated with the Child on a copper throne" is described as being "covered with plates of gold, silver and copper."[16] The statue was sent to Paris to be melted down shortly afterward, but clearly some of the golden leaves sheathing the statue, which Stephen had claimed were the purest gold, had already been pilfered, probably long before as the gold of the throne had been replaced with copper, a fate

---

[11] In the first inventory, "Majestatem Sancte Marie una vestita cum cibori [sic] et botarico I de cristallo," and in the second, "Majestatem Sancte Marie I, vestita cum ciborio cum uno cristallo" (Bréhier, "Inventaires," 35-36).

[12] Rigodon, "Vision," 40; Pourreyron, *Le Culte*, p. 30. The major source for both is Audigier; see note 14 below.

[13] Pourreyron, *Le Culte*, p. 30.

[14] For the martyrology, see Vieillard-Troiekouroff, "La Cathédrale," 216 n. 1. The text is cited by Savaron, *Les Origines*, p. 343 and P. Audigier, "Histoire de la ville de Clermont," Bibl. Nat., fonds français 11846 and 32811-32812, published partially in Etienne Baluze, *Histoire généalogique d'Auvergne*, Paris, 1708, II, p. 39.

Audigier's description which is translated here is taken from Pourreyron, *Le Culte*, p. 31 ("une statue de la Vierge dont la tête est en vermeil, entourée de brillantes pierreries, et dans laquelle Etienne, Evêque d'Auvergne avait renfermé bien des reliques qu'on dit avoir été portées d'Orient par Saint Austremoine"). Rigodon quotes a slightly different wording of the text: "une statue de la Vierge haute de plus de trois pieds qui tient l'Enfant Jesus sur ses genoux. Elle est toute brillante de pierres précieuses. Dans cette statue l'évêque Etienne avait renfermé bien des reliques, que saint Austremoine avait apportées de Rome, comme on le lit dans un ancien livre."

[15] Pourreyron, *Le Culte*, pp. 31, 33.   [16] *Ibid.*, p. 33.

which also befell some of the gold plaques on the figures.[17] There is no evidence as to whether the vermeil head noted in the seventeenth century was original or was also a later replacement.

The statue seen by Robert in his "vision" is thus verified by other textual sources and we may consider it the earliest *sedes sapientiae* for which we have relatively precise and abundant information. We can safely regard it as a work done for Bishop Stephen II shortly after the consecration of the cathedral in 946 and picture it as a three-dimensional gold and wood sculpture of Mary and Christ enthroned. It was under life-size, and the figures were surmounted by a ciborium. It served as a reliquary. The drawing attests to the seated pose of the figures, but this sketch seems to have followed a conventional Madonna and Child image such as would be customary in an Adoration of the Magi scene rather than to have attempted an accurate rendering of the statue of Stephen. The drawing does, indeed, illustrate details of costume and pose which we know in later Throne of Wisdom statues. Since these features are common to other early portrayals of the enthroned Virgin and Child in manuscripts (e.g. Fig. 4) and ivories, however, the drawing does not provide evidence for the Clermont-Ferrand Majesty as being the prototypal source for these aspects of later statues.

On the other hand, the elaborate description of the triumphant contest of the Virgin with the devil, via the bees and the flies, may be something of a veiled apology for the use of a kind of sculpture which was still innovative at this time. The story seems devised to dramatize the Virgin's approval of this form of honor to her, clearly shown in the tale by the cleansing action provided by the virgin bees (*avibus virginibus*). If the insertion of the bee narrative was occasioned by the rarity of this type of sculpture, however, it is curious that Bernard of Angers makes no mention of the statue.[18] Perhaps the explanation is that the Clermont Majesty was only one of a number of statues of the Virgin known in his time. If Stephen's Virgin was an anomaly half a century earlier, it was no longer so at the turn of the century. Much less is known about related examples, but they did exist. Bernard himself had mentioned Rodez Cathe-

[17] Beutler (*Bildwerke*, pp. 39-41) considers the copper original on the basis of comparison with the Essen Madonna. Since this view does not accord with the medieval textual sources and since the Essen Madonna's throne also appears to be an alteration, in the manner of the Orcival Madonna, it is much more likely that all of these works had been plundered. See the discussion of the vandalism of metal-sheathed statues in Chapter I above.

[18] Bernard's visit to Conques, Aurillac, Rodez and the vicinity was avowedly for the purpose of seeing the reliquary statues in the area. His sojourn there in ca. 1013 must have been roughly contemporary with the recording of this story of Robert's vision, and we know from Bégon's inventory (980-1010) that the statue was indeed in Clermont-Ferrand close to Bernard's time there. Ties between Clermont-Ferrand and Conques were close. Bégon was Abbot of Conques and Bishop of Clermont-Ferrand as Stephen had been. It seems odd that Bernard, who was bent upon seeing such statues, could have stayed in Conques for twenty-five days, as he did on his first visit, and have made subsequent visits, without being aware of the Clermont Majesty. His reasons for ignoring it are unknown, but they cannot have been because it was not there. His silence makes us wary of using arguments based upon his omissions in attempting to date other lost statues (e.g. Chartres, Le Puy).

99

dral's golden image of Mary as present at the Rodez synod and his notice provides an early eleventh-century *ante quem* for this work.[19] It would have been roughly contemporary with the late tenth/early eleventh-century Madonna at Ely.

Across the Channel in England there was evidently an early and keen interest in statuary. The gold and silver statues of the Savior, the apostles and Mary made for King Ine (ca. 725) have already been commented upon.[20] At Ely, there were many rich treasures in gold. Among the offerings listed as given by the monks of the abbey to William the Conqueror in 1066 were statues of saints which had been made for Abbot Brithnod (d. 981). They were of wood covered with gold, silver and gems, according to the *Liber Eliensis*.[21] William's plunder also included a gold and silver image of the Virgin enthroned with the Christ Child in her lap. It is described as "a marvelous work" which had been made for Abbot Aelfsinus (981-1019). This would seem to be a third example of a Majesty of Mary from this early period.[22]

In Northern Europe the Essen Madonna (Figs. 28-32) provides another parallel of tenth-century date (ca. 980). It will be discussed below with other early Madonnas which survive to the present day. Rather close to it must have been the work which Stephen Beissel tells us Bishop Gero (969-976) had had made of wood and gold representing the Virgin Mary. Beissel considered this an early *Maiestas*, but unfortunately little further documentation of it can be found.[23] Gero's interest in sculpture—so brilliantly attested by the Gero Cross in Cologne Cathedral today—makes it likely that the prelate commissioned a Madonna of the Throne of Wisdom type as well. At the same time the monumental wood sculpture of a *Palmesel* was being used at Augsburg, according to Gerard's life of St. Ulrich (d. 973).[24] It is generally regarded as the earliest known example of this related genre of statuary. Of course, monumental crucifixes were widely known and much more numerous. They have long been regarded as typical

---

[19] Bouillet, *Liber miraculorum*, I, xxviii, p. 72. The reference is not very explicit and one might be tempted to interpret this golden image as the Majesty from Clermont-Ferrand. However, Bouillet explains that this is impossible since the synod was convoked by Arnaud, Bishop of Rodez, "pour ses seuls diocésains." According to Bouillet, the Madonna was presumably from the cathedral of Rodez which was dedicated to Notre-Dame and in which relics of the Virgin were preserved (*Sainte Foy, vierge et martyre*, Rodez, 1900, p. 489).

[20] Pfeilstücker, *Kunstgut*, p. 184; see Chapter III, note 51 above.

[21] Lehmann-Brockhaus, *Schriftquellen in England*, no. 1524; cf. *Acta Sanctorum*, Junii v, 449.

[22] Lehmann-Brockhaus, *Schriftquellen in England*, no. 1551: "Ob hoc totum quod in ecclesia ex auro et argento residuum fuit, insuper imaginem S. Mariae cum puero suo sedentem in trono, mirabiliter fabrefactam, quam Aelfsinus abbas [a. 981-1019] fecerat de auro et argento, comminutum est."

[23] Beissel, *Verehrung*, p. 162. His source is "Marroccio, *Familia Mariana*, c. 7, 23, Summa Aurea x, Paris, Migne, 896, 1047," which is unknown in libraries in this country. It is questionable whether the silver and wood Madonna mentioned in the inventory of St. Maria im Kapitol of 1405 and sold at auction in 1795—which had evidently been carried in processions in the mid-thirteenth century—is the same statue.

[24] See Chapter II, note 90 above.

images in the round from that period. Such works would have provided a sculptural context for the statues of the Virgin and Child.

Thus we can conclude that medieval artists in the late tenth and early eleventh centuries were familiar with religious sculpture in the round, the Madonna in Majesty being a significant genre of this new repertory of statuary. Judging by later literary evidence, statues of Mary were known throughout the eleventh century. Andreas of Fleury (1043-1056) mentions twice a wood sculpture of the Madonna and Child which was venerated in the time of Abbot Gauzlin (d. 1029) at Châtillon-sur-Loire. The sculpture was in a crypt dedicated to the Virgin. A dreadful fire devastated the church toward 1030. Andreas described the collapse of the ceiling and the billowing vapors which entered the crypt by a small, open door. As already discussed, a shower of burning embers covered the altar table and reduced to ash a reliquary chest there, but the sculptured wood Madonna and Child escaped so completely that not even the curtain hanging in honor about the statue retained the odor of fire. The statue was clearly carved of wood ("ligneo opere sculpta") and there is no indication of its being sheathed with precious metal. It was above the altar. In the year 1029, shortly before the fire, Abbot Gauzlin was borne during his last illness to the crypt of the Virgin to die before the altar and the statue.[25]

[25] For the report of the fire see: Certain, *Miracula*, Lib. v, cap. xi, pp. 209-210; Mortet, *Recueil*, I, pp. 7-9, "[Vers 1030]—Locus illecelebris effectus . . . accidit ut, tempore gloriosissimi abbatis Gauzlini effectus et Bidorcensium archietralis, casualibus flammis correptus in cinerem ejus lignea septa resolverentur; solummodo ex tantae conflagrationis damno opertura capicialis fornicis a foris intacta, caeterisque compaginata combustae ecclesiae appendiciis, merito tantorum amicorum Christi, cum sua vitrea inviolata remansit. Nihilominus memorata sanctae Dei genitricis Mariae crypta eadem eripitur divinae salvationis potentia; testatique sunt qui adfuerant geminas columbas super utramque adstitisse absidam, quae vim totius camini oppositione sui procul abegerint. Verum trabibus conlapsis, laquearibus ambustis, cum aediculam reginae virginum a regione aestuantis incendii ostiolo patenti tota rabies impeteret camini, eoque inveheretur spirantibus auris quo iconia matris Domini cum imagine nostri Redemptoris, ligneo opere sculpta, veneratur, ab illis divinitus auctus . . . ardere videbatur nil laedens. Et cum sui irruptione carbonum hac illacque immitteret congeriem, altarisque compleret tabulam, sacrosanctam quoque reliquiarum reduceret archam, cumque etiam more ferventis ebulliret fornacis, nec aulaea quidem eorum ob honorem in gyro dependens, ignis sensit nidorem, quae adhuc superest ob tantae rei venerationem." Cf. T. Cochard, "Châtillon-sur-Loire, son histoire avant 1789," *Mémoires de la société archéologique et historique de l'Orléanais*, XIV (1875), 115-118, 123; Hubert, *L'Art pré-roman*, p. 138. See Chapter II, note 57 above.

The description of the death of Gauzlin is from the *Vita* by Andreas of Fleury, ed. R. Bautier and G. Labory, *André de Fleury: Vie de Gauzlin, abbé de Fleury (Vita Gauzlini Abbatis Floriacenis Monasterii)*, Paris, 1969, pp. 144-145: "Jamque sese sentiens ad Christum vocari, in criptam Dei genitricis se deferri precepit, in qua idea ipsius matris Domini ex ligno honestissimae arae supereminet insculpta, cum ipsius nostri Redemptoris humanae assumptionis forma, quo ac si jam positus ante tribunal districti judicis, humi prostratus, se suosque quos usque in ultimum diem, Deo disponente, gubernaverat, sub obtentu orationis Jesu Christo commendat."

The above texts, taken together, give the following information relevant to the statue: in a

Somewhat later, other sculptures of Mary appear in the sources. An image of the Virgin, which was probably a statue, was described on the altar at Coutances in Normandy in an account of events between 1049-1093.[26] The Madonna adorned with a golden crown and bracelets at Avallon in 1078 has already been mentioned.[27] In Coventry, England, the statue of the Madonna presented with a necklace by Godiva, Countess of Malmesbury (1040-1080), has also been noted above.[28] Some evidence exists for a silver Virgin at Payerne, the Cluniac monastery in Switzerland. According to Joan Evans it was a late eleventh-century work which was destroyed in 1312.[29] The reliquary statues of the Madonna discussed earlier, i.e. of Abbot Fabritius at Abingdon (1100-1115),[30] Abbot Arnould at Ghent (ca. 1114-1132),[31] at Vézelay (late eleventh to early twelfth century)[32] and Utrecht (ca. 1112-1114),[33] would also belong to this series. In addition there were the famous Virgins at Chartres and Le Puy. Both were lost in the Revolution.

Before her destruction in 1794 Notre-Dame du Puy was the center of a widespread and fervent cult. Her fame drew illustrious and devoted followers. Louis XI was a pilgrim to Le Puy in 1476 and his benefaction resulted in an ornamental aedicula of late Gothic style arranged for the statue. Accordingly the Virgin was moved from the high altar to the new setting on the altar at the Gospel side of the sanctuary. Louis is also

---

crypt at Châtillon-sur-Loire, which was dedicated to the Virgin and was burned in about 1030, a wood sculpture of the Virgin and Child was above (or upon) a beautiful altar; a curtain was hanging around them as a mark of honor.

[26] Mortet, *Recueil*, I, pp. 76-77, interprets this work as a statue: ". . . et ecce ab altari Sancti Johannis processio veneranda uxorum fulgentium cereos ferentium progrediens, ac per circuitum interiorem ecclesiae prope mulierem transitum faciens, ante altare Sanctae Dei Genitricis imaginis constitit, moxque post paululum per chorum transiens, ante majus altare denuo stetit. . . . Miles quidam, in ecclesia stans ante supradictam imaginem Virginis gloriosae, et imaginis pulchritudinem admirans . . . et in candelabro ante imaginem Sanctae Mariae Virginis resedit. . . ." Cf. the image of Mary described as carried in procession at Saint-Benoît-sur-Loire, Albers, *Consuetudines*, v, p. 151.

[27] Bruel, *Recueil*, iv, no. 3518, "imago sancte Marie cum aurea corona et armillis aureis"; see above, Chapter II, note 60.

[28] See above, Chapter II, note 59. The text suggests a statue: ". . . hunc ergo gemmarum circulum collo imaginis s. Mariae appendi iussit" (Lehmann-Brockhaus, *Schriftquellen in England*, I, no. 1131).

[29] J. Evans, *Cluniac Art of the Romanesque Period*, Cambridge, 1950, p. 12.

[30] See Chapter II, note 10 above.

[31] See Chapter II, note 9 above. Note also the sculptures commissioned in this period by Abbot John I of Ypres at the Abbey of Saint-Bertin (1081-1095). He embellished the church and placed at the right and left of the high altar two statues of wood, encrusted with gold, silver and precious stones: "Ligneas quoque duas ymagines, auro argentoque cum lapidibus fabrili arte supertectas, dextra levaque capitanee crucis statuit" (B. Guérard, *Cartulaire de l'abbaye de Saint Bertin de Saint-Omer, France*, Paris, 1840, I, p. 207).

[32] See Chapter II, note 7 above.   [33] See Chapter II, note 49 above.

credited with establishing the tradition of costuming the statue.[34] In the eighteenth century (1723-1729), Louis's donation was replaced by a new aedicula or niche, and the statue was returned at that time to the high altar, where it survived as a *Vierge miraculeuse* until 1794.[35]

Descriptions of these phases of the statue's history have come down to us thickly embroidered with legends regarding the origins of the image. According to a tale recounted by the Abbot of Saint-Vosby in 1471 and repeated by Pierre de Gissey in 1644, she had been found by Jeremiah the Prophet and brought by St. Vosby to Le Puy from the Sudan. Another story had it that she was a seventh-century B.C. statue of indestructible wood brought from the Sudan by St. Louis. The latter account was preferred by Gissey and Brother Theodore, both of whom examined the statue in the seventeenth century.[36] Faujas de Saint-Fond considered it an ancient Egyptian sculpture of Isis, brought from Africa by St. Louis and converted into a Madonna.[37] These preposterous claims echo the theory current in the seventeenth and eighteenth centuries that reliquary statues were imported from the East during the Crusades. Olivier reminds us, on the contrary, that earlier chroniclers of Le Puy simply referred to the work as due to a successor of Clovis.[38]

Numerous copies of the statue were made in later centuries and some of these survive,[39] along with multitudinous representations on seals (from 1209 on), plaques (from the twelfth century on), medals, coins, goldsmith work, and renderings in paintings, engravings and small sculpture. These have been conscientiously collected and studied by Olivier.[40] Of this large mass of material only one engraving (Fig. 24) illustrates the statue free of its heavy vestments and its enframing niche. This was published by Faujas de Saint-Fond in 1778 along with a verbal description. Duranson's eye-witness account of the burning of the statue[41] and these records constitute the chief sources of information on the original appearance of the work.

The statue was taken from the altar on January 19, 1794, and put in the Cathedral Archive to be despoiled of its riches.[42] Presumably some of the gems from the long list of pearls, diamonds, cameos, etc., entered in the cathedral inventory of that date, came from the statue, but this is not explicitly stated. Both Faujas and Duranson say that both figures were made of wood and covered by linen and polychromy, so that it is unlikely

---

[34] Olivier, *L'ancienne Statue*, pp. 24-27. [35] *Ibid.*, pp. 24-25.

[36] *Ibid.*, pp. 17, 22-24; Jacotin and Pascal, "Bibliographie," 50-52.

[37] See Chapter I, note 40 above; Olivier, *L'ancienne Statue*, p. 22; Faujas de Saint-Fond, *Recherches*, pp. 417-428.

[38] Olivier, *L'ancienne Statue*, pp. 22-23.

[39] J. Breck, "A Souvenir of the Black Virgin of Le Puy," *Metropolitan Museum Studies*, I (1929), 155-158; L. Bréhier, "Une Reproduction en pierre de l'ancienne statue de Notre-Dame du Puy," *Revue d'Auvergne*, XLVII (1933), 196-198.

[40] Olivier, *L'ancienne Statue*.

[41] Jacotin, "Duranson"; see Chapter II, note 12 above.

[42] Jacotin, "Duranson," 80.

that the image was sheathed with precious metal. If it did display gems, they might have been set into the wood as cabochons or have served as ornaments of the crown. Faujas says that the statue was of hawthorn or cedar, 2 ft. 3 in. (about 72 cm.) in height. He says that Mary was seated in a stiff manner on a chair with her hands on Christ's knees. Her elongated face was black, showing a long nose and enamelled eyes. Her costume was made up of a long robe, a veil and a crown,[43] and on her feet were shoes. Christ's feet were bare and he wore a tunic. These general features are reproduced in Faujas's engraving (Fig. 24).[44]

Despite such abundant evidence, none of it gives a clue to the statue's date of origin. The costume and black faces were surely alterations in its later history,[45] while the other characteristics would pertain to a Throne of Wisdom statue of any period prior to about 1200. We know something of the medieval activities which centered about the statue. Processions made up of intense crowds are documented from 1254 and pilgrimages were evidently brisk by the end of the tenth century. Bishop Guy of Anjou (975-996) decided that those who died while visiting the altar of the Virgin at Le Puy on pilgrimage (*orationis causa*) might be interred in the cloister of Saint-Pierre le Monastier, an ordinance confirmed sixty years later by Etienne de Mercoeur.[46] We do not know, however, whether those pilgrims who visited her altar came primarily out of devotion to Notre-Dame in general, or to her relics, or to her statue in particular. The chief relic of Mary at Le Puy was her slipper, considered a gift of St. Martial. The age of this tradition is unknown, but it is established that relics of Mary were in Le Puy at least from the ninth century.[47] Apparently they were either enclosed in an altar, along with other relics, or put in a shrine. There is no evidence for assuming the statue was originally conceived as a reliquary, although such an intention seems likely.

The earliest reference to the Le Puy image of Mary would seem to be that found in the donation of Raymond of Saint-Gilles. In preparing to join the First Crusade in 1096 he made a gift of various villages to the cathedral of Le Puy with the stipulation that the feast of St. Giles should be celebrated every year in the sanctuary there, and that during his lifetime a candle should burn on his behalf night and day before the venerated image of the Virgin on the altar, ". . . et ut candela, dum vixero incessanter die ac nocte pro me ante Dei Genitricis venerandam imaginem super altare ardeat."[48]

[43] Theodore describes a crown of pearls, Olivier, *L'ancienne Statue*, p. 16.

[44] Faujas de Saint-Fond, *Recherches*, p. 428. Faujas mentions a small opening 3 in. long in the statue, but it was probably not the relic compartment revealed by the fire in 1794. The latter was closed by a little door which was totally unsuspected, since it had been completely concealed by the linen.

[45] See the discussion on "Black Virgins" in Chapter I; Jacotin and Pascal, "Bibliographie," 50-52, also considered the black faces to postdate the Renaissance.

[46] Olivier, *L'ancienne Statue*, p. 20.   [47] *Ibid.*, p. 19.

[48] C. de Vic and J. Vaissete, *Histoire générale de Languedoc*, Paris, 1738, II, pp. 343-344. Possibly this was an image of the Virgin in two-dimensional form. In view of the context and the evidence of related texts, it seems highly improbable. See Introduction, note 1 above.

In all likelihood this *imago* was the statue of Notre-Dame du Puy. The donation of Raymond of Saint-Gilles thus gives it a possible *terminus ante quem*. An earlier date cannot easily be hazarded. Bernard of Angers does not mention the statue in his passing reference to Le Puy.[49] This is hardly to be considered evidence, however, since he does not refer to the Clermont-Ferrand Majesty of this period either. His silence seems due to other reasons. Since he made a special pilgrimage to Le Puy after his third trip to Conques, ca. 1020, it is tempting to imagine that his interest in Le Puy was stimulated in part at least by the statue of Notre-Dame. This must remain conjecture, however, for the account of his trip is lost.

It is tantalizing that the exact date of a Majesty so important as Notre-Dame du Puy continues to elude us. Some scholars have been inclined to consider it as ancient as the tenth century in view of the date of the related Clermont-Ferrand Madonna. The history of Le Puy's pilgrimage traffic and the number of late tenth- to early eleventh-century statues cited in our previous discussion suggest a vogue which makes a tenth-century date logical, but without further evidence this can remain only a hypothesis.

Another celebrated Majesty, Notre-Dame-sous-terre, the statue of the Virgin at Chartres, provides many parallels to Notre-Dame du Puy. She was equally famous, her origins were also shrouded in obscurity and her demise was similarly due to the iconoclast zeal of the Revolution. Popular tradition ascribed to her a pre-Christian origin, reminiscent of Notre-Dame du Puy's supposed pagan antiquity. According to the legend a statue, carved before the birth of Christ, had been ordered by an early prince of Chartres to be placed beside pagan idols in a secret place where it became the object of a prophetic cult.[50] Although the statue was said to represent a virgin holding a child in her arms, it was known as the *Virgo paritura* (the Virgin about to give birth). Such an apparent inconsistency did not disturb those who held the popular belief that in honoring the statue, one really honored the Virgin Mary herself before the Incarnation of Christ, a presentiment of whom was thought to have existed at Chartres. The origins of these claims are unknown, but their purpose—to establish the temporal priority of the Chartres church—is only thinly veiled. Merlet and Jusselin have disengaged this tradition from the later assertion that the veneration of the Chartres Virgin was due to an ancient cult of Druids whose envoys had supposedly been instructed by Isaiah in

---

[49] Bouillet, *Liber miraculorum*, I, vii, p. 30. According to Bouillet (*ibid.*, p. xiii), Bernard was accompanied by four other Angevins and made a written record of his travels. Unfortunately only a fragment of his recital of this trip is known. It is included by Ménard in his *Ecrivains d'Anjou*, which draws upon the seventeenth-century work of Pierre de Gissey.

[50] E. Lépinois and L. Merlet, *Cartulaire de Notre-Dame de Chartres*, Chartres, 1862-1865, I, pp. 38-39, from the *Vielle Chronique* of 1389: ". . . et ad honorem illius imaginem unius virginis puerum in gremio gestantis fabricari fecisse, quam in secreto loco, justa Idola reconditam, adorabant, quemadmodum in Babilone sicut in legenda aurea legitur, audierant esse factum." This is usually thought to be the earliest textual source but see notes 54 and 66 below. Jusselin, "Tradition," 9; Lépinois, *Histoire*, p. 540; Y. Delaporte, *Les Trois Notre-Dame de la cathédrale de Chartres*, Chartres, 1955, pp. 9-10.

Jerusalem to make a statue of the Virgin.[51] The interpolation of this narrative into Chartrain documents can now be recognized as a sixteenth-century attempt to strengthen
belief in the pre-Apostolic traditions of Chartres by casting the story in the then fash-
ionable imagery of Classical studies; Caesar and Pliny had both written of the Druids
in Gaul.

In any case devotion to Mary began at an early moment in Chartres history. The
famous tunic of the Virgin, which was the chief relic of the city and which accounted
for numerous miracles, was reportedly donated by Charles the Bald (ca. 876) and a
church with a crypt existed at this date. It was built after the fire of ca. 858 by Bishop
Gislebertus. In that year cadavers of Chartrain martyrs, including Bishop Frotbold, were
supposedly thrown into a well following a massacre in the city by the Normans. The
well—called the *Locus Fortis* and thought to have curative powers—was mentioned in
the eleventh century, along with an account of Chartres's earlier "apostolic" martyrs,
Savinien and Potentien, by the monk Paul from the abbey of Saint-Père-en-Vallée, who
thus gave the tales renewed impetus. This ninth-century church burned in 962 and was
repaired by an architect named Teudon, who, like his contemporary Adelelmus in
Clermont-Ferrand, was also a goldsmith. He is credited with the *Sainte Châsse*, a sacred
shrine made for the holy tunic in 970.[52] A later devastation of the church in 1020 occasioned the building of Fulbert's cathedral, which was dedicated in 1037.

In Fulbert's structure, the position of the high altar and the sanctuary of the earlier
church were retained. Arrangements were also made for maintaining the site of the
Puits des Saints-Forts, i.e. the well of the ninth-century martyrs. In addition, Fulbert
made provision for another cult attraction, the cave marking the prison of the "apostolic" martyrs Savinien and Potentien, which was located behind the well. This may
also have been the site of a martyrium or primitive basilica since traces of a Gallo-Roman
monument were observed there by René Merlet, who concluded that the earliest church
at Chartres, possibly ca. 343, was erected on the site of a pagan sanctuary. Fulbert also
had set up in this place an altar in honor of the Virgin. Conforming to tradition, it
would have been directly below the high altar in the upper church. These arrangements
of the crypt would then have included the well, the cave or grotto and the altar of the
Virgin.[53]

The popular attraction of these shrines continued unabated throughout the Middle

[51] R. Merlet, "La Cathédrale de Chartres et ses origines, à propos de la découverte du puits des
Saints-Forts," *Revue archéologique*, XLI (1902), 232-241; Jusselin, "Traditions," 1-13. S. Roulliard,
Parthénie ou Histoire de Chartres, Paris, 1609, and V. Sablon, *Histoire de l'auguste et vénérable
église de Chartres*, Chartres, [1671], both repeat the Druid story; the relevant passages translated
and published by Branner, *Chartres*, pp. 104-105, 107-110, are partially quoted on pp. 107-108 with
his generous permission.

[52] R. Merlet, *La Cathédrale de Chartres*, Paris, 1926, pp. 14-16.

[53] R. Merlet, "Le Puits des Saints-Forts et l'ancienne chapelle de Notre-Dame-sous-terre," *Congrès archéologique de France, Chartres, 1900*, Paris, 1901, 226-255; H. Hilberry, "The Cathedral at
Chartres in 1030," *Speculum*, XXXIV (1959), 561-572; E. Lefèvre-Pontalis, "Le Puits des Saints-Forts
et les cryptes de la cathédrale de Chartres," *Bulletin Monumental*, LXVII (1903), 381-402.

Ages. Louis XI's devotion to the Virgin at Chartres prompted him to have a tabernacle made for the statue, then known as Notre-Dame-sous-terre, which was still in the chapel under the choir in 1471. In the sixteenth century the grotto was rearranged as the site of the Druidical shrine and the *Virgo paritura* identified with Notre-Dame-sous-terre. The cult activities which were practiced there seemed to the Chartres clergy in the seventeenth century to be excessive and they attempted to terminate them by immuring the well and part of the grotto. Efforts to exhume these monuments have been undertaken, but the subterranean appointments at Chartres still remain an archaeological puzzle.[54]

Nevertheless, the chief attraction there, from its conception until its destruction in 1793, was clearly the statue of Notre-Dame-sous-terre. In the sixteenth-century revision the figure was moved to a very grand new installation in the north aisle of the crypt, in which location it was described in 1609 by Sébastien Roulliard[55] and again in ca. 1671 by Vincent Sablon who wrote as follows:

> The first and principal chapel is the one of the Virgin, consecrated by St. Potentianus at the altar where the ancient Druids' idol used to be. This chapel, which until recently had a simplicity recalling that of our elders, is now the richest and most ornate in the world. Its walls are covered with marble; its rail is of the same material; around the altar there is only gold, jasper, and painting; and the place where the people go to pray to the holy Virgin is ornamented with beautiful paintings which cover the walls as well as the vault from top to bottom. Behind this chapel there is a kind of hiding place and next to it is the well of the *Saints forts*. It is at this altar, which is called Notre-Dame-sous-Terre, that the people of Chartres and the pilgrims pay their greatest devotion. It would not be out of place here to describe the Virgin which our ancient Druids put up on this altar. She is seated on a throne holding her Son in her arms. She is black or Moorish in color as are nearly all the images of the Virgin in Chartres, and the Druids are thought to have given her this color because she came from a country more exposed to the sun than ours. The real color of her skin is not known, but one can imagine it from what Solomon, in a prophetic spirit,

[54] Merlet, "L'ancienne chapelle," 239 n. 1, 240-252; Merlet, "Origines," 239-241; Delaporte, *Chartres*, p. 26.

An image of the Virgin is also mentioned in the necrology of Chartres for 1150. Richerius, the archdeacon of Dunois, who died in that year, had decorated the entrance of the cathedral with an image of the Virgin suitably adorned with gold. Charles de Lasteyrie thought this reference meant a gilded wood image located near the entrance to the church, rejecting the more usual view that a gilding of the sculpture of the tympanum was implied. This puzzling reference surely does not relate to the statue of the enthroned Virgin and Christ Child in the crypt. Lépinois, *Cartulaire*, III, pp. 19-20: "Decoravit etiam introitum huius ecclesiae imagine beatae Mariae auro decenter ornata." Ch. de Lasteyrie, "Etudes sur la sculpture française au moyen âge," *Fondation Eugène Piot, Monuments et mémoires*, VIII (1902), 10.

[55] Roulliard, *Parthénie*, N.B. frontispiece, which illustrates the grotto and the Madonna. Cf. Merlet, "L'ancienne chapelle," 241 n. 1; Delaporte, *Chartres*, p. 10, fig. 1.

said—that she was dark but not lacking in beauty. Nicephoras, however, says he saw several paintings made from nature by St. Luke, in which the color of her skin was the color of wheat—which is probably to say that when wheat is ripe it tends to be brownish or a chestnut color.[56]

In 1681, Alexandre Pintard, an historian of Chartres, gave a more objective eye-witness description, preserved in manuscript, from which Lépinois published the following section:

In the chapel erected especially in her honor, the venerable image which appears there, set up in a niche above the altar, is made of wood that seems to be pear wood which the long course of time has given a smoky color. The Virgin is on a chair, holding her Son seated on her knees, while he, with his right hand, gives a blessing and, with his left, carries the orb of the universe. His head is bare and the hair very short. The tunic which covers his body is close-fitting and gathered into pleats by the belt; his face, his hands and his feet, which are bare, have the color of shiny gray ebony. The Virgin is covered, above her tunic, by a mantle of Classical style, in the form of a dalmatic, which, being gathered up over her arms, appears looped in front upon her knees, down to which it descends; the veil which covers her head rests on both her shoulders, from which it is thrown over her back; her face is extremely well executed and well proportioned, oval in form and of a shiny black coloration; her crown is very simple, being adorned on top with fleurons in the form of celery leaves; the chair has four supports, of which the two rear ones are 23 inches high [62.26 cm.], with a spread of one foot [32.48 cm.], the chair [width] included; there is a hollow [space] in back, as if it [the figure of the Virgin] were the shell of a tree, three inches thick [8.12 cm.], wrought with carving [i.e. the carved surface of the figure].

In citing this passage in his discussion of Chartres, Hamon published a final line from Pintard's description which indicates that the total height of the work was "28 pouces 9 lignes" [77.83 cm.].[57]

[56] Branner, *Chartres*, p. 110; see note 51 above.

[57] The passage was published by Lépinois as follows (*Histoire*, p. 541): "Dans la chapelle spécialement érigée en son honneur, la vénérable image qui s'y voit élevée dans une niche au-dessus de l'autel, est faite de bois qui paroist estre du poirier que le long temps a rendu de couleur enfumée. La vierge est dans une chaise, tenant son fils assis sur ses genoux, qui, de la main droite, donne la bénédiction, et, de la gauche, porte le globe du monde. Il a la tête nue et les cheveux fort courts. La robe qui lui couvre le corps est toute close et replissée par le ceinture; son visage, ses mains et ses pieds qui sont découverts, sont de couleur d'ébeine grise luysante. La vierge est revestue, par dessus sa robe, d'un manteau à l'antique, en forme de dalmatique, qui, se retroussant sur les bras, semble arroundie par le devant sur les genoux jusqu'où elle descend; le voile qui lui couvre la teste porte sur ses deux épaules, d'où il se rejette sur le dos; son visage est extrêmement bien fait et bien proportionné, en ovale, de couleur noire luysante; sa couronne est toute simple, garnie par le hault de fleurons en forme de feuilles d'ache; la chaise est à quatre piliers, dont des deux de derrière ont 23 pouces de haulteur, sur un pied de largeur, comprise la chaise, est creuse par le

Pintard's precise description evokes the outlines and details of a typical *sedes sapientiae* statue. It had the familiar characteristics of Throne of Wisdom sculptures from northern France. The hollowed back corresponds to the woodworking technique in that area and the iconographic details are also consistent with those of the region. There is no indication of a relic compartment, which would be unlikely anyway.

In addition to verbal descriptions, a number of reproductions of the lost work are known: a statue in oak at Bergen-op-Zoom;[58] late seventeenth-century engravings by Leroux (Fig. 26) and Barbier, and an anonymous panel painting at Chartres;[59] a drawing by Chanoine Etienne in 1682, also at Chartres (Fig. 25);[60] a drawing made by Barbier for Pintard;[61] a drawing by Claude Chauveau in 1681[62] and two engravings mentioned by M. Lejeune.[63]

The Virgin's celebrated tunic was kept in the *Sainte Châsse* and it had its own "miraculous" history. It was particularly effective in deterring public calamities; and donations were made to it just as they were to the statue, such gifts being recorded from the eleventh century and later.[64] Both the *Châsse* and the statue are represented on

---

derrière comme si c'était une écorce d'arbre de trois pouces d'épaisseur, travaillée en sculpture." Cf. Hamon, *Histoire*, I, pp. 200-201. Delaporte (*Chartres*, pp. 12-14) gives a slightly different wording of the above passage, drawing on A. Pintard, "Histoire chronologique de la ville de Chartres," Chartres, Bibl. Municipale, N.A. MS 29 and Bibl. Nationale, fonds français 32973. The reference to the height of the statue was often repeated in Chartrain documents.

[58] Jusselin, "Traditions"; Merlet, *La Cathédrale*, p. 7.

[59] The engravings of Leroux and Barbier were included in manuscripts (Chartres, Bibl. Municipale, MSS 1011 and 1013) which are now lost. Three similar impressions may be seen in the Musée Municipale des Beaux-arts, Chartres, along with the painting, which is attributed to the French School of the seventeenth century and exhibited as no. 986. Cf. the discussion in Delaporte, *Chartres*, p. 13, fig. 2; Saillens, *Nos Vierges noires*, fig. 15.

[60] "Catalogue des reliques de joyaux de l'église de Chartres," Chartres, Archives départementales, MS G 403, fol. 68r. Our reproduction is based on a photograph made by the Chanoine Yves Delaporte before the manuscript was damaged during the last war. Grateful thanks are extended to him and to Mlle M. Houvet of Chartres who kindly made arrangements for its use. I am also most grateful to M. Jacques Lacour, director of the Services d'Archives d'Eure-et-Loir, who permitted me to consult this and other manuscripts in the Chartres Archives and who gave such courteous assistance to my work.

Etienne's descriptive text, which is close to that of Pintard, is reproduced in L. Merlet, *Catalogue des reliques et joyaux de Notre-Dame de Chartres*, Chartres, 1885, pp. 171-178. Cf. Jusselin, "Traditions," 16-17; Delaporte, *Chartres*, pp. 12-16, fig. 4.

[61] Lépinois, *Histoire*, p. 541.

[62] *Ibid.*, p. 541; Delaporte, *Chartres*, p. 14, fig. 3.

[63] Lépinois, *Histoire*, p. 541. Cf. Delaporte, *Chartres*, p. 20, for other possible reproductions, e.g. at Carmel-de-Chartres.

[64] *Ibid.*, pp. 550-553. Lépinois, *Cartulaire*, III, p. cxlvi. Suger refers to the tunic being borne in procession to avert siege and fire in 1118, in his life of Louis the Fat, A. Lecoy de la Marche, *Oeuvres complètes de Suger*, Paris, 1857, p. 106, "Vie de Louis le Gros," xxv; A. Molinier, *Vie de Louis le Gros par Suger*, Paris, 1887, pp. 91-93.

medieval pilgrim badges from the twelfth century on (Fig. 27) and were evidently carried in procession from at least that date.[65]

Notre-Dame-sous-terre had been the recipient of many gifts. Affluent visitors came even in "bad times" according to Lépinois, who says that in 1338 the receipts for the Holy Image totaled 98 pounds Tournois (2,352 francs in Lépinois's time).[66] Even on the eve of the French Revolution there was renewed interest in her, and Bishop Bonnet had the statue brought up from the crypt and given a new mount in the upper church as late as 1791. Two years later on December 20, 1793, the statue was burned along with other church furnishings in the square before the cathedral. A replica of 1857 is seen at Chartres today.[67]

In spite of the substantial history of the statue, only a few clues emerge as to the date of its origin. Scholars have tended to prefer a late eleventh- to early twelfth-century date, reasoning that an earlier origin would be incompatible with what we know of early eleventh-century activity at Chartres. Proponents of this theory argue that it would be difficult to imagine the statue in the crypt during Fulbert's time (d. 1029). Bernard of Angers had been Fulbert's pupil at Chartres before he made the first of several trips to southern France. He could hardly have written as disparagingly as he did about the statues which he saw in that region if a famous and honored Majesty were familiar to him already in Chartres. At the beginning of his book on the miracles of St. Foy, he describes his reaction to her statue on his initial visit, in ca. 1013. He explicitly states that his own rational point of view, disciplined by the Chartres school, would suffer only images of the crucified Christ in fully plastic form and that consequently he disapproved of the statues he saw for the first time at Conques and Aurillac.[68] One need not infer from these observations that the Chartres Virgin was a product of the mid-twelfth century, as did Emile Mâle.[69] Bernard's remarks merely provide a possible *terminus a quo* for the statue. Any attempt to be more precise about its date involves us in a review of relevant events at Chartres in the eleventh century.

Fulbert became Bishop of Chartres in 1007. As a student under the Bishop, Bernard learned of the miracles of St. Foy in Auvergne. He dreamed of visiting there one day himself, but was called to Angers in 1010 by Bishop Hubert of Vendôme to direct the episcopal school. After three years of some disillusionment over his own teaching experiences, Bernard renewed his decision to visit Auvergne and undertook his trip of ca. 1013.[70] His initial reaction to the reliquary statues he saw and to the superstitious cus-

[65] Forgeais, *Collection*, pp. 28-32; see Chapter II, note 34 above. See also Hamon, *Histoire*, I, pp. 200-202; Drochon, *Histoire*, pp. 344-345; Delaporte, *Chartres*, fig. 26.

[66] Lépinois, *Histoire*, p. 224 n. 2. This reference antedates the mention of the statue in the *Vielle Chronique* of 1389, usually thought to be the earliest textual source for the work (Lépinois, *Cartulaire*, I, pp. 38-39); see note 50 above.

For several centuries the city burned a candle weighing 250 lb. every year before the altar of the Virgin in the crypt, Lépinois, *Histoire*, p. 224 n. 2.

[67] Lépinois, *Histoire*, p. 542; Delaporte, *Chartres*, p. 30, fig. 10.

[68] Bouillet, *Liber miraculorum*, I, xiii, p. 47.

[69] Mâle, *L'Art religieux*, pp. 282-284.   [70] Bouillet, *Liber miraculorum*, p. xii.

toms he witnessed was critical, almost a revulsion. Later, the presence of the sacred relics within the statues and their effectiveness as devotional objects converted him to a wholesale acceptance of them. In particular he became a loyal and devoted adherent of the St. Foy cult, writing a careful account of the miracles induced by the saint through the agency of the statue, and describing the activities in Auvergne which centered about her. It is significant that he dedicated this book to his master, Fulbert.[71] He made two return visits to Conques, the later one in ca. 1020. These trips were followed by a pilgrimage to Le Puy, presumably soon afterward. Meanwhile work began on Fulbert's cathedral, replacing the one destroyed by the fire of 1020. In the new crypt, completed by 1024, Fulbert was careful to maintain the venerable sites of the Puits des Saints-Forts and the grotto, adding an altar especially arranged for the honor of the Virgin; the altar was erected on the traditional site of the *Virgo paritura*. The renewed concern in the eleventh century for the apostolic claims of Chartres has been mentioned.[72] In accord with that concern, Fulbert would wish to show honor to cults which center about the "apostolic" martyrs of Chartres and the *Virgo paritura* who had even anticipated the Virgin Mary. It is an attractive hypothesis that Bernard, returning amid these activities and filled with a new convert's zeal for the effectiveness of holy images, would have convinced his old master, Fulbert, to whom he had dedicated a book on the very subject, that a Majesty of the Virgin and Child, comparable to the St. Foy, would convey with the impact of three-dimensional art those traditional values which the Bishop was eager to assert. While such a conclusion cannot be proved, it gains credibility from the existence at that time of a wood statue of the Madonna and Child at Châtillon-sur-Loire, in the vicinity of Chartres, which was venerated by Abbot Gauzlin prior to his death in 1029. Nor was this a unique example for the period. As previously noted, comparable examples were to be found elsewhere at that time, at Cologne, Ely, etc.; and the Arras Synod of 1025 gave official approbation to such images. The conjecture is reasonable, therefore, that the first Notre-Dame de Chartres in three-dimensional form existed by about 1029.[73]

[71] *Ibid.*, p. 1.

[72] See notes 52 and 53 above; cf. Merlet, "L'ancienne chapelle," 227, 232 and 234-235 regarding Fulbert's recovery from a contagion through the intercession of the Virgin, which may have influenced his commission.

[73] The above conjecture is made with due recognition of alternative possibilities. Fulbert may not have caused such an image to be made or, if he did, the original may have been heavily restored, or even replaced, at a later date. René Merlet thought that a twelfth-century Virgin probably superseded an earlier statue ("Origines," 237). All the copies and verbal descriptions which are known to us date from the seventeenth century and later. The earlier sources assure us that a sculpture of an enthroned Madonna and Child was known in the crypt, but they do not delineate its appearance. The darkened faces of the figures mentioned by Sablon were surely later alterations at Chartres as at Le Puy, since no "Black Virgins" are known prior to the Renaissance. It is probable that the Chartres Virgin was costumed with actual vestments in her later history and that her crown was realistically added in metal. The 1682 drawing of Etienne suggests this (Fig. 25). It is impossible to know when such furbishing might have begun but a post-medieval date is likely, since Louis XI is credited with such at Le Puy. The form of the chair and the poses illus-

From the foregoing discussions several conclusions can be drawn. The Madonnas in Majesty known from literary sources comprise the following: Wessex (ca. 725),[74] Rome (ca. 731-741, ca. 817-824),[75] Clermont-Ferrand (ca. 946), Cologne (ca. 969-976), Ely (ca. 981-1019), Rodez (ca. 1013), Châtillon-sur-Loire (prior to ca. 1029), Coutances (ca. 1049-1093), Avallon (ca. 1078), Coventry (ca. 1040-1080), Payerne (late eleventh century?), Le Puy (prior to ca. 1096), Chartres (after ca. 1013), Abingdon (1100-1115), Vézelay (late eleventh-early twelfth century), Ghent (ca. 1114-1132), Utrecht (ca. 1112-1114). These examples form an unbroken series which loosely spans the early Romanesque period. They suggest a continuous development from Carolingian times on into the twelfth century and evince an international interest in the Throne of Wisdom as an early form of sculpture.

Extant Examples

To trace the stylistic development of the Throne of Wisdom statue prior to 1100, one must turn to Germany and Belgium where enough examples are preserved to permit a more concrete analysis. Of the surviving group of wood Madonnas in Majesty from this period the most important ones are now at Essen, Hildesheim, Paderborn, Walcourt and Brussels (from Hermalle). There are difficulties in establishing a chronology for them. Although the sculptures themselves have come down to us, very little else is known about them because literary evidence is almost totally absent. Only in the case of the Paderborn Madonna is there documentation sufficient to fix the date of the statue independent of stylistic considerations. The supposed dates of the other figures have shifted back and forth with the arguments of successive scholars; the Essen Virgin, for

---

trated in the copies which survive (Figs. 25 and 26) are similar to those of twelfth-century Throne of Wisdom sculptures but might also characterize earlier ones.

Notre-Dame-sous-terre or the *Virgo paritura*, also known as the *Vierge-aux-miracles*, was not the only statue of the Virgin at Chartres in its later history. According to Lépinois, a statue known as the *Virgo dei para* (Virgin Mother of God), probably the Renaissance work more commonly known now as *Notre-Dame du Pilier*, was located sometime before 1506 in the upper church. She was displayed on an altar accessible by flanking staircases. In 1506 she was placed in a niche of the choir screen, supported there by a stone column, and then moved in 1763 to a pier where she stayed until 1791 when she was relegated to the crypt and Notre-Dame-sous-terre replaced her in the upper church. This exchange was short-lived for in December 1793 Notre-Dame-sous-terre was violently thrown to the pavement and was burned before the Royal Portal of the cathedral. A poignant report was submitted by the municipal officer in charge: "It seems that the devotion, which the priests have inspired for this *vierge magotine* which we have burned . . . had called [to Chartres] and animated all the most celebrated artists of the time to construct the church." Lépinois, *Histoire*, p. 542. Cf. Delaporte, *Chartres, passim.*

A silver image of the Virgin with two angels was given to the church by Pierre de Bordeaux in 1261 for the high altar and an alabaster Virgin by Gilles de Condé in 1309 (Lépinois, *Cartulaire,* III, pp. 162, 175).

[74] See Chapter III, note 51 above.   [75] See Chapter III, note 52 above.

example, has been variously dated between ca. 973 and ca. 1050. Formerly this fluid situation prevailed because of the paucity of sculpture recognized as being from the Ottonian period. A stylistic context did not seem to obtain. The corpus of Ottonian sculpture continues to grow, however, and the number of works carved in both stone and wood has only recently been augmented by a group of sculptures which have now been correctly identified as eleventh-century works (e.g. the stone heads from St. Pantaleon, Cologne, the Benninghausen Crucifix), and by other sculptures whose early date and importance were previously not recognized (e.g. the Grossbirkach relief of St. John the Baptist).[76] In this great century of German history, which is still interpreted variously and uncertainly, our Madonnas take their place.

The extant examples form links in a chain which loosely spans the entire Ottonian period. Their stylistic relationships elucidate the formal development of the *sedes sapientiae* type, and in so doing they also illustrate the changes which appear in Ottonian art from the late tenth century to the rising Romanesque style at the end of the eleventh. In surveying this transition a sensitive observer sees a change in tone and mood, a shift from an art marked by gentleness and poignancy of feeling to one in which there rules an ever more cool and dispassionate detachment. Full, massive forms, which are very plastically realized, give way to compact, compressed shapes which are defined by thinly stratified surfaces composed in a rigid formalism. While the early Ottonian work shows an organic coordination of parts resulting in a rhythmic unity of the whole form, distortion is more apparent in the later pieces. The body becomes more angular; it seems more slender in relation to the longer upper torso. The artist dwells upon the articulation of individual units in the composition, particularly the joints and extremities of the body. Distinct contour replaces the soft and relaxed flow of outline in the earlier period. The figure becomes increasingly frontal and gradually yields its freedom to an ever more insistent vertical alignment. In short, this is the period when incipient Romanesque style is being formed. That emergent process receives particular clarification when the morphology of an unchanging composition, fixed by iconographic tradition, is reviewed. By tracing the changes in the Throne of Wisdom statue we are given revealing glimpses of the gestation of Romanesque style.

The golden Madonna at Essen (Figs. 28-32) is clearly the earliest representative of this group.[77] She is also the most plastically conceived. One might expect the oldest

[76] R. Wesenberg, "Die fragmente monumentaler Skulpturen von St. Pantaleon in Köln," *Zeitschrift für Kunstwissenschaft*, IX (1955), 1-28; Fritz, "Benninghausen." For the Grossbirkach relief of ca. 1040, see Munich, Stadtmuseum, *Bayerische Frömmigkeit*, 1960, no. 153.

[77] The gold repoussé statue, formerly in the Minster Treasure, is now in the Minster at Essen. It measures 74 cm. The eyes are set with enamel. Filigree and gems decorate the orb, the book, the nimbus and the knobs of the throne. Numerous restorations are discussed in the text below. As to date, Weerth called it simply "Ottonian." Humann dated it, "somewhere between ca. 970 and the middle of the eleventh century," while Panofsky and Beenken favored a date in the first quarter of the eleventh century. Clemen suggested a late tenth- or early eleventh-century date, mentioning Trier and Cologne as possible places of origin. Schnitzler would date the work ca. 973-982 and attributes it to a Cologne workshop. Swarzenski suggests Mainz or Essen, end of tenth

of all Madonnas sculptured in the round to look particularly archaic and to retain the character of relief sculpture, but such is not the case. Instead of organizing the design about one predominant aspect of the work, the artist has fashioned a number of interesting views for his statue, each with its own three-dimensional composition. An ever changing pattern of curves leads the eye beyond the confines of a single side and draws the observer with a sense of expectancy around the figure. The continuity of the plastic form thus requires the beholder to move about the statue so that its formal meaning may be fully grasped.

Nor can the composition be called a "cylindrical relief," for the articulation of the surface is intimately dependent upon and determined by the organic form of the implied figure. Indeed, it is the relation of drapery to figure which accounts for this early version of the so-called "revolving view." The left arm of the Mother which supports the Child clearly demonstrates the effect (Fig. 31). The prolonged sweep of the graceful gesture, with its gradual dénouement, is intimately related to the head of the Mother where a twist of drapery serves as vortex of a spiral movement curling and unfolding from head to hand. Against this spiraling curve the linear folds of the drapery play a counter theme. In spite of their vertical arrangement, they are not arbitrary or stiff. Each crease varies in the line of its fall and also in its thickness. Its edges are accented by the creasing of the metal and by the lustre of the gold. Ridges and hollows model the surface and give the drapery a plastic quality which accords with, and is conditioned by, the form and movement of the arm. The drapery does not, therefore, exist as an independent calligraphic appliqué. Its play is determined by the form of the figure

---

century. Rosemarie Messerer also assigns the statue a Cologne origin of ca. 980. She provides the most complete as well as the most persuasive study of the work. I should like to express my thanks to her for lending me the typescript of her dissertation. The literature on the statue is too vast to be cited here in full. Among the most important studies are: E. Aus'm Weerth, *Kunstdenkmäler des christlichen Mittelalters in den Rheinland*, II, 1871, p. 31; F. Arens, *Die Essener Münsterkirche*, n.d.; P. Clemen, *Die Kunstdenkmäler der Rheinprovinz*, II (III), *Die Kunstdenkmäler der Stadt und des Kreises Essen*, Düsseldorf, 1893, pp. 47f.; G. Humann, *Die Kunstwerke der Münsterkirche zu Essen*, Düsseldorf, 1904, pp. 251f.; P. Clemen, *Berichte über die Tätigkeit der Provinzkommission für die Denkmalpflege in der Rheinprovinz und der Provinzialmuseum zu Bonn und Trier*, XI, 1906, Düsseldorf, 1907, pp. 7-12; Arens, *Liber Ordinarius*, 4, 33-35, 80-89, 104-107, 168-173, 181-185, 201-207; M. Burg, *Ottonische Plastik*, Bonn and Leipzig, 1922, pp. 52-56; H. Beenken, *Romanische Skulptur in Deutschland*, Leipzig, 1924, no. 11; E. Panofsky, *Die deutsche Plastik des 11. bis 13. Jahrhunderts*, Munich, 1924, p. 73; K. Kästner, *Das Münster in Essen*, Essen, 1930, pls. 31-38; Redlefsen, *Mariendarstellungen*, doctoral dissertation, Kiel, 1937, pp. 12-13; H. Picton, *Early German Art and its Origins*, London, 1939, pp. 129f.; Cologne, Alte Universität, *Romanische Kunst*, ed. H. Schnitzler, 1947, no. 46; Amsterdam, Rijksmuseum, *Uit de Schatkamers der Middeleeuwen*, 1949, no. 7; R. Messerer, *Goldschmiedewerke*; Swarzenski, *Romanesque Art*, nos. 39-40; Köhn, *Der Essener Münsterschatz*, pp. 16-18; R. Wesenberg, *Bernwardinische Plastik*, Berlin, 1955, p. 60; Essen, *Werdendes Abendland*, 1956, no. 498; H. Schnitzler, *Rheinische Schatzkammer*, Düsseldorf, 1957, no. 39, pls. 130, 131, 133; Victor Elbern, *Das Erste Jahrtausend*, Tafelband, Düsseldorf, 1962, no. 370; Essen, Villa Hügel, *Marienbild in Rheinland und Westfalen*, 1968, no. 1.

underneath and the result is an effect of thin fabric pulled across the frame of a human body.

In the structure of the figure, there is a high degree of freedom. No single prominent axis imposes itself. The head of Mary tilts to her left and deep pleats cross the upper torso suggesting a parallel diagonal movement. A similar oblique thrust is stated by the long folds between Mary's knees, the impetus here recalling the diagonal movements above. The treatment of the legs is far in advance of the cylindrical shafts observed in the St. Foy. The knees arch outward and the feet are lightly pressed together in sensitive and self-conscious restraint (Figs. 29 and 30). The gesture of the Madonna's left hand, which barely touches the shoulder of the Child, is light and tentative. Other features show a similar, delicate tension achieved through a lightness of touch: the Child's transitory pose athwart the lap of his Mother—from which he seems about to slide; the highly arched position of Mary's feet, which adds tension to her lower body since all weight is balanced on her toes; the sway of Mary backward and to her left (Fig. 30). The sculpture is thus made up of shapes, planes and lines that tilt and meet at angles to one another, and which are freely arranged in space. The contrast to the rigid grid-like format of later, more columnar forms of the Madonna and Child, where vertical-horizontal relationships prevail, is obvious.

This analysis reveals the comparative freedom of the composition of the Essen statue, which makes it differ from all other sculptures of the Virgin considered in this study. It is a feature which is rooted in Carolingian style, recalling qualities known in ninth-century goldsmith work, e.g. the Lindau Book Cover, the cover of the Munich Codex Aureus or the Arnulf Ciborium. Its prominence in the Essen sculpture indicates that an early date should be postulated for this Madonna.

There are no documents known which help to date the Essen Virgin accurately or to determine in which goldsmith's atelier she was made. A mid-eleventh-century date is surely far too late and even an early eleventh-century date seems unlikely in view of the development of Ottonian style as we now know it. The Paderborn Virgin (Fig. 46) demonstrates that the form of the Madonna in Majesty had crystalized into a formal, ceremonious type by the middle of the eleventh century at least, and the Hildesheim Madonna (Fig. 37), which typifies the Bernwardian period at the beginning of the century, also differs strongly from the Essen Madonna. The Hildesheim statue still shows the full volumes of early Ottonian form, but decided changes in proportion and iconography have already set in, indicating tendencies which will develop further in the course of the century. The tight frontality of the Hildesheim work is such a marked departure from the Essen statue that these figures must be separated by a significant difference in date. Other goldsmith works from the early years of the eleventh century, the Basel Altar or the Aachen Altar, illustrate figures which are close to the Hildesheim Madonna in their vertical emphasis, but are unlike the Essen statue.

The style of the Essen figure is more properly at home in the last third of the tenth century. The monument most closely related to it is the so-called First Mathilda Cross found in the Essen Minster Treasure (Fig. 33).[78] There the lightness of touch in the

---

[78] Köhn, *Der Essener Münsterschatz*, p. 10f.; Elbern, *Das Erste Jahrtausend*, no. 376.

repoussé work is a marked feature. The delicate modeling of the slender Christ is reminiscent of the best views of our Madonna. The parallel pleating of his loin cloth is similar to the treatment of the Madonna's drapery, the ends of folds often being almost identical in pattern. This is particularly noticeable in the folds at the right side of the Crucifix body and those at Mary's left side. In both works there is a tendency to arrange the thin fabric in thick, bulky gatherings.

Moreover, the modulation of the upper torso of the crucified Christ, the bending of the knees and the light placing of the feet, the gentle sway of the body and the relaxed spread of the arms, all recall the character of the Essen statue. Gestures flow freely from the body core and in both there is a balance between the straight lines of the drapery and the softness of organic forms. The roundness of the Madonna's head, back and knees is echoed in the head, arms and legs of the crucified Christ. Even the serpent beneath the cross reveals this plastic proclivity in its graceful coil.

Both the statue and the repoussé crucifix may be related in turn to a group of works which come from Cologne. Monuments from the Cologne school in this period are marked by a predilection for broad, rounded forms. This is evident in manuscripts where overly large discs serve as nimbi for the figures, and arching promontories, caves and shadows fill the backgrounds of scenes (e.g. the Gereon Sacramentary, the Hitda Codex).[79]

The same character is evident in Cologne sculpture. The famous Gero Cross (Fig. 34), for example,[80] shows a liking for sphericity in all parts of the body: the bulbous head, the swelling upper torso with its abdominal "orb," the globular knees and the full hips. Although it is more highly charged with emotional intensity than the Essen crucifix, the similarities are clear: the inclination of the body and the head, details such as the arrangement of the hands or the folding and knotting of the loin cloth. The Mathilda Cross also shows the oversize nimbus of the Cologne school.

In comparing the Gero Cross with the Essen Madonna, it is clear that full volumes are common to both. Christ's rounded abdomen in the former resembles that of the Essen Child. There is also the same parallel creasing of the drapery and a similar treatment of the edges of the folds.

Fortunately the First Mathilda Cross in Essen can be closely dated by internal evidence. The dedicatory enamel at its base depicting donors Abbess Mathilda and Duke Otto of Bavaria indicates an origin between the years 973 and 982. These are the years of Mathilda's appointment as abbess and Otto's death. The dates overlap those of Arch-

---

[79] P. Block and H. Schnitzler, *Die Ottonische Kölner Malerschule*, Düsseldorf, 1967.

[80] For a discussion of parallels between manuscripts and sculpture in the Cologne school, see R. Messerer, *Goldschmiedewerke*. For the Gero Cross, see R. Hamann, "Grundlegung zu einer Geschichte der mittelalterlichen Plastik Deutschlands," *Marburger Jahrbuch für Kunstwissenschaft*, I (1924), 1-48, N.B. 15ff.; R. Hamann, "Studien zur ottonische Plastik," *Städel Jahrbuch*, VI (1930), 5-19; H. Haedecke, "Das Gerokreuz im Dom zu Köln und seine Nachfolge im XI. Jahrhundert," *Kölner Domblatt*, XIV-XV (1958), 42-60; H. Haedecke, *Rheinische Holzkruzifixe von ihren Anfangen bis zur hochromanischen Zeit*, doctoral dissertation, Cologne, 1954; Haussherr, *Ikonographie des Gerokreuzes*; M. Imdahl, *Das Gerokreuz im Kölner Dom*, Stuttgart, 1964.

bishop Gero in Cologne (969-976) who gave the crucifix which bears his name. The Essen Madonna is closest to these two monuments in character and thus must be roughly contemporary. Moreover, Cologne miniatures which compare most convincingly with the Madonna are the earliest of the school, dating from ca. 985-999.[81] These comparisons point to a Cologne origin and to a probable date of ca. 980. This is more or less contemporary with works done for Archbishop Egbert in Trier which reveal a similarity of tone and are more comparable stylistically than works done later at the turn of the century during the time of Otto III or Henry II. Very little is known of the production of the Essen workshop under Abbess Mathilda so that, until the role of this atelier is clarified, one may suppose that Mathilda had the Cross and the Madonna made in nearby Cologne.

Almost nothing is known regarding the later history of the statue. Except for the fourteenth-century references to the figure in the *Liber Ordinarius* already mentioned above in the discussion of the processional function of the *Maiestas*, the literary sources are silent.[82] Close examination of the work itself reveals that it has been subjected to various revisions. The latest restoration affected the sculpture most profoundly. The gold surface had become pitted with many depressions caused by the decay of the lindenwood core which once served as a base for the sheath of gold repoussé leaves. The disintegration of this core had so enfeebled the work that in 1902 the pulverized wood was removed and replaced with an infusion of cement.[83]

Thus the cavity which can be seen now from the underside of the throne is of uncertain date and we can never know the character of any earlier hollow which might have existed there. Accordingly the question of a relic compartment remains an insoluble enigma. An opening might have been intended as a technical precaution as well as providing a receptacle for relics. Moreover, the pierced grating (Fig. 32) which closes this aperture was obviously not made originally for its present position under the throne. It is of gilded copper rather than of gold and is very awkwardly cut for its installation, as our illustration shows. The irregularity of its edges indicates that it was reduced from a larger piece of metal to fit this space. Its design, a geometric pattern of nested crosses, has been compared to the ornament of the throne of the St. Foy statue (Fig. 13) and to the St. Servatius reliquary key.[84] The cut-out crosses at Conques are of extreme simplicity, however, and they resemble the Essen example only in a generic sense. The Essen design is much more convincingly compared with the throne of the Madonna

[81] Bloch and Schnitzler, *Malerschule*, e.g. nos. I (Lectionary of Archbishop Evergar, Cologne, Cathedral Library, Cod. 143, 984-999), II (Evangeliary of St. Gereon, Cologne, Historical Archives, Cod. W. 312, ca. 996), III (Sacramentary of St. Gereon, Paris, Bib. Nat., Lat. 817, ca. 996-1002).

[82] Arens, *Liber Ordinarius*, pp. 4, 33-35, 80-89, 104-107, 168-173, 181-185; see Chapter II, notes 36-37 above.

[83] A complete account of this complicated operation, in which the pulverized interior of the statue was drawn out with suction, is given by Paul Clemen, *Berichte*; see note 77 above. The restoration was carried out by C. A. Beumers, Düsseldorf.

[84] Taralon, "Majesté," pl. 35. For the ninth-century reliquary key of St. Servatius at Maastricht, see Swarzenski, *Romanesque Art*, no. 92.

in the famous Book of Kells (Fig. 35).[85] In both there is an ambiguity of positive and negative elements in the scheme, which is a characteristic of Hiberno-Saxon metalwork. It persists in early medieval manuscript ornament and can also be seen, in varied form, in the bronze railings of the Palace Chapel at Aachen.[86] The grating of the Essen throne seems then to have been an earlier panel, but whether put into place at the time of the execution of the statue or at a later date is indeterminate. The reworking of the throne, done possibly in the Early Middle Ages, would have required some alterations of the grating, which suggests these two copper elements—the grill and the throne—were added contemporaneously.

The throne stands out clearly as an alteration of the original conception of the sculpture. This is evident upon observation because of the use of gilded copper in contrast to the gold of the figure and because of the rough execution of the throne, so that it appears as an impoverishment of the work. One bit of ornament, made up of filigree and gems, and some fragments of gold plate are still visible on the knobs of the chair. These seem to be the last traces of the earlier throne which was probably of gold like the figures. An attempt has been made to see the vestige of supporting rods—which would have been used to carry the figure processionally—in the blunt ends of this throne, but such a conjecture seems unlikely. Since the throne is clearly remade, its present state cannot yield a reliable indication of its original arrangement; nor do these knobs seem to be logically placed for the support of the weight involved. Surely when carried processionally, the statue was supported on a platform of some sort, or on a litter as recorded in the *Liber Ordinarius*, and covered with a canopy or baldachin.[87]

A close examination also reveals that a panel of gold at Mary's right side is preserved from the statue's state prior to the addition of the copper throne. This bit of golden drapery does not form part of the costume of the Madonna. It may orginally have been part of a drape for the throne itself. Such a draped *cathedra* can still be seen in the later wood Majesty from Autun (Fig. 152). A similar arrangement for the Essen Madonna would make sense of the curious panel of gold preserved at the back of the throne. Not belonging to Mary's dress, it might have been part of a cloth covering the throne in a regal and sumptuous manner.

Other changes were also made. The eagle and the miniature Madonna on the dress of the Virgin are later additions. So is the present right hand of the Child, which is of gilded silver. The last is a particularly unfortunate restoration because the gesture of the hand introduces a childlike element which is entirely inappropriate to the original conception. The theory of Redlefsen that the Mother offers the apple to the Child and that there is a warm human relationship between the two figures is quite untenable,[88] since originally the Child undoubtedly made a gesture of benediction, rather than one suggesting an infant's response to his mother. Moreover the Virgin extends the orb, not

[85] E. H. Alton and P. Meyer, *The Book of Kells*, Bern, 1950-1951.

[86] Braunfels, "Bronzewerkstatt," figs. 8-9.

[87] Arens, *Liber Ordinarius*, pp. 170, 184; see Chapter II, note 36 above. The use of rods was proposed by Oslender, "Die goldene Madonna," 34-36.

[88] See note 77 above.

to the Child, but to the observer. The orb has been interpreted as an iconographic reference to Mary's role as the New Eve, but it is more likely an allusion to divine kingship.[89] Here the gesture makes of Mary a graceful mediator. As she extends the sphere her gentle majesty is impressive.

The nimbus of Christ shows a number of losses and small, awkward restorations. Its entire form seems ill related to the rest of the figure. A gilded copper plate supports its back and is rudely attached to the head of the Child with angular braces. The date of this attempt at securing the nimbus can hardly be determined, but the material used suggests that it may have been contemporary with the remaking of the throne in copper.

A nimbus similar to that of the Christ Child was thought by Weerth, and later by Clemen and Schnitzler, to have originally adorned the head of the Madonna. The theory is that the enamels from this hypothetical nimbus were later incorporated into the ornaments of the Theophanu Cross and the Reliquary for the Holy Nail (both in the Essen treasury) when the nimbus was removed.[90] Although the enamels in question all have a similar curvature and surely come from a common earlier source, the supposition that they provided a halo for the Madonna seems unlikely. Should the four pieces from the Nail Reliquary and the six from the Cross be placed side by side, they would form an ellipse larger than necessary for the head of the Virgin and of quite different diameter. Moreover, the head shows no signs of holes where such an ornament would have been attached. Only the holes made for the crown, a later addition which was formerly worn by the Madonna,[91] are visible.

Since the decoration of the Child's nimbus differs from that of his book and his Mother's orb, it seems possible that it too was not part of the original conception. It may have been added in Theophanu's time when the Cross and the Nail Reliquary were made. The enamels for both the Child's nimbus and the reliquaries probably would have come, as Köhn conjectures, from some sort of circular disc on hand in the Essen convent.[92]

These observations lead to the conclusion that the Essen Madonna would have been more splendid originally, with her elaborate golden throne intact, but her form would have been essentially what we see today. The remaking of the throne and the altera-

---

[89] In this case Mary would be portrayed as *regina nostri orbis* (Scheffczyk, *Mariengeheimnis*, pp. 477-496, based on passages from Paschasius Radbertus, *PL*, XCVI, 240-241, among others; and J.L.M. de Gruyter, *De beata Maria regina, Disquisitio positivo-speculative*, Herzogenbosch and Turin, 1934). For a fuller discussion of the Eve-Mary relationship, see: H. Coathalem, S.J., *Le Parallélisme entre la Sainte Vierge et l'église dans la tradition latine jusqu'à la fin du XIIᵉ siècle*, Analecta Gregoriana, LXXIV, Sectio B, no. 27, Rome, 1954, pp. 1-30, for the parallelism prior to the time of Bede; and E. Guldan, *Eva und Maria, Eine Antithese als Bildmotiv*, Graz and Cologne, 1966, p. 111, who points out the association between the orb held by Mary at Essen and imperial insignia. Cf. the Madonna and Child in Majesty portrayed in a manuscript in the Cologne Cathedral Library, MS 141, fol. 5, ca. 1030 (illustrated by Swarzenski, *Romanesque Art*, fig. 172); the Child is seated sideways and the Virgin holds a sphere as at Essen; Essen, *Marienbild*, 1968, no. 2.

[90] See note 77 above.   [91] Schramm, *Herrschaftszeichen*, I, pp. 415ff.

[92] See note 77 above.

tions to the Child's right hand, plus the addition of a few gemmed ornaments, have not seriously altered the basic work. That the sculpture has come down to us so remarkably intact is a wonder which must be due in part to a traditional and continuous veneration which ensured preservation. If this is true, then it is all the more lamentable that we have so little written record about this intriguing Majesty.

Curiously, the feature of the statue most commonly mentioned in the modern literature devoted to it is an iconographic consideration. The profile disposition of the Child reclining athwart the lap of the Virgin has been commented upon repeatedly. Scholars are almost annoyed that the earliest Madonna and Child in the round should not show the strict frontality of later Throne of Wisdom statues. Yet Christ is turned to the side in numerous examples of the Madonna and Child theme from the period of the Essen statue. In our wood and metal sculptures the profile disposition is seen at Paderborn and at Walcourt. Illustrations exist in other media: e.g. the Cuthbert Coffin and the Madonna from the Book of Kells. The repoussé decoration of the Theophanu Book Cover in Essen (1039-1056) (Fig. 36) includes a Madonna and Child in Majesty which shows the Child in profile.[93] The form of the throne is similar and there is a baldachin with curtains which we would normally expect as an honorific enframement for such a statue. That this image is to be interpreted as the Madonna in Majesty is clearly indicated by the formal relationship to the pendant *Maiestas Domini* rendering of Christ above and by the presence of Sts. Spinosa and Waldburg and the Abbess herself below. The Abbess is in the attitude of *proskynesis* at Mary's feet, while the female saints flanking Mary gesture to her in honor. This is clearly a ceremonial and devotional representation of the Madonna enthroned.[94]

Frontal and profile dispositions for the Christ Child can be found in early medieval representations of the Madonna, both with and without attendant Magi. This fact indicates that traditions for both dispositions obtained and demonstrates that the frontality of Christ was an optional feature in either case. A frontal disposition for the Child gradually predominated in the twelfth century, but even then a number of variant poses appeared.

The Child at Essen may seem in a photograph to recline precariously.[95] This is due to the unfortunate preference of photographers for the frontal view. In actual experience, the Child does not seem to the beholder to be insecure. Indeed, as the viewer moves about the statue and the form of the work changes under his gaze, this feature, far from being a distraction, appears to add deftly to the tension and vitality of the work. A similar device can be seen in the bronze doors at Hildesheim whose date (1015)

[93] Essen, *Marienbild*, 1968, no. 3.

[94] The interpretation of this image as a portrait of the local statue of the Madonna is problematic.

[95] A feature which has led some scholars to point to ancient Egyptian statues of Isis as models, an extreme view which seems unnecessary in view of the numerous Christian examples of the iconography which antedate the work. See P. Bloch, "Überlegungen," and the studies of Boll, Weber and Norden, Chapter I, note 40 above.

is only slightly later. There too the dangling feet and the slippery pose of the Child add alertness to the enthroned Madonna group—this time in an Adoration of the Magi scene (Fig. 42).

In sum, then, the Essen Madonna's importance as the earliest *Maiestas* preserved to us, and as the only one which survives with its sheath of gold intact, can hardly be overstressed.[96] In addition to these historical claims, the work also has an impressive character of its own. This is particularly evident when it is seen in relation to its successors.

Turning to the Hildesheim Madonna (Figs. 37-41),[97] we find a very different version of the early medieval *Maiestas* of Mary. The vicissitudes suffered by this sculpture in the course of its history have deprived it of the heads of both Mother and Child and have occasioned other, smaller losses, but fortunately the wood core of the statue is basically intact. The gold metal casing (Figs. 40, 41) was removed in 1950 for the first of a series of restorations under the direction of Joseph Bohland. The detachment of the sheath allowed study of the sculptured wood core. The evidence of early medieval wood carving thus revealed is particularly valuable since such a possibility no longer exists with the Essen Madonna. The blunt ends of nails and the holes made by the tiny metal pegs which formerly held the gold cover in place were made visible, and both carving and joinery could be observed. The figure of the Mother is hollowed inside with a large cavity closed by a wood panel which forms her back (Fig. 39). This panel is carefully carved and fitted so that the figure is conceived fully in the round. Since the same manner was followed later in twelfth-century France, as in the Autun Virgin (no. 87), it is of particular interest to know of this technical precedent. When Joseph Bohland opened the figure he found small bits of wood, presumably taken from the so-called Thousand-Year-Old Rosebush which grows at the apse of the cathedral.[98] An inscription inside the statue records the restoration of Wissocque in 1664 and suggests that the statue was made from the wood of the rosebush.[99] This indefensible theory

[96] Of course, there are other golden Madonnas but their gold sheathing has been lost or replaced, or is of silver or silver gilt.

[97] The statue is due to return to the Cathedral Treasury at Hildesheim after restoration of the heads and hands by sculptor Leo Dierkes of Kevelaer. I should like to thank Prof. Dr. Konrad Algermissen of Hildesheim and Herr Dierkes for their courtesy in allowing me to examine it at leisure. The statue is of lindenwood and measures 56.5 cm. to the shoulder. It has been studied chiefly by Wesenberg, in addition to the following: Kratz, *Der Dom*; *Kunstdenkmäler der Provinz Hannover*, II, *Regierungsbezirk Hildesheim*, IV, *Stadt Hildesheim, Kirchliche Bauten*, 1911, p. 107; J. Braun, *Meisterwerke der deutschen Goldschmiede-Kunst der vorgotischen Zeit*, Munich, 1922, fig. 21; Redlefsen, *Mariendarstellungen*, pp. 15-16; Keller, "Vollskulptur," p. 84; Algermissen, "Marienverehrung"; Wesenberg, *Bernwardinische Plastik*, no. 7, pp. 59-62, 171, pls. 154-155, figs. 111, 112; Essen, *Werdendes Abendland*, 1956, no. 550, pl. 54; Elbern, *Das Erste Jahrtausend*, no. 430; V. Elbern and H. Reuther, *Der Hildesheimer Domschatz*, Hildesheim, 1969, no. 82. For discussion of the gold repoussé sheath, see Chapter I, p. 13.

[98] Wesenberg, *Bernwardinische Plastik*, p. 171.

[99] *Ibid.* Redlefsen, *Mariendarstellungen*, pp. 15-16.

adds little to our knowledge of the early history of the piece.[100] There is no other document so far discovered which assures us that the figure was originally a reliquary and the quasi-relics of the rosebush seem like later insertions. Access to the inner cavity may be had by removing the panel which forms the back of the sculpture. Certainly a great deal could be put inside, including relics. One would expect a more specific receptacle, however, and the matter is uncertain. As discussed in our first chapter, statues were usually hollowed for technical reasons; the effectiveness of this procedure is apparent here. Although the surface of the work is abraded through wear, there is no indication of any cracking or splitting and the statue is amazingly well preserved.

The revealed surfaces of the wood were equally cause for surprise. The extraordinary beauty of its carving was wholly unsuspected beneath the metal casing. During the long process of restoration the character of this carving could be studied carefully. Unlike the St. Foy core, which was left an unworked wood cylinder, the Hildesheim wood core was worked and finished with the greatest care and subtlety. Indeed, it is a true statue which would be complete in itself even without its precious metal enrichment. The vigorous composition, especially evident in a profile view (Fig. 38), the strongly articulated lines of drapery folds and edges which are deeply and crisply carved, and the overall grasp of plastic volume are the achievements of a sculptor working in a powerful tradition. Behind this artist must be a long sculptural development which, although little known as yet, probably reaches back into the Carolingian era. An attempt has been made to sketch the nature of the Carolingian interest in freestanding sculpture in our chapter on origins above. The Hildesheim Madonna is surely a descendant of that earlier sculptural style and one of the oldest existing heirs to it.

The origin of the Hildesheim Virgin is not documented but an approximate date can be assigned to it by stylistic argument. It has often been associated with Bernwardian art of the first quarter of the eleventh century, and clearly its closest relative in style is the tiny Mainz ivory Madonna (Fig. 43) of this period, which is so similar in pose and drapery.[101] The proportions of the figures are alike and the broad, arching knees and heavy upper torso are common to both. Although differences in size and medium should be taken into account, these works are so alike in style and in the plastic conception of the figures that they must be roughly contemporary. The dating of the Mainz ivory ca. 1000 by Nordenfalk, which has been generally accepted, removes any previous doubt about the appropriateness of an early eleventh-century date for the Hildesheim Madonna.

Further confirmation of a Bernwardian date comes from the reliefs on the Hildes-

---

[100] We know that the statue was held in great esteem even prior to the sixteenth century when it was present at the ceremony in which homage was paid to newly elected bishops and when feudal oaths were sworn. Still, the sources explaining these practices cannot be traced before the fifteenth century, making us uncertain of the importance of the statue in eleventh-century life. See Chapter II, notes 38, 46 above, where these matters and the processions of August 1 have already been commented upon.

[101] C. Nordenfalk, "Der Meister des Registrum Gregorii," *Münchner Jahrbuch der bildenden Kunst*, I (1950), 61f.; Essen, *Werdendes Abendland*, no. 426.

heim doors. A comparison of the Madonna of the Magi scene thereon (Fig. 42) with the Hildesheim statue (Fig. 37) reveals a more attenuated style in the former but also a number of similar motifs: the manner in which the head cloth wraps about the neck, and then falls loosely over the shoulders and back, the folds on the sleeves of the Virgin which are handled in the same double-edged manner, the draperies at the sides of the legs and across the lower front of the figure. Allowing for differences of theme, medium and artist, these works seem products of the same school. The Madonna must be somewhat earlier than the doors of 1015, however, inasmuch as it is closer to the plastic forms of Ottonian art at the beginning of the century (e.g. the Bernward Cross, ca. 1006-1007,[102] and the Mainz Madonna, ca. 1000). The years ca. 1000-1010 thus seem most probable. Indeed, Bishop Bernward himself would be a likely patron.

The Hildesheim Virgin can, therefore, be distinguished stylistically from the Essen statue which belongs to an earlier phase of Ottonian art. They derive from different schools, and iconographically the two works also differ substantially. Unlike the Essen statue, the Child in the Hildesheim group does not recline in his Mother's lap, but sits upright, supported between her knees. This position for the Christ Child, centered and frontal, persists to the end of the twelfth century and predominates over other variants in the Romanesque period. The central and frontal position of the Child is not, however, the only new feature. The freedom of the structure of the Essen figures has been replaced by a more rigid ordering of form. The Hildesheim Madonna, although more imposing in its plastic volumes, has not the open, spatial conception of the Essen group, which invites the viewer to circle around it continuously because of its unfolding sequence of curved profiles. The artist who produced the Hildesheim Madonna had a new hieratic conception of the meaning of the group. To realize this objective he organized the composition as a closed, compact mass around a vertical axis which makes the front view dominate, like a facade, and reduces the side views to subordinate entities. Both Mother and Child have been schematized and subjected to a frontal arrangement of almost Egyptian rigidity. The shape of the Child repeats the larger shape of the Mother. The feet of Mary are not tucked together on one side, as in the pose of the Essen Madonna, but placed solidly on the base in a symmetrical and stable arrangement. Also the drapery follows a centralized pattern: the curving folds over the legs are carefully balanced about vertical folds between them; and the balanced disposition of the head cloth, falling over her shoulders symmetrically, is stressed by identical edgings. In the side view there is the same formalism. The knees of the Child repeat the shape of those of the Mother and the line of his back echoes the line of hers.

Happily, the system of design is not allowed to become oppressive. Its rigor is relieved in the side view by curvilinear incisions which delineate drapery, by the rounding of the shoulders of the Mother and the forward slant of the bodies, and by the subtle way in which the Mother's back arches forward and then back again while anchored to the stable, firmly rooted form of the lower torso. In the front view the symmetry and frontality are softened by several factors. The knees of the Mother are not perfectly parallel but splay outward as do those of the Child. Moreover, the drapery of the Child

---

[102] Essen, *Werdendes Abendland*, no. 554.

shows some free variation, as in the oblique folds which pull across his lap to his left knee, in the curvilinear emphasis of the upper drapery which loops over the girdle, or in the inventive edging of the folds.

Such strength of design, set off by sensitive modulations, qualifies the Hildesheim Madonna as an extraordinary work. Its mastery and beauty can be appreciated even in its decapitated state and are convincing evidence that by the early eleventh century freestanding statuary was already an accomplished fact. The ornamental metal sheath was ready to be shed at any time.

The monumental Madonna made for Bishop Imad (1051-1076), which is still preserved in the Paderborn Diözesan Museum (Figs. 44-46), comes from a very different artistic milieu.[103] Although the golden sheath is lost, the figure retains a sculptural beauty

[103] The lindenwood statue measures 112 cm. in height. At some unknown date a small relic compartment was cut into the large oval panel which is set into the back of the figure so as to be almost imperceptible (Fig. 44).

It has always been thought that the sculpture was originally covered with a gold repoussé sheath which was stripped off and melted down in the war of 1762 as tribute to Duke Ferdinand. This information was recorded by Anton Wennecker, the sacristan, who described the removal of the gold, recorded its weight and preserved for us the following fragmentary inscription, previously reported in 1654, which provides the chief support for an attribution to Bishop Imad (1051-1076): ". . . praesulis Immadi . . . tuorum libens eius devotum suscipe munus . . . Salvatorem mundi, quem pariendo tulisti . . . Stephanus protomartyr." At that time Mary evidently wore a crown of gold and pearls, but it seems unlikely that these were original ornaments.

The gesso simulation of a filigree border, visible prior to the most recent restoration, must have been added following the denuding of the statue, but whether immediately or in the restorations recorded for 1866 and 1886 is unknown. The polychromy from these refurbishings was removed under the direction of Alois Fuchs in 1917 and additional conservation treatment was undertaken in 1952. Currently, renewed study of the piece and a thorough technical examination have revealed data apparently inconsistent with some of our former conceptions of the statue's history and the extent of its alterations. New evidence has been found, suggesting a very early polychromy subsequently covered by an early gilded copper sheath of which the principal surviving fragment would be the metal cover of Christ's book. I am extremely grateful to my friend, Dr. Hilde Claussen at the office of the Landeskonservator, Westfalen-Lippe, for her generous courtesy in allowing me to consult the proof of her important publication regarding the restoration of the statue, just as my own book was going to press, and in sending me her new photographs of the sculpture so that these up-to-date views might be included here (Figs. 45 and 46). Dr. Claussen has gathered together and studied anew the texts relevant to the sculpture, including some unknown to Fuchs, and she presents fresh interpretations of them in the light of the recent technical discoveries; for a full description, see H. Claussen and K. Endemann, "Zur Restaurierung der Paderborner Imad-Madonna," *Westfalen*, 1/2 (1970), 1-27. Dr. Claussen's work will attract the most serious attention from scholars. Additional reports from the scientific tests being made will be published in due course.

For the earlier literature on the statue see: *Die Bau und Kunstdenkmäler von Westfalen, Kreis Paderborn*, ed. A. Ludorff, Münster, 1899, p. 98, pl. 44.1; A. Fuchs, "Die goldene Madonna des Bischofs von Paderborn," *Zeitschrift für christliche Kunst*, XXXI (1918), 30-35; E. Lüthgen,

which is apparent even in photographs. Like the Hildesheim Madonna, the Paderborn Virgin was a finished statue before it received its gold cover. In a comparison of the two, however, it is clear that the articulation of the surface is very different. The plastic treatment of projecting folds outlined by shadows in deep cuttings, which was distinctive of the Hildesheim example, does not appear in the later statue. The contours of the Paderborn figure remain fully rounded and the shoulders massive, but its entire surface looks flattened and settled. Even the pleats, which serve to outline the limbs and body, are reduced to mere parallel lines. They never penetrate deeply into the core of the sculpture. It is as if the torso were made up of sheets of wood arranged in thin, sharp-edged layers. Likewise, the lower part of the figure shows this tendency to stratified effect, as the surface is continually stepped back in a series of recessions. The result is a work which is as placid in tone as the carving is in manner. From it emanate the commanding calm and serene stillness of a truly monumental work of art.

The proportions of Mary are still comparable to those of the Hildesheim statue, the upper torso being relatively short and heavy. The lower part of the figure, on the other hand, shows a more rigid parallelism of pleats. An emphatic contrast is the reduced scale of the Child, which is difficult to explain. He is so much smaller in scale than the Virgin that he seems almost marginal in relation to the great woman who towers above him.[104] The Mother is obviously the leading figure and it is her role which is stressed.

The position of the Child on the left knee of Mary is a departure from the Hildesheim Madonna where an axial alignment of figures was seen. If the sculpture were placed at the side of the choir rather than behind the altar, as Alois Fuchs has

---

Romanische Plastik in Deutschland, Bonn and Leipzig, 1923, p. 15; Beenken, *Romanische Skulptur*, no. 12; Panofsky, *Die deutsche Plastik*, p. 79, fig. 9; Hamann, "Ottonische Plastik," p. 7f.; Redlefsen, *Mariendarstellungen*, pp. 13-14; A. Feulner, "Imad Anna oder Imad Madonna," *Pantheon*, XXI (1938), 160; Picton, *Early German Art*, p. 135; Fuchs, *Madonnen*, pp. 7-28 (here are quoted the pertinent ancient documents and sources known to Fuchs); H. Wentzel, *Niederdeutsche Madonnen*, Hamburg, 1940, pls. 14-17; Münster, Landesmuseum für Kunst und Kulturgeschichte, *Altwestfälische Kunst*, ed. P. Pieper, 1947, no. 1; Amsterdam, *Uit de Schatkamers*, 1949, no. 1; H. Eickel, "Die Madonna des Bischofs Imad von Paderborn, ein frühmittelalterliches Kultbild," *Festgabe für Alois Fuchs*, Paderborn, 1950, 45-52; Munich, *Ars Sacra*, 1950, no. 395; Keller, "Vollskulptur"; Münster, *Westfalia Sacra*, 1951-1952, no. 63; Wesenberg, *Bernwardinische Plastik*, p. 60; Essen, *Werdendes Abendland*, 1956, no. 526, pl. 55; Schrade, "Monumentalplastik," p. 61; Elbern, *Das Erste Jahrtausend*, no. 402/403; Corvey, *Kunst und Kultur im Weserraum 800-1600*, 1966, no. 29; Essen, *Marienbild*, 1968, no. 4.

[104] The Madonna was seen by traveling monks Edmund Martène and Ursin Durand in 1718. They were impressed with the golden statue but described it as a representation of St. Anne and Mary ("une figure de Saint Anne d'or massif, donnée autrefois par Imadus, evêque de Paderborn," *Voyage littéraire de deux bénédictins de la Congrégation de Saint-Maur, Second voyage*, Paris, 1724, p. 239, quoted by Fuchs, *Madonnen*, p. 11). The error in identification was probably due not only to the size and position of the Christ Child, but also to the somewhat feminine treatment of the Child. See A. Feulner, "Imad Anna," answered by Fuchs, *Madonnen*, p. 12f., and the recent thorough review of the question by Claussen (see note 103 above).

suggested,[105] an observer in the choir would face the Christ Child and would see the profile of the Virgin's head, which is more interesting than the frontal aspect of it. Indeed, her whole figure is more unified and expressive from the side (Fig. 45). The curve of the back, the looped sleeve and the cascade of the skirt combine in a slowly descending rhythm which expresses with unaffected grace the gentle serenity of the Madonna. Whatever position she occupied originally in the church,[106] the beauty of the design of the figure and its devotional appeal would have been arresting.

The earliest reference to the Paderborn statue is found in a treasure inventory of the late eleventh century. The texts relating to it have been gathered and discussed by Alois Fuchs, however, and need not be repeated here. A series of references to the figure precedes the 1762 record of an inscription which mentions the Virgin as a gift of Bishop Imad (1051-1076).[107]

We can be sure, therefore, that the statue is a work of the third quarter of the eleventh century. Comparison with other sculptures of this quarter, such as the Essen-Werden stone reliefs (Figs. 47a, b),[108] the Werden Crucifix,[109] or the St. George Crucifix,[110] reveals similar stylistic features. The Theophanu Book Cover from Essen

[105] *Madonnen*, p. 9, and my discussion with Professor Fuchs in 1959. See Chapter II, note 23 above.

[106] The placement of the group at the side of the choir is only a conjecture and may simply have been a later medieval arrangement. Were it not for the profile, off-center position of the Child, the figure of Mary would seem more strictly frontal, since the details of her form are arranged with some degree of symmetry, particularly from the knees down. Moreover, the departure from the frontality of the Hildesheim Madonna may also be explained as due to a divergent iconographic stream of influence, relating the Paderborn Madonna to the Virgins at Essen and Walcourt.

[107] For the inventory, dated by Fuchs in the twelfth century, "Die goldene Madonna," 33, see the recent study of B. Bischoff, *Mittelalterliche Schatzverzeichnisse*, I, Veröffentlichungen des Zentralinstituts für Kunstgeschichte in München, IV, Munich, 1967, p. 69; for the other texts, see Fuchs, *Madonnen*, pp. 7ff. For the inscription, see note 103 above. Claussen discusses all of these records in the light of recent evidence (see note 103 above).

[108] The question of the purpose (tomb or altar frontal) and the date of these reliefs is still unsettled. Whether made for Abbot Gero (1050-1063) or for Abbot Adalwig (1066-1081) cannot be decided here, but their style seems to this author appropriate to the later years of the 1050s, or ca. 1060, contemporary with the Imad Madonna. For a recent review of the subject, see R. Wesenberg, "Ein kleiner Bronzekruzifixus aus den Werkstatten der ehemaligen Benedictinerabtei Werden," *Miscellanea Pro Arte, Hermann Schnitzler zur Vollendung des 60. Lebensjahres am 13. Januar, 1965*, Düsseldorf, 1965, 132-143, N.B. 135-141. The subject of an Essen-Werden workshop has been discussed by Schnitzler, *Rheinische Schatzkammer*, p. 34; cf. R. Wesenberg, "Der werdener Bronzekruzifixus und eine Essen-Werdener Schule des 11. Jahrhunderts," *Bewahren und Gestalten, Festchrift zum siebzigsten Geburtstag von Günter Grundmann*, Hamburg, 1962, 157-163.

[109] F. Rademacher, "Der werdener Bronzekruzifixus," *Zeitschrift des deutschen Vereins für Kunstwissenschaft*, VIII (1941), 141-158, dates the Cross ca. 1060-1080; Essen, *Werdendes Abendland*, 1956, no. 491.

[110] Ca. 1067. See Chapter III, note 96 above.

(Fig. 36) is also comparable.[111] Particularly close are the Essen-Werden stone figures where the compactness of silhouette and the modeling of form through nested and echeloned planes of relief strongly resemble their counterparts in the Paderborn Madonna. Since a fire in 1058 caused a refurbishing of Paderborn ecclesiastical appointments, the statue was probably made soon afterward or ca. 1060, a date which is also appropriate for the stone reliefs and the bronze Cross at Werden. Moreover, the affinities to the Essen-Werden reliefs suggest that Imad may even have had the statue made in the Essen-Cologne area.

Almost certainly the Paderborn Madonna was the inspiration for the statue of the Virgin and Child in the Schnütgen Museum in Cologne (Fig. 48).[112] One recognizes the repeated use of the sleeve padding and the somewhat similar position of the Child. The broad folds of the lower legs suggest a sketchy version of corresponding parts of the earlier statue. The long upper torso, however, indicates the approach of the twelfth century and the more slender proportions of Romanesque style. Instead of the rounding of the back of the body and the slope of the front seen in the Paderborn Madonna, the later figure is perfectly erect and vertical. From the side one sees that the figure is uniform in thickness, the waist being small. Such characteristics suggest a date near the turn of the century. The motifs along the edge of the sleeves and at the neck, which relate to works by Roger of Helmarshausen, combined with the above stylistic relations to the Paderborn Madonna, suggest a Westphalian provenance of ca. 1100.[113]

The Madonna now in the Liebieghaus in Frankfurt-am-Main (Fig. 49) has been called an eleventh-century work,[114] but a date early in the twelfth century seems more

[111] Essen, *Marienbild*, 1968, no. 3.

[112] This walnut statue measures 69 cm. in height. It was acquired by the Schnütgen Museum from a private collection in Cologne. The feet, the lower edge of Mary's garments and the left hand of the Child are restored and there are a number of losses including the head of the Child and the right hands of both figures. The arrangement of Christ's left hand can no longer be determined due to a repair which obscures its form. The head of the Virgin has also been tampered with, and Hermann Schnitzler suggests a recarving in the Gothic era. Repairs to the throne and the triangular incision at the neckline are also modifications. The broad treatment of the figure suggests a metal covering, but there are no traces of nail holes so that this hypothesis seems unlikely. There is no indication of a relic cavity in the solid back of the figure. The statue is mentioned in the following: F. Witte, *Die Skulpturen der Sammlung Schnütgen in Cöln*, Berlin, 1912, pp. 32f., pls. 23-24; Lüthgen, *Romanische Plastik*, pl. IX; Redlefsen, *Mariendarstellungen*, pp. 15f.; H. Schnitzler, *Alte Kunst im Schnütgen Museum*, Cologne, 1956, no. 10.

[113] Cf. the portable altar in the Paderborn Cathedral, A. Fuchs, *Die Tragaltäre des Rogerus in Paderborn*, Paderborn, 1916; Münster, *Westfalia Sacra*, 1951-1952, no. 23. Earlier examples of a similar but simplified motif can be found in Mosan art, e.g. the Tongres ivory Crucifix, J. Borchgrave d'Altena, *Art mosan*, Brussels and Paris, 1951, p. 11.

[114] The statue is made of apple wood and measures 52.5 cm. in height. It was acquired by the Museum in 1928 from Krupp in Bendorf who had obtained it from a family in Coblenz. They claimed that it had come from the Siechenhaus, Coblenz. It was restored by the Museum in 1949. The losses of the feet of the Child and some fingers of his right hand are minimal. The head of

appropriate to its style. It marks the beginning of Romanesque tendencies in this series of Madonnas. The figure is related stylistically to the Paderborn Madonna, the drapery over the legs obivously deriving from that source, but a decided emphasis upon the central axis of the group and a rigid alignment of Mother and Child bespeak the approach of the new style. This insistent frontality recalls the Hildesheim Madonna, although the arching forms of the Hildesheim figure have been compressed into a more compact block. Thus the knees of the Hildesheim Madonna arch boldly outward but are strictly parallel in the Frankfurt figure. The folds which loop across the lower legs in the Hildesheim work have disappeared in favor of a thin layering of drapery like that of the Paderborn Madonna. There is only a trace of the greater freedom of older forms in the oblique drapery between the legs of the Child and the rather free folds of the drapery over Mary's breast. Proportions undergo an equally significant change. The upper torso is longer, the lower shorter. The heavy volumes of the earlier statues have thinned and are now contained within a slender, flattened cylinder. The mass of the Child is larger in relation to the Mother, a more perfectly balanced form within a form. The body of the Mother leans forward with a gentleness, however, which relieves the otherwise rigid play of verticals and horizontals, and the strict parallels of Mother and Child. The costume too has changed. The Virgin wears a mantle which is like a paenula in form. It falls over her arms and arcs into her lap. This is the type of garment common for statues of the Madonna in the twelfth century, particularly in France. Its appearance here marks a departure from the tunic of the Paderborn or Essen figures. Gone also is the separate head cloth which hangs to the shoulders, visible in the Hildesheim and Paderborn examples, as here the mantle simultaneously forms a veil for the head of the Virgin. Of interest too is the fact that the statue shows no sign of a relic compartment. Relics might, of course, have been deposited in the space hollowed out at the back of the throne, but there is no evidence to suggest that this large hollow was ever securely closed. By the end of the eleventh century, a reliquary function was evidently no longer likely for a statue of the Madonna in Majesty.

Although Hamann relates the Frankfurt Madonna to Auvergne Virgins of the twelfth century, he nevertheless concludes that it is much earlier.[115] He would date it in the first half of the eleventh century well before the Paderborn Madonna. This possibility seems precluded by the strict verticality of the figure, the elongation of the upper torso and the flattening of the surface treatment, all of which are anticipations of the new twelfth-century style destined to supersede the outmoded forms of early eleventh-century Ottonian art. Since the Paderborn Madonna retains much stronger reminiscences of that earlier Ottonian manner, we are warranted in assuming that the one at Frankfurt is later. A reasonable conjecture is that it belongs to the late eleventh century or, preferably, the early twelfth.

Mary seems reworked, however, while the jewelled brooch is clearly a later addition. There are some traces of an old polychromy. The back of the figure is solid. It is discussed by: Hamann, "Ottonische Plastik," 5-10; W. Müseler, *Geist und Antlitz der romanischen Zeit*, Berlin, 1938, p. 21, pl. 49; *Liebieghaus, Museum alter Plastik, Frankfurt-am-Main*, 1959, no. 9.

[115] Hamann, "Ottonische Plastik," 9.

While we have discussed only a handful of examples of Madonnas prior to 1100, they are distinctive sculptures and are widely enough separated in time to serve as stylistic paradigms for their periods. The lively sensitivity seen in the Essen Virgin, the forceful plasticity of the Hildesheim Madonna and the monumental, yet sensitive, detachment of the Virgin at Paderborn, illustrate the extraordinarily rich and varied development of Ottonian art. The trend from Ottonian to Romanesque style is interestingly demonstrated by a comparison of the side views of each of the figures considered. We turn from the rounded grace of the Essen Madonna (Fig. 31) to the arching thickness of the Hildesheim and Paderborn figures (Figs. 38, 45) and, finally, to the slenderness of the Frankfurt statue (Fig. 49). In the last there is an austere spareness and verticality which will remain the mark of twelfth-century statues, particularly in Germany, but also in France. It makes apparent the emergence of Romanesque style.

Into this skeletal framework it is still somewhat difficult to fit the three Madonnas in Belgium which are possible eleventh-century forerunners of French Romanesque Madonnas. From what remains of the sadly dilapidated Walcourt Madonna (Figs. 50 and 51), one can obtain only a general idea of its original form.[116] The work is of wood covered with silver repoussé in the manner of the Essen and Conques figures. It has suffered many losses and restorations and exhibits a number of ex-voto reliefs applied to the surface, which make it a puzzling pastiche. Nevertheless it is a rare and important work, since it is one of the few early medieval statues which retains most of its original metal casing. If we could remove the seventeenth-century metal masks, we might find more ancient faces which would help considerably in dating the figure; if we could study the carving of the wood beneath the main sheath, we might also discover significant criteria of date. At present only an approximation is possible, based on very inadequate information.

The sculpture is unusual in that a throne for Mary is not at first evident. Long sleeves fall to the ground at the sides of the figure and obscure what must be intended as a simple chair underneath. Also the Christ Child lacks the usual book in his left hand.

[116] The statue is about 63 cm. high and is still to be seen at the church of Notre-Dame, Walcourt. The silver plates covering the figures show innumerable repairs: a Gothic plaque of gilded copper engraved with figures of the Apostles at the back, a copper band of filigree ornament inset with gems at the base, various appliqués to the front of the work, and the heads of both figures which were added in 1626. The Gothic additions can be related to objects in the Walcourt treasury, suggesting a thorough restoration in the thirteenth century. Fragments of ancient textiles and a white corded sachet were found within the statue in 1886 so that it must formerly have been intended as a reliquary. Studies of the statue include: J. Borchgrave d'Altena, "La Vierge de pèlerinage à Walcourt," *La Revue d'art*, xxviii (1926), 56-61; J. Borchgrave d'Altena, "A Propos des Vierges en majesté conservées en Belgique," *Bulletin des musées royaux d'art et d'histoire* (1937), 16-17; J. Borchgrave d'Altena, "Le Trésor et le mobilier de l'église Saint Materne à Walcourt," *Bulletin de la société royale d'archéologie de Bruxelles*, ii (1938), 49-50, 56-57, figs. 34-36; Dom Thierry, *Notre-Dame de Walcourt*; J. Borchgrave d'Altena, *Madones anciennes conservées en Belgique, 1025-1425*, Brussels, 1945, pp. 6-7, pl. i; Lejeune, "Genèse," 48f.; Borchgrave d'Altena, "Madones en Majesté," p. 9; S. Collon, J. Lejeune and J. Stiennon, *Romanische Kunst an der Maas im 11. 12. und 13. Jahrhundert*, Brussels, 1962, p. 154, no. 3.

Reminiscent of the Essen statue is his position with the legs hanging limply over the side of Mary's lap. In marked contrast to the open composition of the Essen group, however, is the compact, almost huddled, effect of the Walcourt Madonna. Her high, angular shoulders, stiffly Romanesque in effect, have a contour very different from the oval form of German figures such as the Hildesheim and Paderborn Madonnas. Some other aspects retain an early character, such as the placing of the legs, not yet strictly parallel, the short upper torso, and the thickening of the silhouette toward the middle of the statue which contrasts with the more uniform shaft typical of a twelfth-century Romanesque Madonna.

Borchgrave d'Altena and Lejeune believe the statue to be the product of an art center in the valley of the Meuse in the eleventh century.[117] This area produced many monuments in metal during the first half of the following century, the famous works of Godefroi and Renier of Huy being among them. They attest to the high level of artistic activity which flourished there in the first half of the twelfth century. Unfortunately, the earlier monuments produced in the area from the period of Bishop Notger (972-1008) and later are lost. Parts of the Hadelin Shrine are among the few remnants of metalwork preserved from the entire eleventh century in the valley of the Meuse.

Owing to the lack of comparative material, any date assigned to the Walcourt Madonna will necessarily be a very tentative one. Although sources document the completion of the church of Saint-Maternus in 1026 by Oduin, the work having begun at the end of the tenth century, there is only legend to support a belief in an equally early date for the Madonna.[118] Nor does stylistic analysis yield results. Until more material is uncovered, we may provisionally accept Borchgrave d'Altena's dating in the second quarter of the eleventh century, soon after the beginning of Oduin's patronage, always bearing in mind that this is only a conjecture. The figure is so much of an anomaly that its date may be much later.

The wood Madonna from Hermalle-sous-Huy (Fig. 52), now in the Musées Royaux d'Art et d'Histoire in Brussels, can also be regarded as an eleventh-century sculpture on the basis of its stylistic affinity to the Cologne doors of St. Maria im Kapitol (ca. 1065).[119] Mary's face, with its protruding eyes and mouth, and the contour of

[117] Borchgrave d'Altena, "Le Trésor," 49-50, 56-57; Borchgrave d'Altena, "La Vierge de pèlerinage," 56-61; Lejeune, "Genèse," 48.

[118] Thierry, *Notre-Dame de Walcourt*, pp. 5-7, 22; Borchgrave d'Altena, "La Vierge de pèlerinage," 56-61. For the legend of the flight of the statue from a fire in the thirteenth century, see Chapter II, note 58 above. This miracle is commemorated in an annual festival in which the statue is carried in procession by young women of the community dressed in white.

According to another Walcourt legend, an oratory was dedicated to Notre-Dame in the ninth century by St. Maternus, Bishop of Tongres. He reportedly carved a wood statue of the Virgin and placed it on the altar of this church which burned in 992. Its rebuilding was undertaken by Wideric and finally completed by Oduin in 1026.

[119] This Madonna, 58 cm. in height, was recently freed from many layers of disfiguring polychromy. The figure of Mary and her throne were originally fashioned from a single block of wood. The Child was carved separately and doweled into place. There is no trace of a reliquary niche

130

her chin find parallels in the depictions of Mary on the doors. Similar features are seen in the Tongres wood head of Christ. The irregular curve of Mary's body, which repeats the arching form of the Christ Child, can also be found in the sculpture of the middle of the century (e.g. Regensburg).[120] This stylistic context suggests an origin in the Meuse area in the second half of the eleventh century—possibly the third quarter—for the Hermalle Madonna and Child.

An eleventh-century date has been projected for the stern-faced Virgin from Evegnée now in the Musée Diocésain, Liège (Fig. 53).[121] Although she wears a veil close to her head in the manner of the Hermalle Madonna and the head cloth falls about the shoulders and back as in the earlier Madonnas at Hildesheim and Paderborn, the extreme simplification of the form of the dress indicates a late rather than an early phase of this style. The frontality of the group and the strictness of the pose, evident in the erect, axial paralleling of Mother and Child and in the constraint of the figures, pertain to the Romanesque period. Therefore, while the work seems to derive from statues of the Hermalle type with respect to its simplified drapery and general composition, and while there is a hint of the Walcourt Madonna's form in the arrangement of the sleeves and in the Child's feet, the simple strength of the Evegnée Virgin nevertheless indicates a twelfth-century date. An origin in the Meuse valley seems likely.

---

in the solid back of the Madonna. Losses and restorations are numerous, affecting in particular the throne, the left hand of the Child (under which the book, the appropriate iconography, can be traced) and his head. The literature on the statue includes: M. Laurent, "Une nouvelle 'Sedes Sapientiae' romane aux Musées d'art et d'histoire," *Bulletin des musées royaux d'art et d'histoire*, IV (1932), 26-31; Borchgrave d'Altena, "A Propos," 16-17; Borchgrave d'Altena, *Madones anciennes*, p. 8, pl. IIIA; Liège, *L'Art mosan et arts anciens du pays de Liège*, 1951, no. 365; J. Borchgrave d'Altena, "Notes au sujet de sculpture en bois," *Bulletin des musées royaux d'art et d'histoire*, XXVII (1955), 4-5, fig. 1; Essen, *Werdendes Abendland*, 1956, no. 485; Brussels, Musées Royaux d'Art et d'Histoire, *Archéologie nationale, industries d'art, folklore*, 1958, no. 39.

For the Cologne doors, see: R. Hamann, *Die Holztüren der Pfarrkirche zu St. Maria im Kapitol*, Marburg, 1926; H. Schnitzler, *Die Holztüren von St. Maria im Kapitol*, Bonn, 1937; P. Bloch, *Die Türflügel von St. Maria im Kapitol*, München-Gladbach, 1959. For the Tongres Christ, see: Bloch, *op. cit.*; Borchgrave d'Altena, *Art Mosan*, no. 58; Liège, *L'Art mosan*, 1951, no. 362.

[120] For the sculptures of St. Emmeran, Regensburg (ca. 1052), see H. Karlinger, *Die Romanische Steinplastik im Altbayern und Salzburg*, Augsburg, 1924. Note also, however, the archaic flattening of the lower body against the front of the throne and the vertical arrangement of the feet which recalls the older manner of the Madonna in the Magi scene at Hildesheim (Fig. 42).

[121] The height of this oak Madonna is 46 cm. (54 cm. according to Lejeune) and comes from the chapel of Notre-Dame at Evegnée. Serious losses affect the throne and the lower portion of the figure of Mary. There is no trace of a relic compartment in her solid back. The iconography is unusual in that Mary holds the support of the throne with her left hand and an orb in her right, rather than securing the Child. Publications include: O. Melon, *La Vierge du Magnificat et la statue de Notre-Dame d'Evegnée*, Liège, 1925; Borchgrave d'Altena, *Madones anciennes*, p. 7, pl. II; Liège, *L'Art mosan*, 1951, no. 363; *Les Collections du Musée Diocésain de Liège*, 1959, no. 40; Borchgrave d'Altena, "Madones en Majesté," 8; Collon-Gevaert, *Romanische Kunst*, no. 4; J. Lejeune, *Liège de la principauté à la metropole*, Antwerp, 1967, pl. 6.

A question might now be raised as to whether all of the sculptures considered in this chapter can be regarded as belonging to the Throne of Wisdom type. Their enrichment with precious sheaths of silver and gold suggests that they were highly revered, in a manner appropriate to a Majesty, yet the examples where Christ is seated in a profile position do present a problem. At first sight the simple human relationship of maternal care seems to outweigh the profound theological meaning of the *sedes sapientiae*. As previously emphasized in connection with the Essen Madonna, the repoussé Madonna and Child on the Theophanu Book Cover is a true Majesty (Fig. 36), conforming to the Throne of Wisdom iconography, in spite of Christ's profile position.[122] Further evidence supporting such a conclusion is that the Walcourt statue shows Christ with his right hand raised in a gesture of benediction (Fig. 51). Very likely this was also the case in the statues at Essen and Paderborn, although the Child's right hand is a later restoration in both cases.

That these statues were considered Throne of Wisdom Majesties, despite the position of Christ, is further borne out by their individual histories. Each played an active role in the ceremonies within the religious communities, as already described. Clearly the numerous surviving twelfth-century examples are related generically to their predecessors, and therefore it is significant that many variants of a frontal pose of Christ appear among the later works. He may be seated obliquely with his ankles crossed or parallel; he may sit on Mary's left or on her right knee; or he may even be in a semistanding position. The main thing is that she is always shown as a throne for him. This is the essence of the *sedes sapientiae* iconography. The character of his pose may vary in accordance with regional interpretations, but a departure from frontality does not nullify the basic iconography.

The examples of Romanesque art in which the enthroned figures are labelled by a medieval inscription referring to the Throne of Wisdom iconography have been mentioned.[123] The Arezzo sculpture (Fig. 1), actually from the early thirteenth century, includes Magi. This is reasonable inasmuch as the typological parallel between Christ and Solomon was strengthened by the presence of the Magi who evoked, in medieval thought, the Queen of Sheba. The profile position for Christ is very common in Magi iconography, and indeed he is shown thus in the Arezzo relief. The inscription, moreover, actually refers to the lap of Mary as the seat of wisdom: IN GREMIO MATRIS: RESIDET SAPIENTIA PATRIS. The Beaucaire relief (Fig. 2), which Hamann relates to the sculpture of Saint-Gilles, has the same inscription; Mary is frontal, but the Child is shown from the side as at Essen, Paderborn and Walcourt. Therefore it must be conceded that a frontal position for the Christ Child is not an indispensable requisite for a Throne of Wisdom sculpture. To sum up, the only invariable conditions for such a statue, as proposed at the beginning of this study, seem to have been: first, that Mary be represented as a throne for Christ; and second, that the statue be readily portable.

[122] Essen, *Marienbild*, 1968, no. 3.

[123] See Chapter I, note 65 above. For discussion of the Beaucaire relief, see Hamann, *St. Gilles*, pp. 190, 358-359, fig. 456.

Conclusion

By combining the information available from literary sources with our knowledge of extant sculpture, a number of conclusions can be drawn regarding the Throne of Wisdom statue prior to 1100. Sculptural representations of Mary and the Christ Child enthroned were known from as far west as Ely, as far north as Cologne and Hildesheim, and as far south as the region about Clermont-Ferrand, an area so broad as to indicate a widespread, international development of the type in the tenth and eleventh centuries. Although some of the statues were made as reliquaries (Clermont-Ferrand, Abingdon, Ghent, Vézelay, Le Puy (?), Paderborn, Walcourt and possibly Essen and Hildesheim), not all of them were. Some were sheathed with precious metal (Clermont-Ferrand, Ely, Rodez, Essen, Hildesheim, Paderborn, Walcourt). It appears that a metal sheath was more likely to be applied in an early work, considering the more numerous later ones which show no evidence of such an overlay (Le Puy, Chartres, Châtillon-sur-Loire, Avallon, Vézelay, Abingdon, Ghent, Hermalle). In spite of this early tendency to mask the wood core, we do know that as early as the creation of the Hildesheim Madonna (ca. 1010), freestanding wood sculpture of the Virgin and Child was being carved in a fully developed form (Fig. 37). The survey we have made indicates that the sheath was no longer thought necessary, even in the first half of the eleventh century. By 1029 it would seem to have been optional, since there is no mention of one at Châtillon-sur-Loire.

The number of statues for which we can, by reason of literary sources or the evidence of extant works, consider a pre-1100 date is modest, sixteen in all. This figure excludes eighth- and ninth-century references which are less specific in character and also omits the examples which were probably made in the very early years of the twelfth century. Nevertheless the figure is large enough to suggest that a respectable number of examples of the type once existed and to indicate that the Throne of Wisdom, as a freestanding form of sculpture, was well established by the opening of the twelfth century. When French Romanesque sculptors began to produce the twelfth-century type of statue which is now most familiar to us, they were heirs to an old tradition and could draw upon a rich inheritance. In order to explain as fully as possible the background to their work, it has been necessary to discuss forerunners which survive in other countries and are helpful in filling the extensive lacunae in the French background. The development of the Throne of Wisdom in the twelfth century in France is our next concern.

CHAPTER V. The Twelfth Century

Regional Styles

THE LITERARY SOURCES reviewed in the last chapter assure us that a number of wood statues of the Madonna were to be seen in France during the opening years of the twelfth century, e.g. at Avallon, Châtillon-sur-Loire, Coutances, Le Puy and Vézelay; and many additional statues must have been produced early in the century. Curiously, only one such French Madonna, from Autun (Figs. 152 and 153, no. 87), has survived to the present day, while those which date from the second half of the twelfth century are very numerous. To a large extent this may be due to chance, yet the extraordinary difference in number does suggest that the popularity, and consequently the production, of the Majesties increased as the century wore on.

The statues were made in workshops all over France, despite the common view that their locus was limited to Auvergne. Without losing sight of the early golden Majesties of Clermont-Ferrand and Rodez, it is evident that early French Madonnas in wood came from ateliers farther north (e.g. Châtillon-sur-Loire, Vézelay, Autun) as well as Auvergne. The Auvergne statues are best known because of the publications of Louis Bréhier who attempted a classification of types in 1943.[1] He distinguished two representative styles: the first was illustrated by Madonnas from Saint-Nectaire, Saint-Rémy-de-Chargnat and Montvianeix (Figs. 75, 76, 60-63, nos. 15, 16, 3), the second by statues such as the Madonna now in the Louvre and those of Marsat and Saint-Flour (Figs. 98-100, 101, 97, nos. 34, 35, 33). Comparing the styles of the two categories, Bréhier thought one to be the outgrowth of the other. In the first group, an incisive, linear style is characteristic. Folds are rectilinear, with crisply cut edges which meet in sharp angles. This manner seemed archaic to Bréhier and he dated it in the beginning of the twelfth century, considering it an index to the early phase of freestanding statuary. The second group also shows a linear style, but the folds coil in a softer manner and the edges are smoothly rounded; they are curvilinear rather than rectilinear in profile. There are patterns of concentric loops as in the first group, but a tendency to simplify passages in the drapery is evident, particularly in the regular vertical folds of the tunic over Mary's knees. Bréhier thought that this second group reflected the influence of later developments in art. Therefore he regarded it as a fuller statement of the *Vierges romanes* type, and he dated it "after 1140." Together the two groups seemed to him to delineate the stylistic development of the century.

[1] Bréhier, "Vierges romanes," 26f.

134

Actually the situation is far more complex. Many styles obtained in the twelfth century, and Auvergne knew only a few of them. The two styles isolated by Bréhier do not represent a stylistic evolution but are in reality two parallel modes, contemporary to one another and basically similar in aesthetic conception. They simply illustrate the varying products of different workshops. The broad range of style which can be observed in France is due to variations in manner which correspond to regional preferences rather than to date.

Unhappily almost no historical documentation exists for the preserved Majesties so that their specific dates can rarely be hazarded. Analogies with relief sculpture in stone may provide a stylistic context and an approximate date. Although the hieratic severity of the wood Madonnas sometimes makes them seem retarded in style, there are enough close parallels to stone sculpture to indicate that their creators were aware of the stylistic innovations of the age. While some examples illustrate the persistence of a taste for calligraphic articulation of surface into the late twelfth century, even when contrary ideas were evolving, others show a response to the force of stylistic change which eventually brought about the Gothic movement in art. The influence of the jamb figures of Saint-Denis and Chartres was particularly strong, for we see the unmistakable reverberations of their styles in wood sculptures where Mary appears as a crowned queen with hair dressed in long strands bound with ribbon and in robes which illustrate fashions and mannerisms of the cathedral facades. Formal notions can also be traced to the second atelier at Saint-Denis and to Senlis, and can likewise be related to the style in stone at Mantes, Angers and Le Mans.

Although they were decidedly different in function, the wood statues resembled their counterparts in stone and shared their stylistic history. Consequently the wood statues are particularly useful in supplementing our knowledge of early medieval sculpture, e.g. in documenting styles when preservation is poor in stone and in giving us a clearer idea of the loci of workshop traditions. Since the wood statues constitute an international phenomenon, they portray very clearly the dissemination of styles transmitted across the frontiers of France to receptive centers in the Rhine and Meuse valleys and even in Alpine regions in Switzerland, Austria and Spain.

The statues which come from the Auvergne are distinguishable as a group even though they exhibit considerable variety. The woodworking technique of the area has already been commented upon[2] and need only be reviewed here. The sculptures are likely to be of walnut and are made of many pieces of wood which have been fitted together through skillful joinery so as to simulate a solid statue. The heads of the Mother and Child are usually doweled into place along with other small forms, such as the hands of the Child. The sculpture is carved carefully on all sides, the back being given particular attention. The total height ranges from approximately 70 to 82 cm.[3] The Christ Child usually wears a tunic with a *himation* (stole) or mantle wound about his shoulders and he is barefooted. Mary wears more elaborate robes: a tunic with long

[2] See pp. 16-19 above.

[3] For a discussion of measures, see Chapter I, pp. 15-16 above.

sleeves covered by a paenula, which is made from a large circular piece of fabric with an opening for the head similar to a chasuble. It forms a cloak-like veil and then drapes over the shoulders and arms and falls into the lap in an intricate play of pleats. The edges of the sleeves of Mary's tunic and its skirt, which drapes over her legs, are visible beneath the paenula. Normally she wears no crown and only a few strands of her hair are revealed beneath her veil. Christ is represented bareheaded. Mary supports him with both hands, while he holds the book in his left hand and makes the gesture of benediction with his right. The throne is usually arcaded, but its form is variable, as is the position of the Child.

Most distinctive of all, however, is the scheme of the drapery folds. In this the sculptor finds a vehicle for his creative genius. Like calligraphy or the fluting on columns, the pleats of the drapery form an abstract pattern expressive of intense energy. The scrolls and ovals which animate the surfaces serve also, like contour lines, to make the bodies tangibly apparent. They give the figures immediacy and presence while at the same time suggesting by the abstract linear configuration forms which are hieratically remote. The effectiveness of this combination of tangibility and transcendence is one of the outstanding accomplishments of the Auvergne sculptor.

The Morgan Madonna in the Metropolitan Museum in New York (Figs. 54-56, no. 1) is an excellent representative of a first group of Auvergne Virgins which exhibit that combination. Since the statue is obviously the work of an outstanding artist and since his name is unknown, we may refer to him for convenience as the "Morgan Master" after this masterpiece. The statues which relate to it stylistically are numerous (nos. 1-29) and include, as closest relatives, Notre-Dame de Claviers and Notre-Dame de Montvianeix (nos. 2-3). The Madonna at Heume l'Eglise (no. 4) is also a near relative though more remotely connected. Other related examples are Notre-Dame d'Aubusson and the Madonna at Parentignat (nos. 5 and 6) as well as Madonnas at Saint-Rémy-de-Chargnat, Saint-Laurent-Chabreuges and Chanaleilles (nos. 16-18).

Stylistically this group of Madonnas is characterized by intricate drapery patterns (Figs. 54-64). The body of the Virgin is wrapped in layers of crisp pleats, and the linear edges of these folds form vigorous rhythms which curve over the shoulders, dip low in back and loop over and between the legs of the Madonna. Occasionally the formation of the folds can become highly inventive and fanciful, attaining great beauty, as for example in the work from Montvianeix (Fig. 61). The arching catenaries of the Morgan Madonna's drapery (Fig. 54) contrast with the vertical creasing of the Child's mantle. Parallel folds cascade over his knees and terminate in an agitated zigzag hemline which is further set off by the hairpin folds of the tunic below. These rhythms are so strong that, despite the rigid frontality of the Child's pose, there is an excitement in the work. The same drive is conveyed by the confident, forward thrust of the Madonna's powerfully plastic arms and shoulders. Notre-Dame de Montvianeix demonstrates this order of vitality particularly well (Figs. 60-63). In combination with an energetic linearism in the drapery, the poses of both Mary and Christ are dramatically askew, tilting forward and to the left, so that the majestic frontal composition is enlivened with an indication of alertness. The facial expressions, although imperious, are

136

keen, with fleeting smiles of hauteur which temper the awesomeness of the Throne of Wisdom image. In the example of Notre-Dame de Claviers (Fig. 58) the theme is played in another key, as it were. The proportions of both Mother and Child are more elongated while the course of drapery folds moves in tighter curves. The energy of the design, heightened thereby, enhances the severity of the commanding expression.

Despite such differences in tone and varying states of preservation, these three statues are most probably the work of a single sculptor's hand. In technical details, so revealing of the artist's touch, the Morgan Madonna and Notre-Dame de Montvianeix are intimately related.[4] This is also apparent in the poses, proportions, drapery and particularly in the rendering of the physiognomies. In a comparison of Notre-Dame de Claviers and the Morgan Madonna, the facial features (Figs. 56 and 57) are so close as to make analysis and further argument hardly necessary. It is a reasonable conclusion, therefore, that all three statues are the work of the Morgan Master.

As further confirmation of the above conclusion, these three statues seem to reveal a definite artistic personality and something of its development. A comparison between Notre-Dame de Montvianeix and the Morgan Madonna indicates that in carving the former the artist was still somewhat tentative about his work. There are hesitancies in execution and a less proficient and elaborate technique. Trials are made with the fold system which occasionally reveals wavering edges, particularly in the back, whereas similar folds are executed with utter ease in the Morgan Madonna and in Notre-Dame de Claviers as well. The sureness of the hand of the master as we follow the course of the knife and the chisel in the Morgan Madonna indicates an artist who has established his style and exercises it deftly. His more accomplished technique is evident in the hair of Mary, which is more finely and intricately carved, and in the fold strata, which are again more elegantly cut, the ridges being raised and undercut to give greater clarity to the style. Details of the throne are also carved with more finesse, closer attention is given to ornamental edges, and the joinery is more elaborate. Both the silhouette, with its double curve at the back, and the pattern of folds are highly complex. Surely the Morgan Madonna is in the master's mature style. There is greater freedom in Notre-Dame de Montvianeix, as if the artist had not yet settled upon a formula for the fold system and as if, with youthful bravura, he enjoyed the broadly coursing folds which he turns into sinuous designs spread with intriguing, deviant symmetry across the pair of figures. Carving of details is delicate but this subtlety does not detract from the overall expression of the work, which is particularly poignant. The Montvianeix statue is one of the great masterpieces in its genre. The relationships among Notre-Dame de Montvianeix, the Morgan Madonna and Notre-Dame de Claviers suggest that Notre-Dame de Montvianeix is the earliest of the three while Notre-Dame de Claviers and the Morgan Madonna represent the artist's developed manner, but it would be hard

[4] A similar use of the knife and the chisel, revealed for the latter by the "chatter" marks, can be discerned, along with a like handling of doweling in the joinery process. This is particularly evident in the thrones where a similar treatment of plinths, bases and capitals is combined with identical joinery, even though the Morgan Madonna's throne, unlike the other, is one-storied. Both thrones have octagonal bases.

to determine a relative chronology for the last two sculptures. The Madonna at Heume l'Eglise (Figs. 64a and b, no. 4) must be closely associated with this triad, especially the Morgan Madonna, even if it is not by the Morgan Master's own hand, because the poses, proportions and linear rhythms of these works are all apparent in it.

A style similar to that of the Morgan Master, although inferior in quality, is seen in the related figures at Aubusson and Parentignat (Figs. 65 and 66). In both there is a comparable formula for the drapery, but an additional vertical panel which falls between the legs of the Madonna distinguishes the type. The two-storied throne is also characteristic. Other statues which follow this manner are discussed in the Register (nos. 5-13).

A second variant of the Morgan Master's work is seen at Saint-Rémy-de-Chargnat, Saint-Laurent-Chabreuges and Chanaleilles (Figs. 76-78, nos. 16-18). The throne is two-storied in the usual way and the poses are similar, although Mary's proportions are broader. The fully rounded shoulders are emphasized by the prominent nesting of folds, while the ends of the paenula are pulled forward over the arms. A horizontal band encircles the upper arm as ornamentation and a similar one runs from the neckline into the lap. The Child's drapery is slightly different than in the Morgan Master's work with a single set of broadly designed folds between the legs. Additional examples may be found in the Register (nos. 19-29).

A second stylistic group of Auvergne Majesties is represented by Notre-Dame-la-Brune from Saint-Pourçain-sur-Sioule, now in Tournus (Fig. 89, no. 30). Although this sculpture is heavily gilded and polychromed, its form represents the style of the group very clearly. Other members are Notre-Dame d'Orcival, Notre-Dame de Saint-Flour, now in Lyon (Musée des Beaux-Arts), the Madonnas in the Louvre and in the Martin Collection, New York, and the Madonnas at Chalus-Lembron and Marsat (Figs. 90-102, nos. 31-36). These statues are similar to those of the Morgan group, but the pose of the Child is usually different. He is often seated rather precariously, being poised obliquely on Mary's right knee or more or less centered in her lap. He appears active. Sometimes his legs are asymmetrically placed, turning to his left, and alternately covered by smooth drapery over one leg and a fall of folds over the other.

The robes of Mary and Christ are the same as those we have already observed in the Morgan Madonna type, but the fold system has a different character. The paenula fits closely over the head and falls across the shoulders into the lap in the same manner, and is articulated by a series of hanging loops reminiscent of the other except that over the arms they lose precision and appear crumpled or softly coiled. At the wrist the sleeve of the tunic falls into an elaborate drooping fold which hangs almost to the floor. The folds over Mary's legs are vertical and arranged in parallel fashion. Most characteristic is the inverted pleating of this drapery, which is found in every example and is particularly clear in the Tournus Madonna (Fig. 89). Over each ankle and between the legs are pleats which turn in, while alternating folds project outward in the usual manner.

At the back of the statue there is another scheme for the drapery. A continuous shaft of vertical folds fans outward and then curves symmetrically upward to the shoulders (Figs. 91, 99). The throne is ordinarily of two stories with four colonnettes below and arcades above, forming a cathedra-like box. It may be interestingly ornamented with decorative patterns of lozenges, frets and the like, but it is nevertheless heavier than its counterpart in the Morgan Madonna type and it exhibits simpler joinery.

The statues of a third category of Auvergne Madonnas (nos. 45-54) are illustrated very well by Notre-Dame de Saugues (Fig. 112, no. 45), the outstanding member of the group. Excellent examples of it are also to be seen at Monistrol d'Allier and La Chomette (Figs. 113-115, nos. 46 and 47) which, along with Saugues, are located in the Haute-Loire. The Madonna in this case wears priestly garb: the simple paenula becomes a chasuble, and over it is worn the archepiscopal pallium which is decoratively treated with an ornamental design and fastened by a large circular brooch. A second ornamental band may extend down the center of the sleeves and another down the center of the back. Symmetrically curving folds are arranged on either side of the pallium, adorning both the front and the back of the chasuble. Both the ecclesiastical vestments and their decorative features are a departure from the relatively simple clothing worn by Madonnas of the Tournus group. The basic conception of the Saugues type of statue, however, remains the same. The Child is similarly seated with the legs slightly turned and the drapery is similarly arranged. Mary's skirt is given the same vertical emphasis with the use of the inverted pleat system we have observed and the throne is of like four-columned form. Thus the Saugues group is really a variant of the Tournus style. It is the same basic statue with decorative additions.

In Notre-Dame de Saugues (Fig. 112) the familiar formula is executed in an especially interesting manner. The edges of the drooping oval folds in the chasuble are scored with an incision which parallels the contour of the fold and gives it salience. The creases of the sleeves are handled in similar fashion. The fineness of the work and the effectiveness of its expression are best seen in the head of Mary where an aristocratic, high-cheekboned visage, elegantly framed in an oval coif, presents an eloquent statement of majesty.

The three categories thus isolated through formal analysis are seen to be closely related, with the latter two particularly like one another. The differences among them are too slight for us to imagine one group as much earlier than the other. It is more likely that we are dealing with the production of two nearly contemporary ateliers, one of them being responsible for the style of the Morgan Master and its sub-variants, and the other for the sculptures of the Tournus and Saugues groups. The two supposed ateliers might, of course, be two manners practiced within a single shop or nothing more than two regional traditions with local variations. Without further documentation we cannot be more precise.

Attempts at the localization of the ateliers must also be very speculative. There is no certainty that even the statues which are still in churches have never been moved. As portable sculptures, they could easily have been displaced during their later histories. Yet the strong attachment of a country parish, or even a whole town, to its own Majesty would have normally awakened resistance to any threat of losing its beneficent presence. The Orcival Madonna, for example, is documented as being in her present setting since at least 1375. Also it seems significant that all the examples under discussion come from a relatively small area of France, the pre-1791 royal Province of Auvergne. Montvianeix, Aubusson, Parentignat, Saint-Rémy-de-Chargnat and Mailhat are in the Puy-de-Dôme, the first two near Thiers, and the last three near Issoire. Chanaleilles and Saint-Laurent-Chabreuges are further south in the more rugged Haute-Loire, and Notre-Dame de Claviers, Moussages, is from further west in the mountainous Cantal. Clermont-Ferrand thus suggests itself as a possible center of production for this group of statues. The Tournus type is represented by sculptures from Saint-Pourçain-sur-Sioule, Orcival, Chalus-Lembron, Marsat and Saint-Flour, towns which are located in the Puy-de-Dôme, except for the first, Saint-Pourçain-sur-Sioule, which is in Allier and the last, Saint-Flour, in the Cantal, south of Brioude. Examples of the Saugues type, our third group, are found chiefly in the Haute-Loire. Saugues itself, Monistrol d'Allier and La Chomette are a few kilometers south of Brioude. All the sites mentioned for the three styles are within a 150-kilometer radius of Clermont-Ferrand. Of course, the modern departments of France do not indicate medieval political boundaries. Moreover, the distribution pattern is not clear enough to associate an individual manner with a specific area. The three styles intermingle and are represented irregularly in all the departments discussed here, so that precise localizations are not readily discernible.

The dating of the three styles is also difficult. Unfortunately no dated sculptures in stone have yet been found which are close enough to the Morgan Master's work to help in dating his production or to suggest a chronology for the related statues. The Tournus group, however, can be related to several Romanesque relief sculptures which survive in Auvergne. The outstanding parallel is found in the figure of the Madonna enthroned in the Magi scene from the south portal of Notre-Dame-du-Port in Clermont-Ferrand (Fig. 110), which has already been discussed.[5] The throne is similar and the Child's position is identical though reversed. The drapery patterns for Mary's paenula and tunic, which are the identifying hallmarks of this group, are the same. Indeed, the inverted pleating of the skirt of the tunic is evident also in the other figures of the tympanum and lintel. In the past the stone reliefs have been dated loosely in the third quarter of the twelfth century or later, but only on the basis of conjecture. The sole surviving document indicates that work on the church was still in progress in 1185, which hardly constitutes evidence for the date of the carvings or for the vogue of this particular style. A recent student of the Notre-Dame-du-Port sculptures, Anne Lewis Miller, placed them ca. 1160 chiefly on the basis of internal stylistic evidence.[6]

A second parallel in stone is seen in the relief of the Madonna enthroned (Fig. 111) at Espalion-Perse (Aveyron), but it is even more problematic.[7] The drapery patterns, the physiognomic type and the throne are clearly related to the Tournus manner and a chronological association between this relief and our statues can justifiably be assumed, but the Perse sculpture is no better documented than the wood Madonnas. The history

[5] See Chapter II, note 65 above.

[6] *Ibid.*

[7] A. K. Porter, *Romanesque Sculpture of the Pilgrimage Roads*, Boston, 1923, fig. 405; *Vierges romanes*, pl. 79.

of the church is very sketchily known.[8] Perse was an ancient priory which had been donated to Conques in 1060 by Hugh of Colmont. Relations between the two monasteries, Conques and Perse, are established for the twelfth century as well. Since the sculptures which concern us have been rearranged several times, however, these records are of little assistance. Although the Perse relief does not help to date the wood Madonnas, it does amplify the stylistic context within which the portable statues must ultimately be evaluated.

The capitals at Mozat (Puy-de-Dôme) also show some stylistic affinity to the wood sculptures, although in a less specific idiom. The angel of the *quem quaeritis* scene and the Marys who approach the tomb show similar drapery mannerisms.[9] The arrangement of the folds of the mantle over the legs of the angel is very like the drapery of the typical Christ Child in our group. The Easter capital at Mozat, like the other capitals there and like the related capitals at Saint-Julien de Brioude and at Orcival, can be dated only in an approximate manner, in the middle third or second half of the twelfth century.

Looking further afield to monumental stone sculptures preserved in northern France, we find material which is better dated, but scholars have tended to consider the wood Madonnas of Auvergne conservative by comparison with more northern styles and have therefore been reluctant to use the latter for dating the Madonnas through formal comparisons. A stylistic lag is normally assumed for remote and mountainous Auvergne, and it is thought to have participated little in the artistic advances achieved by the Ile-de-France during the second half of the century. Yet we have no real evidence that this is so. Quite possibly those stylistic innovations of the 1170s and 1180s were echoed in a regional manner in Auvergne. Although the hieratic iconography of the Throne of Wisdom theme permitted little change in its basic composition, progressive sculptural qualities are evident. The sinuous and looping rhythms of both the Morgan and Tournus groups may be interpreted as the Auvergne response to avant-garde changes in regions of France further to the north. In any case the Auvergne Madonnas described here may safely be assigned, on the basis of general stylistic appraisal, to the second half of the twelfth century. One may reasonably venture to be more specific and assign an approximate date in the middle years of the second half of the century on the basis of the wider frame of reference provided by the stone sculptures which we found to be analogous. Such a period would make them contemporary with their more northern counterparts to be discussed below.

Another distinctive style which is loosely related to that of the Auvergne Madon-

[8] B. de Gaulejac, "Espalion: Eglise de Perse," *Congrès archéologique de France, Figeac, Cahors et Rodez, 1937*, Paris, 1938, 445-458; L. Saltet, "Perse et Conques, rapports entre deux portails voisins du douzième siècle," *Bulletin de la société archéologique du midi de la France*, XLVI (1917-1921), 72-92; H. Affre, "Notice archéologique sur l'église de Perse," *Congrès archéologique de France, Rodez, Albi, Mans, 1863*, Paris, 1864, 262-266; P. Merimée, *Notes d'un voyage en Auvergne*, Paris, 1836, pp. 192-194. The Last Judgment sculptures at Perse have been related to the Conques tympanum on the basis of iconographic similarities (Saltet, *op. cit.*) but stylistic resemblances between the Perse and Conques reliefs are not apparent.

[9] Porter, *Sculpture*, figs. 1225-1226.

nas is represented by Notre-Dame de Laurie (Fig. 122, no. 55) and by an example in the Philadelphia Museum (Fig. 123, no. 56). In these sculptures the Virgin is carved as a solid figure with the head separately doweled as in the Auvergne examples we have discussed. The figure of the Child is also separate and is placed on Mary's left knee. There is a paenula for Mary but it has an agitated hemline which forms a pattern of short, thick folds falling symmetrically about a longer center fold, and, in contrast to both Morgan and Tournus styles, it is completely undifferentiated above. The long, drooping sleeves recall the Tournus type of Madonna, however, as does the two-storied throne. Although little is known of this group of sculptures and it is not large enough to yield clear clues as to its extent, the fact that a small, relatively modern replica of Notre-Dame de Laurie exists in the church of Saint-Julien, Brioude, suggests that the type may have been widespread and that its production may have been localized in Laurie where the cult of Notre-Dame de Laurie was centered.

Also related to Auvergne is a small group of Majesties sheathed with base metal. These sculptures are made of wood and encased in plates of lead, tin or copper which seem to have been cast in moulds, as at Thuir (Pyrénées-Orientales), Châteauneuf-les-Bains (Puy-de-Dôme) and Prunières (Lozère). Marcel Durliat cites Bost's claim that the same mould was used for the Thuir and Châteauneuf-les-Bains statues (Figs. 124 and 125, nos. 57 and 58) along with Spanish examples (see the discussion under no. 57). The Prunières Madonna (Fig. 126, no. 59) was also made in this way. The resemblances among them are indeed remarkable, a result which such a system of reproduction would inevitably effect. The vestments of Mary, who wears a chasuble, plus pallium, recall the Madonnas of the Saugues group (nos. 45ff.) so that the possibility of these metal statues deriving from that source can be considered. However, crowns for both Mary and the Christ Child are featured in the metal statues and there is greater emphasis upon ornamental details such as gemmed borders. The treatment of the draperies is much broader and freer, and the style as a whole seems more appropriate to the thirteenth century than to the late twelfth. Despite their date discussion of these figures is included here because of the interesting evidence they present of the persistence of the metal-sheathed Majesty in the later period. These works were gilded in imitation of the earlier repoussé statues in precious metal but, as with most such simulations of gold and silver in baser metal, the lesser value of the product betrays the more modest aims of its artists.

From the Auvergne, which has traditionally been regarded as the preeminent domain of the *sedes sapientiae* statue, or even the only area where it flourished in the twelfth century, we can turn to other parts of France where the type was also prevalent in the late Romanesque period, as we now know. Two such areas in the southern and central part of France, which are no longer represented by important examples of the type but are none the less significant in a generic sense as indicating its widespread development, are the Pyrenees and an area located in the present department of Allier.

Statues from the Pyrenees introduce styles quite different from the stylistic families found in Auvergne. Two groups may be distinguished: those of the Pyrénées-Orientales and those of the Hautes-Pyrénées. The group in the Pyrénées-Orientales is well represented by the Madonna at Corneilla-de-Conflent (Fig. 127, no. 60), and includes Madonnas from Odeillo, Err, Prats-Balaguer, Montbolo and Planès (Figs. 128-132, nos. 61-65).[10] The most distinctive feature in this region is the throne, which is formed by columnar supports decorated with a spiral twist topped by a large pommel. The Child is usually supported on one knee of the Madonna, who is heavily proportioned, has broad facial features and normally, as in Auvergne, lacks a crown, although there are some exceptions. The drapery is strongly stylized, with a simple scheme of symmetrical, chevron-shaped folds falling over the legs and a vertical pleat in the center. A mantle of classical type reveals the decorative neckline of the tunic beneath it. The ornamental qualities of the group suggest that these sculptures, which now seem very modest in execution, have lost much of their original interest through heavy overpainting, faulty restoration and poor preservation.

In the Hautes-Pyrénées the statues are taller (about 79-83 cm. in contrast to 66-72 cm. in the Pyrénées-Orientales) and more slender in proportion, the effect of height being exaggerated by the Madonna's long, columnar neck, and by her high, peaked crown. She wears a cope instead of a mantle or paenula and a short veil as a head-cloth under her crown. The Child is centered in her lap and holds the book while making the gesture of benediction in the usual way. Also distinctive of the style is the detail that simple knobs terminate the four supports of the throne. A characteristic of the joinery is that the Child and the hands of the Virgin are often carved separately and doweled into place. The stylistic treatment is very broad, with drapery patterns reduced to skeletal schemes: a tunic made up of simple, inverted pleats over the legs and covered by a smooth, unworked cope which reveals the tunic's long flaring sleeves. The leading representative of this modest manner is the Madonna in the museum at Saint-Savin (Fig. 134, no. 67). A second Madonna in the local church at Saint-Savin and sculptures at Luz and Aragnouet are also members of the group (Figs. 135-137, nos. 68-70). The degree to which the style has been reduced to essentials, and the fact that the general form of the figures follows models known in the north of France, suggest that these Pyrenean works are of the late twelfth and early thirteenth century. Despite their date and *retardataire* manner, they are included here because of their interest as indicating the spread of Romanesque style across the southern frontiers of France. Affinities to Spanish sculpture are marked, but beyond the scope of the present discussion.[11]

[10] As this is a style which spans the Pyrenees, examples can be seen in Spain, e.g. the Madonna in the Cloister at Solsona (A. Malraux, *Le Musée imaginaire de la sculpture mondiale*, Paris, 1954, I, p. 487) and the Madonna from Urgel in the Barcelona Museum (no. 15936; W. Cook and J. Gudiol Ricart, *Pintura e imagineria románicas, Ars Hispaniae*, VI, Madrid, 1950, fig. 307). They are in turn related to the Virgin de la Selva in Gerona Cathedral (J. A. Sanchez-Perez, *El Culto Mariano en Espagna*, Madrid, 1943, pl. 201; Barcelona, *El Arte Romanico*, 1961, no. 261; Cook and Gudiol Ricart, *Pintura e imagineria*, fig. 301) and the Virgin at Montserrat, patroness of Catalonia (Sanchez-Perez, *El Culto Mariano*, pl. 160; Cook and Gudiol Ricart, *Pintura e imagineria*, fig. 304). The Altar of Angustrina illustrates the manner in which a Majesty could be combined with a baldachin and incorporated in a retable (Cook and Gudiol Ricart, *Pintura e imagineria*, fig. 159).

[11] See Cook and Gudiol Ricart, *Pintura e imagineria*, figs. 353, 354, 377-380.

Other Madonnas from the Pyrenees do not conform to recognizable stylistic categories in France but may be mentioned in passing: e.g. the Virgin from the church at Bourg-Madame, Hix (Fig. 138, no. 71) and Notre-Dame de Targassonne (Fig. 141, no. 74).

The famous statue known as Notre-Dame du Rocamadour (Puy-de-Dôme) is dressed with actual garments and is so enshrouded with veneration that it is difficult for the visitor to assess its antiquity (Fig. 143, no. 78). In photographs showing the sculpture without these encumbrances, it is seen to have distinctive though rustic form: tall, slender proportions, a narrow waist, thin arms covered by long trailing sleeves which descend to a broad triangle at the wrist, and a curious, bird-like face. The Child is seated on Mary's left knee and both wear crowns. These general features are also seen in Madonnas at Blesle (Haute-Loire) and Bellevaux-en-Bauges (Savoie), and in one formerly in a private collection at Frankfurt (nos. 75 and 76, Fig. 142, no. 77). The last two sculptures are closely related in style, showing comparable draperies. Despite the widespread locations of these examples, the similarities suggest a generic relationship which indicates still another type of French Romanesque Madonna in Majesty, whose localization can not yet be determined.

North of the Puy-de-Dôme we encounter a group of sculptures whose distinctive style is illustrated by a number of examples now in Nancy (Figs. 147, 149 and 150, nos. 82, 84 and 85). Mary wears a separate head-cloth as a veil and a robe which has wide, triangular sleeves edged with a simple band and articulated by nested, segmental folds which spin out from the elbow. The skirt is marked by two prominent folds at each side and two in front. The tunic is not visible. Mary holds the Child, who wears a distinctive tunic and a crown, in the center of her lap, supporting him with both hands. Since these sculptures are very curious technically, showing hollowing and joinery inconsistent with their style, and since they are closely related to garbled versions of Romanesque Madonnas (Fig. 108, no. 43, Fig. 148, no. 83) which are even more clearly replicas of medieval works, the antiquity of the group is certainly in question; but the particular fold arrangement for Mary's skirt and the form of her clothing in general are to be seen at Vernouillet (Allier) and at Souvigny (Allier). These two statues (Figs. 145 and 146, nos. 80 and 81) differ from each other in that Mary has a separate veil at Souvigny, but the smocked sleeves of the tunic are similar, the thrones are very like and there are other affinities, particularly in the pleating of Mary's skirt. The Souvigny statue itself, however, appears to be a renewal or a replica of a Romanesque Madonna, possibly modeled in part after Notre-Dame de Vernouillet. Therefore, the existence and extent of such a postulated regional style is problematic, although the recensions considered here do support belief in a Romanesque antecedent. A Madonna at Monteignet (Allier) also shows affiliation with the group, particularly in the pattern of the lower drapery (Fig. 144, no. 79). Since it is clearly an ancient, twelfth-century sculpture the Allier area suggests itself as a possible locale for such works. The questionable examples mentioned above are included for discussion here because they have interest in documenting an otherwise lost type of the *Vierge romane*.

144

Even more important than Auvergne for an understanding of the development of the *sedes sapientiae* statue during the twelfth century is Burgundy, where the wood Madonna in Majesty was known quite early. According to our literary sources, the type existed in Avallon and Vézelay in the opening years of the century,[12] but the sole survivor which has come down to us from before 1150 is the beautiful example from Autun, now in the Cloisters in New York (Figs. 152 and 153, no. 87). Its stylistic character is closely related to the Gislebertus workshop of ca. 1130 in Autun, as is indicated by its animated linear treatment of drapery—particularly the incisions and ridges, which are rhythmically gathered in groupings, twisted into spiral whorls and pleated into accordion-like edgings—and by the delicate emotional tone which also recalls Gislebertus. Such high quality gives it the uniqueness of a great work of art. Certain of its characteristics recur in another, somewhat later, Burgundian example, Notre-Dame de Bon Espoir in the church of Notre-Dame at Dijon (Figs. 154 and 155, no. 88). Tentatively we may conjecture, therefore, that there was a Burgundian manner for Romanesque Majesties.

Unfortunately, radical alterations to the Dijon Madonna's face have given her an ominous, distracting look. If one can ignore the face while analyzing the work as a whole, it will be recognized as an interesting and significant example. Common to it and the Autun Madonna are such persistent features as Mary's crown and veil, the type of costume, the finely ribbed drapery and also the technical execution, both figures of Mary being carved from single pieces of wood which have been hollowed in back rather than joined, as was the practice in Auvergne.

Clearly later in date than the Madonna from Autun, the Majesty at Dijon betrays influences of new stylistic developments in the Ile-de-France and other areas of northern France, which begin to assert themselves while blending with its earlier, native Burgundian characteristics. Vigorously surviving is the preference for linear articulation of surface by curvilinear and angular patterns, which enliven the form and add decorative interest. The propensity is evident in the veil, ornamented with a cascade of chevrons below a whorl at each shoulder, and also appears in the designs of the robe. Contrasting with such indigenous delight in surface patterns of line is a quite different use of arching folds over the abdomen and of concentric circles at the breast to express the organic structure under the surface, conveying a sense of a substantial body and its slumping weight. This new assertive corporeity is in marked contrast to the barrel-like trunk of the Autun Madonna whose calligraphically animated surfaces and flipped-up fold at the hemline have decorative independence and are not motivated by the structure of the body. They are inextricably related to the total, formal expression of the sculpture, but that expression does not depend upon the dictates of organic reality. In the Dijon example, on the contrary, the artist's awareness of the human body, with its real attributes, as the basic motif is evident in the more massive form of the figure, its suggestion of substantial weight, the greater thrust of the knees and the projecting arms of Mary. The materiality of the latter is obtruded by an ingenious arrangement of the

[12] See above, pp. 32ff., 102.

145

veil, which falls about the arms in graceful contraposition (Fig. 155). It hangs over Mary's right arm but is tucked below her left, indicating the volume of each and their separateness from the abdomen. The long, slender tresses of hair, bound their full length with ribbon, follow the edge of the veil and serve as an armature undulating across the three-dimensional form and arching over to stress the forward thrust of the head. At Mary's right shoulder the veil's irregular edge contrasts with the robe beneath, convincingly suggesting layers of fabric in depth. The tunic and robe function similarly in defining Mary's skirt below.

The use of the tunic, robe, veil and hair as vehicles for new stylistic ideas—specifically the rendering of more lifelike forms—has hardly reached a classicizing stage. Still, these changes are in accord with the formal conceptions which were also evolving in northern France in the second half of the twelfth century. Indeed, the hair style which featured long braids or tresses bound with ribbon was a fashion so generally popular in that area as to awaken the ire of St. Bernard. It emerged in monumental sculpture with the Saint-Denis column statues now destroyed (Fig. 156)[13] and can be seen at Chartres (Figs. 160 and 161),[14] Etampes (Fig. 158)[15] and Corbeil (Essonne, formerly Seine-et-Oise),[16] Ivry-la-Bataille (Eure)[17] and Saint-Loup-de-Naud (Seine-et-Marne),[18] as well as at Saint-Bénigne in Dijon, as known from Plancher's engravings.[19]

The circular stylization at the breast is also prevalent in these locales, e.g. at Chartres (Fig. 159), Etampes (Fig. 158), Châteaudun (Eure-et-Loire),[20] Saint-Quentin-les-Beauvais (Oise),[21] Vermenton (Yonne),[22] etc., and at Saint-Denis[23] (Fig. 157). To what extent they may have derived it from the art of various centers farther west in France is an intriguing but unresolved problem. We do know, however, that decorative spirals and whorls occur with the greatest frequency in the Romanesque period in Burgundy.[24] They may well have passed from centers such as Autun and Vézelay to Saint-Denis, Etampes and Chartres, where they were metamorphosed and, of course, blended with other ingredients to form a style which spread widely and became a supraregional manner. It seems to function as an intermediary lull between Romanesque and Gothic, not quite belonging to either. Its terminal function with respect to Romanesque is to quiet the dynamics of the latter. In contrast to the complex linear webs which

[13] For the engraving made from Montfaucon's drawing (Fig. 156) and for other examples, see Montfaucon, *Monumens*, I, pls. VIII, XVII.

[14] Cf. Katzenellenbogen, *Chartres*, pls. 28, 30, 33.

[15] Porter, *Sculpture*, figs. 1463-1464.

[16] *Ibid.*, fig. 1467.   [17] *Ibid.*, fig. 1478.   [18] *Ibid.*, fig. 1493.

[19] Dom Plancher, *Histoire générale et particulière de Bourgogne*, Dijon, 1739, opp. p. 503.

[20] Porter, *Sculpture*, figs. 1425-1427.

[21] *Ibid.*, fig. 1432.   [22] *Ibid.*, fig. 1500.

[23] Cf. *ibid.*, figs. 1441, 1444; Montfaucon, *Monumens*, pl. XVI.

[24] I. Forsyth, "The Mabon Madonna," *Mary, Throne of Wisdom*, Collegeville, Minn., 1963, pp. 4-10. Examples in Burgundy are too numerous to mention individually. A notable instance is the series of elegant whorls of the Cluny ambulatory capitals. A particularly interesting detail of the circular stylization at the breast occurs in the Vézelay tympanum where the Assyrians are represented, M. Aubert, *Les Richesses d'art de la France, La Bourgogne*, Paris, 1927, I-II, pl. 27.4.

animated figures with such energy and excitement, such transports of ecstasy, at Autun and Vézelay, a simpler, more static linearity followed in the new "intermediate" style. It is equally schematized but more restrained, e.g. circles replace spirals. The febrile tempo of Romanesque Burgundy seems visibly slowed in anticipation of the more pliant, more earthbound style ahead, as if this intermediate manner represented the moment of reflection necessary for the advent of a new style, the Gothic. Such a *détente*, preparatory to a new departure in art, can be compared to that which occurred at the end of the Middle Ages.

For all its linearity, the intermediate style was coincident with advances in the natural rendering of the human form; the new sense of tangibility in the figures at Chartres and Saint-Denis has often been noted. Perhaps their *détente* character represents the experimental period necessary to make the traditional technique of abstract line express the new interest in natural form. The success of the experiment is evident in the Dijon Madonna, apparently a Burgundian reflection of the intermediate style developing in the Ile-de-France. The style ran on into the fourth quarter of the twelfth century in some areas of France while in others it was replaced sooner by the developments stimulated by the second atelier at Saint-Denis, Senlis and, above all, Mosan art. The Dijon Majesty can therefore be dated in a general sense to the third quarter of the century, probably in its early years. Less characteristic but related examples from the Burgundian area are discussed in the Register (nos. 89-95; Figs. 162-167).

In Lorraine the style of the latter half of the twelfth century has been appraised as developing from Burgundian roots.[25] The most representative Madonna in Majesty which has come down to us from this period in Lorraine (Figs. 168 and 169, no. 96) is at Mont-devant-Sassey (Meuse). As in Burgundy, the statue is hollowed out in back; Mary wears a separate veil; she is crowned and she holds the Child, also crowned, centered in her lap. These features recall Notre-Dame de Bon Espoir in Dijon as do the revealed strands of hair which wind into her lap.

In his account of the style of the Lorraine region, Norbert Müller-Dietrich has emphasized the close parallels which exist between the stone reliefs from the apse cycle of the church at Verdun-sur-Meuse and our nearby wood Madonna at Mont-devant-Sassey. Included among the Verdun reliefs is an Annunciation scene in which Mary is represented with long tresses and Gabriel's hair is coiffed in orb-like curls. Both of these features appear in the wood sculpture and there is a strong resemblance between the rendering of the garments in each case.[26] If the Adam Master of Verdun was responsible for both the wood and stone sculptures, as Müller-Dietrich asserts, then the Madonna at Mont-devant-Sassey would date soon after 1147, the time of the completion of the Verdun works. However, another parallel for the long, free hair style and

[25] Müller-Dietrich, *Romanische Skulptur*, pp. 70, 164. Léon Pressouyre expresses reservation about Müller-Dietrich's theories and presents an alternate explanation, which stresses the importance of Mosan influence, in "Reflections sur la sculpture du XIIème siècle en Champagne," *Gesta*, IX/2 (1970), n. 36.

[26] Müller-Dietrich, *Romanische Skulptur*, pp. 81-84 nn. 314-325, fig. 40.

curious garment of Mary is found in the figure of the Queen of Sheba among the embrasure statues at Saint-Loup-de-Naud (Seine-et-Marne). These column statues have recently been dated around 1160-1162.[27] An even closer parallel to the Mont-devant-Sassey Majesty is the Madonna in stone from the previously discussed Adoration of the Magi scene on the tympanum of the Lorraine church at Pompierre, which appears to represent a performance of the *Officium Stellae* (Fig. 7).[28] The Virgin and Child there seem a rendition in stone of our wood Madonna in Majesty and they are so close in style that they must be contemporary. In addition to identical costumes, both have heavy-jowled, square faces and a massive immobility. The blockiness of the figures seems a local characteristic, known also at Verdun and Metz. Unfortunately, the Pompierre reliefs are dated only in an approximate manner to the second half of the twelfth century. That they recall the Chartrain style of the middle of the century in a number of ways, particularly in the rendering of the draperies of the Three Kings, tells little regarding date since Ile-de-France mannerisms lingered long in this area. Still, considering all of the comparisons cited here as a group, a date in the third quarter of the century seems appropriate for both the wood sculpture and the stone tympanum.

To sum up, stylistic analysis of the wood Madonna at Mont-devant-Sassey reveals a mixture of formal elements: some seemingly due to local influences, such as the traits which can be seen at Verdun and Metz, and others evidently coming from further afield, since they are known in Burgundy and in monuments created under the influence of Ile-de-France ateliers.

It is the greatest good fortune that we have one wood Majesty which is the key to a more precise chronology for a final group (nos. 102-108). The handsome Romanesque Madonna in the Fogg Museum of Art at Harvard University (Figs. 178-181, no. 102) shows a remarkable affinity, in its overall style and details, to the Coronation tympanum at Senlis whose date in the 1170s, first proposed by Sauerländer, is now generally accepted (Fig. 182).[29] Mary wears a crown in both cases; her hair is coiffed in the same fashion; and her veil similarly descends in long, thinly pleated, vertical folds which fall directly over her right shoulder but are flipped capriciously over her left. The exu-

[27] Pressouyre, "Reflections," 23; the usual dating of ca. 1167 depends upon F. Salet, "Saint-Loup-de-Naud," *Bulletin monumental*, XCII (1933), 129-169, N.B. 166. The sculptures are illustrated in Porter, *Sculpture*, fig. 1453.

[28] Müller-Dietrich, *Romanische Skulptur*, pp. 92-103, stresses the contribution of Metz in explaining the style of the tympanum; see the discussion in Chapter II, notes 67-68 above; cf. Schmoll Gen. Eisenwerth, "Sion," for an explanation of the iconography.

[29] The literature on Senlis is vast, including the following basic studies: M. Aubert, *Monographie de la cathédrale de Senlis*, Senlis, 1910; Pia Wilhelm, *Die Marienkrönung am Westportal der Kathedrale von Senlis*, doctoral dissertation, Hamburg, 1941; W. Sauerländer, "Die Marienkrönungsportale von Senlis und Mantes," *Wallraf-Richartz Jahrbuch*, XX (1958), 115-162; W. Vöge, "Das Westportal der Kathedrale von Senlis und der plastische Stil am Ende des 12. Jahrhunderts," *Bildhauer des Mittelalters, Gesammelte Studien von Wilhelm Vöge*, ed. E. Panofsky, Berlin, 1958, 54-59; Katzenellenbogen, *Chartres*, pp. 56ff.

berant rhythm of this last motif is almost a hallmark of the Senlis style. The Virgin's cope is also similarly treated in both examples, with folds fanning radially from a brooch at her throat to the smoothly moulded contours of her shoulder where the fabric is pulled taut to reveal the substance of the body before descending over her arms and knees in further fine folds. The Child's draperies are modeled in like fashion, the thickly gathered folds of his mantle being flung diagonally across the chest in a pattern followed also on the column statues at Senlis.[30] With her left hand the Fogg Madonna secures bunched folds from the end of Christ's mantle against his chest; the motif of drapery clasped in one hand is a feature of the Senlis style, as illustrated by the column statues of David or Abraham, or Mary in the tympanum. It is also present in works which are related to Senlis, such as the torso from Notre-Dame, Paris, now in the Cluny Museum.

The strong features of Mary's face in the wood statue, although fashioned broadly, are subtly expressive of alertness tempered by a tragic gentleness. It is a face very like that of the sister figure in the stone tympanum. The face of Christ resembles that of the angels on the archivolt fragment from Notre-Dame, Paris, now in the Louvre, which Sauerländer has associated with Senlis. Despite the loss of most of the original crown and the forehead, it is a memorable one. The high cheek bones, the subtly modulated gradations of surface, especially sensitive about the firmly rounded chin and in the slight indentations at the corners of the mouth, express patrician graciousness. A similar loftiness of mien radiates from the superb heads from Mantes[31] and recalls some of the sculptures at Châlons-sur-Marne.[32] The entire group represents a late stage in the sculptural genealogy analyzed by Sauerländer, which extends from ca. 1160 to ca. 1185, and includes Notre-Dame in Paris, Saint-Denis (Valois Portal), Senlis, Mantes and Châlons-

[30] Sauerländer, "Senlis," figs. 65, 67.

[31] The Mantes heads have been the subject of active discussion recently. Cf. M. Aubert, "Têtes gothiques de Senlis et de Mantes," *Bulletin monumental*, XCVII (1938), 8-11; J. Bony, "La Collégiale de Mantes, les circonstances historiques," *Congrès archéologique de France, Paris-Mantes, 1946*, Paris, 1947, 201-202; Sauerländer, "Senlis," 148-150; L. Grodecki, "La 'Première sculpture gothique,' Wilhelm Vöge et l'état actual des problèmes," *Bulletin monumental*, CXVII (1959), 283-284; Cleveland Museum of Art, *Treasures from Medieval France*, ed. W. Wixom, 1967, no. III, 37; Raleigh, The North Carolina Museum of Art, *Sculpture and Decorative Art, A Loan Exhibition of Selected Art Works from the Brummer Collection of Duke University*, ed. R. Moeller, 1967, no. 10; Providence, Rhode Island, Museum of Art, Rhode Island School of Design, *The Renaissance of the Twelfth Century*, ed. S. Scher, 1969, no. 57; L. Pressouyre, "Sculptures retrouvées de la cathédrale de Sens," *Bulletin monumental*, CXXVII (1969), 114; New York, *1200*, 1970, nos. 2-4.

[32] L. Pressouyre, "Sculptures du premier art gothique à Notre-Dame-en-Vaux de Châlons-sur-Marne," *Bulletin monumental*, CXX (1962), 359-366; W. Sauerländer, "Skulpturen des 12. Jahrhunderts in Châlons-sur-Marne," *Zeitschrift für Kunstgeschichte*, XXV (1962), 97-124; W. Sauerländer, "Twelfth-century Sculpture at Châlons-sur-Marne," *Acts of the 20th International Congress of the History of Art, New York, 1961, Studies in Western Art, I, Romanesque and Gothic Art*, Princeton, 1963, 119-128; L. Pressouyre, "Fouilles du cloître de Notre-Dame-en-Vaux de Châlons-sur-Marne," *Bulletin de la société nationale des antiquaires de France*, 1964, 23-28; Cleveland, *Treasures*, 1967, III, 27; Paris, Louvre, *L'Europe gothique, XIIe-XIVe siècle*, 1968, nos. 3-19, N.B. nos. 5, 19; New York, *1200*, 1970, no. 7; Pressouyre, "Reflections."

sur-Marne.[33] The Fogg statue fits comfortably within this context. Since its closest parallels are the works preserved from the Senlis atelier, particularly the Coronation tympanum, it may be attributed to a Senlis master and assigned a date close to that of the tympanum in the 1170s.

These conclusions are significant since the Fogg *sedes sapientiae* is a critical figure in discussion of our final group of statues. Its localization clarifies the positions of the others. The Majesty at Jouy-en-Josas known as La Diège (Fig. 183, no. 103) has already been compared to Senlis by Sauerländer.[34] The handling of the veil with its long, trailing, vertical folds, the loop of fabric under Mary's left hand, the knot in Christ's mantle, are all familiar Senlis features. In the radial folds of the cope, La Diège resembles the Fogg Majesty as well, and there are other details which make the association close. Consequently a place of origin in the Senlis area and an approximate date in the 1170s seem appropriate also for La Diège.

The Madonna at Limay (Fig. 184, no. 104) follows in this suite, its affiliation with La Diège being evident in the chair-like throne, the curious iconography of angels supporting the Christ Child, and in the dress of the Virgin. The more relaxed tone and the more gracefully curving movement of the thicker drapery suggest some of the sculptures at Mantes, particularly figures of the north portal. The heavy, almost baroque swirls of the angels' drapery and of the folds over Christ's left thigh in the wood sculpture invite comparison with the angels of the Mantes tympanum and support a date soon after 1175 and an origin in the same area, which Limay's proximity to Mantes would also suggest.[35]

A helpful comparison for these three wood statues is provided by the stone Madonna from Saint-Martin, Angers (Maine-et-Loire), in the Yale University Art Gallery (Figs. 188a, b).[36] The Madonna's veil was once wound about her head in an enfram-

---

[33] Sauerländer's penetrating and convincing analysis has been generally accepted by students of the period. See: W. Sauerländer, "Beiträge zur Geschichte der Frühgotische Skulptur," *Zeitschrift für Kunstgeschichte*, XIX (1956), 1-34; idem, "Senlis"; idem, "Die kunstgeschichtliche Stellung der Westportale von Notre-Dame in Paris," *Marburger Jahrbuch für Kunstwissenschaft*, XVII (1959), 1-12; idem, "Art antique et sculpture autour de 1200, Saint-Denis, Lisieux, Chartres," *Art de France*, I (1961), 47-56; idem, "Châlons-sur-Marne"; idem, "Twelfth-century Sculpture"; idem, *Von Sens bis Strassburg, Beiträge zur kunstgeschichtlichen Stellung der Strassburger Querhausskulpturen*, Berlin, 1966. Cf. L. Grodecki, "A Propos de la sculpture française autour de 1200," *Bulletin monumental*, CXV (1957), 119-126; E. Kitzinger, "Byzantium and the West in the Second Half of the Twelfth Century: Problems of Stylistic Relationships," *Gesta*, IX/2 (1970), 49-56, N.B. 54.

[34] See the discussion in the Register, no. 103. [35] See Register, no. 104.

[36] G. Forsyth, *The Church of Saint-Martin at Angers*, Princeton, 1953, pp. 175-176 nn. 41-42; A. Mussat, *Le Style gothique de l'ouest de la France, XII-XIII siècles*, Paris, 1963, pp. 206-208; L. Schreiner, *Die frühgotische Plastik Südwestfrankreichs, Studien zum Style Plantagenet zwischen 1170 und 1240*, Cologne and Graz, 1963, pp. 7-18; L. Schreiner, "Style Plantagenet: Entwicklung und Deutung, 1180-1220 und die Rezeption in Westfalen," *Akten des 21. Internationalen Kongresses für Kunstgeschichte in Bonn, 1964, Stil und Überlieferung in der Kunst des Abendlandes*, I, Berlin, 1967, 155-163; New York, *1200*, 1970, no. 8.

ing, oval twist before drooping over her left arm in the telltale, Senlis manner, and the draperies over her knees relate her to other wood sculptures in this final group (Figs. 186, 187, 189, nos. 106-108), which also shows some affinities to Le Mans sculpture; these are discussed in detail in the Register. The pattern of distribution indicated by the possible places of origin for the entire group is therefore of great interest. As far as we can determine, the sculptures come from Senlis, Villetain near Jouy-en-Josas, Limay, Paris, Le Mans and Saumur, all within the northwestern area of central France. Their production in the 1170s and 1180s would also connect some of them, notably those from Le Mans and Saumur, with the early Plantagenet style.

A final comment may be made about the position of this particular group of wood Madonnas within the broader context of the period. The group demonstrates nicely the spread of a Senlis manner southwestward as far as Anjou. The presence of Senlis ideas to the east, in Champagne, has already been widely recognized, the sculptures at Châlons-sur-Marne being a most visible manifestation. The role of Mosan art in inducing this stylistic phenomenon has also been discussed in the specialized literature devoted to the period.[37] The puzzling fact which emerges from our present study is that little of the Senlis manner is discernible in the wood sculpture produced on the eastern borders of France in Lorraine. This is particularly curious in that Verdun-sur-Meuse, in the Mosan area, could be expected to give some immediate reflection of the germinative style in which Nicholas of Verdun might at that time have been reared, and to give some hint of the Mosan artistic impulses which were about to be disseminated widely, perhaps as far as Senlis itself.[38] If Verdun harbored such nascent stirrings at that time, they are not reflected in the retarded fashion of the Majesty of Mont-devant-Sassey.[39] Nearby Châlons-sur-Marne, on the other hand, does seem to have absorbed Mosan ideas, and it was certainly receptive to the fashion issuing from Senlis.[40] The stylistic situation in the

[37] Sauerländer, "Senlis"; Sauerländer, "Twelfth Century Sculpture"; Pressouyre, "Reflections."

[38] We have noted earlier the stylistic connection between the Lorraine Majesty at Mont-devant-Sassey and the conservative work of the Adam Master at Verdun (see pp. 147-148 above).

[39] Distinctions between traditions in metalwork and monumental sculpture should be kept in mind. They have been discussed by Pressouyre with regard to stone sculpture and metalwork in Champagne, "Reflections." Apparently metalwork was the progressive art in the Mosan area.

[40] See Pressouyre, "Reflections." Cf. note 33 above. A manuscript miniature which is clearly related to the early style of Nicholas of Verdun (British Museum MS Harley 1585, fol. 13, portrait of a physician) illustrates a seated figure whose draperies are reminiscent of Senlis because of their fine radial folds fanning out to the shoulder and knees in the manner of the Fogg Madonna and because of the handling of the ends of the paludamentum, which recalls Senlis along with Châlons-sur-Marne. The miniature has been dated ca. 1160 and attributed to Liège (with a question mark, by Swarzenski, *Romanesque Art*, fig. 483), but a later date in the century, along with a possible Champagnesque origin, has also been suggested (Grodecki, "La première Sculpture gothique," 287 n. 1). Sauerländer has related the miniature to Senlis and Mantes style considering it to be of Mosan origin, ca. 1160 ("Senlis," 141-142, fig. 84; see n. 72 for the earlier literature).

Note also that the Burgundian Madonna at Thoisy-le-Désert (Fig. 163, no. 90) bears some comparison with the Senlis group of Majesties and its stone relatives: the curious type of crown

whole eastern area was obviously very complex and is only now being explained. No matter how it is eventually evaluated, clearly the style at Senlis was strong enough to impress itself upon the character of sculpture produced all the way from Angers to Châlons-sur-Marne in the 1170s and 1180s, a development which can be recognized as a major trend affecting the course of stone sculpture style in this period.

Conclusion

From our study of more than a hundred French sculptures of the Throne of Wisdom subject, a number of conclusions can be drawn. Since our concern has been limited to a single theme, a clear demonstration of the evolution of style might be expected. Indeed, the forerunners to French sculpture which are still preserved in Germany and Belgium from the eleventh century, discussed in Chapter IV, do illustrate the unfolding course of Ottonian art in an exemplary way. The same is true in a general sense for the twelfth-century sculptures in France. The Autun Madonna (Figs. 152 and 153, no. 87) may be seen as preparatory to the Dijon Madonna (Figs. 154 and 155, no. 88) which in turn has a close relationship to Mont-devant-Sassey (Figs. 168 and 169, no. 96). This series of three sculptures illustrates the dissemination of Burgundian stylistic traits as they are admixed with formal ideas radiating from the first atelier at Saint-Denis and from Chartres. Unfortunately, however, we do not have examples preserved in sufficiently large numbers from every decade of the century to allow analysis of similar progressions for all periods. The sculptures are numerous for the second half of the century, particularly from the decades of the 70s and 80s. During these years we can establish a rough chronology, but it can hardly be called "Darwinian." The Morgan Master's work (Figs. 54-63, nos. 1-3) seems to be contemporary with the Lorraine Majesty at Mont-devant-Sassey (Figs. 168 and 169, no. 96) and with the Madonnas in the Senlis group (Figs. 178-181, 183-187, 189, nos. 102-108). But these groups represent parallel, regional styles which coexist without one inexorably leading to another. They simultaneously express the sculptural preferences of the region while reflecting to greater or

---

is reminiscent of Limay (Fig. 184, no. 104), the looped drapery held in Mary's right hand recalls Jouy-en-Josas and the Fogg Madonna (Figs. 183, 178, nos. 102-103), and the mobility of the Child suggests Saint-Martin, Angers (Fig. 188). The drapery differs in form, however.

The elegantly elongated Madonna in the Boston Museum which reflects currents of Mosan art—see H. Swarzenski, "A Vierge d'Orée," *Bulletin of the Museum of Fine Arts*, Boston, LVIII (1960), 64-83—and has been compared with similar sculpture in western France, particularly the tomb of Eleanor of Acquitaine at Fontevrault (ca. 1204-1210, A. Erlande-Brandenburg, "La Sculpture funéraire en France vers 1200," paper read at the symposium, "The Year 1200," Metropolitan Museum of Art, March 25, 1970), also compares stylistically with the Madonna enthroned from the church of Saint-Yved, Braisne (Aisne), of ca. 1205-1216 (Paris, *L'Europe gothique*, 1968, no. 35) and with the north transept sculptures at Chartres, of ca. 1204-1210 (Swarzenski, *loc. cit.*). Therefore the Boston Madonna must date from shortly after 1200, unfortunately too late for further discussion here. For a study of this style in manuscript painting, see F. Deuchler, *Der Ingeborg Psalter*, Berlin, 1967.

lesser degree the course of change affecting the production of art in the century as a whole. Our study has allowed us to discern style clusters which help to localize wood-sculpture centers in the second half of the twelfth century. Clermont-Ferrand, Corneilla-de-Conflent(?), Dijon, Senlis and Verdun seem to have harbored ateliers, or at least groups of wood sculptors, working in a distinguishable manner. Rather than constituting a workshop which produced Throne of Wisdom statues in quantity and according to standardized patterns, each of these centers appears to have functioned as the nexus of a style which cannot be geographically circumscribed, which overlaps that of neighboring areas, absorbing and transmitting ideas in the creation of a local manner, and which is more or less distinct and more or less vital. The range of variety within each style is such that fixed workshops with controlled standards seem less likely than concentrations of independent artists working in accord with regional traditions. The existence of itinerant ateliers would seem to be ruled out as being unnecessary because the statues themselves were so mobile.

Although the Madonnas we have studied are difficult to date and place exactly, this has proved to be relatively possible with some examples from the last few groups of statues discussed (nos. 87-108). We may take heart that it will some day be realizable for Auvergne sculptures as well, when that area is better studied and understood. In any case, it can no longer be thought that Auvergnat wood sculptors were hopeless rustics, provincially removed from the main artistic streams affecting stylistic developments in the twelfth century. The artists of the wood sculptures seem to have experienced the same delight in innovation which stimulated the stone sculptors. Statues made in Burgundy or northern France such as the Autun Majesty at the Cloisters (Figs. 152 and 153, no. 87) and the Senlis Majesty at the Fogg (Figs. 178-181, no. 102) speak with such concentration and clarity in the artistic language of their ambience and period that we can conclude that their masters were tapping vital currents. The distillation of the period is too strong in them for us to believe that their artists lagged behind the van or were remotely out of touch. On the contrary, the wood sculptors seem to have shared the same ideas and to have reacted to the same sources of inspiration as their fellow artists in stone. The demands of the *sedes sapientiae* subject matter prevented them from experimenting with iconography, but stylistically, they were just as likely to try out new motifs as their confrères. No claim is made here that a single sculptor carved both in stone and wood. Because of technical demands and because of what we know of the organization of wood ateliers in the thirteenth century,[41] this seems unlikely, but surely it was possible. Adelelmus, the earliest creator of a Throne of Wisdom statue on record, was sculptor, architect and goldsmith at once.[42]

The stone representations of the Throne of Wisdom most readily called to mind are the beautiful sculptures of the Madonna enthroned in the tympana at Chartres (Royal Portal), Reims, Bourges and Notre-Dame, Paris. Curiously, none of these has an exact approximation in wood. Majesties in wood use motifs seen in the column statues of mid-twelfth-century Saint-Denis and Chartres, but the particular costume worn by Mary in the tympana cited, the style of her drapery and the character of Christ's tunic

[41] See Chapter I, note 34 above.   [42] See pp. 96-97 above.

as he makes his gesture have not yet been found in wood parallels. Were it not for the strong evidence of the literary sources, the existence of eleventh-century wood Madonnas outside France and the fortunate survival of the Autun Majesty, one might have falsely interpreted this inconsistency as a *terminus post quem* for the vogue of the French *Maiestas*. As it is, the influence of these particular enthroned Madonnas in stone upon the production of wood Majesties is subject to question.

In the light of this situation, Hamann's theory that the enthroned Madonna from the Chartres tympanum served as a model for Auvergne Majesties must be modified. He quite rightly pointed out that the wood sculptures of Auvergne are not the source for Chartres (Royal Portal) style, but one cannot agree with his simultaneous conclusion that the Auvergne Madonnas represent a regression.[43] When we realize that the regional styles of the Madonnas are for the most part contemporary with one another, the Morgan Master's work can be understood as the Auvergne counterpart to the phase of style represented by the second Saint-Denis atelier, Senlis and Mantes, rather than a holdover of early Romanesque style from Languedoc or Burgundy, or even a later interpretation of Chartres (Royal Portal). The looping, elliptical draperies of the Morgan Master reveal a rhythmic mode of sensibility which is more attuned to the ebullience of Senlis style than to the rigid tenor of the Chartres portal. If the crisp carving of the Morgan Master's work is seen as an element native to his individual manner and beloved in the area where he worked, rather than an archaism, the relationship becomes clear. Sauerländer's claim that the sources of the Senlis style were to be found in the second Saint-Denis atelier rather than the first, and in the archivolts of the St. Anne portal at Notre-Dame, Paris, rather than in the tympanum,[44] is therefore a view which our findings would support.

The evidence which we have presented, spanning several centuries from Carolingian times to 1200, indicates that the wood representation of the Madonna as the Throne of Wisdom was a phenomenon which originated in the late Carolingian period, developed profoundly in the Ottonian era and flowered in Romanesque times. For all its iconographic distinctness, its stylistic course paralleled that of monumental sculpture in stone. When there are lacunae in the latter, it can provide significant information on the history of medieval style. Nevertheless, the object of the present study has not been to buttress the otherwise well-supported stylistic studies of Romanesque stone sculpture, but to reveal something of the intrinsic interest of these works in wood.

When installed in their churches, these handsome sculptures had a lofty function. Although occasionally serving as reliquaries, they were not fashioned chiefly for that purpose; nor were they meant solely to satisfy the needs of private piety. The majestic, hieratic visualization of the *sedes sapientiae* which they afforded to local altars as well as to processions, dramas and other ceremonies within the community, made them authentic representatives of the Virgin and her Son. Behind them stood the belief that "the truly divine had entered into experienced history, into verifiable reality. This,

[43] Hamann, "Madonna," 99.
[44] See note 33 above, N.B. "Senlis," figs. 71-73, and "Notre-Dame in Paris," 1-12.

154

according to Christianity, was what happened in the Incarnation."[45] The statues were visible demonstration that the Incarnation was not merely abstract and remote history. Through their agency its message could be comprehended as a perpetually meaningful reality. The authors of the official stand taken in the *Libri Carolini* were not quite ready to indulge this function of art, fearing idolatrous results. Such reluctance was overruled as sculpture's power to evoke this dogma, central to Christian thought, was realized. In the veneration of the image devotion passed to the prototype so that the worshiper, in a vicarious sense, stood before God incarnate.

The process by which sculpture was accepted as having religious validity in the West, bears many similarities to the emergent cult of images in the East. There, religious images "acquired the position and function which imperial images had enjoyed."[46] Their entrance into religious life was chiefly fostered by the "desire to make the presence of the Deity and of the saints and the succour which they could be expected to give, visually palpable."[47] In the West that palpability was given additional reality through the use of the third dimension and it was endowed with an expression of transcendence through the use of a *Maiestas* pose.

In view of their *raison d'être*, the formal response which these sculptures show to the stylistic forces which shaped the art of their periods is of the greatest interest. They were evidently not considered as detached from the mainstream of art, or in any way exclusively privileged with a formal stylistic canon of their own. Nor were they conceived of as simple vessels devoid of aesthetic value because of their exalted role as intermediaries between two worlds, the material and the immaterial. Their artistic quality suggests that, even for such an important commission as the creation of a sculpture intended to have a transcendental function, the artist and his style could not be separated. The momentous achievement of the Romanesque Throne of Wisdom is not that it sanctioned the cult statue in the Christian Church,[48] but that its style conveyed so convincingly the medieval vision of humanity and divinity interfused. The felicitous blend of tangibility and abstraction which is peculiar to Romanesque style was perfectly consonant with the essential meaning of the image.

[45] G. Ladner, "Gibbon's Problem after Two Centuries," *The Transformation of the Roman World*, ed. L. White, Jr., Berkeley and Los Angeles, 1966, 69.

[46] Kitzinger, "Images," 125. This article gives eloquent explanation of the genesis of the image cult in the East.

[47] *Ibid.*, 149.   [48] *Ibid.*, 85.

Register of Principal Examples

The symbol § indicates that the author has personally examined the sculpture. Inclusion in the Register does not imply authentication of the statue. Replicas are sometimes listed when useful in documenting Romanesque style and demonstrating distribution of types. Unless otherwise noted, the sculpture is found in the only church of the town mentioned; the name of the statue, as distinguished from the church, is in italics. M.H., followed by a date, indicates when classified by the Monuments Historiques, Paris. *Liste des objets meubles* indicates the list of portable works of art maintained by the Monuments Historiques in Paris; local listings can also be consulted in its offices in the departments of France.

§ 1. [Figs. 54-56, Frontispiece]
NEW YORK, METROPOLITAN MUSEUM OF ART

> Acc. 16.32.194
> Ex collections: Morgan, Hoentschel, Molinier
> Walnut, polychromed
> H. 78.7 cm.

> Second half 12th century

This Majesty was the gift of John Pierpont Morgan to the Metropolitan Museum in 1916. Except for the loss of both hands and feet of the Child, the work is well preserved.

Although a rectangular break in the breast of the Madonna may conceal a relic cavity, the carelessness of the cutting of this aperture and the manner in which the panel was inserted after the splitting of the wood above had been sustained, indicate that it is was not a part of the original conception of the statue. However, in the back of Mary's left shoulder (Fig. 55) another panel has been so skillfully fitted into the body of the sculpture and its carving incorporated into the drapery system that it is almost invisible to the naked eye. It appears to be original. Its purpose is unknown, but it may possibly conceal a cavity in the manner of the Vézelay Madonna (see pp. 32-36 above), in addition to relieving pressure caused by expansion and contraction of the wood.

The facial type of the Virgin and Child and the drapery of the figures relate the carving very closely to Notre-Dame de Claviers (no. 2), and Notre-Dame de Montvianeix (no. 3) and, more distantly, to the Madonna at Heume l'Eglise (no. 4). These statues are surely products of the same Auvergne workshop, and the first three, at least, are probably by the hand of the same master. Technical details of the first three (such as the handling of the chisel, doweling and joinery) also argue for a single source. Because this sculpture most clearly represents a widespread type, it is referred to as the "Morgan Madonna" in the text, and its artist as the "Morgan Master" (see the discussion under no. 3 and in the text pp. 136-138). Other related Madonnas are at Aubusson (no. 5) and Parentignat (no. 6).

BIBLIOGRAPHY: A. Pératé and G. Brière, *Collections Georges Hoentschel*, Paris, 1908, I, 11, pl. XXI; J. Breck, *Metropolitan Museum of Art, Catalogue of Romanesque, Gothic and Renaissance Sculpture*, New York, 1913, no. 108, pl. p. 109; J. Breck and M. Rogers, *The Pierpont Morgan Wing, the Metropolitan Museum of Art*, New York, 1925, fig. 11; M. Freeman, "A Romanesque Virgin from Autun," *Metropolitan Museum of Art Bulletin*, n.s. VIII (1949), ill. p. 114; *Art Treasures of the Metropolitan*, New York, 1952, pp. 48, 220, no. 37; Forsyth, "Magi and Majesty," 215-222.

§ 2. [Figs. 57-59]

MOUSSAGES (CANTAL),

SAINT-BARTHELEMY

Notre-Dame de Claviers

M.H. 30-6-1908
Wood, polychromed
H. 81 cm.

Second half 12th century

The cleaning of this Majesty by M. Maimponte in 1958 (see Enaud) revealed afresh its distinguished character: viz. the interesting early polychromy, the fine carving, the air of imperiousness in the expression, and the clear association with the Morgan Madonna (no. 1). Notre-Dame de Claviers approximates the Morgan Majesty in size, pose, facial treatment and drapery patterns, even though its proportions as a whole are more svelte. Also close are Notre-Dame de Montvianeix (no. 3) and the Madonna at Heume l'Eglise (no. 4). To the present author these four sculptures are products of the same Auvergne workshop and the first three, at least, are probably from the hand of a single sculptor (called the Morgan Master in the text, see the discussion under no. 3 below). More distantly related are the Madonnas at Aubusson and Parentignat (nos. 5-6). The throne of Notre-Dame de Claviers is restored and both hands and feet of the Christ Child are missing. There is no compartment cut into the reverse of the statue. The colors preserved are a blue mantle over red dress for Mary, a carmine mantle over a blue tunic with gilt borders for the Child.

An early tradition which claimed this statue to be one given to Claviers by Raoul de Scorailles before his departure for the Holy Land in 1098 (see Chabau) was discredited by Dr. Cany in favor of a twelfth-century date.

Although the statue was formerly carried annually to the mountain chapel of Jailhac where it was venerated during the summer months of the year, it is now replaced there by a replica. Notre-Dame de Claviers herself has been permanently installed in a niche in the northeast wall of the sanctuary of the church of Saint-Barthélémy.

BIBLIOGRAPHY: J. Chabau, *Sanctuaires et pèlerinages de la Vierge dans le voisinage de Saint-Flour*, Paris, 1888; H. Delmont, *Guide du Cantal*, Aurillac, n.d.; Bréhier, "Vierges romanes," figs. 17, 29, 55; Dr. Cany, "Les trois Offrandes du Sire Raoul de Scorailles," *Bulletin historique et scientifique de l'Auvergne*, LXIII (1943), 195-203; *Liste des objets meubles ou immeubles par destination classés parmi les monuments historiques*, Dept. Cantal, Paris, 1951, p. 41 (the statue is dated in the eleventh century here); Gybal, *L'Auvergne*, p. 100; Aurillac, *Orfèvrerie*, 1959, no. 25; F. Enaud, "L'Exposition d'art sacré de Haute-Auvergne," *Les Monuments historiques de la France*, V (1959), 191; A. Beaufrère, *Richesses de la France, Le Cantal*, LXIII (1965), 130, 141; A. Muzac, *Sculpture romane de Haute-*

Auvergne, Aurillac, 1966, pls. 42-46; For-syth, "Magi and Majesty," 215-222, n. 2.

§ 3. [Figs. 60-63]

PRIVATE COLLECTION

Notre-Dame de Montvianeix

From the chapel of Saint-Victor-
Montvianeix (Puy-de-Dôme)
Walnut, traces of polychromy
H. 68 cm.

Second half 12th century

According to Bréhier, this Madonna comes from the chapel at Saint-Victor-Montvianeix where she was known as Notre-Dame de Montvianeix. He records ("Notre-Dame de Montvianeix") that black paint covering the faces of both Mother and Child was removed along with other superficial polychromy in 1931, revealing the medieval conception of color for the statue: flesh tints for the faces and hands, a blue mantle over a red dress for Mary and a red mantle over a green tunic for the Child; the garments were ornamented with gilded borders. Traces of this scheme survive. Serious losses are minor: the left hand of Christ (inaccurately restored some decades ago), the fingers of his right hand, his feet and all but one column from the upper story of Mary's throne. There is slight insect damage to parts of the surface and there are some repairs to the base. A small circular opening (diam. 1.12 cm.) in the back accommodates a dowel and could hardly have contained a relic. The joinery in the sculpture is impressive, the statue being composed from at least eighteen separately carved pieces of wood which have been doweled together so that the seams are almost imperceptible. Traces of fine linen beneath the original polychromy survive in some areas.

This sculpture is a particularly handsome piece and has long been admired. Its close relationship to the Morgan Madonna and to Notre-Dame de Claviers (nos. 1 and 2) is apparent in the faces, postures, poses, proportions, drapery patterns and, more specifically, in technical details such as joinery and carving technique. Also closely related is the Madonna at Heume l'Eglise (no. 4), although its quality is less outstanding.

These first three sculptures are probably the work of a single artist from Auvergne whom I have called the Morgan Master (see the discussion in the text, pp. 136-138). The elegance of his style is well expressed by the drapery of this statue. It is reduced to a system of abstract lines which express through their subtle undulations of ovals, loops and cascades a gentle, lyrical mood. The linear system serves at the same time to outline and model the simplified forms. Inner mood and outer form are one, as in music. Particularly felicitous is the carving of the heads. The surfaces of their simple oval forms are modulated into facial expressions of youthful confidence, with a fleeting smile of petulance. The majestic, formal character is thus interpreted with sensitivity and the result is a sculpture of subtle vitality.

Unfortunately it is not yet possible to localize the oeuvre of the Morgan Master or to date individual examples, but the distribution of these three statues and the sculptures related to them (e.g. the Madonna at Heume l'Eglise, no. 4, Notre-Dame d'Aubusson, no. 5, and the Madonna at Parentignat, no. 6) suggests a locus northeast and southwest of Clermont-Ferrand in the Puy-de-Dôme. Their affinity to the stone sculpture of Notre-Dame-du-Port at Clermont-Ferrand (Figs. 5, 110) suggests that the Master may have centered his work in Clermont.

BIBLIOGRAPHY: L. Bréhier, *L'Art chrétien*, Paris, 1918, p. 223, no. 3; Bréhier, "Clermont," 209; Bréhier, "Notre-Dame de Montvianeix," 193-198 (in which a date of ca. 1150 is postulated); Bréhier, "Communication," 383-384; Bréhier, "Vierges romanes," figs. 1, 43; A. Malraux, *Le Musée imaginaire de la sculpture mondiale*, 1, *La Statuaire des origines à 1900*, Paris, 1952, figs. 467-468; Gybal, *L'Auvergne*, p. 100; W. Messerer, *Romanische Plastik*, Munich, 1964, fig. 61, pp. 44-47.

§ 4. [Figs. 64a and 64b]
HEUME L'EGLISE (PUY-DE-DOME)

Wood, polychromed
H. 74 cm.

Second half 12th century

The cleaning and restoration of this sculpture during the late 1960s—chiefly affecting Mary's hands, the tip of her nose and her throne, the tip of Christ's nose, his feet (?) and minor areas of surface damage—brought to light another Majesty attributable to the workshop of the Morgan Master. Although the statue is not as high in quality or as well preserved as the closely related pieces discussed above (Figs. 54-63, nos. 1-3), and despite the fact that the present restoration of polychromy makes it impossible to detect features of the sculptor's personal technique (such as chisel strokes), the Morgan Master's style is immediately apparent in the fold system of Mary's paenula, the character of her coiffure and the expansive proportions of her torso, which are very like those of the Morgan Madonna (no. 1). The treatment of the tunics of Mary and the Child, on the other hand, is less elaborate. Owing to the modern restoration of the faces, particularly the noses, comparison of facial types is difficult. In any case the statue surely comes from the Morgan Master's immediate circle, if not from his own hand.

A small recess cut into the back of the statue, possibly for relics, appears to be a later alteration of the work.

BIBLIOGRAPHY: Bréhier, "Vierges romanes," 26; Gybal, *L'Auvergne*, p. 100; B. Craplet, *Eglises romanes en Auvergne*, Clermont-Ferrand, 1969, p. 34.

§ 5. [Fig. 65]
AUBUSSON (PUY-DE-DOME)
Notre-Dame d'Aubusson

M.H. 25-9-1961
Wood, polychromed
H. 79 cm.

Second half 12th century

Heavy overpaint conceals much of this sculpture. What can be discerned appears to be of twelfth-century date, of interesting character and rather good condition. The work easily finds a place within the stylistic context represented by the Morgan Madonna (no. 1). In overall effect it is closest to the Madonna at Parentignat (no. 6). It is also very like Notre-Dame-de-Montvianeix (no. 3), even with respect to minor details such as the circular opening covered by fine linen on the reverse which is probably a technical precaution. Traces of the linen survive visibly in several areas of the surface. Also related are Notre-Dame de Claviers (no. 2) and several others (nos. 7-11).

BIBLIOGRAPHY: Bréhier, "Vierges romanes," fig. 54; Gybal, *L'Auvergne*, p. 98; *Liste des objets meubles*, Dept. Puy-de-Dôme, 1957, p. 4 (hand insert; dated here "XIIIe siècle").

§ 6. [Fig. 66]
PARENTIGNAT (PUY-DE-DOME),
CHATEAU DE LASTIC

From Usson
Wood, polychromed
H. 82 cm.

Second half 12th century

Despite heavy, disfiguring layers of polychromy, this is an interesting example of the Morgan Madonna type of Majesty (nos. 1-5). It exhibits a two-storied throne and drapery which is almost identical to that of Notre-Dame d'Aubusson (no. 5). The feet of the Child and some portions of the base of the statue are lost.

BIBLIOGRAPHY: Previously unpublished.

§ 7. [Fig. 67]
MOLOMPIZE (CANTAL), VAUCLAIR CHAPEL

Notre-Dame de Vauclair

> M.H. 4-11-1908
> Wood, polychromed
> H. 73 cm.
>
> Second half 12th century (?)

Despite many alterations and renewals, this work conforms in general to the type of the Morgan Madonna (no. 1). It resembles in particular the examples at Aubusson and Parentignat (nos. 5, 6) and that at Moussages (no. 2). Little of what must once have been a twelfth-century sculpture survives, however, as, in the opinion of the author, restorations include the heads of Mary and the Child, his hands, his feet and the throne. The glass cabochon at Mary's throat appears to be a later addition. There is a small rectangular niche, possibly for relics, cut in the back of the figure of Mary. Before the recent restoration, dark paint made the Madonna a *Vierge noire.*

BIBLIOGRAPHY: Delmont, *Guide du Cantal*; A. de Chalvet de Rochemonteix, *Les Eglises romanes de Haute-Auvergne*, Paris and Clermont-Ferrand, 1902; Bréhier, "Vierges romanes," fig. 36; *Liste des objets meubles*, Dept. Cantal, 1951, p. 40; Gybal, *L'Auvergne*, p. 102; Aurillac, *Orfèvrerie*, 1959, no. 26; Enaud, "Exposition," 191; *Vierges romanes*, pls. 37, 39-42; Beaufrère, *Richesses*, 130, 135.

8. Fig. [68]
COLOGNE, BURG COLLECTION (formerly)

> Wood
> Measurements unavailable
>
> 12th century (?)

The present location of this statue, which has been lost since World War II, is unknown. It seems to derive from the Morgan Madonna group (nos. 1-6), and its closest relatives are Notre-Dame d'Aubusson and Notre-Dame de Vauclair (nos. 5, 7).

BIBLIOGRAPHY: Hamann, "Madonna," pl. XXXVIIIC.

§ 9. [Fig. 69]
SAINT-GERVAZY (PUY-DE-DOME)

Notre-Dame de Saint-Gervazy

> M.H. 5-12-1908
> Wood, stained black
> H. 81 cm.

This statue is a replica of a Romanesque Majesty made at some unknown but relatively recent date after the manner of the group represented by Madonnas at Aubusson, Parentignat, etc. (nos. 5, 6). A relic compartment is cut into the back and there are small losses.

BIBLIOGRAPHY: Bréhier, "Vierges romanes," figs. 4, 8, 58; Gybal, *L'Auvergne*, pp. 90, 100; *Liste des objets meubles*, Dept. Puy-de-Dôme, 1957, p. 33; *Vierges romanes*, pls. 33-36, 38, p. 103.

§ 10. [Fig. 70]
NANCY, PRIVATE COLLECTION I

> From Saint-Cirgues (Puy-de-Dôme)
> Wood, traces of polychromy
> H. 73 cm.
>
> Second half 12th century (?)

In addition to a number of breaks in the surface, the feet of the Child are lost. The anomalous character of the style (e.g. the thin ridges which mark the drapery folds and the treatment of the back of the statue) makes it difficult to date this attractive sculpture, even though its general form shows it to derive from the group of the Morgan Madonna (cf. nos. 1-6).

BIBLIOGRAPHY: Bréhier, "Vierges romanes," fig. 51; Paris, Petit Palais, *La Vierge dans l'art français*, 1950, no. 135; Gybal, *L'Auvergne*, pp. 90, 100; M. Aubert, *L'Art roman en France*, Paris, 1961, p. 288.

§ 11. [Fig. 71]

GENEVA, MUSEE D'ART ET D'HISTOIRE

Legs Baird No. 12.143
Wood, polychromed
H. 92 cm.

Second half 12th century

Characteristics of both Morgan and Tournus types of Madonnas are seen here, suggesting that this sculpture is a provincial work, perhaps even from beyond the frontiers of France but based upon Auvergne models (nos. 1-6; 30-34). The throne and the hands of the Virgin have been restored, the feet of the Christ Child are lost and the surface has been recently polychromed.

BIBLIOGRAPHY: L. Bréhier, "Une Vierge romane au musée de Genève," *Genava*, VI (1928), 79-91, figs. 1, 3; W. Deonna, *Ville de Genève, Musée d'art et d'histoire, Collections archéologiques et historiques, Moyen âge et temps modernes*, Geneva, 1929; Bréhier, "Vierges romanes," fig. 28; P. Bouffard, "Vierges romanes et gothiques du Valais," *Genava*, n.s. 1 (1953), 18; Gybal, *L'Auvergne*, p. 102.

12. [Fig. 72]

ROUEN, MUSEE DEPARTEMENTAL DES ANTIQUITES DE LA SEINE-MARITIME

Said to come from Brioude
(Haute-Loire)
Wood, polychromed
H. 71 cm.

12th century (?)

Acquired by the Museum in 1887 from a dealer in Rouen, this statue has been frequently mentioned in the literature on *Vierges romanes*. In his discussion of it, Bréhier first evolved his theory of the chronology of the two styles of Madonnas from Auvergne, considering the Rouen example a member of the early group and dating it ca. 1125-1130. However, the dating criteria he relied upon (e.g. the throne at Vauclair, the figure at Bredons, nos. 7, 25) have since proved to be non-Romanesque. The fact that Bréhier could not find close parallels to what he described as a very stiff style in this work may be due to its being a replica of a twelfth-century Madonna. There is a cavity in the back of the statue, presumably intended for relics, which is now closed (cf. nos. 7, 9, 14, 25).

BIBLIOGRAPHY: Bréhier, *L'Art chrétien*, figs. 100-101; Mâle, *L'Art religieux*, p. 287 n. 2; *Musée des antiquités de la Seine-Inférieure, Guide du visiteur*, Rouen, 1923, pp. 29-30; Bréhier, "Clermont," 207; L. Bréhier, "Une Vierge romane de Brioude au musée de Rouen," *Almanach de Brioude*, Brioude, 1925, 1-8; Hamann, "Madonna," pl. XXXVIIg; A. Gardner, *Medieval Sculpture in France*, New York, 1931, p. 20; Bréhier, "Vierges romanes," p. 12; P. Pradel and E. Sougez, *Sculptures romanes des musées de France*, Paris, 1958, fig. 21; Paris, Louvre, *Chefs-d'oeuvre romans des musées de province*, 1957-1958, no. 62.

13. [Fig. 73]
LA ROCHELAMBERT (HAUTE-LOIRE),
CHATEAU

Wood, polychromed
H. 79 cm.

12th century (?)

Although this statue resembles Majesties of the Saint-Rémy-de-Chargnat type (nos. 16-19) and surely derives from them, technical inconsistencies make the date of the sculpture problematic. Other Madonnas attributed to the Romanesque period are in the Rochelambert collection (see Salmann).

BIBLIOGRAPHY: *Art and Auctions*, II, 4 (1958), 88-89; G. Salmann, "The Castle of La Rochelambert," *Connoisseur*, CLVII (1964), 3-7.

§ 14. [Fig. 74]
PARIS, MUSEE DE CLUNY

Inv. no. 9.270
Oak, polychromed
H. 80 cm.

Early 13th century (?)

The statue was acquired by the Museum in 1875. Losses, such as the Child's feet, and restorations are visible. A slight depression in the breast which was probably intended for a cabochon, appears to be a later alteration. An aperture in the back may have served as a reliquary niche. The statue is related to the group represented by the Morgan Majesty and seen at Aubusson and Parentignat (nos. 5, 6). The heaviness of the style suggests a late work, probably to be dated at the beginning of the thirteenth century.

BIBLIOGRAPHY: Fleury, *Vierge*, II, pl. CXXXII; E. Haraucourt, F. de Montremy, and E. Maillard, *Musée des thermes et de l'hôtel de Cluny, Catalogue général*, II, *Catalogue des bois sculptés et meubles*, Paris, 1925, no. 2; Hamann, "Madonna," pl. XXXVIIIb.

§ 15. [Fig. 75]
SAINT-NECTAIRE (PUY-DE-DOME)
Notre-Dame du Mont-Cornadore

M.H. 25-2-1899
Wood, polychromed
H. 69 cm.

Second half 12th century (?)

A recent cleaning of the face, carried out in May 1954, removed several layers of paint while the robe still shows an old polychromy of indeterminate date. A small niche in the back for relics is rudely closed with a hinged lock which, along with some minor restorations to Mary's hands, seems a later alteration. The Child's right hand and both feet are lost. The patterns of the drapery and the arrangement of the throne, which seem contemporary in execution, differ from the leading examples of Madonnas in Auvergne. The Virgin here wears a mantle rather than a paenula, draped with curious asymmetry. Its folds are heavily delineated in contrast to the usual dynamics of Auvergne drapery style. The pleating over the legs and the fussy hemlines over and between Mary's knees are anomalous. Since the proportions of the figures are also curious, the possibility of the statue being a later renewal of a Romanesque image should be considered.

BIBLIOGRAPHY: Marquis de Fayalle, "Le Trésor de l'église de Saint-Nectaire," *Congrès archéologique de France, Clermont-Ferrand, 1895*, Paris, 1897, 301-302; Marquis de Fayalle, "Oeuvres d'orfèvrerie en Auvergne," *Congrès archéologique de France, Clermont-Ferrand, 1924*, Paris, 1925, 447-448; Mâle, *L'Art religieux*, p. 287; Bréhier, "Vierges romanes," figs. 32, 38, 42; Gybal, *L'Auvergne*, ill. p. 94, p. 100; *Liste des objets meubles*, Dept. Puy-de-Dôme, 1957, p. 33; *Auvergne romane*, La Pierre-qui-vire, 1958, p. 161, fig. 23 after p. 128.

§ 16. [Fig. 76]
SAINT-REMY-DE-CHARGNAT
(PUY-DE-DOME)

Notre-Dame de Saint-Rémy

> M.H. 21-10-1902
> Wood, polychromed
> H. 80 cm.
>
> Second half 12th century

A recent cleaning has restored much of the original attractiveness of this sculpture. The drapery system follows the pattern of the Morgan Madonna, and the two-storied throne is like that of Notre-Dame d'Aubusson (nos. 1, 5); but decorative elaboration—namely the ornamental bands across the upper arms and down the center of the paenula and the treatment of its ends, pulled forward in graceful gatherings over the lower arms—make this a distinctive variant of the Morgan Madonna style. The Saint-Rémy-de-Chargnat manner is known in many examples, e.g. Saint-Laurent-Chabreuges, Chanaleilles, etc. (nos. 17ff.). Relics, traditionally identified as fragments of the Virgin's clothing, are reported to have been enshrined within the statue in 1732 and a niche is said to have been cut into the back of the sculpture to receive them. The present location of the Majesty, in an aedicula high above the altar, makes it impossible to examine the reverse side of the work and verify the presence of the compartment.

BIBLIOGRAPHY: Pourreyron, *Le Culte*, pp. 265-266; Bréhier, "Vierges romanes," figs. 2, 3, 46; *Liste des objets meubles*, Dept. Puy-de-Dôme, 1957, p. 33.

§ 17. [Fig. 77]
SAINT-LAURENT-CHABREUGES
(HAUTE-LOIRE), ENTREMONT CHAPEL

Notre-Dame d'Entremont

> M.H. 13-2-1929
> Wood, polychromed
> H. 78 cm.
>
> Second half 12th century

Freed of overpaint in a recent cleaning, the statue nevertheless suffers from losses and awkward renewals. The throne is remade, as are parts of the Child, notably the head. The distinctive bands about the arms relate the sculpture most closely to Saint-Rémy-de-Chargnat and Chanaleilles (nos. 16, 18).

BIBLIOGRAPHY: *Liste des objets meubles*, Dept. Haute-Loire, 1958, p. 31.

§ 18. [Fig. 78]
CHANALEILLES (HAUTE-LOIRE)

Notre-Dame du Villeret d'Apchier

> M.H. 22-7-1958
> Wood, traces of polychromy; the faces are black
> H. 67 cm.
>
> Second half 12th century

Substantial losses have deprived the sculpture of the throne, the lower part of the figure of Mary and the hands and feet of the Child; in addition there is serious surface deterioration. The head of the Child has been preserved, though kept separate from the rest of the sculpture until recently. A small cylindrical cavity (diameter 2.5 cm.) is visible in the back, probably intended as a technical precaution. The drapery scheme follows the Saint-Rémy-de-Chargnat variant of the Morgan Madonna type (nos. 16ff.) which is characterized by decorative bands across the upper arms of the Madonna, a vertical strip descending into the Madonna's lap and the paenula pulled forward over the arms.

The statue was preserved during the Revolution by a family in Villeret, whose heirs safeguarded the head of the Child until 1957 when it was presented to the Curé of Chanaleilles. It has been reunited with the rest of the sculpture, and the whole is to be installed in the now restored, early medieval church at Chanaleilles where the statue is greatly venerated as patroness for children at Baptism.

BIBLIOGRAPHY: *Liste des objets meubles*, Dept. Haute-Loire, 1958, p. 10, hand insert.

§ 19. [Fig. 79]
MAILHAT, NEAR LAMONTGIE
(PUY-DE-DOME)

Notre-Dame de Mailhat
  Wood, polychromed
  H. 60 cm.
  Second half 12th century (?)

The statue is poorly preserved, being disfigured by thick overpaint and many small losses. It follows the Saint-Rémy-de-Chargnat variant of the Morgan type of Madonna (nos. 16ff.), but its small size and anomalous details suggest that it is a derivative work of uncertain date. A compartment in the back of the Virgin (6.5 x 6 cm.) appears to have been a relic niche. A second Madonna in Majesty exists at Mailhat which also derives from a Romanesque model (no. 44).

BIBLIOGRAPHY: Bréhier, "Vierges romanes," figs. 47, 53; Gybal, *L'Auvergne*, p. 100.

§ 20. [Fig. 80]
WASHINGTON, D.C., COLLECTION OF
MR. AND MRS. ROBERT SARGENT
SHRIVER, JR.

Ex collections: French and Co.;
  Demotte, Paris
Wood, polychromed
H. 81.3 cm.
Second half 12th century (?)

The right hand and right foot of the Child are lost and his left hand is restored. The throne and base have suffered some damage and loss as well, and the piece has been variously polychromed. The reverse side reveals two small circular cavities. The closest relative to the Shriver Majesty is the Madonna in the Giraud Collection, Geneva (no. 21). A dryness, seen in the excessive stylizations, and an exaggerated grimness in expression are common to both. Similarities in drapery, costume and pose are also evident. Both are like the group of Saint-Rémy-de-Chargnat (Puy-de-Dôme, no. 16), which includes Haute-Loire examples from Saint-Laurent-Chabreuges (no. 17) and Chanaleilles (no. 18), and surely derive from that group even if not of comparable antiquity. Also related stylistically are the Madonnas in the Bührle Collection (no. 22) and the Duke University Museum (no. 23). In the United States the statue has been exhibited in Cincinnati (1956), Dallas (1958) and Houston (1959).

BIBLIOGRAPHY: Dallas, Museum of Fine Arts, *Religious Art of the Western World*, 1958, no. 42.

21. [Fig. 81]
GENEVA, GIRAUD COLLECTION

  Said to come from near
    Besse-en-Chandesse (Puy-de-Dôme)
  Walnut, polychromed
  H. 72 cm.
  Second half 12th century (?)

The hands and feet of the Child and Mary's left foot are lost. The right hand of Christ and the throne have been partially replaced by later alterations. The surface has suffered some erosion through insect damage and repainting. In facial type and expression the piece resembles the Madonna in the Shriver Collection (no. 20) very closely and conforms in general to a group typified by the Madonnas from Saint-Rémy-de-Chargnat (Puy-de-Dôme) and Saint-Laurent-Chabreuges (Haute-Loire) among others (cf. nos. 16-18, 22). Although its date is uncertain, the Giraud Majesty clearly depends upon this group for its style. There is a circular cavity on the reverse of the statue.

BIBLIOGRAPHY: Previously unpublished.

22. [Fig. 82]

ZURICH, BÜHRLE COLLECTION

Ex collections: Brummer; Demotte,
  New York
Walnut, polychromed
H. 67 cm.

Second half 12th century (?)

The feet of the Child are lost and some of the surface of the work has suffered from insect damage. The statue conforms iconographically and stylistically to the group of Madonnas typified by Saint-Rémy-de-Chargnat (nos. 16ff.) which represent a variant of the Morgan Master's style (nos. 1-6). It must derive from this context even though its exact antiquity is unknown. Its closest affiliation is to the Madonnas in the Giraud Collection, the Shriver Collection and at Duke University (nos. 21, 20, 23).

BIBLIOGRAPHY: L. Réau, *Collection Demotte, La Vierge en France, XII-XVII siècle*, New York, 1930, pl. 1, pp. 8-9; P. Muratoff, *La Sculpture gothique*, Paris, 1931, pl. xx; D. Wild, "Zur Ausstellung der Sammlung Bührle," *Alte und Neue Kunst*, Heft ½, 1958, 10-11; Zurich, Kunsthaus, *Sammlung Emil G. Bührle*, 1958, no. 19.

23. [Fig. 83]

DURHAM, NORTH CAROLINA, DUKE
UNIVERSITY ART MUSEUM

Ex collections: Brummer; Speyer
Wood, traces of polychromy
H. 72.1 cm.

Second half 12th century (?)

This sculpture is said to have been formerly in the collection of Mrs. Edgar Speyer, whence it came to the Brummer Collection and then to Duke University. There are losses and repairs to the throne and base, and the Child's right hand is missing. A small round cavity, probably for a cabochon, is seen at Mary's throat and a similar opening is visible on the reverse side. Although the question of its antiquity is unresolved, this Majesty is closely related in style and type to the Madonnas in the Shriver, Giraud and Bührle Collections (nos. 20-22), and derives from the group typified by Saint-Rémy-de-Chargnat (no. 16, Puy-de-Dôme).

BIBLIOGRAPHY: Raleigh, The North Carolina Museum of Art, *Sculpture and Decorative Art, A Loan Exhibition of Selected Art Works from the Brummer Collection of Duke University*, ed. Robert C. Moeller, 1967, no. 9, pp. 30-31; *Art Journal*, XXVII, 2 (1967/1968), p. 184.

24. [Fig. 84]

RALEIGH, THE NORTH CAROLINA
MUSEUM OF ART

Ex collections: French and Co.; Blair
Wood, traces of polchromy
H. 74 cm.

Second half of 12th century (?)

Acquired in 1962 from French and Co. and formerly in the collection of Mrs. Chauncey Blair in Chicago, this sculpture has been subjected to substantial revision. Restorations of indeterminate date include the heads of Mary and the Child, the throne with its cushion, and the base. The date of the remaining carving is still an open question. In type the sculpture conforms to the manner of the Morgan Madonna following the Puy-de-Dôme examples at Aubusson and Parentignat (nos. 5, 6) and their relatives. A circular cavity and indications of a closing panel are visible on the reverse side.

BIBLIOGRAPHY: *Bulletin of the Art Institute of Chicago*, VII, 4 (1914), p. 58.

25. [Fig. 85]
BREDONS (CANTAL) I

M.H. 21-10-1902
Formerly in the church at
    Albepierre-Bredons
Oak, polychromed
H. 80 cm.

From photographs this statue appears to be a relatively recent replica of the Saint-Rémy-de-Chargnat type of Auvergne Majesty (nos. 16ff.). It was stolen in 1959 and has not reappeared. Local legend holds that the Virgin was brought from the Holy Land by St. Louis. A second, fragmentary statue survives from the Romanesque period in Bredons (no. 49).

BIBLIOGRAPHY: Chalvet de Rochemonteix, *Eglises romanes*, pp. 75-77.

§ 26. [Fig. 86]
THIERS (PUY-DE-DOME), PRIVATE COLLECTION

Notre-Dame de Montpeyroux

From the chapel of the Château of
    Montpeyroux, Puy-Guillaume
    (Puy-de-Dôme)
Wood, polychromed
H. 58.5 cm.
Second half 12th century (?)

A recent cleaning and restoration is evident and accounts for the new right hand of Mary, repairs to Christ's left hand and right foot, and extensive renewal of the throne. Niches in the back of the sculpture were probably used to secure the statue to a panel rather than to provide relic compartments. The work departs from even its closest relatives in the style of its drapery patterns, the presence of the crown for the Christ Child, the position of the Child's book and the character of the throne. Such deviations suggest the derivative manner of a provincial workshop. The bands on the sleeves and vertical strip at the center of the drapery of the upper torso relate this Madonna to the Saint-Rémy-de-Chargnat group, particularly Notre-Dame d'Entremont at Saint-Laurent-Chabreuges (no. 17) and to the statue at Chauriat (no. 27).

BIBLIOGRAPHY: Bréhier, "Vierges romanes," figs. 12, 18.

§ 27. [Fig. 87]
CHAURIAT (PUY-DE-DOME)

M.H. 30-9-1911
Wood, polychromed and gilded
H. 64 cm.

Second half 12th century (?)

Like Notre-Dame de Montpeyroux at Thiers (no. 26), this statue differs decidedly even from its closest parallels. The drapery formula, with bands across the upper arms and a vertical strip at the center, is like that of the Saint-Rémy-de-Chargnat group (nos. 16ff.), but the proportions of the figures and the faces differ, and the folds are handled more broadly. There are curious, anomalous features such as the position of the book and the nature of the throne, indicating a derivative workshop and a production of an unknown, later date.

BIBLIOGRAPHY: *Liste des objets meubles*, Dept. Puy-de-Dôme, 1957, p. 9.

§ 28.

AUBUSSON (PUY-DE-DOME), CHAPEL OF
NOTRE-DAME D'ESPINASSE

Notre-Dame d'Espinasse

> M.H. 20-5-1933
> Wood, polychromed
> H. 50 cm.

The rusticity of this sculpture is apparent beneath its heavy polychromy, and although there is a distant resemblance to its sister statue at Aubusson (no. 5), in that both follow Auvergne styles in rendering the Virgin and Child, it shows greater stylistic affiliation to the Madonna at Chauriat (no. 27). In its present state a date can hardly be conjectured. Notre-Dame d'Espinasse is the center of a cult which can be documented from the seventeenth century, and she is known as a *Vierge miraculeuse*. A compartment in the back may once have served as a receptacle for relics.

BIBLIOGRAPHY: J. Decouzon, *Notre-Dame d'Espinasse*, Clermont-Ferrand, 1953; *Liste des objets meubles*, Dept. Puy-de-Dôme, 1957, p. 5.

§ 29. [Fig. 88]

ECHLACHE (PUY-DE-DOME)

> Wood, polychromed
> H. 72 cm.

A replica of a Romanesque Majesty, copied after a member of the Saint-Rémy-de-Chargnat group (nos. 16ff.).

BIBLIOGRAPHY: Bréhier, "Vierges romanes," fig. 27; Gybal, *L'Auvergne*, p. 100.

§ 30. [Figs. 6, 89]

TOURNUS (SAONE-ET-LOIRE),
SAINT-PHILIBERT

Notre-Dame-la-Brune

> M.H. 4-7-1903
> Said to be from Saint-Pourçain-sur-Sioule (Allier)
> Wood, gilded and polychromed
> H. 73 cm.
>
> Second half 12th century

Repainted and gilded in 1860, this Majesty is related stylistically to Notre-Dame d'Orcival (no. 31), Notre-Dame de Chalus-Lembron (no. 36), Notre-Dame de Saint-Flour (no. 33), and their relatives. It is even closer to the image of the Virgin carved in stone over the south portal of Notre-Dame-du-Port in Clermont-Ferrand (Fig. 5). There the Child's position is similar but reversed. The correspondences between the thrones, evident even though the chair has been restored in the Tournus sculpture, and the drapery, which shows almost identical concentric folds over the Virgin's breast and inverted pleats over her lower legs, are striking. The same features may be found in the other figures of the portal. These affinities suggest a close link between this type of Majesty and a Clermont-Ferrand workshop. Unfortunately the portal sculptures cannot be dated with precision, but a place in the third quarter of the twelfth century is stylistically appropriate.

In 1850 M. Canat observed a small compartment of uncertain antiquity in the reverse of the figure of the Virgin. The relics within were examined in 1860 and identified by inscribed notes thought to be of twelfth-century date. In this same year the Bishop of Autun decreed that the image might be carried in procession outside the church only in rare circumstances and for extraordinary needs. The tradition of presenting children to the statue seems to date from after the Revolution.

In 1733 Juénin explained that the name Notre-Dame-la-Brune was due to the obscurity or darkness of the chapel where the altar of Notre-Dame was located. Although he does not specifically mention the statue, his reference to Notre-Dame-la-Brune seems to apply to the sculpture, indicating that the Majesty had been moved from Saint-Pourçain-sur-Sioule, a dependency of Saint-Philibert, before his time. Although there is no literary evidence to support the tradition which claims that the statue comes from Saint-Pourçain-sur-Sioule, the close stylistic resemblances to the Clermont-Ferrand relief sculpture make an Auvergne origin clear and the Saint-Pourçain-sur-Sioule provenance likely.

BIBLIOGRAPHY: P. Juénin, *Nouvelle histoire de l'abbaie royale et collégiale de Saint Filibert et de la ville de Tournus*, Dijon, 1733, p. 232; M. Canat, "Note sur l'église abbatiale de Tournus," *Congrès archéologique de France, Auxerre, Cluny et Clermont-Ferrand, 1850*, Paris, 1851, p. 105; Curé, *Saint-Philibert*, p. 333f.; Hamann, "Madonna," p. 95, pl. XXXVIIIa; J. Virey, "Saint-Philibert de Tournus," *Congrès archéologique de France, Dijon, 1928*, Paris, 1929, 412; Gardner, *Medieval Sculpture*, p. 20; Bréhier, "Vierges romanes," fig. 31; J. Vallery-Radot, *Saint-Philibert de Tournus*, Paris, 1955, pls. 58-60, pp. 210-211; *Liste des objets meubles*, Dept. Saône-et-Loire, 1956, p. 43; Gybal, *L'Auvergne*, p. 98; *Bourgogne romane*, La Pierre-qui-vire, 1958, fig. 17, p. 44; Forsyth, "Magi and Majesty," pp. 215-222, n. 20.

§ 31. [Figs. 90-94]
ORCIVAL (PUY-DE-DOME)

Notre-Dame d'Orcival

M.H. 27-1-1897
Walnut covered with gilded silver and copper plate; the hands and faces are painted.
H. 74 cm.
Second half 12th century

The restoration of this important sculpture under the auspices of the Monuments Historiques in 1959 allowed detailed, archaeological study (see Enaud) which clarified the seventeenth-, eighteenth-, and nineteenth-century alterations to the work. The disfiguring brass and copper-gilt repairs of the nineteenth century have now been removed and the original silver and vermeil sheath revealed in so far as possible. Losses to the revetment have been carefully restored in modern equivalents (by M. Lucien Toulouse), with due respect for the subtle alternations of the original silver and silver gilt (cf. Beaulieu, no. 101). These restorations include much of the silver socle and columns of the throne, small parts of the vermeil chair, large sections of the vermeil drapery covering the knees and legs of the Virgin along with some of her sleeves and veil, Christ's vermeil *himation*, his silver tunic and some of the vermeil cover of the book. The hands of Mary (and a small fragment of simulated lace at her right wrist) are from the seventeenth century. The right forearm of Christ was redone in the eighteenth century. The heads of both figures are purportedly original and were never intended to be covered with metal.

The claim that the copper patching was done in the seventeenth century, which is so often repeated in the literature on the subject, was pointed out as erroneous by Abbé Bernard Craplet (*Auvergne romane*), who adduced seventeenth-century texts to demonstrate the high regard the statue enjoyed in that period. He notes that in 1631 the aldermen of Clermont took their vows before the statue and that in 1651 J.

Branche, historian of Louis XIV, admired the image ("beau à ravir") and commented on its excellent preservation. Neither of these references would suggest a revision of the work at that time, but the archaeological evidence indicates that the hands of the Virgin were replaced then. In 1769, according to Craplet, who draws on a quotation from Chanoine Chardon, the people of Clermont bore the expense of replacing some of the silver leaves (evidently chiefly for the tunic of Christ). The exact date of the clumsy nineteenth-century restoration in copper is not known.

During the recent dismantling of the work, other interesting features were revealed. The basic wood core was found to be very well preserved. Its form resembles a finished sculpture of no little merit. Although the folds of the drapery are skillfully carved in the wood surface and seem complete, they actually correspond only in summary fashion to the more intricate repoussé decoration of the metal sheath. The original areas of this revetment, now particularly visible at the back and sides of the statue, show work of extreme delicacy and refinement. The simulated fabric of Mary's overgarment is gracefully draped and patterned with a trilobed fleurette. It is edged with rich borders showing a circle motif (Fig. 93). Fragments of similar borders survive at the neckline and near the hem of the tunic. These were all done by a light and accomplished hand, and some of the drooping folds, especially those near the Virgin's right wrist, have great elegance. The ornament of Mary's long sleeves (Fig. 94) is done in a heavier repoussé manner, comparable to the enframement of the throne (Figs. 91, 94) where antique intaglios, gems and filigree are imitated (stamped as directed by Theophilus, *De Diversis Artibus*, see p. 13 above). Within these frames decorative arcades and spandrels are very nicely finished with beaten designs, in-

cluding fluted pilasters, imbricated bases, stylized acanthus capitals, beaded abaci and archivolts, and charming miniature towers. The cushion of the chair and its surround show further repoussé of interesting character. Also noteworthy is the original fragment of the book cover with embossed letters (a and ω) and simulated fastenings. By rare good fortune, not only is the original wood largely preserved but also much of the metal sheath which originally covered it. The preservation of both teaches much about Romanesque sculpture, particularly when studied in relation to the comparable metal-sheathed Majesty at Hildesheim, a forerunner which is older by a century and a half.

In attempting to determine the origins of the Orcival Majesty, the Marquis de Fayalle related its ornament to that decorating the bust of St. Baudimus in Saint-Nectaire. He considered them products of the same Limoges workshop. The improbability of this conjecture can be readily seen by a comparison of photographs recording the recent restorations of both works. When the St. Baudimus bust was examined, its wood interior was also studied and photographed. Neither the wood core, which is rough and almost completely unworked, nor the broadly dry and insipid stylization of motifs articulating the copper-gilt sheath of the saint, bear any but the most distant relation to the Orcival Virgin. A more apt comparison is with the figure of St. Chaffre in Monastier; its wood surface was fully carved beneath the silver repoussé of the head and the bust, but the treatment of draperies and borders is less skillful than on the Orcival Madonna.

The Orcival Majesty is most plausibly related to a Clermont-Ferrand workshop represented by Madonnas at Tournus, Marsat, Chalus-Lembron, etc. (nos. 30ff.), since the throne, pose of the figures, costumes and so forth all conform to the pattern discernible in this group. Civil ties with Clermont in Orcival's history have already been noted. The Madonna thus provides evidence for an outstanding goldsmith atelier in Clermont-Ferrand at this time.

Popular belief credits Notre-Dame d'Orcival with countless miracles, including protection of the city from fire in 1641 (Drochon). Although modern taste has allowed the removal of the gemmed crowns given in the 1875 coronation ceremony, the Madonna's reputation as a wonder worker is undiminished. The tradition that relics of the Virgin from Pont l'Abbé were brought to Orcival from Rocamadour in the ninth century is noted by Rupin as substantiated in a thirteenth-century chronicle (Bibl. nat. fonds français, Colbert, no. 10307,5), but this does not guarantee the same relics were enshrined in the statue when it was made in the twelfth century. Evidence for the belief that relics were hidden in a compartment beneath the metal was provided when a rectangular aperture was uncovered during the recent restoration. Although it seems very likely that this cavity was originally meant to contain relics, at the same time it should be noted that the cutting of the opening seriously disrupts the folds which articulate the reverse side of the figure (cf. the Autun Madonna, no. 87, where the cavity and drapery are carefully adjusted to one another), and there is no indication that it was originally closed with a panel. The possibility of it being an alteration cannot be ruled out.

Rupin also refers to the incident which took place in 1375 when Louis II, Duke of Bourbon, participated in a pilgrimage to Orcival and raised his fleur-de-lis pennon to the venerated image after delivering Auvergne from the English at Roche-Sardaine. The site was already a renowned pilgrimage center, as indeed it is today. A replica of the Majesty is carried annually in procession on August 15 (see Drochon for the description by Branche).

BIBLIOGRAPHY: Abbé Caillau, *Histoire critique et religieuse de Notre-Dame de Rocamadour*, Paris, 1834; A. Michel, *L'ancienne Auvergne et le Velay, histoire, archéologie, moeurs, topographie*, III, Moulins, 1847, p. 162; Fleury, *Vierge*, II, p. 214; Drochon, *Histoire*, pp. 998-1000; E. Rupin, *L'Oeuvre de Limoges*, Paris, 1890, p. 469, fig. 521; Fayalle, "Le Trésor," 303-304; Bréhier, "Les Origines," 892f.; Mâle, *L'Art religieux*, p. 287, n. 2; Fayalle, "Oeuvres d'orfèvrerie," 447-448; Hamann, "Madonna," p. 95, pl. XXXVIId; Hamann, "Ottonische Plastik," 9-10; Gardner, *Medieval Sculpture*, p. 20; Pourreyron, *Le Culte*, pp. 129-150; Bréhier, "Vierges romanes," fig. 5; Couturier de Chefdubois, *Mille Pèlerinages*, p. 115; Gybal, *L'Auvergne*, p. 101; *Liste des objets meubles*, Dept. Puy-de-Dôme, 1957, p. 23; *Auvergne romane*, pp. 76-78, ill. opp. p. 76; F. Enaud, "Remise en état de la statue de la Vierge à l'Enfant d'Orcival," *Les Monuments historiques de la France*, VII (1961), 79-88; *Vierges romanes*, pls. 15-19, p. 200.

§ 32. [Figs. 95, 96]

NEW YORK, METROPOLITAN MUSEUM OF ART, LOANED BY MR. AND MRS. A. B. MARTIN

L. 48.44

Ex collections: Major Lambert d'Audenarde; Baron Edmond de Rothschild; Baron Maurice de Rothschild

Wood, polychromed

H. 68 cm.

Second half 12th century

This statue was acquired in 1939 by Ernest Brummer for the Martin Collection from Lambert in Paris who, according to one account, had purchased it at Riom.

This particularly fine sculpture retains much of its original attraction in spite of the heavy insect damage to the surface, the loss of the lower part of the group, which has been rudely sawn off, and the missing forearms of the Virgin along with large parts of the body of the Child. Stylistic adherence to the Tournus group of Madonnas, localized about Clermont-Ferrand (cf. nos. 30ff.), is nevertheless clear. The figure of the Virgin closely resembles Notre-Dame d'Orcival (no. 31) where the handling of folds, particularly on the reverse side, is similar. Even more striking is the resemblance to Notre-Dame de Saint-Flour (no. 33) where Mary's head is elongated in much the same manner. The wistful expression in both faces suggests a common hand. However, the drapery of the Martin Madonna is less schematically rendered, with softer and more varied form.

There is no direct evidence of a relic compartment in the work, although cabochon jewels were evidently added to the Virgin's mantle (over the forehead and at the throat) at some time in the statue's history and these could have enclosed relics. A small opening in the crown of the head must originally have been a technical precaution, the plug now being lost. It is interesting that Notre-Dame de Saint-Flour shows a similar cavity. Smaller holes in the reverse side of the Martin Madonna preserve their plugs which were concealed beneath the painted surface. The statue was thinly covered with cloth and gesso to prepare it for polychromy. As to the wood joinery, it follows the common practice that the hands of Mary, her head, the right arm of Christ and his feet were carved from separate pieces of wood and fixed with dowels to the basic sculpture. The remnants of the throne in this work demonstrate that the joinery of these statues could be very complex.

BIBLIOGRAPHY: T. Hoving, "Valuables and Ornamental Items: The Collection of Mr. and Mrs. Alastair Bradley Martin," *The Metropolitan Museum of Art Bulletin*, XXVIII (1969), 153; H. Bober, "A Majesty of Saint Mary from Auvergne," forthcoming catalogue of the Martin Collection.

§ 33. [Figs. 97a and 97b]
LYON, MUSEE DES BEAUX-ARTS

Notre-Dame de Saint-Flour

> M.H. 21-8-1928
> Said to come from one of the churches of Saint-Flour (Cantal)
> Ex collections: Gilbert; Lesme; Demotte, Paris; Brimo and Roussilhe
> Wood, polychromed
> H. 71.5 cm.

Second half 12th century

This particularly fine statue was purchased in 1934 for the Lyon Museum. According to André Muzac, it had long been preserved by the Gilbert family of Saint-Flour and was said to have come from a local church where it was known under the name of Notre-Dame de Pegros. Its condition is marred by ornamental bands of gilded copper about the neck, back, shoulders and throne. They must once have been even more extensive judging by the traces of nailheads in the polychromed surface of the work. They look like additions to the sculpture, possibly of late medieval date, rather than being vestiges of an original metal sheath. The hands of the Child are lost while the feet of Mary and the back of the throne have been remade. There is a small cavity in the head of the Virgin and a depression near the neck which probably once held a jewel. Relics may have been inserted in both, but at what date would be uncertain.

The sculpture is closely related to the Tournus group (nos. 30ff.), especially the

Madonna from the Martin collection now in the Metropolitan Museum (no. 32), but the Child here is even more lively.

BIBLIOGRAPHY: Lyon, *Catalogue de l'exposition diocésaine d'art religieux*, 1936, no. 6; Bréhier, "Vierges romanes," figs. 16, 44, 49; *Liste des objets meubles*, Dept. Cantal, 1951, p. 43; R. Jullian, *Catalogue du musée de Lyon*, III, *La Sculpture du moyen âge et de la renaissance*, Lyon, 1954, pp. 30-33, pls. I, II; Aurillac, *Orfèvrerie*, 1959, no. 41; Muzac, *Sculpture romane*, pl. 10.

§ 34. [Figs. 98-100]

PARIS, LOUVRE

Inv. R.F. 987
Wood, polychromed
H. 84 cm.

Second half 12th century

When the statue was acquired by the Museum in 1894, an unconfirmed report from the dealer assigned the sculpture to the Forez. Bréhier supposed that its origins would have been in the region of Ambert (Puy-de-Dôme). Without further evidence, however, this remains an open question; the statue does indeed show affinities to the Tournus type of Madonna (nos. 30ff.), but it is in a class by itself because of the exceptional finesse of the carving. Particularly distinctive is the aristocratic elegance of Mary expressed by the haughty gesture of her hand with its long, tapering fingers, the proud set of her features and the harmonious rhythms of draperies and proportions. This Majesty is a composition of unusual vitality and grace.

An unfortunate rectangular panel in front, evidently cut into the drapery at some later date, may have been a reliquary niche. The head of Mary is separable in the usual manner. Losses include both hands of Christ, the toes of his right foot and Mary's left hand. A deterioration of the surface is visible in many areas (Mary's right foot,

Christ's left knee, etc.). The traces of color indicate a probable repainting in the Baroque era.

BIBLIOGRAPHY: A. Michel, *Musée national du Louvre, Catalogue sommaire des sculptures du moyen âge, de la renaissance et des temps modernes*, Paris, 1897, no. 37; P. Vitry and G. Brière, *Documents de sculpture français du moyen-âge*, Paris, 1906, pl. XXXVII, 3; P. Vitry, "Une tête de Christ du XIIe siècle," *Monuments Piot*, XVI (1909), 138; C. Pourreyron, *Les Vierges romanes et le culte marial en Auvergne*, Clermont-Ferrand, 1920; Mâle, *L'Art religieux*, p. 286; P. Vitry and M. Aubert, *Musée national du Louvre, Catalogue des sculptures du moyen âge, de la renaissance et des temps modernes*, I, Paris, 1922, no. 69; Lüthgen, *Romanische Plastik*, pl. LV; Porter, *Sculpture*, no. 1484; Hamann, "Madonna," p. 96, pl. XXXIXb; Bréhier, "Vierges romanes," figs. 13, 37, 41; M. Aubert, *Musée national du Louvre, Description raisonnée des sculptures du moyen âge, de la renaissance et des temps modernes*, I, *Moyen âge*, Paris, 1950, no. 32; Gybal, *L'Auvergne*, p. 102, ill. p. 82; Forsyth, "Magi and Majesty," 215-222.

§ 35. [Fig. 101]

MARSAT (PUY-DE-DOME)

Notre-Dame de Marsat

M.H. 25-2-1899
Walnut, painted and gilded
H. 80 cm.

Second half 12th century (?)

Although the throne is obviously remade, the recent gilding renders determination of any other restorations and alterations very difficult. The hands of the Child look restored and one can detect the outline of a book, the appropriate iconography, beneath the thick coat of gesso and gilt above his left arm. The faces and hands of both Mary and the Child were blackened, presumably about 1830 (cf. Craplet). In 1939 the figures were ceremoniously crowned but these metal ornaments have now been removed.

Gregory of Tours in his *In gloriam martyrum* referred to relics of the Virgin Mary preserved in the chapel in the village of Marsat where he had a vision. There is no present evidence of a relic compartment in the statue wherein these might have been housed subsequently.

This handsome Madonna is related in style to the Majesty of similar type, but lesser quality, at Tournus (no. 30). Also related is the Virgin in Lyon, Notre-Dame de Saint-Flour (no. 33) and the Martin Madonna in New York (no. 32), among others. Despite this reassuring context, the glib manner and some curious details in the Marsat work are disturbing. Whether the present sculpture preserves or skillfully replaces the original twelfth-century Majesty is uncertain, largely owing to the heavy gilt incrustation.

BIBLIOGRAPHY: Fleury, *Vierge*, II, p. 217, pl. CXXIX; Fayalle, "Le Trésor," 304; Mâle, *L'Art religieux*, p. 287, n. 2; Bréhier, "Clermont," 209; Hamann, "Madonna," p. 95, pl. XXXVIIf; Pourreyron, *Le Culte*, pp. 215-216; Bréhier, "Vierges romanes," fig. 52; Couturier de Chefdubois, *Mille Pèlerinages*, p. 121f.; Gybal, *L'Auvergne*, p. 100, ill. p. 68; *Auvergne romane*, p. 221; Craplet, *Richesses*, 66-68; *Vierges romanes*, pls. 43-47.

§ 36. [Fig. 102]

CHALUS-LEMBRON (PUY-DE-DOME)

M.H. 20-10-1913
Wood, polychromed
H. 72 cm.

Second half 12th century

Except for the restored head of Christ and the loss of his right hand, the statue is well preserved. Its thick polychromy makes the character of the carving difficult to dis-tinguish, however, and may account for the otherwise puzzling weakness of the drapery folds of Mary's tunic. The affiliation to the Tournus group of Madonnas (nos. 30ff.) is nevertheless clearly indicated by the position of the Child, his drapery, Mary's robe and her throne. A compartment is cut into the otherwise solid back of the Virgin.

BIBLIOGRAPHY: Bréhier, "Vierges romanes," fig. 24; *Liste des objets meubles*, Dept. Puy-de-Dôme, 1957, p. 9.

§ 37. [Fig. 103]

CLERMONT-FERRAND, MUSEE BARGOIN I

Wood, polychromed and gilded
H. 65 cm.

Second half 12th century

The Christ Child is lost from the lap of Mary where the dowel which held him is visible, and the rest of the statue is ill preserved, showing serious surface deterioration. Thick layers of a floral gilt and other polychromy obscure the character of the carving, but the statue clearly derives from the Tournus group (nos. 30ff.).

The Museum owns a second Auvergne Madonna, of different type (no. 51).

BIBLIOGRAPHY: A. Audollent, *Le Musée de Clermont-Ferrand*, Clermont-Ferrand, 1908, p. 20, fig. 12; Hamann, "Madonna," pl. XXXVIIb; Paris, *Chefs-d'oeuvre*, 1957-1958, no. 61.

§ 38. [Fig. 104]

NEW YORK, METROPOLITAN MUSEUM OF ART

Bequest of Michael Dreicer, 1921;
    Acc. 22.60.21
Wood, originally polychromed and
    gilded
H. 66 cm.

Second half 12th century

This statue is only loosely related to the Tournus Madonna type (nos. 30ff.). Its style, particularly as evident in the form of the throne and the drapery patterns, indicates a workshop dependent upon such Auvergne influence, but the doweling of forms differs decidedly from the Auvergne manner so that the localization of this piece is still uncertain. A cavity in the breast indicates the later addition of a cabochon. The work is very roughly cut on the reverse.

BIBLIOGRAPHY: J. Breck, "The Michael Dreicer Collection," *Metropolitan Museum of Art Bulletin*, XVII (1922), 108; M. Freeman, "Romanesque Virgin," 114; Chapel Hill, North Carolina, William Hayes Ackland Memorial Art Center, *An Exhibition of Medieval Art*, 1961, no. 7.

39. [Fig. 105]

CHASSIGNOLES (HAUTE-LOIRE)

Notre-Dame de Chassignoles

Wood
H. 76 cm.
Second half 12th century

According to Bréhier, the statue was found in an attic in a village near Chassignoles in a poor state of preservation. The serious deterioration of the surface and a number of losses and awkward repairs are conspicuous. The drapery patterns are unusual in some passages (e.g. over the breast of Mary) but in conjunction with the remains of the throne, they suggest a possible affiliation with the Tournus group of Majesties (nos. 30ff.).

BIBLIOGRAPHY: Bréhier, "Vierges romanes," fig. 40; Gybal, *L'Auvergne*, p. 98.

40. [Fig. 106]

VERGHEAS (PUY-DE-DOME)

Notre-Dame de l'Assomption

M.H. 28-2-1899
Wood, polychromed
Measurements not available

Early 13th century

This statue is an interesting illustration of thirteenth-century changes in Auvergne statues of the Virgin, noticeable particularly in the draping of the separate veil for Mary, the freedom of her pose which breaks the frontal silhouette, the lively position of the Child, etc. A compartment in the back of the throne may have been used for relics.

BIBLIOGRAPHY: Fleury, *Vierge*, II, p. 215; Fayalle, "Le Trésor," 305; Pourreyron, *Le Culte*, pp. 286-288; Bréhier, "Vierges romanes," figs. 30, 45.

§ 41. [Fig. 107]

TOURZEL-RONZIERES (PUY-DE-DOME)

Notre-Dame de Ronzières

M.H. 5-12-1908
Wood, polychromed
H. 75 cm.
13th century (?)

This statue has been credited with many miracles, which accounts for the numerous votive gifts in the church and explains the stained glass windows which illustrate its "discovery" by shepherds and a bull. There is, however, little possibility that the present sculpture dates from the Romanesque period. Many alterations have affected the head—carved separately and possibly renewed—and the throne. The drapery, insofar as it is distinctive, conforms to later, thirteenth-century style. A recent restoration was carried out in 1969.

BIBLIOGRAPHY: Fleury, *Vierge*, II, p. 215; *Liste des objets meubles*, Dept. Puy-de-Dôme, 1957, p. 71; *Vierges romanes*, pls. 61-64.

§ 42.

SAINTE-MARIE-DES-CHAZES
(HAUTE-LOIRE)

Notre-Dame des Chazes

M.H. 20-10-1913
Wood, polychromed
H. 84 cm.

12th century (?)

This statue is venerated in a small chapel across the river from Saint-Julien-des-Chazes. It was cleaned in the early 1960s, but its character is still very difficult to assess. The throne is clearly modern and the heads and hands look remade. The figure of Mary is solid but the form of her tunic and the fold pattern in the drapery are completely anomalous.

BIBLIOGRAPHY: F. Fabre, A. Achard and N. Thiallier, "Cinq statues en bois du XIIe et due XIIIe siècle," *Congrès archéologique de France, Le Puy, 1904*, Paris, 1905, 567-568; Bréhier, "Vierges romanes," figs. 15, 22; *Liste des objets meubles*, Dept. Haute-Loire, 1958, p. 31; *Vierges romanes*, p. 138, pls. 51-54.

§ 43. [Fig. 108]

NANCY, PRIVATE COLLECTION II

Sainte-Marie de Verdun

Oak, polychromed
H. 70 cm.

Garbled in iconography, style and technique, this Madonna, which was found in Verdun, appears to be a fairly recent replica of a Romanesque statue from Auvergne.

BIBLIOGRAPHY: Gybal, *L'Auvergne*, pp. 94, 102.

§ 44. [Fig. 109]

MAILHAT, NEAR LAMONTGIE
(PUY-DE-DOME), PRIVATE COLLECTION

Wood, polychromed and gilded
H. 71 cm.

Losses are minimal in the case of this heavily polychromed and gilded sculpture, which appears to be a replica of a Romanesque work. There is a compartment in the back, presumably for relics. The statue is commonly cited as a twelfth-century work, but its relative modernity is evident in its execution and in such curious anomalies as the nimbus for the Child and the exceptional dress of Mary. There is little stylistic affiliation with a second statue of the Virgin in Mailhat (no. 19).

BIBLIOGRAPHY: Bréhier, "Vierges romanes," fig. 26; Evans, *Cluniac Art*, fig. 43; *Vierges romanes*, pls. 59-60.

§ 45. [Fig. 112]

SAUGUES (HAUTE-LOIRE)

Notre-Dame de Saugues

M.H. 10-6-1905
Wood, polychromed
H. 70 cm.

Second half 12th century

Although some damage to the base has caused the loss of Mary's feet and the throne is modern, this sculpture is the outstanding example of a group of Majesties in which Mary wears ecclesiastical vestments, i.e. a chasuble and archepiscopal pallium (cf. nos. 46-49).

A dark coat of varnish applied prior to 1904 as a conservation measure was removed shortly after 1960, revealing early polychromy and enhancing the aristocratic elegance of this beautiful work.

BIBLIOGRAPHY: Fayalle, "Le Trésor," 298; Mâle, *L'Art religieux*, p. 285; Bréhier, "Vierges romanes," fig. 20; *Liste des objets meubles*, Dept. Haute-Loire, 1958, pl. 31; Aubert, *L'Art roman*, p. 288; *Vierges romanes*, pls. 55-58.

§ 46. [Figs. 113, 114]
MONISTROL-D'ALLIER (HAUTE-LOIRE), CHAMPELS CHAPEL

Notre-Dame d'Estours
M.H. 10-6-1905
Wood, polychromed
H. 72 cm.
Second half 12th century

In a recent restoration the Child's head, his hands and his feet were remade after the original manner and eroded surfaces were consolidated. The throne is a renewal from an earlier restoration of unknown date. The sculpture belongs to the group represented by Notre-Dame de Saugues (no. 45), in which the Virgin wears the chasuble and pallium, as here, and Christ is also seated with his knees turned to the side (cf. nos. 47-48).

Notre-Dame d'Estours is venerated in the Romanesque chapel of Champels in a dramatic mountain setting and is honored with an annual pilgrimage on the first Sunday in September.

BIBLIOGRAPHY: A. Lascombe, *Histoire et légende de Notre-Dame-des-Tours*, Le Puy, 1891; Fayalle, "Le Trésor," 298, 305; Fabre, Achard and Thiallier, "Cinq statues," 566, pl. 1; Mâle, *L'Art religieux*, p. 287, n. 2, fig. 180; Bréhier, "Vierges romanes," fig. 56; *Images de Notre-Dame*, La Pierre-qui-vire, 1954, fig. 31; Gybal, *L'Auvergne*, p. 100; *Liste des objets meubles*, Dept. Haute-Loire, 1958, p. 17.

§ 47. [Fig. 115]
LA CHOMETTE (HAUTE-LOIRE)

M.H. 21-8-1925
Wood, polychromed
H. ca. 71 cm.
Second half 12th century

Losses of the feet of Mary and the Child, repairs to the throne and some damage to the surface of the work have not obscured the considerable interest of this sculpture. A recent cleaning has made its affiliation with the Saugues group of Majesties (nos. 45ff.) apparent. The pallium and chasuble are given particularly felicitous ornamental treatment here.

BIBLIOGRAPHY: Bréhier, "Vierges romanes," p. 22; *Liste des objets meubles*, Dept. Haute-Loire, 1958, p. 13.

§ 48.
SAINT-MARTIN-DE-LENNE (AVEYRON)

Notre-Dame de Lenne
M.H. 2-10-1938
Wood, polychromed
H. ca. 69 cm.
Second half 12th century (?)

According to the Monuments Historiques, this statue was completely restored in 1936 when the base of the sculpture, the feet and right hand of the Child were remade. Exaggerated grimness of expression and excessive stylization of form suggest that the present work is a relatively recent replica of a statue of the Saugues group (cf. nos. 45ff.), from which it clearly derives. A particularly close relation exists with Notre-Dame d'Estables, a modern statue of similar type at Estables, where there is also an annual pilgrimage.

BIBLIOGRAPHY: Rodez, *Notre-Dame en Rouergue*, ed. J. Bousquet, 1951, pp. 11, 17; *Liste des objets meubles*, Dept. Aveyron, 1953, p. 21.

§ 49. [Fig. 116]

BREDONS (CANTAL) II

From Albepierre-Bredons
Wood
H. 50 cm.
Second half 12th century

This mutilated statue, now in extremely fragile condition, must once have been an interesting Majesty of the Saugues type (nos. 45ff.). Traces of pallium and chasuble are visible and an expressive face can be seen, but little else survives. It is stylistically unrelated to a second statue from Bredons (no. 25).

BIBLIOGRAPHY: Aurillac, *Orfèvrerie*, 1959, no. 39.

50. [Fig. 117]

COLOGNE,

SELIGMANN COLLECTION
(formerly)

Walnut, polychromed
H. 58 cm.
Second half 12th century

The present location of this statue, lost during World War II, is unknown. Despite the missing right hand and feet of the Christ Child and the damage to the head of Mary, which was cut back to provide support for a crown, the statue clearly derives from the Saugues group in Auvergne (nos. 45ff.), although the dryness of the carving suggests a workshop at some remove.

BIBLIOGRAPHY: O. von Falke, P. Clemen and G. Swarzenski, *Die Sammlung Dr. Leopold Seligmann*, Cologne and Berlin, n.d., no. 135.

§ 51. [Fig. 118]

CLERMONT-FERRAND,

MUSEE BARGOIN II

Notre-Dame de Vernols

From Vernols (Cantal)
Wood, polychromed
H. 73 cm.
Second half 12th century (?)

Despite frequent mention of this statue in the literature on the subject, its Romanesque date may be seriously questioned. The exactness of its similarity to Notre-Dame de Saugues (no. 45), the freshness of its execution, the anomalous presence of a crown fashioned in the wood of the sculpture and a curious sophistication in details, indicate a replica made after a member of the Saugues group at some unknown date.

Another Madonna from Auvergne may be seen in the Museum's collection (no. 37).

BIBLIOGRAPHY: Delmont, *Guide du Cantal*; Bréhier, *L'Art chrétien*, figs. 127, 128; Bréhier, "Clermont," 207; Hamann, "Madonna," pl. XXXIXa; Gardner, *Medieval Sculpture*, p. 20; Bréhier, "Vierges romanes," fig. 34; Dr. Cany, *Vierges romanes de la Haute-Auvergne*, Souillac, 1943; Gybal, *L'Auvergne*, p. 102, ill. p. 91; Aurillac, *Orfèvrerie*, 1959, no. 42.

52. [Fig. 119]

ROME, PRIVATE COLLECTION

Wood, polychromed
H. 64 cm.
Second half 12th century

The statue has suffered losses, e.g. the feet, right hand and head of the Christ Child, and its surface is eroded in some areas, e.g. the top of Mary's head. Iconographically it is affiliated with the Saugues group of Majesties, but the style is weak, indicating a more distant derivation from Auvergne models (cf. nos. 45ff.).

BIBLIOGRAPHY: "Una mostra di antichi sculture lignee, Arezzo," *Emporium*, 1956, 264; Milan, Museo Poldi Pezzoli, *Mostra di sculture lignee medioevoli*, 1957, no. 6, pls. 16, 17.

§ 53. [Fig. 120]
ZURICH, KUNSTHAUS

> Inv. no. 1948/10, loan of the Vereinigung Zürcher Kunstfreunde
> Wood, polychromed
> H. 73.5 cm.
>
> After 1200

A strongly stylized version of the Saugues group of Madonnas (nos. 45ff.), this statue has suffered the loss of Mary's feet and most of the figure of the Christ Child. The many departures from French models, e.g. the thinner proportions, more severe facial type, more schematic drapery, the rigorous symmetry and the variations in the throne, suggest a provincial work of at least thirteenth-century date, produced outside of France though inspired by an Auvergne prototype.

BIBLIOGRAPHY: *Kunsthaus Zurich Sammlung*, Zurich, 1958.

§ 54. [Fig. 121]
PARIS, MUSEE DES ARTS DECORATIFS

> Peyre 519 Inv. 314
> Wood, polychromed
> H. 74 cm.
>
> 13th century

The statue, acquired by the Museum in 1905, is poorly preserved, the Christ Child and the right hand of Mary being lost and the surface showing some areas of deterioration. The late date of the sculpture is evident in the advanced modeling of the figure of Mary, the plastic treatment of the folds and the broad manner in which the work is executed. The figure is interesting, nevertheless, in illustrating the persistence of the Saugues type of Madonna (nos. 45ff.) into the thirteenth century. A small rectangular aperture in the back was probably intended for relics.

BIBLIOGRAPHY: Bréhier, "Vierges romanes," fig. 10; Gybal, *L'Auvergne*, p. 102.

§ 55. [Fig. 122]
LAURIE (CANTAL)

Notre-Dame de Laurie

> M.H. 4-11-1908
> Wood, polychromed
> H. 73 cm.
>
> Second half 12th century

Heavily repainted over a linen base, the sculpture shows repairs to the throne, a restored right hand for Mary and losses and alterations to the Child (his torso and head, hands and feet). A glass cabochon has been added at the neck of Mary. A small compartment in her back, possibly for relics, measures about 7 cm. square.

The asymmetrical position of Christ on Mary's left knee and the distinctive drapery for Mary—an active fold system below contrasting with the undifferentiated surface of the paenula above—make this statue differ from most Auvergne Majesties. The handling of the folds of Mary's tunic, however, shows it to be a variant which is rooted in Auvergne style. Closely related in iconography is the Madonna now in the Philadelphia Museum of Art (no. 56). A small relatively modern replica of the Laurie statue is venerated in Saint-Julien, Brioude, indicating a widespread cult, issuing from the pilgrimage center of Laurie where devotion to Notre-Dame de Laurie is of some antiquity and where this type of statue may be localized.

BIBLIOGRAPHY: Chabau, *Sanctuaires*, p. 592; Delmont, *Guide du Cantal*; *Liste des objets meubles*, Dept. Cantal, 1951, p. 38; Aurillac, *Orfèvrerie*, 1959, no. 27.

§ 56. [Fig. 123]

PHILADELPHIA, MUSEUM OF ART I

Acc. no. 45-25-70
From the Cantal (?)
Ex collections: Barnard; Demotte
Wood, polychromed
H. 58 cm.

Second half 12th century

The statue was acquired by the Museum from the Barnard Collection. It is in very poor condition, having undergone repeated renewals of polychromy and repairs (the nose of the Virgin, her right hand, the feet of the Child, the throne). Moreover, the surface suffers from insect damage, the back of the base and the throne have been cut and altered and Christ's left hand is lacking. A small compartment cut into the back of the Virgin measures about 7 x 7 cm., but there is no further evidence of its presumed use for relics.

Stylistically and technically, the sculpture is very close to Notre-Dame de Laurie (no. 55). The position of the Child on the left knee of Mary, the technique of carving the heads separately, the presence of a compartment, the *maroufle* surface, the costumes, the drapery and the form of the throne are all similar. An earlier attribution of the Philadelphia statue to the Ile-de-France (Weinberger) now seems unlikely since the statue follows the manner of the south-central area of France rather than the north in technical matters and in style.

BIBLIOGRAPHY: M. Weinberger, *The George Grey Barnard Collection*, New York, 1941, no. 70.

§ 57. [Fig. 124]

THUIR (PYRENEES-ORIENTALES)

Notre-Dame-de-la-Victoire

Wood covered with lead sheathing, formerly polychromed and gilded
H. 54 cm.

Beginning of the 13th century (?)

This statue, sheathed with lead plates formerly polychromed and gilded in imitation of goldsmith work, is related to a group which, according to A. Bost (see Durliat), were all covered with plates cast from the same mould: the Madonnas at Châteauneuf-les-Bains (Puy-de-Dôme, no. 58), Saint-Georges-de-Batailles (Loire) and examples in Spain (from Plandogau, now in the Museum in Barcelona, and a lost Madonna formerly in the Vallin Collection, Barcelona). The statue of Prunières (Lozère, no. 59) is also related. Because of the use of moulds, it is extremely difficult to attempt to date this group of figures, but some stylistic affiliation to the Saugues type of Madonna (nos. 45ff.), known particularly in the Haute-Loire, is evident and the group may have derived from that source. The awkward repairs made to Notre-Dame-de-la-Victoire during a former attempt at conservation (Durliat) were removed in the recent restoration. The base is inscribed: MATER DEI.

Local legend ascribes a venerable history to the statue as a miracle worker, and she still has a vital cult: a Saturday office is celebrated in her honor; annual processions on October 7 commemorate her intervention in an epidemic of 1631; she is invoked as protection against sterility; she is said to have assured the victory of Charlemagne at Thuir against an Islamic invasion, while providing a spring which "miraculously" appeared at the site for the benefit of the soldiers—accounting for the foundation of a monastery built by Charlemagne at the spot and for her name, Notre-Dame-de-la-

Victoire. Buried for protection, she was "rediscovered" fortuitously by shepherds at the present site of Thuir. Her name, however, can be traced back only to the Battle of Lepanto (1571).

BIBLIOGRAPHY: L. de Bonnefoy, "Epigraphie roussillonaise," *Bulletin de la société agricole, scientifique et littéraire des Pyrénées-Orientales*, XVII (1868), 101-168; Fleury, *Vierge*, II, pl. CXVIII; J. A. Brutails, "Notes sur l'art religieux en Roussillon," *Bulletin archéologique*, 1893, 366-367; M. Durliat, "La Chasuble et la Vierge de Thuir," *Les Monuments historiques de la France*, n.s. 1 (1955), 176-181; C. Duprat, "Sculptures du Roussillon associées aux croyances populaires," *Arts et traditions populaires*, V (1957), 332; Paris, *Trésors*, 1965, no. 586; P. Auzas, "Statuette de la Vierge en Majesté en Lozère," *Bulletin de la société nationale des antiquaires de France* (1966), 66-74.

58. [Fig. 125]

CHATEAUNEUF-LES-BAINS
(PUY-DE-DOME),

CHAPEL OF SAINT-VALENTIN

M.H. 5-12-1904
Wood, covered with copper
H. 56.5 cm.

Beginning of the 13th century (?)

According to A. Bost (see Durliat), this Madonna, Notre-Dame-de-la-Victoire, Thuir (Pyrénées-Orientales), and the Madonna from Saint-Georges-de-Batailles (Loire) were all made from the same mould. See the discussion under no. 57.

BIBLIOGRAPHY: Bréhier, *L'Art chrétien*, p. 223, n. 3; Pourreyron, *Le Culte*, p. 193; Durliat, "Vierge de Thuir," 176-181; *Liste des objets meubles*, Dept. Puy-de-Dôme, 1957, p. 9.

59. [Fig. 126]

PRUNIERES (LOZERE)

M.H. 4-5-61
From the chapel of Saint-Jean d'Apcher
Pine, covered with lead and tin, polychromed
H. 37.5 cm.

13th century (?)

A late, rustic example of the cast sculptures of the Madonna such as those at Thuir (Pyrénées-Orientales) and Châteauneuf-les-Bains (Puy-de-Dôme); see the discussion under no. 57. After its discovery at Apcher in 1960 by the priest of Prunières, Abbé Paudevigne, and Dr. C. Morel of Mende, the statue was restored and disfiguring polychromy removed. A reliquary compartment was cut into the heavy wood throne at some unknown date.

BIBLIOGRAPHY: *Liste des objets meubles*, Dept. Lozère, 1954, hand insert; P. Auzas, "Statuette de la Vierge en Majesté en Lozère," *Bulletin de la société nationale des antiquaires de France* (1966), 66-74.

60. [Fig. 127]

CORNEILLA-DE-CONFLENT
(PYRENEES-ORIENTALES)

M.H. 6-5-1901
Wood, polychromed
Measurements not available

Second half 12th century

The drapery, pose of the Mother with hands extended, the position of the Child on her left knee and the distinctive throne with spiral colonnettes relate this statue to the Madonnas from Odeillo, Err, Montbolo and Prats-Balaguer (nos. 61-64).

BIBLIOGRAPHY: Cook and Ricart, *Pintura et imagineria*, fig. 302, pp. 306-307; M. Durliat, *La Sculpture romane en Roussillon*, Perpignan, 1952, p. 14; M. Durliat, "L'église de Corneilla-de-Conflent," *Congrès archéo-*

logique de France, Le Roussillon, 1954, Paris, 1955, 276-277; *Liste des objets meubles,* Dept. Pyrénées-Orientales, 1956, p. 13; Duprat, "Sculptures du Roussillon," 329-338; M. Durliat, *Roussillon roman,* La Pierre-qui-vire, 1958, p. 238.

61. [Fig. 128]
ODEILLO (PYRENEES-ORIENTALES)

Notre-Dame de Font-Romeu

> M.H. 14-11-1907
> Wood, gilded
> H. 66 cm.

Second half 12th century

The statue is carried processionally to Font-Romeu in the summer and back to Odeillo on the feast on September 8 and is often costumed. The right hand of Christ has been remade and the gilding is modern. The spiral columns of the throne, the asymmetrical position of Christ and the drapery style relate this work closely to the Madonna at Corneilla-de-Conflent (no. 60). Cf. also the Madonnas at Err and Montbolo (nos. 62, 64). A local legend claims the statue was found in a forest.

BIBLIOGRAPHY: Abbé Rous, *Histoire de Notre-Dame-de-Font-Romeu,* Lille, 1890; *Liste des objets meubles,* Dept. Pyrénées-Orientales, 1956, p. 23; Duprat, "Sculptures du Roussillon," 330-331.

62. [Fig. 129]
ERR (PYRENEES-ORIENTALES)

> M.H. 5-12-1908
> Wood, polychromed
> Measurements not available

Late 12th-early 13th century

Although little is known about this statue, its general character indicates its relation to the Corneilla-de-Conflent group (nos. 6ff.). It is a *retardataire* example of

the style and probably dates from the late twelfth century, or the beginning of the thirteenth. It is heavily overpainted.

BIBLIOGRAPHY: *Liste des objets meubles,* Dept. Pyrénées-Orientales, 1956, p. 15.

63. [Fig. 130]
PRATS-BALAGUER
(PYRENEES-ORIENTALES)

> M.H. 30-3-1954
> Wood, covered with leaves of tin, plastered and varnished to give the impression of gold; the face is repainted.
> H. 72 cm.

Late 12th-early 13th century

The statue derives from the type represented by Corneilla-de-Conflent (nos. 6ff.), but differs in that the Virgin wears a crown and the Christ Child, centered in his mother's lap, has a cross-legged pose. The more plastic treatment of the drapery indicates a later date, i.e. late twelfth- or early thirteenth-century. The head of Mary has been cut back to provide support for a crown.

BIBLIOGRAPHY: *Liste des objets meubles,* Dept. Pyrénées-Orientales, 1956, p. 31; Lourdes, Musée Pyrénéen, *La Vierge dans l'art et la tradition populaire des Pyrénées,* 1958, no. 72.

64. [Fig. 131]
MONTBOLO (PYRENEES-ORIENTALES)

> M.H. 14-11-1907
> Wood
> Measurements not available

Late 12th-early 13th century

Although derived from the Corneilla-de-Conflent type (nos. 6ff.), this Madonna illustrates the advent of Gothic style in the Pyrénées-Orientales, as indicated particularly by the freer drapery. Both figures wear crowns.

BIBLIOGRAPHY: *Liste des objets meubles,* Dept. Pyrénées-Orientales, 1956, p. 21.

65. [Fig. 132]
PLANES (PYRENEES-ORIENTALES)

Notre-Dame de Planès
> M.H. 12-2-1892
> Wood, polychromed
> H. 54 cm.

Late 12th-13th century (?)

This heavily featured Madonna is seated on a throne decorated wtih spiral columns in the manner of the Virgins at Corneilla-de-Conflent and Odeillo (nos. 6off.). A restoration in 1952 chiefly involved repairs to the hands of Mary and Christ's right arm and hand. The statue is very much venerated in the area.

BIBLIOGRAPHY: Fleury, *Vierge,* II, pp. 277-278; H. Sabarthez, "L'Eglise triangulaire de Planès," *Bulletin de la société agricole, scientifique et littéraire des Pyrénées-Orientales,* XXXVI (1895), 123-124.

66. [Fig. 133]
CAZARILH-LASPENES (HAUTE-GARONNE)

> M.H. 24-2-1959
> Wood, traces of polychromy
> H. 35 cm.

Late 12th-13th century (?)

This ill-preserved statue seems to relate to the sculptures produced in the Pyrenees (cf. nos. 67ff.). Owing to overpaint and serious wear, however, its date is problematic.

BIBLIOGRAPHY: *Liste des objets meubles,* Dept. Haute-Garonne, 1955, p. 8, hand insert; Lourdes, *La Vierge,* 1958, no. 39.

67. [Fig. 134]
SAINT-SAVIN (HAUTES-PYRENEES), MUSEUM

> M.H. 30-10-1914
> Wood, traces of polychromy and gilt
> H. 82.5 cm.

Late 12th century

An old legend in the region attributed a Syrian origin to this sculpture which was thought to have been brought by Crusaders from the East. Heavily incrusted with overpainting, the statue was recently restored. It serves as representative of a family of sculptures in the area (cf. nos. 68ff.), which illustrate Mary as a figure with long, slender proportions, seated on a simple, four-posted throne, and wearing a crown, a cope—instead of a paenula—and a short, separate veil over her head. The child is likely to be centered in her lap as here and is normally crowned. The draperies are usually reduced to simple broad forms, with minimal articulation of folds. The Child and the hands of the Virgin (which have been lost in this work) are ordinarily carved separately and doweled into place.

BIBLIOGRAPHY: *Liste des objets meubles,* Dept. Hautes-Pyrénées, 1956; Lourdes, *La Vierge,* no. 10, pl. 2; *Vierges romanes,* pls. 13-14.

68. [Fig. 135]
SAINT-SAVIN (HAUTES-PYRENEES)

La Vierge de Castère
> M.H. 21-3-1904
> Wood, polychromed
> Measurements not available

Late 12th-13th century

Little is known of this sculpture which, from its appearance, belongs to the type represented by another Madonna at Saint-Savin (no. 67). Cf. the statues at Luz and Aragnouet (nos. 69-70).

BIBLIOGRAPHY: *Liste des objets meubles*, Dept. Hautes-Pyrénées, 1956.

69. [Fig. 136]

LUZ (HAUTES-PYRENEES), SAINT-SAUVEUR

Wood, traces of polychromy
H. 79 cm.

Late 12th-early 13th century

Despite disfiguring polychromy, the affiliation of this sculpture to the Saint-Savin group is apparent (nos. 67ff.). It was found in the little church in the valley of Barèges by Chanoine Maréchal, the Curé-doyen of Luz.

BIBLIOGRAPHY: *Liste des objets meubles*, Dept. Hautes-Pyrénées, 1956, p. 8; Lourdes, *La Vierge*, 1958, no. 9, pl. 1.

70. [Fig. 137]

ARAGNOUET (HAUTES-PYRENEES), LE PLAN CHAPEL

Notre-Dame d'Aragnouet

M.H. 23-2-1959
Wood, polychromed
H. 82 cm.

Beginning of the 13th century (?)

Known in Aragnouet as the *Trône de Sagesse*, this statue is a *retardataire* example of the Saint-Savin type of Madonna (nos. 67ff.). The rusticity of the work, which makes its date problematic, also relates it to the "Black Virgin" at Dorres (no. 73). The Child and the hands of the Virgin are lost.

BIBLIOGRAPHY: *Liste des objets meubles*, Dept. Hautes-Pyrénées, 1956, p. 1; Lourdes, *La Vierge*, 1958, no. 3; *Vierges romanes*, pls. 1-3.

71. [Fig. 138]

HIX (PYRENEES-ORIENTALES), BOURG-MADAME

Notre-Dame de la Cerdagne

Wood, polychromed
H. 68 cm.

13th century

The statue shows some of the features of the Hautes-Pyrénées group represented by Saint-Savin (nos. 67ff.), but it is much more developed in style, indicating a thirteenth-century date and the influence of still another stylistic tradition.

BIBLIOGRAPHY: J. Sarrèté, "Notre-Dame de la Cerdagne," *Bulletin de la société agricole, scientifique et littéraire des Pyrénées-Orientales*, XLIV (1903), 299-318; *Liste des objets meubles*, Dept. Pyrénées-Orientales, 1956; Lourdes, *La Vierge*, 1958, no. 69, pl. 16.

72. [Fig. 139]

MANOSQUE (BASSES-ALPES)

Notre-Dame de Romigier

M.H. 5-11-1948
Wood, polychromed
H. ca. 75 cm.

Late 12th century (?)

Related to the statues of the Hautes-Pyrénées in dress, i.e. a cope rather than a paenula for the Virgin and crowns for both Christ and Mary (cf. nos. 67ff.), this *Vierge noire* is a very modest sculpture which is difficult to date. It is the object of some veneration at Manosque where legend holds that it was discovered after being buried in a sarcophagus by the Saracens, the place of its entombment being indicated by bulls to a peasant. It is credited with numerous miracles.

BIBLIOGRAPHY: F. Cabrol, H. Leclerq, et al, *Dictionnaire d'archéologie chrétienne et de liturgie*, Paris, 1907-1953, s.v. "Manosque"; *Liste des objets meubles*, Dept. Basses-Alpes, 1956, p. 7; M. Letellier, *Histoire d'une Vierge Noire*, Osny, 1969.

73. [Fig. 140]
DORRES (PYRENEES-ORIENTALES)

M.H. 26-5-1932
Wood
H. 86 cm.

13th century (?)

A *Vierge noire* which is much venerated in its community, this statue is of very rude form. The provincial character of the style indicates a work well after 1200.

BIBLIOGRAPHY: P. Robin, "L'Art roman du Roussillon," *Le Point*, XXXIV-XXXV (1947), 33; *Liste des objets meubles*, Dept. Pyrénées-Orientales, 1956, p. 13; G. Duby, *The Making of the Christian West, 980-1140*, Geneva, 1967, p. 100.

74. [Fig. 141]
TARGASONNE (PYRENEES-ORIENTALES)

M.H. 30-3-1954
Wood, polychromed
H. 70 cm.

12th-13th century (?)

Only distantly related to the Saint-Savin type of Madonna (nos. 67ff.), this statue shows stylizations which indicate a late date. The surface is heavily overpainted.

BIBLIOGRAPHY: *Liste des objets meubles*, Dept. Pyrénées-Orientales, 1956, p. 35.

§ 75.
BLESLE (HAUTE-LOIRE)

M.H. 5-9-1925
From Saint-Etienne-sur-Blesle
Wood, traces of polychromy
H. ca. 73 cm.

Late 12th century

The figure of Mary has suffered serious damage from wood cracks, notably in the lap where a dowel originally secured the lost figure of the Christ Child. Traces of a crown, a separate head-cloth, an ornamental robe decorated with a circular motif in imitation of metal designs and a knotted girdle are apparent, but the distinctive feature is the silhouette of Mary, which is marked by slender proportions, a narrow waist and long sleeves which fall in a prominent triangular design. The back of the figure is solid except for a compartment which may have been used for relics. The throne, which was once colonnaded, shows many losses. The sculpture is related to Madonnas at Bellevaux-en-Bauges (Savoie) and Rocamadour (Lot) (cf. nos. 76, 78).

BIBLIOGRAPHY: L. Bréhier, *La Statue-reliquaire de Saint-Etienne-sur-Blesle*, Brioude, 1934; *Liste des objets meubles*, Dept. Haute-Loire, 1958, p. 29.

76.
BELLEVAUX-EN-BAUGES (SAVOIE)

Notre-Dame de Bellevaux

Wood, polychromed
Measurements not available

Late 12th century (?)

Despite modern embellishments, which include a crown for Mary and an orb for the Child, such features of this statue as the long, narrow proportions of the face and figure, the thin arms and the prominent triangular sleeves recall the Madonnas at Blesle and Rocamadour, and, in particular, one in a private collection at Frankfurt (nos. 75, 77, 78). The Madonna has been very much revered and is honored with votive gifts, pilgrimages, etc.

BIBLIOGRAPHY: R. Oursel, *L'Art religieux du moyen-âge en Savoie*, Ars Sabaudiae, Annecy, 1956, pl. XXII.

77. [Fig. 142]

FRANKFURT-AM-MAIN,
PRIVATE COLLECTION (formerly)

Poplar, polychromed
H. 81 cm.

Late 12th century

This statue is said to have been sold in 1924; its present whereabouts is unknown. Although Hamann rejected the northern French origin proposed for this work by Schmitt and Swarzenski, in favor of an association with unnamed works of an Umbrian-Tyrolian-Swiss tradition, the facial features, drapery details and proportions of the figure relate this Madonna clearly to the Virgin at Bellevaux-en-Bauges (Savoie), and more distantly to sculptures at Rocamadour (Lot) and Blesle (Haute-Loire) (nos. 76, 78, 75). The back is hollowed out, however, in the manner of a more northern type. The Christ Child is lost.

BIBLIOGRAPHY: O. Schmitt and G. Swarzenski, *Meisterwerke der Bildhauerkunst in Frankfurter Privatbesitz*, Frankfurt-am-Main, 1921, I, fig. 2; Hamann, "Madonna," 133, pl. LXh.

§ 78. [Fig. 143]

ROCAMADOUR (LOT)

Notre-Dame de Rocamadour

Wood, polychromed and partially covered with plaques of oxidized silver; the faces are blackened.
H. 76 cm.

End of the 12th century (?)

Much has been written about this poorly preserved sculpture, chiefly because of its preeminence as the cult statue of Rocamadour. Legends describe the following: her origin (carved by a third-century hermit identified as St. Amadour himself, the patron saint of Rocamadour, or, according to another tale, by St. Luke); her "rediscovery" in ca. 1166 (when the body of St. Amadour was found); her many celebrated visitors (Henry II of England, St. Louis, Blanche of Castille, Louis XI, etc.); the munificent donations made to her (a forest in 1190, a tapestry in 1170, etc.); and her many extraordinary miracles. Pilgrimages can be traced to the late twelfth century, and references to the statue are documented from 1235 (when Notre-Dame de Rocamadour was profaned by a skeptic), so that, despite the impoverished state of the present work, a twelfth-century statue must have existed in Rocamadour. Because of its religious importance and resulting inaccessibility, verification of the statue's antiquity by a close inspection is not possible. The custom of vesting the figure with actual garments evidently began in the fifteenth century, and a reliquary compartment was let into the hollow of the throne at some unknown date. The proportions of the figure with its narrow waist and very thin arms, plus the long trailing sleeves of the costume and the presence of crowns, suggest affiliation with Bellevaux-en-Bauges (Savoie) and, more distantly, Blesle (Haute-Loire). Cf. nos. 76, 75.

BIBLIOGRAPHY: Caillau, *Notre-Dame de Rocamadour*; Forgeais, *Collection*, p. 52f.; E. Rupin, *Roc-Amadour*, Paris, 1904, pp. 289-292; Saillens, *Nos Vierges noires*, p. 151; M. Vloberg, *La Vierge et l'Enfant dans l'art français*, Paris and Grenoble, 1954, p. 107f.

§ 79. [Fig. 144]

MONTEIGNET (ALLIER)

M.H. 30-8-1924
Wood, traces of polychromy
H. 84 cm.

Late 12th-13th century

Substantial damage to the statue includes serious surface deterioration and the loss of the head, hands and feet of the Child, most of the throne and parts of the figure of Mary. The Virgin's head is affixed with a dowel; and there is a small niche (about 6 x 8 cm.) covered with a panel in the otherwise solid back, best explained as a receptacle for relics. The statue is related in drapery style to Notre-Dame de Vernouillet (no. 80) where, despite some substantial differences, the pleating of Mary's skirt is almost identical.

BIBLIOGRAPHY: *Liste des objets meubles*, Dept. Allier, 1954, p. 11.

80. [Fig. 145]
VERNOUILLET (ALLIER),
MUSEE COMMUNAL DE BOURBON
L'ARCHAMBAULT

Notre-Dame de Vernouillet

From the chapel of the priory of
    Vernouillet, Bourbon-Archambault
Wood, polychromed
H. 86 cm.

Late 12th-13th century (?)

There are similarities to Auvergne style in the galleried throne and in the position of the Child, but the throne is higher and more massive. The sleeves of Mary's paenula also recall Auvergne, yet the simple, unworked fabric over the shoulders and breast do not follow the pattern of that region. Since the smocked sleeves of the tunic and the distinctive vertical folds of the skirt find parallels in Madonnas from the Allier region, particularly at Souvigny (no. 81), but also at Monteignet (no. 79), the Vernouillet sculpture must be part of a regional group whose model is unknown but whose manner may be seen in these recensions. The antiquity of the statue is difficult to determine without extensive cleaning and subsequent examination.

BIBLIOGRAPHY: Bréhier, "Les Origines," 892;

Bréhier, *L'Art chrétien*, p. 233, n. 3; Bréhier, "Vierges romanes," figs. 14, 48.

§ 81. [Fig. 146]
SOUVIGNY (ALLIER), SAINT-PIERRE
(SACRISTY)

M.H. 23-12-1918
Wood, varnished
H. 72 cm.

After 1200

The head of Mary has been lost as has the entire Christ Child, once secured by a dowel in Mary's lap, and a number of small breaks are visible. The figure is hollow, the back being closed with a panel between the shoulders (cf. no. 85).

Although the two-storied throne, the clothing of the Virgin (a tunic with smocked sleeves, a wide-sleeved robe and a separate veil for the head), the style of the drapery (particularly the folds at the sides and at the hemline of the Virgin's skirt, and in the sleeves) and the technical character of the sculpture (the panel on the back) relate the figure clearly to the Allier group (nos. 80ff.), the freshness of the execution indicates a close replica of a Romanesque work, perhaps modeled in part on Notre-Dame de Vernouillet (no. 80).

BIBLIOGRAPHY: F. Deshoulières, "Souvigny," *Congrès archéologique de France, Moulins, Nevers, 1913*, Paris, 1916, 216-217; Hamann, "Madonna," p. 97 n. 1, pl. xxxvid; Evans, *Cluniac Art*, fig. 26; *Liste des objets meubles*, Dept. Allier, 1954, p. 27.

§ 82. [Fig. 147]
NANCY, PRIVATE COLLECTION III

Oak (?), polychromed
H. 87 cm.

After 1200

The technical inconsistency of the separately carved head of Mary combined with a hollow interior, in addition to the incompleteness of drapery passages, make the statue appear to have derived from Romanesque style at some post-1200 date. It is clearly affiliated with other Madonnas in this collection (nos. 83-85) and is distantly related to Notre-Dame de Souvigny (no. 81). Characteristic of the group are: Mary's long wide sleeves, edged with a single band as a border; folds of an almost circular pattern on her arms, and a separate veil for her head; a throne normally solid, except for two examples where it is colonnaded (nos. 84 and 85).

BIBLIOGRAPHY: Bréhier, "Vierges romanes," figs. 21, 50; Paris, *La Vierge*, 1950, no. 136; Gybal, *L'Auvergne*, pp. 95, 102.

§ 83. [Fig. 148]

NANCY, PRIVATE COLLECTION IV

Said to have come from Chagny (Saône-et-Loire), Burgundy
Wood, polychromed
H. 86 cm.

After 1200

Closely related to other Madonnas in this collection (nos. 82, 84-85), the statue is carved from a single, solid piece of wood, a fact which accounts for the ruptures in the back. This is contrary to the technique normally consistent with the style it illustrates, suggesting that several Auvergne models have been followed in its creation at some post-Romanesque date.

BIBLIOGRAPHY: Gybal, *L'Auvergne*, pp. 95, 102.

§ 84. [Fig. 149]

NANCY, PRIVATE COLLECTION V

Wood, polychromed
H. 64 cm.

After 1200

The head of Mary is carved separately but the rest of the figure is a solid. Closely related to other Madonnas in this collection (nos. 82, 85, particularly the latter, which seems to be by the same hand), and affiliated stylistically with the Madonna in Souvigny (no. 81), the statue appears to derive from Romanesque models but to date from well after 1200.

BIBLIOGRAPHY: Gybal, *L'Auvergne*, pp. 99, 102.

§ 85. [Fig. 150]

NANCY, PRIVATE COLLECTION VI

Said to come from Saint-Victor-la-Rivière (Puy-de-Dôme)
Oak, polychromed
H. 64 cm.

After 1200

The completely hollowed-out interior of this statue extends up between the shoulders so that the head of Mary is not doweled into the figure in the usual way but is held in place by a board across the back, affixed to the shoulders. The statue is closely related to other members of this collection, particularly no. 84 which has an almost identical fold system and presents remarkably similar physiognomies. Such striking similarities suggest that these two sculptures are by the hand of the same artist, who worked with Romanesque models at some unknown date. Statues in Besson and Cincinnati may be related stylistically to this group (see Appendix I).

BIBLIOGRAPHY: Gybal, *L'Auvergne*, pp. 99-100.

§ 86. [Fig. 151]

MEILLERS (ALLIER)

M.H. 14-11-1907
Wood, polychromed
H. 87 cm.

12th century (?)

Little from the Romanesque period can be seen in this work. The entire Christ Child, the hands and feet of Mary and the throne are all modern restorations. The figure of Mary is older, but owing to its anomalous character, neither age nor provenance can be determined. There are some similarities to the Madonna now at Saint-Denis (no. 105), for example in the drapery of Mary's skirt.

BIBLIOGRAPHY: Mâle, *L'Art religieux*, p. 287 n. 2; Hamann, "Madonna," pl. xxxvic; Bréhier, "Vierges romanes," fig. 11; *Images de Notre-Dame*, figs. 29, 34; *Liste des objets meubles*, Dept. Allier, 1954, p. 11; Gybal, *L'Auvergne*, pp. 85, 100; *Vierges romanes*, pl. 24.

§ 87. [Figs. 152, 153]

NEW YORK, METROPOLITAN MUSEUM OF ART, THE CLOISTERS

Acc. 47.101.15
From Autun
Ex collections: Brummer; Terret
Birch, originally polychromed
H. 101.5 cm.

Second quarter 12th century

The statue was purchased by the Museum in 1947 from the Brummer Gallery in New York. Brummer acquired it from the collection of Abbé Victor Terret, Autun. The loss of the head and parts of the right hand of the Christ Child, the fleur-de-lis finials from the Virgin's crown and large parts of the throne is somewhat mitigated by the preservation of slight traces of early polychromy and some of the lapis lazuli for the Virgin's eyes. At the back of her figure there is a large rectangular opening. The carving of the drapery terminates neatly just short of this aperture, suggesting that the compartment is original. Remains of

dowels indicate that the cavity was once closed with a panel which would have given the Majesty the appearance of a sculpture intended to be seen from all sides (cf. the Hildesheim Madonna, Fig. 39). Since the church of Saint-Lazare at Autun possessed a piece of the Virgin's veil, Margaret Freeman thought that the statue was carved to enshrine this relic. The comparable example of the Vézelay Madonna would also suggest this (pp. 32ff.); however, the interior in this case seems hollowed out for technical reasons, which would explain why the cavity is larger than normal for a relic compartment.

The Virgin, her throne and the figure of Christ were all carved from a single block of wood, which may account for the extreme flatness of the Child. His head was cut separately and doweled into place. The drapery spread over the throne, on which the Virgin sits in queenly fashion, is an interesting detail reminiscent of the Essen Madonna (Fig. 31).

In style the statue is typically Burgundian. The subtly varied treatment of the surface, with parallel incised lines, "corrugated" folds, delicately outlined whorls, zigzag edges and even a tossed-up hemline, all are traits of style pointing clearly to the Gislebertus workshop of ca. 1130 in Autun. The Madonna of Gislebertus' great tympanum is similar in form. Abbé Terret believed that the wood statue came from one of the churches of Autun or from a neighboring village. The sensitive interpretation of the Madonna, her tragically reluctant proffer of the Child, and the understated vitality of the forms make this a work of simple power, suggesting that it may indeed have been done for the church of Saint-Lazare itself. Grivot and Zarnecki consider it to have been there at least until the upheavals of the eighteenth century. Drapery details, the type of dress and technical structure relate the work to Notre-

Dame de Bon Espoir (no. 88) as well as to earlier Burgundian sculpture in stone.

BIBLIOGRAPHY: V. Terret, *La Sculpture bourguignonne aux XIIe et XIIIe siècle*, Autun, 1925, II, p. 63, ill. frontispiece; Hamann, "Madonna," p. 104, pl. XVIVc; Boston, Museum of Fine Arts, *Arts of the Middle Ages, 1000-1400, A Loan Exhibition*, 1940, no. 168; M. Freeman, "A Romanesque Virgin from Autun," *Metropolitan Museum of Art Bulletin*, n.s. VIII (1949), 112-116; D. Grivot and G. Zarnecki, *Gislebertus, Sculptor of Autun*, New York, 1961, p. 176; P. Quarré, "La Vierge en Majesté d'Autun aux Cloisters de New York," *Congrès de l'association bourguignonne des sociétés savantes*, Mâcon, 1963, 60-61, illus.

§ 88. [Figs. 154, 155]
DIJON (COTE-D'OR), NOTRE DAME

Notre-Dame de Bon Espoir

M.H. 7-8-1901
Oak (?), polychromed
H. 84 cm.

Third quarter of the 12th century

This Majesty has suffered the loss of the Christ Child, most of the original throne, the forearms of the Virgin, her feet and part of the lower drapery. The Child, which had been carved separately, is supposed to have been destroyed in 1794 during the Revolution. If the 1772 drawing of Calmelet (see Oursel) is as accurate as it seems, the other damage must have occurred even earlier. Such erosion may be a natural result of the frequent moving about of this popular but fragile object of devotion in the course of religious ceremonies and processions. One of the best known "Black Virgins," she has played a conspicuous part in the religious life of Dijon. Her reputation as a *Vierge miracu-leuse* dates primarily from the sixteenth century when a procession, bearing the figure through the streets in 1513, heralded the peace which delivered the city from German and Swiss invaders. Townspeople note that a similar deliverance took place in 1944, on the very anniversary of that earlier event, and willingly attribute it also to Notre-Dame de Bon Espoir. The rendering of the Madonna in a tapestry commemorating the early sixteenth-century incident suggests that the blackening of the face must have come somewhat later. In any case, by 1591 it was black (see Drouot). Out of respect for tradition the face was darkened again in 1945, even though the restoration in that year had revealed natural flesh tints to be a part of the medieval polychromy beneath the later paint. The face has recently been restored to its original light color.

A modern panel closes the back of the sculpture, which must originally have been hollowed from its base to the Virgin's shoulders and was probably closed in similar fashion. The depression at the neck for a jewel is a later alteration along with changes in the features of the face. Victor Petit's engraving (Fig. 154) shows the statue before some of these revisions. Petit reported a restoration of polychromy in ca. 1820.

The statue is variously published as a work of the eleventh century, but its style is hardly compatible with such an early date. Beyond the "primitive" character of the face, due chiefly to unfortunate alterations of the nose and eyes, is a very interesting sculpture. The fluid drapery which pliantly winds over the arms and is finished with finely articulated folds and edges, the full forms of the torso and the revealed coiffure of long strands of hair bound with ribbon are all features which emerge about 1150, and may be seen at Chartres, Saint-Denis, Notre-Dame, Paris (Figs. 156, 158,

189

160, 161) and Saint-Bénigne, Dijon (Dom Plancher, *Histoire générale et particulière de Bourgogne*, Dijon, 1739, opp. p. 503). Particularly distinctive are the circular motifs in the drapery which relate this work to the Madonna from Autun in New York (no. 87), as well as to the stone sculptures mentioned above.

BIBLIOGRAPHY: Abbé Gaudrillet, *Histoire de l'image miraculeuse de Notre-Dame de Bon Espoir*, Dijon, 1733; V. Petit, "Visite des monuments de Dijon," *Congrès archéologique de France, Dijon, 1852*, Paris, 1853, 60-63; A. Caumont, "Sur une Excursion à Arras," *Bulletin monumental*, XX (1854), 120-122, ill. p. 121; Hamon, *Histoire*, VI, p. 354; Fleury, *Vierge*, II, p. 223; Drochon, *Histoire*, p. 1033; J. Thomas, "Comment la Statue miraculeuse de Notre-Dame de Bon Espoir a été conservée pendant la Revolution; nouveaux détails," *Bulletin d'histoire, de littérature et d'art religieux du diocèse de Dijon*, XIX (1901), 1-7; E. Fyot, *Eglise, Notre-Dame de Dijon*, Dijon, 1910, p. 164, fig. 22; J. Vallery-Radot, "Notre-Dame de Dijon," *Congrès archéologique de France, Dijon, 1928*, Paris, 1929, 70; H. Drouot, "La Ligue et le règne d'Henri IV en Bourgogne, études et documents, VI, Dijon à l'automne de 1589," *Mémoires de l'académie des sciences, arts et belles-lettres de Dijon* (1932), 12-13; C. Oursel, *L'Eglise Notre-Dame de Dijon*, Paris, 1941, pp. 90-91; P. Quarré, "La Statue de Notre-Dame de Bon Espoir à Dijon et son ancienne polychromie," *Mémoires de la commission des antiquités de la Côte-d'or*, XXIII (1947-1953), 190-197; Paris, *La Vierge*, 1950, no. 128, pl. I; Dijon, Musée, *Le Diocèse de Dijon*, 1957, no. 172, pl. III; *Liste des objets meubles*, Dept. Côte-d'Or, 1957, p. 43; Forsyth, "The Mabon Madonna," 4-12; Duby, *Christian West*, ill. p. 101.

§ 89. [Fig. 162]
VIEVY (COTE-D'OR)

M.H. 22-7-1959
From the chapel of Veuvrailles
Wood, traces of polychromy
H. 98 cm.
Second half 12th century

This is an unassuming example of a *Maiestas* showing Mary dressed in simple, somewhat illegible garments. She does have a separate veil for her head, however, and both she and the Christ Child wear crowns. The statue is hollowed in back in the manner usual for this area. The long oval face of Mary suggests affinity to Notre-Dame de Bon Espoir, Dijon (no. 88).

BIBLIOGRAPHY: *Liste des objets meubles*, Dept. Côte-d'Or, 1957, p. 126.

§ 90. [Fig. 163]
THOISY-LE-DESERT (COTE-D'OR)

M.H. 1-12-1913
Wood, polychromed
H. 103 cm.
Early 13th century

Heavy overpaint makes it difficult to detect possible restoration and to discern the character of the drapery which must represent a paenula, robe and tunic for Mary despite the indications of the modern polychromy. The apparent plumpness of the faces and the softness of the folds suggest a rather late date, probably well into the thirteenth century. Particularly interesting, however, is the metamorphosis of Romanesque ideas which we see here: e.g. the motif of Mary holding a fold of drapery from Christ's mantle in her right hand, a detail which is known in the stone sculptures of the last quarter of the twelfth century at

Senlis, Châlons-sur-Marne, etc. (see the discussion under no. 102), and the lively rendering of the Christ Child (his knees turn to the left, one toe curls up childishly, while the gesture of his right hand and his facial expression are keenly alert). Both figures are crowned (cf. no. 104).

The sculpture differs technically from the usual form of Majesty in this area in that the figure of Mary is solid while a pentagonal compartment has been hollowed in the back of the throne; whether it was used for relics or not is unknown. The two rear supports for the throne are lost.

BIBLIOGRAPHY: York, Art Gallery, *Art from Burgundy*, 1957, no. 8; *Liste des objets meubles*, Dept. Côte-d'Or, 1957, p. 119; Dijon, *Le Diocèse de Dijon*, 1957, no. 177; P. Quarré, *Guide artistique de la France*, Paris, 1968, p. 409; Dijon, Musée, *Canton de Pouilly-en-Auxois (Côte-d'Or): Statues, XIIIᵉ au XVIIᵉ siècle*, 1969, no. 26.

91.

MONTMORENCY-BEAUFORT (AUBE)

M.H. 31-1-25
Wood, polychromed
H. 60 cm.

12th-13th century

An extremely modest work of seemingly late manufacture, the statue resembles somewhat the one at Thoisy-le-Désert (Côte-d'Or, no. 90) where Christ is similarly seated on Mary's left knee and where her chasuble has a related form.

BIBLIOGRAPHY: *Liste des objets meubles*, Dept. Aube, 1958, p. 7.

§ 92. [Fig. 164]
WORCESTER, MASSACHUSETTS,
WORCESTER ART MUSEUM

Acc. 1933.160
Walnut, polychromed
H. 91.8 cm.

After 1200

This puzzling piece lacks the right hands of Mary and the Christ Child, the head of the Child and most of what was once a high-backed, paneled throne.

The traditional attribution to Autun, based on an unsupported assertion made by the dealer (Durlacher Bros.) from whom the sculpture was purchased in 1933, has been queried recently (Cahn) in favor of a Spanish Romanesque provenance. Renewed study has led the present writer to reassess the antiquity of this work and reverse an earlier opinion regarding the Burgundian origins of the statue (Haering). Features such as the asymmetrical folds over the torso, the confused delineation of the costume, uncertain execution of the drapery and a wood-carving technique which would be anomalous in the Romanesque period, in addition to the freedom in the rendering and proportioning of the forms, all argue against a twelfth-century date.

BIBLIOGRAPHY: H. Comstock, "Romanesque Sculpture from Autun," *Connoisseur*, XCIV (1934), 263, fig. p. 264; *Worcester Art Museum Annual Report*, 1934, pp. 12, 15, 28; *Bulletin of the Worcester Art Museum*, XXIV, no. 4 (1934), 103, 105-108; Worcester Art Museum, *Art Through Fifty Centuries*, 1948, p. 36, fig. 47; *News Bulletin and Calendar*, Worcester Art Museum, XIX, no. 1, October, 1953, p. ii; S. L. Faison, *A Guide to Art Museums in New England*, New York, 1958, p. 187, fig. 8; Haering, "Cult Statues," no. 11; Forsyth, "The Mabon Madonna," 4-12; W. Cahn, "Romanesque Sculpture in American Collections. II. Providence and Worcester," *Gesta*, VII (1968), 56-57.

§ 93. [Fig 165]

COLLEGEVILLE, MINNESOTA,
ST. JOHN'S ABBEY,
LADY CHAPEL

Ex collections: Mabon; Brummer;
  Demotte, New York
Walnut, formerly polychromed
H. 93 cm.

Second half 12th century

In 1962-1963, Mr. and Mrs. James B. Mabon arranged for the cleaning of this statue, then in their New York collection. C. J. Langlais, former conservator at the Metropolitan Museum of Art in New York, removed the many layers of polychromy and gesso, thereby revealing the unusual fold system carved in the wood underneath. Careful study of the exposed surface of the statue and a technical examination of the work as a whole by Professor Mojmir Frinta indicated that, at an unknown period prior to the repeated repaintings, some of the carving had been renewed (when in the Demotte Collection the statue was already covered by the repaintings). Recutting is particularly apparent in the folds over Mary's right breast, which have been fashioned by a chisel in non-Romanesque fashion, and is evident in the character of some of the insect damage. The renewal of the carving also seems to have affected the heads of the Virgin and the Child, the former having been scraped and reduced in perimeter. Despite these alterations there is no doubt regarding the Romanesque origin of the sculpture, which is evinced particularly by the nature of the insect damage visible in its hollow interior. Most of the remaining parts of the sculpture retain their original character and the folds over the knees of the Madonna have survived intact. These suggest a Burgundian provenance and an origin in the second half of the century. The author is grateful to Professor Julius Held and to Professor Mojmir Frinta for consulting on these matters.

After the recent cleaning, the sculpture was consolidated and both hands of the Child and the feet and right hand of Mary were restored. The work was presented to St. John's Abbey by Mr. and Mrs. Mabon and formally enshrined in the Lady Chapel there on October 24, 1963. A very similar work, perhaps a copy, exists in the De Kolb Collection in New York.

BIBLIOGRAPHY: I. Forsyth, "The Mabon Madonna," *Mary, the Throne of Wisdom*, Collegeville, Minnesota, 1963, 4-10.

94. [Fig. 166]

BILLY-CHEVANNES (NIEVRE)

M.H. 20-1-1958
Wood, traces of polychromy
H. ca. 88 cm.

Second half 12th century (?)

Despite major losses and deterioration (the entire Child, both hands of Mary and large parts of the throne, in addition to surface erosion), this statue seems to be a Romanesque work. The figure proportions and the dress of Mary suggest a relationship to Burgundian sculpture (cf. nos. 88, 89).

BIBLIOGRAPHY: Previously unpublished.

§ 95. [Fig. 167]

NEVERS (NIEVRE), MUSEE LAPIDAIRE DE LA PORTE DU CROIX

Wood, traces of polychromy
H. 90 cm.

Late 12th-13th century (?)

Ill-preserved (the entire Christ Child and both hands of Mary are lost and there is serious surface deterioration) and modest in execution, this statue is extremely difficult to place and date. The presence of a crown and separate veil for Mary, the simple throne and the long, thin proportions relate it distantly to Burgundian sculptures (cf. nos. 88, 89).

BIBLIOGRAPHY: Hamann, "Madonna," pl. LXIII.

§ 96. [Figs. 168, 169]
MONT-DEVANT-SASSEY (MEUSE)

M.H. 20-4-1913
Oak, polychromed
H. 99 cm.

Third quarter 12th century

A recent cleaning has restored interest to this sculpture which was heavily encrusted with disfiguring polychromy. There are minor losses: part of the right hand of Mary, fragments of the feet of the Child and bits of the crowns along with some deterioration of the surface. The throne has been largely remade. Mary's garments (a curious paenula-like mantle fastened by a round brooch, a robe, a tunic and a separate veil for the head), her hair (arranged in long waving strands which fall into her lap), the presence of crowns, the Child's hair (with its pattern of orb-like curls) and the rendering of the drapery for both figures, all indicate a work from the third quarter of the twelfth century. Reiners had assigned the statue to the thirteenth century, comparing it with the stone sculptures of Mont-devant-Sassey, and his dating was followed by Fels and Aubert. Recently, Norbert Müller-Dietrich has corrected this late dating by pointing out the close parallels which exist between the wood statue and the stone sculptures of the apse cycle at Verdun. He has postulated the Adam Master of Verdun as a possible artist for the wood Majesty, which would allow a date in the years following completion of the

Verdun sculptures in 1147. Affinities to the Pompierre tympanum reliefs, whose style is consonant with the third quarter of the century, should also be considered. The massive, voluminous form of the Mont-devant-Sassey Virgin, with her broadly modeled, square-featured face and her thick drapery, which is sometimes unworked and sometimes articulated with chevron-shaped, segmental or vertical folds (cf. no. 88), finds its stone counterpart in the tympanum figures. Along with Verdun, Metz, and other sculptures studied by Müller-Dietrich, these monuments illustrate a distinctive Lorraine style which must have been influenced by developments in the Ile-de-France as well as by Burgundy.

The figure of Mary is hollowed out in back from the shoulders to the base and there is no indication of a reliquary compartment. Mary holds an apple which may be an allusion to her role as the "new Eve" (see Chapter IV, note 89).

BIBLIOGRAPHY: Reiners and Ewald, *Kunstdenkmäler zwischen Maas und Mosel*, pp. 62, 65; Hamann, "Madonna," p. 99, pl. XLId; C. Aimond, *L'Eglise de Mont-devant-Sassey (Meuse), Histoire et description*, Bar-le-Duc, 1933, p. 73; Fels, "Mont-devant-Sassey," 471-487; Saint-Rouin, *La Vierge dans l'art lorrain et champenois*, 1958, no. 1; Aubert, *Cathédrales*, p. 547; Müller-Dietrich, *Romanische Skulptur*, pp. 81-84 nn. 314-325.

97. [Fig. 170]
VIC (MOSELLE)

Notre-Dame d'Allyn

Wood, polychromed
H. 63 cm.

Late 12th century (?)

This venerated statue has suffered numerous losses (e.g. Mary's and Christ's hands, his left leg, parts of Mary's crown, all of her throne) and awkward restorations (e.g. Mary's feet). In costume the figures seem related to Mont-devant-Sassey (no. 96), but the modest execution and the simplification of style show the sculpture to derive from a provincial workshop.

BIBLIOGRAPHY: E. Morhain, "La Vierge romane de Vic," *Les Cahiers Lorrains*, XI (1959), 9-11.

§ 98. [Fig. 171]
JOUHE (JURA)

Notre-Dame de Montroland

M.H. 15-7-1958
Oak, polychromed
H. 73 cm.

12th-13th century

Despite the rusticity of the statue, a fervent cult attends upon Notre-Dame de Montroland. Credited with many miracles and carried annually in pilgrimage, she is considered responsible for saving the church of Jouhe from devastation in 1793. The simple garments of Mary, a tunic and a veil, and the plain throne are hardly distinctive. There is a compartment in the back of the sculpture thought to have held relics. Both figures are heavily polychromed and gilded, except for certain areas where the exposed wood reveals considerable surface erosion. Also there are several small losses. The long oval face of Mary suggests a possible relationship to Burgundian Madonnas (cf. no. 88, 89).

BIBLIOGRAPHY: J. Jeannez, *Notes historiques sur Notre-Dame de Mont-Roland et sur le Prieuré de Jouhe*, 1856; P. A. Pidoux, *L'Image miraculeuse de Notre-Dame de Mont-Roland vénerée à Jouhe*, 1908; M. Ferry, *Vierges comtoises, le culte et les images de la Vierge en Franche-Comté, en particulière dans le diocèse de Besançon*, Besançon, 1946, pp. 9, 20-21, 43; P. Pfister, *Notre-Dame de Jouhe*, 1947; *Liste des objets meubles*, Dept. Jura, 1947, p. 16, hand insert.

§ 99. [Fig. 172]
MOUZIEY-TEULET (TARN)

M.H. 30-12-1954
Wood, traces of polychromy
H. 85 cm.

Late 12th-early 13th century

Parts of Mary's face, her left hand and Christ's face, hands and feet are damaged, there is some surface erosion and the original throne is lost. The present base for the group and some details of the crowns are restored. The sculpture is unusual in apparently being made of two pieces of wood with a seam along the length of Mary's sleeves. Although the proportions and the reverse silhouette are reminiscent of Auvergne Majesties, the solid back with its drapery limited to details carved at the shoulders is unlike these examples. The presence of a crown for Mary and the character of her garments (a cope, tunic, separate veil and the rolled fold at the hem of her dress) suggest possible affiliation with western France (nos. 102ff.). At the same time the crown for the Child relates the group to the Madonna at Mont-devant-Sassey (no. 96). The simulation of very thin fabric, pleated in sharp, linear folds, and the developed treatment of the faces suggest a date in the late twelfth or early thirteenth century when the absorption of these varied stylistic ideas might be expected in this part of France.

BIBLIOGRAPHY: *Les Monuments historiques de la France*, n.s. 1 (1955), 192; *Liste des objets meubles*, Dept. Tarn, 1955, p. 13.

§ 100. [Fig. 173]

POITIERS (VIENNE), ABBEY OF SAINTE-CROIX

Notre-Dame de Grâce

M.H. 9-6-1965
Wood (said to be oak), polychromed
H. 96 cm.

After 1200

The abbey's history is exceptionally venerable, tracing its origins to Queen Radegunde, and famous early medieval treasures are preserved there, but an early date can hardly be claimed for its Madonna in Majesty. While losses such as Mary's hands, forearms and parts of the throne are conspicuous and Christ's right hand is evidently a recent restoration, modern polychromy prevents close examination of the rest of the work. Fleury's drawing, published in 1878, indicates that these changes, along with the addition of the inscription at the base, must have been made after his recording of the figure. On the other hand, the cutting across Mary's forehead, which would have altered the piece to accommodate a crown, is already visible in his illustration.

There is no apparent evidence of joinery or hollowing of the figure of Mary which appears to be carved from a single, solid piece of wood. This unusual feature, along with the modest execution of the work and the blurred character of the upper drapery, makes the entire sculpture seem relatively modern. Nevertheless, iconography, proportions and the pattern of the lower draperies (which recalls Madonnas at Meillers, no. 86, and Saint-Denis, no. 105) imply a Romanesque model. Since Romanesque Majesties are very rare in this part of France, Notre-Dame de Grâce is of particular interest in preserving reminiscences of such sculpture in Poitou.

According to Fleury, the statue was credited with the delivery of the city in the twelfth century, when it reputedly kept the city's keys from the enemy, an event commemorated by an annual procession until 1794.

BIBLIOGRAPHY: Fleury, *Vierge*, II, pp. 278-279; R. de Lasteyrie, "Vierge en bois sculpté provenant de Saint-Martin-des-Champs (XIIᵉ siècle)," *Gazette archéologique*, IX (1884), 324 n. 3.

§ 101. [Figs. 174-176]

BEAULIEU (CORREZE)

M.H. 25-6-1891
Wood, covered with silver and vermeil repoussé leaves
H. 60 cm.

Second half 12th century

Despite many vicissitudes, this extraordinary *Maiestas* has survived basically intact from the Middle Ages. The freshness of its appearance gives it a surprisingly modern look which belies its documented history. According to Rupin ("Statue"), the Madonna escaped the perils of the Revolution through the efforts of the Mlles Albert, who successfully hid it. Three centuries earlier it had been saved from the invasion and sack of Admiral Coligny in 1569, according to Armand Vaslet, a Huguenot; quoting statutes of 1432, he recorded that on high feast days the sculpture was displayed upon the altar as an object of veneration. Rupin had Vaslet's manuscript in hand as source for this information. According to M. Banchereau (in an unpublished manuscript quoted by Lefèvre-Pontalis, "Beaulieu"), the statue had also been mentioned in an inventory of 1482. In the mid-nineteenth century it was appreciated, notably by Texier, who included a description of it in his *Dictionnaire d'orfèvrerie*. He particularly admired the many Classical intaglios which are visible as ornaments in the borders of Mary's tunic, and the cameo of her mantle. Some of the former represent Roman deities (Mars, Jupiter, etc.). The cameo, probably from Trajan's time, is obviously an addition to the original statue since it has been set directly across an elegantly cased fold in Mary's drapery. Likewise the crowns with their filigree and intaglios seem to be borrowings and not originally intended for these figures because, when placed on the heads, they obscure some of the attractive details of the metal sheath and do not fit properly. There are other minor changes, chiefly small losses and restorations which affect the throne, the left foot of Mary, her right hand and knee.

Where the precious metal sheath has been well preserved, the sophistication of the medieval goldsmith's work is apparent. Particularly effective is the alternation of silver and of silver-gilt (vermeil). Thus Mary's robe is silver while her mantle, veil and shoes are silver-gilt; Christ's tunic is silver but his hair and the edge of his mantle are vermeil. Such alternations of hue and sheen produce an effect of subtle splendor. As noted in discussion of Notre-Dame d'Orcival (no. 31), its sheath is similarly made up of silver and vermeil but additional variation in texture is provided in the present case by small-scale diaper patterns decorating the neck edge of Christ's tunic and the lining of Mary's mantle. While the seams which join the silver and vermeil leaves are skillfully hidden by creases of simulated fabric, as at Orcival, the drapery is rendered here with greater bravura, as evident in the hemline of Mary's robe before restoration (Fig. 175) or in her tunic, and the folds are terminated dashingly by a decorative motif made up of three horizontal strokes of the repoussé iron.

The attire of the Virgin includes a short veil, with agitated hemline, which covers her head, a robe with wide sleeves which falls over a close-fitting tunic, and pointed, beaded shoes; in addition she wears a chlamys-like mantle or paludamentum,

which is a very unusual feature. The Child sits on a draped cushion on Mary's left knee and wears the usual tunic with a mantle wrapped about it, while holding the book with his left hand. In this case it is open and is inscribed IHS XPS.

The date of the statue has not been agreed upon. Ordinarily it is vaguely assigned to the twelfth century, as Rupin suggested. Evans had placed it in ca. 1100, but recent opinion has dated it much later, even at the beginning of the thirteenth century (Paris, *Trésors*, 1965; Paris, *L'Europe gothique*, 1968). Nevertheless, a twelfth-century date may be correct. The chlamys worn by the Virgin begins to appear in stone relief sculpture in the middle of the twelfth century. An approximation of it may be seen as the mantle for the stone Virgin in the cloister at Solsona (Porter, *Sculpture*, fig. 552), and it serves as a cloak for a queen in the right portal of the west facade at Chartres, among the column statues usually attributed to the Saint-Denis Master (Fig. 160). Indeed, the elongated proportions of our Virgin, her narrow waist, slightly projecting breasts and swelling abdomen are features of the Saint-Denis Master's figure style. A similar manner of representing the human form is seen in western France, e.g. at Parthenay, Perignac and Aulnay, etc. (Porter, *Sculpture*, nos. 985, 991, 1018-1024, 1045-1057). A curious mannerism in the drapery—namely, the decorative terminals for the drapery folds—also has a parallel in mid-twelfth-century stone sculpture. It appears in the altar frontal from Carrières-Saint-Denis, now in the Louvre, as an ornamental detail in the draperies of all the figures (Fig. 177). These comparative examples indicate a context for our silver statue in the twelfth century, preferably the second to third quarter. By the early thirteenth century, figure proportions had altered, particularly in goldsmith work, and no longer showed such marked sinuosity of silhouette or such elongation as here (cf. Hildburgh, "Enamelled Images").

Limoges has been claimed as the place of origin for the piece (Rupin, "Statue"). No arguments have been put forth in support of this attribution, and it is difficult to accept it unreservedly in view of the Limoges work we have from the period, but a convincing alternative has yet to be proposed.

There is no indication of a relic compartment (Lèfevre-Pontalis, "Beaulieu"). Although I have not seen the inner core of wood, M. Enaud ("Vierge") reports that it is only sketchily carved. If so, it would be unlike the more fully worked wood sculptures which were similarly intended to receive metal foil sheaths at Hildesheim, Orcival, Monastier, etc.

BIBLIOGRAPHY: J. Texier, *Dictionnaire d'orfèvrerie*, Paris, 1857, col. 1043; E. Rupin, "Statue de la Vierge en bois recouvert de plaques d'argent, XIIe siècle, Eglise de Beaulieu (Corrèze)," *Bulletin de la société scientifique, historique et archéologique de la Corrèze*, II (1879), 231-244 and III (1880), 171-179, 343-346; L. Palustre, "La Vierge de Beaulieu," *Bulletin monumental*, XLVI (1880), pp. 597-600, 826-829; R. de Lasteyrie, "La Vierge de Beaulieu," *Revue des société savantes*, III (1881), 270-277; Rupin, *L'Oeuvre de Limoges*, pp. 80-85, figs. 151-154; Vitry and Brière, *Documents de sculpture français*, pl. XXXVII, 4; E. Lefèvre-Pontalis, "A quelle École faut-il rattacher l'église de Beaulieu (Corrèze)?" *Bulletin monumental*, LXXVIII (1914), 60-61; E. Lefèvre-Pontalis, "Beaulieu," *Congrés archéologique de France, Limoges, 1921*, Paris, 1923, 388-390; Deschamps, "Etude sur la renaissance," 34 n. 1; Evans, *Cluniac Art*, p. 27; Vloberg, *La Vierge*, p. 105; *Liste des objets meubles*, Dept. Corrèze, 1959, p. 5; *Limousin romane*, La Pierre-qui-vire, 1960, p. 89; Enaud, "Vierge," 86; Paris, *Trésors*, 1965, no. 389; Paris, *L'Europe gothique*, 1968, no. 379.

§ 102. [Figs. 178-181]
CAMBRIDGE, MASSACHUSETTS, FOGG ART MUSEUM

Gift of Friends of the Fogg, Acc. no. 1937.29
From Senlis (Oise) (?)
Wood, traces of polychromy
H. 70 cm. (with modern support: 92 cm.)

1170s

This fine piece of sculpture was acquired from a New York dealer in 1937 and underwent conservation treatment in order to arrest erosion of the surface due to insect damage. Already missing were: the hands, the feet and sections from the top of the head and the lower torso of Christ; the left hand of Mary, the fingers of her right hand and the entire lower section of the work, which includes the lower legs and feet of Mary, the base and the throne. In her original state the Madonna probably would have been enthroned in a high-backed chair which would have abutted against the hollow back of the sculpture.

Although these losses have robbed the sculpture of some of its former grandeur, its high quality is nevertheless immediately apparent. The carving is handled with finesse and the expression is very strong. Moreover the work has important art-historical significance. It provides the most authentic extant example in wood of the famous style of the Senlis stone atelier. Mary's crown, her distinctive veil, with its long, fluted folds falling the length of the torso before curving over her arms, and her cope itself, with its large gemmed brooch and fine, radial folds fanning across the shoulder, are all approximations of the costume of the Virgin in the Mary Portal at Senlis, ca. 1170 (Fig. 182). The figure of the Fogg Child also finds parallels there. This is particularly true of the Child's head, which originally supported a crown with trefoil finials, and his mantle, which is gathered in a thick fold beneath the right hand of Mary. These features can be seen in the Senlis jamb sculptures and in the closely related fragments of figures preserved from the St. Anne Portal, Notre-Dame, Paris, e.g. the torso in the Cluny Museum and the archivolt with angels in the Louvre (see Sauerländer, "Senlis," figs. 67-77). Thus the stylistic context indicates that the Fogg Madonna originated in a wood atelier in the Senlis area during the 1170s.

These features also appear, with remarkable similarity, in the wood Madonna known as La Diège at Jouy-en-Josas (no. 103). The Jouy Mother and Child have the same costumes and poses, the hands of Mary being reversed. Whether the angel motif at the base of the Jouy statue was originally included in the missing portions of the Fogg sculpture is impossible to determine from its present state, but this seems unlikely. Nevertheless, the style of the two works is very close. Sauerländer related the Jouy Madonna to Senlis (see discussion under no. 103) chiefly on the basis of drapery mannerisms and physiognomies.

Other Majesties which belong to the group represented by these two Virgins are the Madonnas at Limay (no. 104) and at Saint-Denis (no. 105, originally from Saint-Martin-des-Champs, Paris). The fact that there are overtones in the Fogg sculpture of the earlier, mid-twelfth-century style of Chartres, Saint-Denis and other Ile-de-France churches and their relatives is not surprising since these, along with the works of the later Saint-Denis atelier, are among the sources of the Senlis style. The Fogg Madonna demonstrates that this was eloquently expressed in wood as well as stone. Its appeal lies in its delicate balance of waning Romanesque and incipient Gothic forms. A firm, full-bodied, plastic vigor and a Romanesque rhythm still control the work, but new and subtle modulations of surface sensitize and lighten the features even as they soften the draperies in an unforgettable mingling of gentleness and strength.

BIBLIOGRAPHY: *Boston Evening Transcript*, April 3, 1937; *Magazine of Art*, XXX, 11 (1937), p. 671; Haering, "Cult Statues," 1960, no. 103; A. Shestack, "A Romanesque Wooden Sculpture of the Madonna and Child Enthroned," *Fogg Art Museum Acquisitions*, 1965, Cambridge, Mass., 1965, 20-26; Forsyth, "Magi and Majesty," 215-222.

§ 103. [Fig. 183]
JOUY-EN-JOSAS (YVELINES, formerly SEINE-ET-OISE)

La Diège

M.H. 11-4-1902
From a chapel in Villetain
Wood, polychromed
H. 140 cm.

ca. 1170s

Popularly called La Diège (from *Dei Genetrix*), this Majesty is said to have been venerated by pilgrims until the eighteenth century in a chapel of the priory of the Célestins in Villetain (Yvelines), and to have been preserved, after an uncertain history during the Revolution, by the Mallet family who offered it to the church in Jouy-en-Josas in 1850. It was restored and repainted in 1863 by M. Excoffier, under the supervision of Viollet-le-Duc. Until the recent restoration of 1968-1969, when the nineteenth-century paint was removed and the piece studied afresh, there was widespread skepticism about the degree of preservation, due chiefly to the distraction of the florid polychromy. This was in spite of the description of 1856 which indicates that the original iconographic features were followed fairly closely in Viollet-le-Duc's treatment (Guilhermy, "Description des localités de l'ancien diocèse de Paris," Paris, Bibl. Nat. MS Nouv. Acq. fonds français

6113, fol. 391r; for excerpts, see Sauerländer, "Senlis"). It is now clear that the following details are modern replacements: the central finial of Mary's crown, the ornament at her throat, the thumb and forefinger of her right hand, Christ's left hand and orb, the fingers of his right hand, his left foot, the hands and part of the feet of the angels, parts of Mary's feet, the base and part of Mary's dress at her left side, most of her cushion and all of her throne (now removed). The rest of the work is an amazingly well-preserved sculpture of the twelfth century. The back of the group is hollowed out just below Mary's shoulders in the manner usual for this part of France, and there is some insect damage to the surface here. The new repainting has been handled with restraint, restoring to the sculpture much of its former interest.

The Madonna is of particular art-historical importance for its unusual iconography of the angels supporting the Christ Child (cf. Limay, no. 104), and for its use of stylistic features which are known in the carved stone figures of the Mary portal at Senlis (Oise). Parallels to Senlis physiognomies and drapery mannerisms—particularly apparent here in the loop of fabric beneath Mary's left hand—were pointed out by Sauerländer. In addition, the trailing ends of Mary's veil, the swinging folds which course across her lap and the identical border motif of her tunic relate the wood and stone sculptures very closely. These many affinities indicate an origin in the Senlis area and a possible date in the 1170s. La Diège also compares stylistically with a group of wood Majesties which includes the Madonnas from Limay (no. 104) and Saint-Denis (no. 105, originally from Saint-Martin-des-Champs, Paris) as well as the sculpture in the Fogg Museum (no. 102). They demonstrate the style of the 1170s as articulated in Mantes, Paris and Senlis respectively. The Fogg Madonna is the closest relative to La Diège among these.

The enthroned Virgin and Child in stone from Saint-Martin, Angers, is similarly costumed and may also be compared, although more distantly.

BIBLIOGRAPHY: Fleury, *Vierge*, II, pl. CXXIII; M. Gavin, "Notice sur la Diège," *Bulletin de la commission des antiquités de Seine-et-Oise*, IX (1897), 35; P. Coquelle, *Les Objets mobiliers classés de Seine-et-Oise*, Mondidier, 1906, p. 6; P. Coquelle, "Texte explicatif," *Album des objets mobiliers artistiques classés de Seine-et-Oise, Mémoires et documents de la société historique et archéologique de Corbeil*, IX (1910), p. 3, pl. 3; M. Aubert, *French Sculpture at the Beginning of the Gothic Period, 1140-1225*, Florence and Paris, 1929, p. 51, n. 68; *Liste des objets meubles*, Dept. Seine-et-Oise, 1945, p. 43; Paris, *La Vierge*, 1950, no. 140, pl. 8; Vloberg, *La Vierge*, pp. 117-118, ill. p. 114; Sauerländer, "Senlis," 131; *Vierges romanes*, pls. 75-77.

§ 104. [Fig. 184]
LIMAY (YVELINES, formerly SEINE-ET-OISE)

M.H. 15-5-1909
From the hermitage of Saint-Sauveur, Limay
Wood, traces of polychromy
H. 94 cm.

1170s-1180s

Surface erosion has been retarded by a recent restoration and the work is fairly well preserved.

Although the presence of a tiny bird in Christ's hands is most unusual, the iconography of the angels supporting the Child relates the statue to La Diège in Jouy-en-Josas (no. 103). It may also be associated stylistically with the Madonna now at Saint-Denis (no. 105) and, more generally, with the Fogg Madonna (no. 102). While Sauerländer is surely right in rejecting its close adherence to the immediate artistic circle of Senlis ("Senlis"; see the discussion under no. 103), the poses, throne and costumes point to some part of the Ile-de-France area. Rather than antedating La Diège as Sauerländer suggests, it is affiliated with the sequel to Senlis style visible at Mantes. Among other features, the posture of Christ with his legs crossed, the thick, curving folds of drapery slung robustly about the body, the furling folds at the sides of Mary's skirt and various details of the angels, are all very similar to the style of the North Portal at Mantes (after 1175). Sauerländer convincingly derives this style from Mosan art infiltrated by Ile-de-France features, and he delineates the stylistic relations which link Mantes with Senlis and the second atelier of Saint-Denis ("Senlis," N.B. figs. 81, 82; cf. his later views in "Twelfth Century Sculpture," 119-128, figs. 28, 31, 39). Thus a date in the late 1170s or 1180s and an origin in the Mantes area seem most likely, as Limay's proximity to Mantes would indeed suggest.

BIBLIOGRAPHY: P. Coquelle, "Texte explicatif," *Album des objets mobiliers artistiques classés de Seine-et-Oise, Mémoires et documents de la société historique et archéologique de Corbeil*, IX (1910), p. 3, pl. 4; *Liste des objets meubles*, Dept. Seine-et-Oise, 1945, p. 45; Paris, *La Vierge*, 1950, no. 141; Sauerländer, "Senlis," 132, n. 45.

§ 105. [Fig. 185]
SAINT-DENIS (SEINE-SAINT-DENIS, formerly SEINE)

Notre-Dame de Saint-Denis

From Saint-Martin-des-Champs, Paris
Oak, polychromed
H. 142 cm.

Second half 12th century (?)

Formerly venerated as Notre-Dame de la Carole in an ambulatory chapel of Saint-Martin-des-Champs, Paris, the statue was removed by Lenoir in 1792 to the "musée des monumens français" and then, when objects in the museum were dispersed, it was placed in the abbey church of Saint-Denis. Various legends antedating this transfer were related by Lenoir, but they add little to the history of the sculpture. The Monuments Historiques restored the work in 1934, and since then it has been very much admired and often reproduced in publications.

Losses are minor: the left hand of Christ and part of his right, as well as bits of Mary's right hand. Presumably there were at one time additional attributes such as an orb in Mary's extended hand. Some traces of polychromy and gilding survive from what must formerly have been a very splendid ornamentation, judging by the remaining replicas of gems set into the garments and crown.

Features such as the high-backed throne, plus the tall crown and the cope worn by Mary, are characteristic of Majesties from northwestern France (N.B. nos. 103, 104). Similar costumes appear in the area, but the exaggerated fineness in the pleating of the draperies here is curious. The stylization of the patterns is more extreme than any known in the mid-twelfth century at Saint-Denis and Chartres and even at Etampes. Moreover, the freedom in the precarious asymmetry of the Child's pose is unusual. Similar attitudes can be found in the second half of the century (e.g. Saint-Martin, Angers, Fig. 188) and are common indeed from 1200 on (see Hamann, 84ff.). The pose troubled Hamann, who called it non-French and attributed its presence here to the influence of a Rhenish (Mosan?) metalwork tradition. R. de Lasteyrie was impressed with the freshness of the statue's preservation in 1884 but dismissed lightly the possibility of a modern restoration. To the present author there are details in dress and a manner of execution inconsistent with

Romanesque style. Clearly the statue can be traced back to Lenoir's time, but a more definite date and explanation can hardly be hazarded.

BIBLIOGRAPHY: A. Lenoir, *Histoire des arts en France prouvée par les monumens*, Paris, 1811, p. 233; Fleury, *Vierge*, II, pl. CXXIII; R. de Lasteyrie, "Vierge en bois sculpté provenant de Saint-Martin-des-Champs (XIIᵉ siècle)," *Gazette archéologique*, IX (1884), 317-324, pl. 42; P. Vitry and G. Brière, *L'Eglise abbatiale de Saint-Denis*, Paris, 1908, p. 76; E. Lefèvre-Pontalis, "Eglise de Saint-Martin-des-Champs à Paris," *Congrès archéologique de France, Paris, 1919*, Paris, 1920, 121-122; Hamann, "Madonna," 84-86, pl. XXXD; Aubert, *French Sculpture*, pp. 50-51, pl. 44A; Gardner, *Medieval Sculpture*, p. 19; Evans, *Cluniac Art*, p. 31, fig. 32; Paris, *La Vierge*, 1950, no. 139, pl. 7; S. Crosby, *L'Abbaye royale de Saint-Denis*, Paris, 1953, pls. 86, 87; Vloberg, *La Vierge*, pp. 116-117, ill. p. 115.

§ 106. [Fig. 186]

BALTIMORE, THE WALTERS ART
GALLERY

> Acc. no. 27.255
> Walnut, polychromed
> H. 94.5 cm.
>
> After 1200

Neither the losses to this sculpture (the hands and feet of the Child, the base of the group including the feet of Mary and the bulk of her throne) nor the damage to parts of its surface obscure its interest. The finely featured faces, the slender proportions of the figures and the skillful portrayal of thin fabric, which is given special prominence in the curious twist of cloth about Mary's neck, are all managed with particular ease. In these features, specifically in the handling of the head of the Madonna, the work is related to the fragmentary sculpture now on loan to the Philadelphia Museum (150-1931-21; see no. 107). If the Philadelphia Madonna did originate in Le Mans, which seems likely, then the origins of the Walters Madonna may also be sought in this area. Curiosities such as the extreme elongation of the left hand of Mary, the rigidity of her right hand, the uncommon arrangement of costumes, etc., are difficult to reconcile with a Romanesque date; they may indicate a work derived from the Angevin style of ca. 1180 but produced sometime after 1200 when Gothic influences had begun to assert themselves in wood sculpture (cf. the stone Madonna from Saint-Martin, Angers, now at Yale, Fig. 188, and the Madonna at Saumur, no. 108).

The statue has been carved so as to be hollow in back from just below the shoulders of Mary to the base. The work has recently been treated in the Museum's laboratory for removal of overpaint and conservation. It was acquired from H. Daguerre in 1927.

BIBLIOGRAPHY: D. Glass, "Romanesque Sculpture in American Collections. V. Washington and Baltimore," *Gesta*, IX/1 (1970), 56-57.

§ 107. [Fig. 187]

PHILADELPHIA, MUSEUM OF ART II,
LOANED BY RAYMOND PITCAIRN

> Acc. no. 150-1931-21
> Said to come from the church of Brentel at Le Mans (Sarthe)
> Ex collections: Demotte, Paris; Moreau-Néret
> Wood, polychromed
> H. ca. 113 cm.
>
> Second half 12th century (ca. 1180?)

This sculpture has suffered some serious damage. The dowel in Mary's lap indicates that the figure of the Child was once secured there. Also lost is Mary's left hand, which was similarly doweled into place, and her right shoulder is in fragmentary condition. A break on this side of the statue continues to the base where a modern panel supports the work. The figure was hollowed to extreme thinness up to a level just below the shoulders; the resulting fragility probably accounts in part for the losses. The face is heavily repainted.

A stylistic feature which especially distinguishes the work is the fluent fold system of the drapery. Despite concentric circles and other nested patterns, the forms are gently modulated, suggesting a rather late hand. The long, slender proportions and the treatment of the head, which is adorned with a crown and a finely fluted veil twisting about the shoulders, relate this figure to the Walters Madonna (no. 106). The fashion of the lower hemlines closely resembles the Madonna from Saint-Martin, Angers, now in the Yale University Art Gallery (Fig. 188), which is usually dated ca. 1180. The sheaf of vertical pleats in the skirt is identical and the asymmetrical fall of the robe is very close. The Angers Madonna also shows a similar arrangement for Mary's veil. If the Pitcairn Madonna does indeed come from Le Mans, as reported by Réau and as implied by the clear affinities to stone sculpture in the area (e.g. Le Mans Cathedral, south portal; Angers Cathedral and Saint-Martin), then it may well represent a contemporary but little-known wood atelier in the Sarthe valley. Like the stone sculpture it would seem to have depended heavily upon Ile-de-France models of the middle of the century and interpretations of them in the second Saint-Denis style of ca. 1170.

BIBLIOGRAPHY: Réau, *Collection Demotte, La Vierge en France*, pl. 2, pp. 8-9.

§ 108. [Fig. 189]
SAUMUR (MAINE-ET-LOIRE)

Notre-Dame de Nantilly

M.H. 11-1-1897
Wood, polychromed
H. ca. 100 cm.

Late 12th century (?)

Although the freshness of this sculpture makes it appear to have been renewed long after the Romanesque period, it is of interest in illustrating the Angevin style of ca. 1180. The pleating of the tunic of Mary, the asymmetrical fall of her robe, and the winding of the veil about her head, even its fall in long vertical folds over her shoulder, follow the drapery manner of the stone Madonna from Saint-Martin, Angers (Fig. 188) now in the Yale University Art Gallery, and can be compared with the Madonna on loan to the Philadelphia Museum from the Pitcairn Collection (no. 107). The crown and hands of Mary seem fairly recent in the Saumur work and the Child, fitted with a brass pin into Mary's lap, is undoubtedly a modern addition. Rohault de Fleury reproduced an engraving of the Madonna, in which the Child is lacking, and also published a drawing which shows the figure in its present state. He commented on the heavily restored polychromy which made it difficult to determine the antiquity of the entire work even in his day.

BIBLIOGRAPHY: Fleury, *Vierge*, II, pp. 162-163, pl. CXXX; A. Rhein, "Notre-Dame de Nantilly, Saumur," *Congrès archéologique de France, Saumur*, 1910, Paris, 1911, I, 12-18; *Liste des objets meubles*, Dept. Maine-et-Loire, 1947, p. 21; Schreiner, *Die frühgotische Plastik Südwestfrankreichs*, pp. 15-16, fig. 8.

§109. [Fig. 190]

SOISSONS (AISNE)

From Presles-et-Thierry
Wood, polychromed
H. 74.5 cm.

12th-13th century

Modest in quality and ill-preserved, this statue is nevertheless interesting as indicating the extent of Romanesque style in northern France. Technically deficient, the work has suffered seriously from two ruptures in the back. The base is worn, the hands of the Child are lost and the surface of the work has eroded badly. Weakly executed folds, heavy proportions and a solid structure indicate a provincial origin, while the separate veil for Mary and the drapery folds suggest a possible affiliation with the Allier group (nos. 81ff.). There is a small circular niche in the back of Mary, once closed with a panel, which presumably held relics at one time.

BIBLIOGRAPHY: Previously unpublished.

110.

MENDE (LOZERE)

Notre-Dame de Mende

M.H. 22-8-1950
Walnut, polychromed
H. ca. 80 cm.

After 1200 (?)

The loss of the Christ Child, Mary's forearms, parts of her feet and almost all of the throne, in addition to the damage caused by a large rupture in the back of the figure, have seriously affected the appearance of the statue which is currently being restored. According to J. Bounial, traces of an original silver sheath are visible at Mary's feet.

Fleury reported the local tradition that this *Vierge noire* was brought from the Holy Land in 1253 where it had supposedly been carved earlier by Frankish monks. Such claims are associated with other Romanesque Madonnas, notably Notre-Dame du Puy, whose later history is also recalled at Mende by the fact that in 1857 a roll of parchment was found in the compartment between the shoulders of the carved back of Notre-Dame de Mende. It was inscribed with the words "capelli Beatae Mariae Virginis." An inventory of the many other relics and their authentications found therein was made at that time. The inventory of 1380 simply mentions a statue of the Blessed Virgin Mary, but it may well have been this one. The statue is said to have been severely damaged during the Wars of Religion in the sixteenth century and hidden during the Revolution for security; its veneration was revived in the nineteenth century, culminating in its coronation on December 18, 1893.

The softly rounded forms of the body, its slump and the fluent style of the drapery suggest a work after 1200.

BIBLIOGRAPHY: Fleury, *Vierge*, II, p. 243; M. Balmelle, "Notre-Dame de Mende," *Lozère Nouvelles*, August 11, 1946; *Liste des objets meubles*, Dept. Lozère, 1954, p. 3; J. Bounial, "La Statue de Notre-Dame de Mende," typescript in the Archives départementales, Mende, 1955; E. Delmas, *Les Madones de chez nous*, Mende, 1957, pp. 3-7.

Sculptures which follow the French Romanesque type of Madonna in Majesty, and which have been attributed to the period, are also found in the following locations:

Arceau (Côte-d'Or)
M.H. 5-11-1923; *Liste des objets meubles*, Dept. Côte-d'Or, 1957, p. 5.

Authezat (Puy-de-Dôme)
M.H. 5-12-1908; Fleury, *Vierge*, II, p. 214; Bréhier, "Vierges romanes," fig. 39; *Liste des objets meubles*, Dept. Puy-de-Dôme, 1957, p. 5.

§Auzat (Puy-de-Dôme)
M.H. 22-4-1955; *Liste des objets meubles*, Dept. Puy-de-Dôme, 1957, p. 5.

§Avioth (Meuse)
Reiners and Ewald, *Kunstdenkmäler zwischen Maas und Mosel*, p. 201; M. Dumolin, "Avioth," *Congrès archéologiques de France, Nancy et Verdun, 1933*, Paris, 1934, 462-463.

§Beaune (Côte-d'Or)
M.H. 9-8-1901; Fleury, *Vierge*, II, pl. CXXVIII; Quarré, "La Statue de Notre-Dame de Bon Espoir," 197 n. 2; *Liste des objets meubles*, Dept. Côte-d'Or, 1957, p. 11.

Besson (Allier), Private Collection
M.H. 15-4-1965

La Bourboule (Puy-de-Dôme), Private Collection
Bréhier, "Vierges romanes," fig. 19.

§Bryn Athyn, Pennsylvania, Pitcairn Collection
The Art News, XXIX (1931), 31, 34; *The Arts*, 1931, 468, 473.

Calmeilles (Pyrénées-Orientales)
M.H. 2-4-1908; *Liste des objets meubles*, Dept. Pyrénées-Orientales, 1956, p. 7.

Camelas (Pyrénées-Orientales) M.H. 5-12-1962; *Liste des objets meubles*, Dept. Pyrénées-Orientales, 1956 (hand insert).

§Chappes (Allier)
M.H. 23-12-1918; Fleury, *Vierge*, II, p. 252; *Liste des objets meubles*, Dept. Allier, 1954, p. 7.

§Chastreix (Puy-de-Dôme)
M.H. 20-5-1958; Bréhier, "Vierges romanes," fig. 35; *Liste des objets meubles*, Dept. Puy-de-Dôme, 1957, p. 8 (hand insert); *Vierges romanes*, pls. 48-50.

§Chazeuil (Allier)
Vierges romanes, pl. 4.

§Cincinnati Art Museum
Magazine of Art, XXXIX (1946), opp. 353; *Guide to the Cincinnati Art Museum*, Cincinnati, [1956], p. 14; *Sculpture Collection of the Cincinnati Art Museum*, Cincinnati, 1970, p. 123.

Clermont-Ferrand (Puy-de-Dôme), Private Collection in Riom
Riom, Musée Mandet, *Collections privées d'Auvergne*, ed. J. Lugand and J. Nougaret, 1970, no. 2.

§Clermont-Ferrand (Puy-de-Dôme), La Providence
Pourreyron, *Le Culte*, pp. 72-73; Bréhier, "Vierges romanes," fig. 25.

§Cusset (Allier)
  M.H. 23-12-1918; *Liste des objets meubles*, Dept. Allier, 1954, p. 7.
§Dauzat-sur-Vodable (Puy-de-Dôme), Roche-Charles
  Bréhier, "Vierges romanes," fig. 23; Gybal, *L'Auvergne*, p. 100.
§Estables (Aveyron)
  Rodez, *Notre-Dame en Rouergue*, ed. J. Bousquet, 1951, pp. 9, 17.
§Illier-Laramade (Ariège)
  M.H. 17-6-1960; *Liste des objets meubles*, Dept. Ariège, 1956, p. 6 (hand insert).
§Iré-les-Prés (Meuse)
  Saint-Rouin, *La Vierge*, 1958, no. 2.
§Lamarche (Vosges), Aureil-Maison
  M.H. 22-12-1947; *Liste des objets meubles*, Dept. Vosges, 1957, p. 15.
Madrid, Museo Arqueologico Nacional
  Cook, *Pintura et imagineria*, p. 363; Barcelona, *El arte romanica*, 1961, no. 1680.
§Massaic (Cantal)
  Aurillac, *Orfèvrerie*, 1959, no. 40.
§Meymac (Corrèze)
  M.H. 12-11-1908; *Liste des objets meubles*, Dept. Corrèze, 1959, p. 13.
§Moulins (Allier)
  M.H. 7-4-1902; Fleury, *Vierge*, II, pl. CXXVII; *Liste des objets meubles*, Dept. Allier, 1954, p. 15.

§New York, New York, De Kolb Collection
  E. De Kolb, *Romanesque Madonnas*, New York, 1961; Notre Dame, Indiana, University of Notre Dame Art Gallery, *The De Kolb Collection of Romanesque Art*, ed. S. Ferber, 1969.
Pavie (Gers)
  M.H. 1-7-1905; *Liste des objets meubles*, Dept. Gers, 1964.
§Philadelphia, Museum of Art
  Art News, XXIX (1931), 34.
§Pouilly-en-Auxois (Côte-d'Or)
  M.H. 2-12-1907; *Liste des objets meubles*, Dept. Côte-d'Or, 1957, p. 91.
Reims (Marne), Institut Maintenon
  Saint-Rouin, *La Vierge*, 1958, no. 3.
Reims (Marne), Private Collection
  Saint-Rouin, *La Vierge*, 1958, no. 4.
Remiremont (Vosges)
  M.H. 20-6-1907; *Liste des objets meubles*, Dept. Vosges, 1957, p. 21.
Rochelambert (Haute-Loire), Château
  Salmann, *Connoisseur*, 3-7
St. Louis, Missouri, City Art Museum
Saulzet-le-Froid (Puy-de-Dôme)
Turlande (Cantal)
  Olivier, *L'ancienne Statue*, p. 14; Beaufrère, *Richesses*, p. 141.
§Valempoulières (Jura)
  M.H. 15-7-1958; *Liste des objets meubles*, Dept. Jura, 1947, p. 36 (hand insert).

Appendix II

Belgian, German and Swiss versions of the Madonna in Majesty are numerous and include some remarkable Romanesque works of art. Notable examples appear in the following collections:

Alsemberg, Notre-Dame
Antwerp, Private Collection
Basel, Museum
§Berlin, Staatliche Museen
Bern, Historisches Museum
§Bonn, Rheinisches Landesmuseum
Brixen, Diözesan Museum
Brussels, Stoclet Collection
§Buschhoven, Parish Church
Chiemsee, Private Collection
§Cologne, Schnütgen Museum
Disentis, Klostermuseum
Dresden, Altertumsmuseum
Dublin, Hunt Collection
Einsiedeln, Birchler Collection
Familleureux (Hainaut), Parish Church
§Frankfurt-am-Main, Liebieghaus
Freiburg, Minster
Garsen, Notre-Dame
§Hannover, Niedersächsische Landesgalerie
§Hartford, Wadsworth Athenaeum
Helsingfors, Historical Museum
§Hoven-Zülpich, Klosterhoven

Koblenz, St. Castor (formerly)
§London, Victoria and Albert Museum
§Louvain, Saint-Pierre
Milte, Rectory
§Munich, Bayerisches Nationalmuseum
§Münster, Diözesan Museum
§Nuremberg, Germanisches
   Nationalmuseum
§Paderborn, Diözesan Museum
Petersberg-bei-Halle, St. Peter
Rheydt, Private Collection
§Stuttgart, Württembergisches
   Landesmuseum
§Sürth-bei-Köln, Private Collection
§Thuin (Hainaut), church of Notre-Dame
   du Val
Tongres (Hainaut), Notre-Dame
§Trier, Bischöfliches Museum
Villers-Notre-Dame (Hainaut),
   Notre-Dame
§Werl, Abbey Church
Wil, Stadtmuseum
§Zurich, Schweizerisches Landesmuseum

Detailed bibliographies may be found in the author's "Cult Statues." Particularly useful studies are the following:

BELGIUM: Borchgrave d'Altena, "A Propos"; idem, *Madones anciennes*; idem, "Madones en Majesté."

GERMANY: G. Fiensch, "Eine Madonna im Diözesan Museum zu Münster," *Festschrift Martin Wackernagel*, Graz, 1958, 37-52; P. Halm and G. Lill, *Die Bildwerke des Bayerischen Nationalmuseums*, I, *Die Bildwerke in Holz und Stein vom XII. Jahrhunderts bis 1450*, Augsburg, 1924, nos. 14, 63, 65; Hamann, "Madonna"; G. von der Osten, *Katalog der Bildwerke in der niedersächsischen Landesgalerie, Hannover*, Munich, 1957, no. 4; K. A. Wirth, "Ein Skulpturenfragment in der ehemaligen Klosterkirche Huysburg," *Zeitschrift für Kunstgeschichte*, XXI (1958), 170-175; Wolters, "Die Madonna von Schillingskapellen"; Essen, *Marienbild*, 1968.

Cf. the discussion of earlier Madonnas from Germany in Chapter IV above.

SWITZERLAND: Baier-Futterer, *Kataloge des schweizerischen Landesmuseum*; Baum, "Romanische Marienbilder"; T. Brachert, "Drei romanische Marienbilder aus der Schweiz," *Schweizerisches Institut für Kunstwissenschaft, Jahresbericht*, 1964, 53-87; F. Gysin, *Holzplastik vom 11. bis zum 14. Jahrhundert aus dem schweizerischen Landesmuseum*, Zurich and Bern, 1958.

Swedish and Spanish Madonnas are even more numerous and have not been listed here. See A. Andersson, *Medieval Wooden Sculpture in Sweden*, II, *Romanesque and Gothic Sculpture*, Stockholm, 1966, Sanchez-Perez, *El culto Mariano*, and M. Trens, *Iconografia de la Virgen en el arte español*, Madrid, 1946, for relevant material. For comparable Italian sculptures, also not listed here, see G. Castelfranco, "Madonne romaniche in Legno," *Dedalo*, III (1930), 768-778, and Milan, *Mostra di sculture*, 1957.

Selected Bibliography

Aachen, Rathaus, *Karl der Grosse*, 1965.
—— *Unsere liebe Frau*, 1958.
Adhémar, Jean, *Influences antiques dans l'art du moyen âge français*, Studies of the Warburg Institute, VII, London, 1937.
Ahsmann, H., *Le Culte de la Sainte Vierge et la littérature française profane du moyen âge*, Utrecht, 1930.
Albers, Bruno, *Consuetudines monasticae*, I, *Consuetudines Farfensis*, Stuttgart and Vienna, 1900; IV, *Consuetudines Fructuariensis*, Monte Cassino, 1911; V, *Consuetudines Monasterium Germaniae, necnon S. Vitonis Virdunensis et Floriacensis Abbatiae, monumenta saeculi decimi continens*, Monte Cassino, 1912.
Algermissen, Konrad, "Die Geschichte der Marienverehrung in der Diözeses Hildesheim," *Unsere Diözese, Zeitschrift des Vereins für Heimatkunde im Bistum Hildesheim*, 1954, 1-28.
Amsterdam, Rijksmuseum, *Uit de Schatkamers der Middeleeuwen*, 1949.
Andersson, Aron, *Medieval Wooden Sculpture in Sweden*, II, *Romanesque and Gothic Sculpture*, Stockholm, 1966.
Antwerp, Musée Royal des Beaux-arts, *De Madonna in de Kunst*, 1954.
Anz, Heinrich, *Die lateinischen Magierspiele*, Leipzig, 1905.
Arens, Fritz, *Der Liber Ordinarius der Essener Stiftskirche*, Paderborn, 1908.
L'Art gaulois, La Pierre-qui-vire, 1956.
Aubert, Marcel, *L'Art roman en France*, Paris, 1961.

—— *Cathédrales et abbatiales romanes de France*, Grenoble, 1965.
—— *French Sculpture at the Beginning of the Gothic Period, 1140-1225*, Florence and Paris, 1929.
—— "Notre-Dame-du-Port à Clermont-Ferrand," *Congrès archéologique de France, Clermont-Ferrand, 1924*, Paris, 1925, 27-59.
Aurillac, Maison Consulaire, *Orfèvrerie et statuaire romane de Haute-Auvergne*, ed. André Muzac, 1959.
Auvergne romane, La Pierre-qui-vire, 1958.
Baier-Futterer, Ilse, *Kataloge des schweizerischen Landesmuseums in Zurich, Die Bildwerke der Romanik und Gotik*, Zurich, 1936.
Barcelona, Palacio Nacional de Montjuich, *El arte romanico*, 1961.
Bauch, Kurt, "Imago," *Beiträge zur Philosophie und Wissenschaft, Wilhelm Szilasi zum 70. Geburtstag*, Munich, 1960, 9-28.
Baum, Julius, "Romanische Marienbilder im schweizerische Landesmuseum," *Anzeiger für schweizerische Altertumskunde*, XXVII (1925), 215-227.
Baum, Paull Franklin, "The Young Man Betrothed to a Statue," *Publications of the Modern Language Association of America*, XXXIV (1919), 523-579.
Beaufrère, Abel, *Richesses de la France, Le Cantal*, LXIII (1965), 127-141.
Beenken, Hermann, *Romanische Skulptur in Deutschland*, Leipzig, 1924.
Beissel, Stephen, *Die Geschichte der Ver-*

ehrung Marias in Deutschland, Freiburg-im-Breisgau, 1890.

Benton, John F., *Self and Society in Medieval France, The Memoirs of Abbot Guibert of Nogent*, New York, 1970.

Bernard, Auguste, *see* Bruel.

Beumann, Helmut, "Grab und Thron Karls des Grossen in Aachen," *Karl der Grosse*, IV, *Das Nachleben*, Düsseldorf, 1967, 9-38.

Beutler, Christien, *Bildwerke zwischen Antike und Mittelalter*, Düsseldorf, 1964.

——— "Documents sur la sculpture carolingienne, I," *Gazette des beaux-arts*, CIV (1962), 445-455.

Bevan, Edwyn, *Holy Images*, London, 1940.

Blindheim, Martin, *Main Trends of East-Norwegian Wooden Figure Sculpture in the Second Half of the Thirteenth Century*, Oslo, 1952.

Bloch, Peter, "Nachwirkungen des Alten Bundes in der christlichen Kunst," *Monumenta Judaica*, Handbuch, Eine Ausstellung im Kölnischen Stadtmuseum, 1963-1964, Cologne, 1964, 735-781.

——— "Überlegungen zum Typus der Essener Madonna," *Kolloquium über frühmittelalterliche Skulptur, 1968*, Mainz, 1969, 65-69.

——— and Schnitzler, Hermann, *Die Ottonische Kölner Malerschule*, Düsseldorf, 1967.

Boll, F., *Aus der Offenbarung Johannis*, Berlin, 1914.

Borchgrave d'Altena, Joseph, *Art mosan*, Brussels and Paris, 1951.

——— *Madones anciennes conservées en Belgique, 1025-1425*, Brussels, 1945.

——— "Madones en Majesté, A propos de Notre-Dame d'Eprave," *Revue belge d'archéologie et d'histoire de l'art*, XXX (1961), 3-114.

——— "A Propos des Vierges en majesté conservées en Belgique," *Bulletin des musées royaux d'art et d'histoire*, 1937, 16-17.

——— "La Vierge de pèlerinage à Walcourt," *La Revue d'art*, XXVIII (1926), 56-61.

Bouillet, Auguste, *L'Eglise et le trésor de Conques*, Mâcon, 1892.

——— *Liber miraculorum Sancte Fidis*, Collection de textes pour servir à l'étude et à l'enseignement de l'histoire, Paris, 1897.

——— *Sainte Foy, vierge et martyre*, Rodez, 1900.

Branner, Robert, *Chartres Cathedral*, Norton Critical Studies in Art History, New York, 1969.

Braun, Joseph, *Der christliche Altar in seiner geschichtlichen Entwicklung*, Munich, 1924.

——— *Das christliche Altargerät in seinem Sein und in seiner Entwicklung*, Munich, 1932.

——— *Die Reliquiare des christlichen Kultes und ihre Entwicklung*, Freiburg im Breisgau, 1940.

Braunfels, Wolfgang, "Karls des Grossen Bronzewerkstatt," *Karl der Grosse*, III, *Karolingische Kunst*, Düsseldorf, 1967, 168-202.

Bréhier, Louis, *L'Art chrétien*, Paris, 1918.

——— "La Cathédrale de Clermont au Xe siècle et sa statue d'or de la Vierge," *La Renaissance de l'art français*, VII (1924), 205-210.

——— "Communication à propos de l'origine des Vierges noires," *Académie des Inscriptions et Belles-Lettres, Comptes rendus des séances, 1935*, Paris, 1935, 379-386.

——— "Deux inventaires du trésor de la cathédrale de Clermont au Xe siècle," *Etudes archéologiques, Mémoires de la société des "Amis de l'Université de Clermont-Ferrand," Supplément à la "Revue d'Auvergne,"* II, Clermont-Ferrand, 1910, 34-48.

——— "Notes sur les statues de Vierges romanes, Notre-Dame de Montvianeix et la question des Vierges noires," *Revue d'Auvergne*, XLVII (1933), 193-198.

—— "Les Origines de la sculpture romane," *Revue des deux mondes*, X (1912), 870-901.

—— "Vierges romanes d'Auvergne," *Le Point, revue artistique et littéraire*, XXV (1943), 12-33.

Brett, Gerard, "The Automata in the Byzantine 'Throne of Solomon,'" *Speculum*, XXIX (1954), 477-487.

Bruel, Alexandre, *Recueil des chartres de l'abbaye de Cluny, formé par Auguste Bernard*, Paris, 1876-1903.

Brunel, Clovis, *Les Miracles de Saint Privat*, Collections de textes pour servir à l'étude et à l'enseignement de l'histoire, Paris, 1912.

Bruyne, Edgar de, *Etudes d'esthétique médiévale*, Bruges, 1946.

Burg, Margaret, *Ottonische Plastik*, Bonn and Leipzig, 1922.

Busch, Harald, and Lohse, Bernd, *Pre-Romanesque Art*, New York, 1966.

Cabaniss, J. Allen, "Agobard of Lyons," *Speculum*, XXV (1951), 50-76.

Caillau, A. B., *Histoire critique et religieuse de Notre-Dame de Rocamadour*, Paris, 1834.

Caumont, Arcise, "Sur une excursion à Arras," *Bulletin monumental*, XX (1854), 89-123.

Certain, Eugène de, *Les Miracles de Saint Benoît (Miracula Sancti Benedicti)*, Paris, 1858.

Chabau, J. B., *Sanctuaires et pèlerinages de la Vierge dans le voisinage de Saint-Flour*, Paris, 1888.

Chalvet de Rochemonteix, Adolphe de, *Les Eglises romanes de la Haute-Auvergne*, Paris and Clermont-Ferrand, 1902.

Chambers, Edmund K., *The Mediaeval Stage*, London, 1903.

Chevalier, Ulysse, *Cartulaire de l'abbaye de St. Chaffre du Monastier*, Paris, 1884.

Clemen, Paul, *Berichte über die Tätigkeit der Provinzkommission für die Denkmalpflege in der Rheinprovinz und der Provinzialmuseum zu Bonn und Trier*, XI, 1906, Düsseldorf, 1907.

Cleveland Museum of Art, *Treasures from Medieval France*, ed. William Wixom, 1967.

Colin, J., "La Plastique 'greco-romaine' dans l'empire carolingien," *Cahiers archéologiques*, II (1947), 87-114.

Collon-Gevaert, S., LeJeune, J., and Stiennon, J., *Romanische Kunst an der Maas im 11., 12., und 13. Jahrhundert*, Brussels, 1962.

Cologne, Erzbischöflichen Diözesan-Museum, *Achthundert Jahre Verehrung der Heiligen Drei Könige in Köln, 1164-1964*, Kölner Domblatt, XXIII-XXIV, 1964.

Cook, Walter and Gudiol Ricart, José, *Pintura e imagineria románicas*, Ars Hispaniae, VI, Madrid, 1950.

Corvey, *Kunst und Kultur im Weserraum, 800-1600*, 1966.

Courson, Aurélien de, *Cartulaire de l'abbaye de St. Sauveur de Redon*, Paris, 1863.

Couturier de Chefdubois, C. de, *Mille Pèlerinages de Notre-Dame, Region B*, Paris, 1953.

Craplet, Bernard, "Vierges romanes," *Richesses de la France, Le Puy-de-Dôme*, XLIV (1960), 66-68.

Curé, Henri, *Saint-Philibert de Tournus*, Paris, 1905.

Delaporte, Yves, *Les Trois Notre-Dame de la cathédrale de Chartres*, Chartres, 1955.

Delius, Walter, *Geschichte der Marienverehrung*, Munich and Basel, 1963.

Delmont, H., *Guide du Cantal*, Aurillac, n.d.

Deschamps, Paul, "Etude sur la renaissance de la sculpture en France à l'époque romane," *Bulletin monumental*, LXXXIV (1925), 6-98.

—— "L'Orfèvrerie à Conques, vers l'an mille," *Bulletin monumental*, CVI (1948), 75-93.

Dijon, Musée, *Le Diocèse de Dijon*, 1957.

Dobrzeniecki, Tadeusz, "A Romanesque Statue of the Virgin and Child in the National Museum in Warsaw," *Bulletin du musée national de Varsovie*, VI (1965), no. 2-3, 33-42.

Donovan, Richard, *The Liturgical Drama in Medieval Spain*, Pontifical Institute of Medieval Studies, Studies and Texts, no. 4, Toronto, 1958.

Drochon, Jean Emmanuel B., *Histoire illustrée des pèlerinages français de la très Sainte Vierge*, Paris, 1890.

Duby, Georges, *The Making of the Christian West, 980-1140*, Geneva, 1967.

Duchesne, L., *Liber Pontificalis*, Paris, 1886-1892.

Duplès-Agier, Henri, *Chroniques de Saint-Martial de Limoges, publiées d'après les manuscrits originaux pour la société de l'histoire de France*, Paris, 1874.

Duprat, Clémence, "Sculptures du Roussillon associées aux croyances populaires," *Arts et traditions populaires*, V (1957), 329-338.

Durand-Lefébvre, Marie, *Art gallo-romain et sculpture romane*, Paris, 1937.

―――― *Etude sur l'origine des Vierges noires*, Paris, 1937.

Durliat, Marcel, "La Chasuble et la Vierge de Thuir," *Les Monuments historiques de la France*, n.s. I (1955), 176-181.

Einem, Herbert von, "Die Monumentalplastik des Mittelalters und ihr Verhältnis zur Antike," *Antike und Abendland*, III (1948), 120-151.

Elbern, Victor, *Das Erste Jahrtausend*, Tafelband, Düsseldorf, 1962.

Enaud, François, "L'Exposition d'art sacré de Haute-Auvergne," *Les Monuments historiques de la France*, n.s. V (1959), 190-192.

―――― "Remise en état de la statue de la Vierge à l'Enfant d'Orcival," *Les Monuments historiques de la France*, n.s. VII (1961), 79-88.

Espérandieu, Emil, *Recueil général des bas-reliefs, statues, et bustes de la Gaule romaine*, Paris, 1907-1955.

―――― *Recueil général des bas-reliefs, statues, et bustes de la Germanie romaine*, Paris and Brussels, 1931.

Essen, Villa Hügel, *Marienbild in Rheinland und Westfalen*, 1968.

―――― *Werdendes Abendland an Rhein und Ruhr*, 1956.

Evans, Joan, *Cluniac Art of the Romanesque Period*, Cambridge, 1950.

Fabre, F., Achard, A., and Thiallier, N., "Cinq statues en bois du XIIᵉ et du XIIIᵉ siècle," *Congrès archéologique de France, Le Puy, 1904*, Paris, 1905, 564-569.

Faujas de Saint-Fond, B., *Recherches sur les volcans éteints du Vivarais et du Velay*, Paris and Grenoble, 1778.

Fayalle, Marquis de, "Oeuvres d'orfèvrerie en Auvergne," *Congrès archéologique de France, Clermont-Ferrand, 1924*, Paris, 1925, 443-449.

―――― "Le Trésor de l'église de Saint-Nectaire," *Congrès archéologique de France, Clermont-Ferrand, 1895*, Paris, 1897, 292-306.

Fayen, Arnold, *Liber traditionum Sancti Petri Blandiniensis, Cartulaire de la ville de Gand—Oorkondenboek der Stad Gent, I, Livre des donations faites à l'abbaye de Saint-Pierre de Gand, depuis ses origines jusqu'au XIᵉ, avec des additions jusqu'en 1273*, Ghent, 1906.

Feulner, Adolph, "Imad Anna oder Imad Madonna," *Pantheon*, XXI (1938), 160.

Fichtenau, Heinrich, "Byzanz und die Pfalz zu Aachen," *Mitteilungen des Instituts für Österreichische Geschichtsforschung*, LIX (1951), 1-54.

―――― *The Carolingian Empire, The Age of Charlemagne*, Oxford, 1957.

Fleury, Rohault de, *La Sainte Vierge, Etudes archéologiques et iconographiques*, Paris, 1878.

Forgeais, Arthur, *Collection de plombs his-*

toriés trouvés dans la Seine, II, *Enseignes de pèlerinages*, Paris, 1863.

Forsyth, Ilene H., "The Mabon Madonna," *Mary, Throne of Wisdom*, Collegeville, Minnesota, 1963, 4-10.

———— "Magi and Majesty: A Study of Romanesque Sculpture and Liturgical Drama," *The Art Bulletin*, L (1968), 215-222.

———— *See also* Haering

Francovich, Géza de, "Arte carolingia ed ottoniana in Lombardia," *Römisches Jahrbuch für Kunstgeschichte*, VI (1942-1944), 115-252.

Frank, Grace, *The Medieval French Drama*, Oxford, 1954.

Freeman, Ann, "Theodulph of Orléans and the Libri Carolini," *Speculum*, XXXII (1957), 663-705.

Freeman, Margaret, "A Romanesque Virgin from Autun," *Metropolitan Museum of Art Bulletin*, n.s. VIII (1949), 112-116.

Fritz, Rolf, "Der Krucifixus von Benninghausen, ein Bildwerk des 11. Jahrhunderts," *Westfalen*, XXIX (1951), 141-153.

Froning, Richard, *Das Drama des Mittelalters*, Darmstadt, 1964 (reprint of orig. ed., Stuttgart, 1891-1892).

Fuchs, Alois, "Die goldene Madonna des Bischofs von Paderborn," *Zeitschrift für christliche Kunst*, XXXI (1918), 30335.

———— *Von Kreuzen, Madonnen und Altären*, Paderborn, 1940.

Gantner, Joseph, and Reinle, Adolf, *Kunstgeschichte der Schweiz*, I, Frauenfeld and Leipzig, 1936.

Gardner, Arthur, *Medieval Sculpture in France*, New York, 1931.

Gauthier, Marie-Madeleine, "Le Trésor de Conques," *Rouergue roman*, La Pierre-qui-vire, 1963, 98-145.

Grabar, André, "La Représentation de l'intelligible dans l'art byzantin du moyen âge," *Actes du VIᵉ congrès international d'études byzantines, Paris, 1948*, Paris, 1951, II, 127-143.

———— "La 'Sedia di San Marco' à Venise,"

Cahiers archéologiques, VII (1954), 19-34.

———— "Le Trône des martyrs," *Cahiers archéologiques*, VI (1952), 31-42.

Graham, Rose, and Clapham, A. W., "The Monastery of Cluny, 910-1155," *Archaeologia*, LXXX (1930), 143-178.

Grivot, Denis, and Zarnecki, George, *Gislebertus, Sculptor of Autun*, New York, 1961.

Grodecki, Louis, "La 'première Sculpture gothique,' Wilhelm Vöge et l'état actual des problèmes," *Bulletin monumental*, CXVII (1959), 265-292.

Guérard, Benjamin, *Cartulaire de l'abbaye de Saint Bertin de Saint-Omer*, France, I, Collections des cartulaires de France, III, Paris, 1840.

Guldan, Ernst, *Eva und Maria*, Graz and Cologne, 1966.

Gybal, André, *L'Auvergne, berceau de l'art roman*, Clermont-Ferrand, 1957.

Habicht, Victor, *Maria*, Oldenburg, 1926.

Haering, Ilene E., "Cult Statues of the Madonna in the Early Middle Ages," unpublished Ph.D. dissertation, Columbia University, 1960.

———— *see also* Forsyth.

Hamann, Richard, *Die Abteikirche von St. Gilles und ihre künstlerische Nachfolge*, Berlin, 1956.

———— "Die salzwedeler Madonna," *Marburger Jahrbuch für Kunstwissenschaft*, III (1927), 77-144.

———— "Studien zur ottonische Plastik," *Städel Jahrbuch*, VI (1930), 5-19.

Hamon, André Jean Marie, *Notre-Dame de France ou histoire du culte de la Sainte Vierge en France, depuis l'origine du christianisme jusqu'à nos jours*, Paris, 1861-1866.

Hardison, O. B., Jr., *Christian Rite and Christian Drama in the Middle Ages, Essays in the Origin and Early History of Modern Drama*, Baltimore, 1965.

Harnack, Adolph von, *History of Dogma*, trans. N. Buchanan, New York, 1961.

Haussherr, Reiner, *Der tote Christus am Kreuz, Zur Ikonographie des Gero-kreuzes*, doctoral dissertation, Bonn, 1963.

Hefele, Charles, *A History of the Councils of the Church*, trans. W. Clark, v, Edinburgh, 1896.

Heitz, Carol, *Recherches sur les rapports entre architecture et liturgie à l'époque carolingienne*, Paris, 1963.

Henderson, George, *Chartres*, Harmondsworth, 1968.

Hildburgh, W. L., "Medieval Copper Champlevé Enamelled Images of the Virgin and Child," *Archaeologia*, XCVI (1955), 115-158.

Hirn, Yrjö, *The Sacred Shrine*, 2nd ed., Boston, 1957.

Hourlier, Jacques, "Saint-Odilon bâtisseur," *Revue Mabillon*, LI (1961), 303-324.

Hubert, Jean, *L'Art pré-roman*, Paris, 1938.

Images de Notre-Dame, La Pierre-qui-vire, 1954.

Jacotin, A., "Mémoire de Antoine-Alexis Duranson sur le département de la Haute-Loire," *Mémoires de la société agricole et scientifique de la Haute-Loire*, XII (1902-1903), 47-111.

———— and Pascal, L., *Bibliographie du Velay et de la Haute-Loire*, published under the auspices of the Société agricole et scientifique de la Haute-Loire, I, Le Puy, 1903.

James, E. O., *The Cult of the Mother Goddess*, London, 1959.

Jantzen, Hans, *Ottonische Kunst*, 2nd ed., Hamburg, 1959.

Jusselin, Maurice, "Les Traditions de l'église de Chartres," *Mémoires de la société archéologique d'Eure et Loir*, XV (1915-1922), 1-26.

Kantorowicz, Ernst, *The King's Two Bodies, A Study in Mediaeval Political Theology*, Princeton, 1957.

———— *Laudes Regiae, A Study in Liturgical Acclamations and Mediaeval Ruler Worship*, Berkeley and Los Angeles, 1958.

Katzenellenbogen, Adolf, *The Sculptural Programs of Chartres Cathedral*, Baltimore, 1959.

Keller, Harald, "Zur Enstehung der sakralen Vollskulptur in der ottonischen Zeit," *Festschrift für Hans Jantzen*, Berlin, 1951, 71-90.

Kitzinger, Ernst, "The Coffin of St. Cuthbert" in *The Relics of St. Cuthbert*, ed. C. F. Battiscombe, Durham, 1956, 202-304.

———— "The Cult of Images in the Age before Iconoclasm," *Dumbarton Oaks Papers*, VIII (1954), 83-150.

———— "Some Icons of the VII Century," *Late Classical and Medieval Studies in Honor of Albert Mathias Friend, Jr.*, Princeton, 1955, 132-150.

Knögel, Elsemarie, *Schriftquellen zur Kunstgeschichte der Merovingerzeit, Bonner Jahrbücher*, CXXXX-CXXXXI (1936), 1-258.

Köhn, H., *Der Essener Münsterschatz*, Essen, 1955.

Kötting, Bernhard, *Peregrinatio Religiosa, Wallfahrten in der Antike und das Pilgerwesen in der alten Kirche*, Regensburg and Münster, 1950.

Kratz, J., *Der Dom zu Hildesheim*, Hildesheim, 1840.

Kreusch, Felix, "Kirche, Atrium und Portikus der Aachener Pfalz," *Karl der Grosse*, III, *Karolingische Kunst*, Düsseldorf, 1965, 463-533.

———— *Über Pfalzkapelle und Atrium zur Zeit Karls des Grossen, Dom zu Aachen*, Beiträge zur Baugeschichte IV, Aachen, 1958.

Ladner, Gerhart, "The Concept of the Image in the Greek Fathers and the Byzantine Iconoclastic Controversy," *Dumbarton Oaks Papers*, VII (1953), 1-34.

Lasareff, Victor, "Studies in the Iconography of the Virgin," *The Art Bulletin*, XX (1938), 26-65.

Lawrence, Marion, "Maria Regina," *The Art Bulletin*, VII (1924-1925), 150-161.

Lehmann-Brockhaus, Otto, *Die Kunst des X. Jahrhunderts im Lichte der Schriftquellen*, Leipzig, Strasbourg and Zurich, 1935.

———— *Lateinische Schriftquellen zur Kunst in England, Wales und Schottland vom Jahre 910 bis zum Jahre 1307*, Munich, 1955-1960.

———— *Schriftquellen zur Kunstgeschichte des 11. und 12. Jahrhunderts für Deutschland, Lothringen und Italien*, Berlin, 1938.

Lejeune, Jean, "Genèse de l'art Mosan," *Wallraf-Richartz Jahrbuch*, XV (1953), 47-73.

Lépinois, Eugene de, *Histoire de Chartres*, Chartres, 1854.

———— and Merlet, Lucien, *Cartulaire de Notre-Dame de Chartres*, Chartres, 1862-1865.

Lesne, Emile, *Histoire de la propriété ecclésiastique en France*, III, *L'Inventaire de la propriété, Eglises et trésors des églises du commencement du VIIIᵉ à la fin du XIᵉ siècle*, Mémoires et travaux des facultés catholiques de Lille, XLIV, Lille, 1936.

Lespinasse, René de and Bonnardot, François de, *Les Métiers et corporations de la ville de Paris, XIIIᵉ siècle, Le Livre des métiers d'Etienne Boileau*, Paris, 1879.

Liste des objets meubles ou immeubles par destination classés parmi les monuments historiques, Paris, 1943-.

Lourdes, Musée Pyrénéen, *La Vierge dans l'art et la tradition populaire des Pyrénées*, 1958.

Lüthgen, Eugen, *Romanische Plastik in Deutschland*, Bonn and Leipzig, 1923.

Mabillon, Jean, *Museum Italicum, seu collectio veterum scriptorum ex bibliothecis Italicis*, Paris, 1724.

Magistretti, Marcus, *Monumenta veteris liturgiae Ambrosianae*, I, *Pontificale in usum ecclesiae mediolanensis, necnon ordines Ambrosiani ex codices saec. IX-XV*, Milan, 1897.

Mâle, Emile, *L'Art religieux du XIIᵉ siècle en France*, Paris, 1922.

———— *La Fin du paganisme en Gaule*, Paris, 1950.

———— "Les Rois mages et le drame liturgique," *Gazette des beaux-arts*, LII (1910), 261-270.

Mansi, J. D., *Sacrorum conciliorum nova et amplissima collectio*, Venice, 1759-1798.

Marraccii, Hippolytus, *Polyanthea Mariana*, Cologne, 1710.

Marette, Jacqueline, *Connaissance des primitifs par l'étude du bois*, Paris, 1961.

Martène, Edmund and Durand, Ursin, *Voyage littéraire de deux religieux bénédictins da la Congrégation de Saint-Maur*, Paris, 1717.

Meer, F. van der, *Maiestas Domini, Théophanies de l'Apocalypse dans l'art chrétien*, Studi di antichità cristiana, Pontificio istituto di archeologia cristiana, XIII, Rome and Paris, 1938.

Mérimée, Prosper, *Notes d'un voyage en Auvergne*, Paris, 1838.

Merlet, René, *La Cathédrale de Chartres*, Paris, 1926.

———— "La Cathédrale de Chartres et ses origines, à propos de la découverte du puits des Saints-Forts," *Revue archéologique*, XLI (1902), 232-241.

———— "Le Puits des Saints-Forts et l'ancienne chapelle de Notre-Dame-sous-Terre," *Congrés archéologique de France, Chartres, 1900*, Paris, 1901, 226-255.

Messerer, Rosemarie, *Ottonische Goldschmiedewerke im Essener Münsterschatz*, doctoral dissertation, Munich, 1950.

Meyendorff, Jean, "L'Iconographie de la sagesse divine dans la tradition byzantine," *Cahiers archéologiques*, X (1959), 259-277.

Meyer, Eric, "Reliquie und Reliquiar im Mittelalter," *Eine Gabe der Freunde für Karl Georg Heise*, Berlin, 1950, 55-66.

Migne, J. P. (ed.), *Patrologiae cursus completus, Series Latina* [PL], Paris, 1844-

1904; *Series Graeca* [PG], Paris, 1857-1866.

Milan, Museo Poldi Pezzoli, *Mostra di sculture lignee medioevoli*, 1957.

Miller, Anne Lewis, "The Sculptural Decoration of Notre-Dame-du-Port: Its Place in Romanesque Sculpture of the Auvergne," unpublished Ph.D. dissertation, Johns Hopkins University, 1964.

Montfaucon, Bernard de, *Les Monumens de la monarchie françoise*, Paris, 1729.

Moreau, Edouard de, *Histoire de l'église en Belgique*, Brussels, 1945.

Mortet, Victor, "Note sur la date de rédaction des coutumes de Cluny dites de Farfa," *Millénaire de Cluny, Congrès d'histoire et d'archéologie tenu à Cluny, 1910*, Mâcon, 1910, I, pp. 142-145.

———— *Recueil de textes relatifs à l'histoire de l'architecture en France, XIe-XIIe siècles*, I, Collection de textes pour servir à l'étude et à l'enseignement de l'histoire, Paris, 1911.

Müller-Dietrich, Norbert, *Die Romanische Skulptur in Lothringen*, Munich and Berlin, 1968.

Munich, Bayerische Staatsbibliothek, *Ars Sacra, Kunst des frühen Mittelalters*, ed. A. Böckler, 1950.

Münster, Landesmuseum für Kunst und Kulturgeschichte, *Westfalia Sacra*, 1951-1952.

Muzac, André, *Sculpture romane de Haute-Auvergne*, Aurillac, 1966.

New York, Metropolitan Museum of Art, *The Year 1200*, ed. Konrad Hoffmann, The Cloisters Studies in Medieval Art, I, 1970.

Norden, E., *Die Geburt des Kindes*, Leipzig, 1924.

Nordenfalk, Carl, "Der Meister des Registrum Gregorii," *Münchener Jahrbuch der bildenden Kunst*, I (1950), 61-77.

Olivier, P., *L'ancienne Statue romane de Notre-Dame du Puy, vierge noire miraculeuse, essai d'iconographie critique*, Le Puy-en-Velay, 1921.

Oslender, F., "Die goldene Madonna," *Das Münster am Hellweg*, XI (1958), 34-56.

Panofsky, Erwin, *Die deutsche Plastik des 11. bis 13. Jahrhunderts*, Munich, 1924.

Paris, Louvre, *Chefs-d'oeuvre romans de musées de province*, 1957-1958.

———— *L'Europe gothique XIIe-XIVe siècles*, 1968.

Paris, Musée des Arts Décoratifs, *Les Trésors des églises de France*, 1965.

Paris, Petit Palais, *La Vierge dans l'art français*, 1950.

Pfeilstücker, Suse, *Spätantikes und germanisches Kunstgut in der frühangelsächsischen Kunst, nach lateinischen und altenglischen Schriftquellen*, Berlin, 1936.

Pfister, F., *Der Reliquienkult im Altertum*, Giessen, 1909-1912.

Picton, Harold W., *Early German Art and its Origins*, London, 1939.

Piper, F., "Maria als Thron Salomos und ihre Tugenden bei der Verkündigung," *Jahrbücher für Kunstwissenschaft*, V (1873), 97-137.

Poole, Reginald Lane, *Illustrations of the History of Medieval Thought and Learning*, 2nd ed., New York, 1960.

Porter, Arthur Kingsley, *Romanesque Sculpture of the Pilgrimage Roads*, Boston, 1923.

Pourreyron, C., *Le Culte de Notre-Dame au diocèse de Clermont en Auvergne*, Nancy, 1936.

Pressouyre, Léon, "Reflections sur la sculpture du XIIème siècle en Champagne," *Gesta*, IX/2 (1970), 16-31.

Quarré, Pierre, "La Statue de Notre-Dame de Bon Espoir à Dijon et son ancienne polychromie," *Mémoires de la commission des antiquités de la Côte-d'Or*, XXIII (1947-1953), 190-197.

Réau, Louis, *Collection Demotte, La Vierge en France, XII-XIV siècle*, New York, 1930.

Redlefsen, Ellen, *Mariendarstellungen*, doctoral dissertation, Kiel, 1937.

Reiners, H. and Ewald, W., *Kunstdenkmäler zwischen Maas und Mosel*, Munich, 1921.

Rigodon, René, "Vision de Robert, abbé de Mozat, au sujet de la basilique de la Mère de Dieu edifiée dans la Ville des Arvernes, relation par le diacre Arnaud (Ms de Clermont 145, fol. 130-134)," *Bulletin historique et scientifique de l'Auvergne*, LXX (1950), 22-55.

Roulliard, Sébastien, *Parthénie ou histoire de Chartres*, Paris, 1609.

Rupin, Ernest, *L'Oeuvre de Limoges*, Paris, 1890.

Sabbe, E., "Le Culte marial et la genèse de la sculpture médiévale," *Revue belge d'archéologie et d'histoire de l'art*, XX (1951), 101-125.

Saillens, Emile, *Nos Vierges noires, leurs origines*, Paris, 1945.

Saint-Rouin, *La Vierge dans l'art lorrain et champenois*, 1958.

Salmann, George S., "The Castle of La Rochelambert," *Connoisseur*, CLVII (1964), 3-7.

Saltet, Louis, "Perse et Conques, rapports entre deux portails voisins du XIIe siècle," *Bulletin de la société archéologique du midi de la France*, XLVI (1917-1921), 72-92.

Sanchez-Perez, José Augusto, *El culto Mariano en Espagna*, Madrid, 1943.

Sauerländer, Willibald, "Die kunstgeschichtliche Stellung der Westportale von Notre-Dame in Paris," *Marburger Jahrbuch für Kunstwissenschaft*, XVII (1959), 1-56.

——— "Die Marienkrönungsportale von Senlis und Mantes," *Wallraf-Richartz Jahrbuch*, XX (1958), 115-162.

——— *Von Sens bis Strassburg, Beiträge zur Kunstgeschichtlichen Stellung der Strassburger Querhausskulpturen*, Berlin, 1966.

——— "Skulpturen des 12. Jahrhunderts in Châlons-sur-Marne," *Zeitschrift für Kunstgeschichte*, XXV (1962), 97-124.

——— "Twelfth-century Sculpture at Châlons-sur-Marne," *Acts of the 20th International Congress of the History of Art, New York, 1961, Studies in Western Art*, I, *Romanesque and Gothic Art*, Princeton, 1963, 119-128.

Savaron, Jean, *De sanctis ecclesiis et monasteriis Claromontii*, Paris, 1608, reprinted in *Les Origines de Clairmont*, ed. P. Durand, Paris, 1662, pp. 341-365.

Schade, H., "Die Libri Carolini und ihre Stellung zum Bild," *Zeitschrift für katholische Theologie*, LXXIX (1957), 69-78.

Scheffczyk, Leo, *Das Mariengeheimnis in Frömmigkeit und Lehre der Karolingerzeit*, Leipzig, 1959.

Schlosser, Julius von, *Quellenbuch zur Kunstgeschichte des abendländischen Mittelalters, Ausgewählte Texte des vierten bis fünfzehnten Jahrhunderts*, Quellenschriften für Kunstgeschichte, VII, Vienna, 1896.

——— *Schriftquellen zur Geschichte der Karolingischen Kunst*, Quellenschriften für Kunstgeschichte, n.s. IV, Vienna, 1892.

Schmoll Gen. Eisenwerth, J. A., "Sion-Apokalyptisches Weib—Ecclesia Lactans," *Miscellanea Pro Arte, Hermann Schnitzler zur Vollendung des 60. Lebensjahres am 13. Januar, 1965*, Düsseldorf, 1965, 91-110.

Schnitzler, Hermann, *Rheinische Schatzkammer*, Düsseldorf, 1957.

Schrade, Hubert, "Zur Frühgeschichte der mittelalterlichen Monumentalplastik," *Westfalen*, XXXV (1957), 33-64.

Schramm, Percy Ernst, *Herrschaftszeichen und Staatssymbolik*, Schriften der Monumenta Germaniae historica, XIII, Stuttgart, 1955-1956.

Schreiner, Ludwig, *Die frühgotische Plastik Südwestfrankreichs, Studien zum Style Plantagenet zwischen 1170 und 1240*, Cologne and Graz, 1963.

Stoddard, Whitney S., *The West Portals of Saint-Denis and Chartres*, Cambridge, Mass., 1952.

Swarzenski, Hanns, *Monuments of Roman-esque Art*, Chicago, 1954.

Taralon, Jean, "Majesté de Sainte Foy," *Les Trésors des églises de France*, Paris, Mu-sée des Arts Décoratifs, 1965, no. 534, 289-294.

———— "La nouvelle Présentation du trésor de Conques," *Les Monuments historiques de la France*, n.s. 1 (1955), 121-141.

Theophilus, *The Various Arts*, trans. C. R. Dodwell, London, 1961.

Thierry, Dom, *Notre-Dame de Walcourt*, Walcourt, 1938.

Thompson, Stith, *Motif-Index of Folk Lit-erature*, Bloomington, Indiana, 1955-1958.

Tournai, Cathédrale, *La Madone dans l'art en Hainaut*, 1960.

Trens, M., *Iconografia de la Virgen en el arte español*, Madrid, 1946.

Usener, Karl, *Les Débuts du style roman dans l'art mosan: L'art mosan*, Paris, 1953.

Vezin, Gilberte, *L'Adoration et le cycle des mages*, Paris, 1950.

Vieillard-Troiekouroff, May, "La Cathé-drale de Clermont du Vᵉ au XIIIᵉ siècle," *Cahiers archéologiques*, XI (1960), 199-247.

Vierges romanes, La Pierre-qui-vire, 1961.

Vitry, Paul and Brière, Gaston, *Documents de sculpture français du moyen-âge*, Par-is, 1906.

Vloberg, Maurice, *La Vierge et l'Enfant dans l'art français*, Paris and Grenoble, 1954.

Vöge, Wilhelm, *Die Anfänge des monu-mentalen Stils im Mittelalter*, Strasbourg, 1894.

———— "Ein kölner Holzbildhauer aus ro-manischer Zeit," *Monatshefte für Kunst-wissenschaft*, 1 (1908), 1113-1115.

Volbach, Wolfgang, *Elfenbeinarbeiten der Spätantike und des frühen Mittelalters*, Mainz, 1952.

Wallach, Liutpold, "The Unknown Author of the Libri Carolini. Patristic Exegesis, Mozarabic Antiphons and the Vetus Latina," *Didascaliae. Studies in Honor of Anselm M. Albareda*, New York, 1961, 469-516.

Weber, W., *Die aegyptisch-griechische Terrakotten*, Berlin, 1914.

Wellen, G. A., *Theotokos, Eine ikono-graphische Abhandlung über das Gottes-mutterbild in frühchristlichen Zeit*, Utrecht and Amsterdam, 1961.

Wesenberg, Rudolf, *Bernwardinische Plas-tik*, Berlin, 1955.

Wiepen, E., *Palmsonntagsprozession und Palmesel*, Bonn, 1903.

Wilm, H., *Das Gotische Holzfigur*, Leip-zig, 1923.

Wolters, A., "Die Madonna von Schillings-kapellen," *Form und Inhalt, Kunst-geschichtliche Studien Otto Schmitt zum 60. Geburtstag*, Stuttgart, 1950, 51-66.

Wormald, Francis, "The Throne of Solo-mon and St. Edward's Chair," *De Artibus Opuscula XL, Essays in Honor of Erwin Panofsky*, New York, 1961, 532-539.

Wrangham, Digby S., *The Liturgical Poet-ry of Adam of St. Victor*, London, 1881.

Wright, Edith, *The Dissemination of the Liturgical Drama in France*, Bryn Mawr, 1936.

Young, Karl, *The Drama of the Medieval Church*, Oxford, 1933, 2nd ed., 1962.

———— "Dramatic Ceremonies of the Feast of the Purification," *Speculum*, XV (1930), 97-102.

Index

Aachen, 82; Palace Chapel, bronzes in, 73, throne of Charlemagne, 88, 90, Fig. 22
Abingdon, 2n1, 19n35, 36, 102
Adam, *see* Christ as second Adam
Adam Master, *see* Verdun
Adam of St. Victor, 24, 26, 28n67, 28-29, 59
Adelelmus, artist and architect, 67, 90, 96-97
adoratio, 72n55
Adoration of the Magi: iconographic tradition, 52n70; play, 49, 52-54. *See also* Epiphany play
Aelfsinus, Abbot of Ely, 100
Agobardus, 71n55
Aldric of Le Mans, 73
Allier, locale of a group of statues, 144, 185-86
Ambert, *see* Paris, Louvre
Andreas of Fleury, 48, 101
Andrew of Crete, 24
Angelelme of Auxerre, 73
Angers, Saint-Martin, *see* New Haven, Conn., Yale University Gallery of Art
Antwerp, Plantin-Moretus Museum, Sedulius manuscript, M.17.4, 50, Fig. 4
Aragnouet (Hautes-Pyrénées), 183, Reg. 70, Fig. 137
Arceau (Côte-d'Or), 205
Arezzo relief, 26, 132, Fig. 1
Arnould, Abbot of Ghent, 36, 102
Arras Synod, 93-94
ateliers, 134, 139, 153
Athanasius, 24
Aubusson (Puy-de-Dôme), 138, 159, 167, Reg. 5, 28, Fig. 65
Augsburg, *Palmesel* of Ulrich, *see* *Palmesel*
Aurillac, statue of St. Gerald, 2n1, 10n4, 12, 39, 63, 79
authentication, 5, 156
Authezat (Puy-de-Dôme), 205
Autun, statue from, *see* New York, Metropolitan Museum of Art

Auvergne: styles of, 135-41; styles related to, 141-42, 178, 194; style of Morgan Master, 154; workshops, 134
Auxerre, crucifix, 73
Auzat (Puy-de-Dôme), 205
Avallon: image of Mary, 2n1, 48, 102; image of St. Lazarus, 79
Avioth (Meuse), 205

baldachin, *see* ciborium
Baltimore, The Walters Art Gallery, 201, Reg. 106, Fig. 186
Beaucaire relief, 26, 132, Fig. 2
Beaulieu (Corrèze), 13, 15, 195-97, Reg. 101, Figs. 174-76
Beaune (Côte-d'Or), 205
Bede, 24n57, 81
Belgium, statues in, 5n5, 207. *See also* Brussels; Liège; Walcourt
Bellevaux-en-Baugues (Savoie), 184, Reg. 76
benching, 19
Benninghausen Crucifix, 78
Bern, Bürgerbibliothek, Cod. 120, 90n157, Fig. 23
Bernard (Vendée), mother goddess from, 64, Fig. 11
Bernard of Angers, *Liber miraculorum*: attitudes toward images, 10n4, 81, 84-85, 99, 105, 110-11; gems in statues, 10; processions, 40; pagan images, 63; reliquary statues, 12, 36, 79, 81; statue of St. Foy, 69, 78-79; stucco statues, 9n1; terminology, 11n1
Bernard, Abbot of Beaulieu, 41. *See also* Conques, St. Foy
Bernerior, companion of Bernard of Angers, 63
Bernward, Bishop of Hildesheim, 123
Besse-en-Chandesse (Puy-de-Dôme), *see* Geneva, Private Collection
Besson (Allier), 205

Beutler, C., theory of, 6, 76n82

Billy-Chevannes (Nièvre), 192, Reg. 94, Fig. 166

birch, 16

Birkenbringhausen Crucifix, 78

Black Virgins, *see Vierge noire*

Blesle (Haute-Loire), 184, Reg. 75

Boso, King of Burgundy, bust given by, 77

Boston, Museum of Fine Arts, 152n40

La Bourboule (Puy-de-Dôme), 205

Bredons (Cantal), 166, 177, Reg. 25, 49, Figs. 85, 116; statue of St. Peter, 79

Bréhier, L., theory of, 5-6, 31, 38, 49-50, 68, 134, 161

Brioude, *see* Rouen

bronze: atelier in Aachen, 73-74; equestrian statuette, 74

Brussels, Musées Royaux d'Art et d'Histoire, 130-31, Fig. 52

Bryn Athyn, Pennsylvania, 205

Burgundy, type of statue, 16, 145-47, 152

Byzantine icons, compared to Throne of Wisdom statues, 12, 20, 49, 60

cabochon gems, 37

Caesarius von Heisterbach, relation of miracles, 3n2

Calmeilles (Puy-de-Dôme), 205

Cambrai, stucco image, 9n1, 39

Cambridge, Mass., Harvard University, Fogg Museum of Art, 148-50, 197-98, Reg. 102, Figs. 178-81

Cappenberg, Frederick Barbarossa, bust of, 80

Caroline Books, *see Libri Carolini*

Carolingian: Renaissance, 7, 82-83; sculpture, 67-77, 81-82, 91

Carrières-Saint-Denis, *see* Paris, Louvre

Cazarilh-Laspènes (Haute-Garonne), 15, 182, Reg. 66, Fig. 133

centers of production, 152-53

Chagny (Saône-et-Loire), *see* Nancy, Private Collection IV

Châlons-sur-Marne (Marne), 149-52

Chalus-Lembron (Puy-de-Dôme), 138, 173, Reg. 36, Fig. 102

Chanaleilles (Haute-Loire), 45n48, 138, 163-64, Reg. 18, Fig. 78

Chappes (Allier), 205

Charlemagne, 62, 71-73, 82-83, 89. *See also* Aachen, Palace Chapel

Chartres Cathedral: Bishop Fulbert's church, 106, 111; column statues of the Royal Portal, 146, 153, Figs. 159-61; Incarnation Portal, 29-30, 153; legend of "pre-Christian" statue of the Virgin (*Virgo paritura*), 59, 62, 105-07, 111; relics of the Virgin (tunic), 32, 44, 106, 109-10; statue of Notre-Dame-sous-terre, 2n1, 43, 95, 99n18, 102, 105-11, 112n73, Figs. 25-27

Chartres, *Vielle Chronique* (1389), 105n50, 110n66

Chassignoles (Haute-Loire), 174, Reg. 39, Fig. 105

Chastreix (Puy-de-Dôme), 205

Châteauneuf-les-Bains (Puy-de-Dôme), 180, Reg. 58, Fig. 125

Châtillon-sur-Loire, statue of the Virgin, 2n1, 39, 48, 101, 111

Chauriat (Puy-de-Dôme), 166, Reg. 27, Fig. 87

Chazeuil (Allier), 205

La Chomette (Haute-Loire), 139, 176, Reg. 47, Fig. 115

Christ as second Adam, 93

chrysotriclinos, 82, 86

Chur, 15n26

Church, Mary as symbol of, 23

ciborium, 49, 57

Cincinnati Art Museum, 205

civil ceremonies, 45

Classical renascence of Charlemagne, *see* Carolingian Renaissance

Claudius of Turin, 71n55

Claviers, *see* Moussages

Clermont-Ferrand: Bibl. Municipale, MS 145, 31, 49-50, 95, Fig. 3; golden Majesty of Mary, 1n1, 10, 49-50, 90-91, Fig. 3, destruction of, 14, 98-99, episode of the flies and the bees, 96-97, location, 39, making and history of, 95-100, models for, 67, 90-91, prototype for Throne of Wisdom statues, 31, 68, in relation to the St. Foy, 68, as a reliquary, 31-32, 77; goldsmith atelier, 170; Musée Bargoin, I, 173, Reg. 37, Fig. 103, II, 177, Reg. 51, Fig. 118; Notre-Dame-du-Port, south portal, 51, 140, 167, Figs. 5, 110; Private Collection in Riom, 205; La Providence, 205; style center, 140, 152-53

Cluny: Palm Sunday ceremony, 41-42; statue of St. Peter, 2n1, 37n15, 39, 41-42, 79

Collegeville, Minn., 192, Reg. 93, Fig. 165

Cologne: Burg Collection (formerly), 160, Reg. 8, Fig. 68; Gero Cross, 77, 100, 116-17,

Fig. 34; St. George Crucifix, 78; Schnütgen Museum, 127, Fig. 48; statue of the Virgin, 100; Seligmann Collection (formerly), 177, Reg. 50, Fig. 117

Conques, statue of St. Foy, 11n1, 10n4, 14, 31, 39, 44, 63, 85, Figs. 13-15; date of, 67-69, 81; miracles, 41-42; in procession, 40; as a reliquary, 12, 77-79

Constantine Porphyrogenitus, *Book of Ceremonies*, 86-87

Corneilla-de-Conflent (Pyrénées-Orientales), 143, 153, 180-81, Reg. 60, Fig. 127; as a type, 143, 180-82

Council, Second Nicene, *see* Council, Oecumenical, Seventh

Council, Oecumenical: Second, Constantinople I (381), 86-87; Third, Ephesus (431), 24, 87; Fourth, Chalcedon (451), 24; Seventh, Nicaea II (787), 7, 71, 91, 94; Eighth, Constantinople IV (869-870), 81, 87

Coutances, 39, 102

Coventry, 2n1, 48, 102

crucifixes, Ottonian, 77-78

crypts, 39

cult: of images in the East, 155; of relics, 61, 80, 82

cult statues, 2

curtains, 48, 57-58, 101

Cusset (Allier), 206

dating, 15, 152-54

Dauzat-sur-Vodable (Puy-de-Dôme), Roche-Charles, 206

Deschamps, P., theory of, 6

"détente" style, 147

devotional practices, 48-49

Dijon, Notre-Dame de Bon Espoir, 15n26, 22, 44, 145-47, 188-90, Figs. 154, 155

Dorres (Pyrénées-Orientales), 184, Reg. 73, Fig. 140

dowels, 17

Druchbert, Abbot of Mozat, 96-97

Dublin, Trinity College, Book of Kells, 118, Fig. 35

Durandus, William, 28

Durham, North Carolina, Duke University Museum, 165, Reg. 23, Fig. 83

Echlache (Puy-de-Dôme), 167, Reg. 29, Fig. 88

effigies, 11n1

Eighth General Synod, *see* Council, Oecumenical, Eighth

Einhard, 66, 83

Ely, 2n1, 100

Epiphany play, 49, 53-59

Erlauer, *Three Kings Play*, 58n89

Err (Pyrénées-Orientales), 181, Reg. 62, Fig. 129

Espalion-Perse (Aveyron), relief, 140-41, Fig. 111

Essen: First Mathilda Cross, 115-17, Fig. 33; golden Madonna, 2n1, 11, 13-15, 43, 99n17, 100, 112-21, 129-30, 188, Figs. 28-32; *Liber Ordinarius*, 43, 117-18; silver Madonna, 43; Theophanu Book Cover, 120, 126-27, 132, Fig. 36

Essen-Werden, reliefs, 126-27, Figs. 47a, b

Estables (Aveyron), 206

Etampes, column statues, 146, Fig. 158

Ethelwold of Winchester, 53n72

Etienne de Boileau, *Livre de métiers*, 18

Etimasia, 86, 88, 90

Eve, 93, 119, 193. *See also* Mary, as the New Eve

Evegnée, *see* Liège, Musée Diocésain

Evron, 44n44

Fabritius, Abbot of Abingdon, 36

Fogg Madonna, *see* Cambridge, Mass., Harvard University, Fogg Museum of Art

folk idols, 65, 67

forerunners of French Romanesque Throne of Wisdom statues, 92ff

forgeries, 5

Foy, St., *see* Conques

Frankfurt-am-Main: Liebieghaus, 52, 127-29, Figs. 9, 49; Private Collection (formerly), 144, 185, Reg. 77, Fig. 142; Synod (794), 71n55

freestanding sculpture, revival of, 6, 67-86, 91. *See also* Carolingian sculpture

Fulbert, Bishop of Chartres, 10n4, 106, 110-11. *See also* Chartres Cathedral

Fulchoinus, dean of Saint-Médard-de-Soissons, 76

Gauthier de Coincy, 46

Gauzbert, artist at Limoges, 79

Gauzlin, Abbot of Fleury, 101

Geneva: Musée d'Art et d'Histoire, 161, Reg. 11, Fig. 71; Private Collection, 164-65, Reg. 21, Fig. 81

Gerald, St., *see* Aurillac

Germanus, St., 75
Germany, statues in, 208. *See also* Essen; Hildesheim; Paderborn
Gero, Archbishop of Cologne, 77, 100, 116-17. *See also* Cologne
Gerresheim Crucifix, 78
Ghent, 2n1, 36, 102
gifts of Magi, symbolism, 27-29, 54, 59
Gildardus, St., 76
Gislebertus of Autun, 145, 188
Godiva, Countess of Malmesbury, 48, 102
gold: foil; repoussé; *see* repoussé
Guibert l'Illuminé, 69, 78
Guibert of Nogent, 24-25, 40n25, 62n6

Hamann, R., theory of, 5, 154
Hautes-Pyrénées, type of statue, 16, 142-43
heads, carved separately, 17
height of statues, 15-16
Henry VI, Emperor, 90, Fig. 23
Hermalle-sous-Huy, *see* Brussels, Musées Royaux
Heume l'Eglise (Puy-de-Dôme), 138, 159, Reg. 4, Figs. 64a, b
Hildesheim: bronze doors, 122-23, Fig. 42; golden Madonna, 13, 15, 18, 43, 45, 115, 121-24, 128-30, Figs. 37-41
Hix (Pyrénées-Orientales), Bourg-Madame, 183, Reg. 71, Fig. 138
hollowing the statue, 17-18
Honorius of Autun, 28
Hugh of Arles, King, 77
Hugh of Poitiers, 32-34, 39

icona, 1n1
Iconoclast Controversy, 61, 83
iconography, 22-30, 86-90, 120, 132
idea, 2n1
idol, 9, 10n4. *See also* folk idols
Illier-Laramade (Ariège), 206
Imad, Bishop of Paderborn, 124, 126-27
images: transcendental role of, 7, 61, 84, 91, 155; as proxies, 9, 49, 59-60, 91, 154-55. *See also* cult of images
imago, 2n1, 70n52
imperial images, 7, 84, 155
Incarnation dogma, 1, 4, 9, 24, 26, 155 and *passim*
"intermediate" style, 147
Iré-les-Prés (Meuse), 206
Isis, 20, 29
Italy, statues in, 208

John Belethus, 23n55
John of Damascus, 24
joinery, 16-19
Jonas of Orleans, 72n55
Jouhe (Jura), 194, Reg. 98, Fig. 171
Jouy-en-Josas (Yvelines), 150, 198-99, Reg. 103, Fig. 183

Keller, H., theory of, 6, 68, 76-78

Lamarche (Vosges), Aureil-Maison, 206
Lambach, Epiphany play, 55-56
Laurie (Cantal), 141-42, 178-79, Reg. 55, Fig. 122
lead sheathing, cast in moulds, 142, 179-80
Liber miraculorum Sancte Fidis, *see* Bernard of Angers
Liber Pontificalis, 66, 70, 82
Libri Carolini, 7, 9n1, 62-63, 69, 71-73, 82, 84, 89n154, 155
Liège, Musée Diocésain, 131, Fig. 53
Limay (Yvelines), 150, 199-200, Reg. 104, Fig. 184
Limoges, statue of St. Martial, 39, 79
linen, applied to wood, 19
lindenwood, 16
literary sources, statues known from, 92ff, 112
liturgical drama, 49-59; beginnings of, 53n72
location of statues, 38-40
Lorraine, style of, 147-48, 151, 193
Lothar, King, statue of, 76
Louis, St., 20, 103
Louis XI, King, 102-03, 107, 185
Luz (Haute-Pyrénées), 183, Reg. 69, Fig. 136
Lyon, Musée des Beaux-Arts, 138, 171-72, Reg. 33, Figs. 97a, b

Madonna in Majesty, 1, *passim*. *See also* Throne of Wisdom
Madrid, Museo Arqueologico Nacional, 206
Magi, *see* gifts of
Magna Mater, 29, 62
Maiestas, 1n1
Maiestas Sanctae Mariae, *see* Throne of Wisdom
Mailhat near Lamontgie (Puy-de-Dôme), 164, Reg. 19, Fig. 79; Private Collection, 175, Reg. 44, Fig. 109
Mainz, ivory Madonna, 122, Fig. 43
Majesty, concept in Carolingian times, 6, 88-89
Manosque (Basses-Alpes), 183-84, Reg. 72, Fig. 139

Le Mans: crucifix of Aldric, 73; statue from, 201-02. *See also* Philadelphia Museum of Art II

Mantes, portal sculpture, 149-50, 200

"Marriage" with the Virgin, 45-47

Marsat (Puy-de-Dôme), 21-22, 138, 172-73, Reg. 35, Fig. 101

Martial, St., *see* Limoges

Mary: as the Church, 23; epithets, 93; as the Great Intercessor, 93; importance in the eleventh century, 92-93; as the New Eve, 119, 193; as the Queen of Heaven, 29, 93; *regina nostri orbis*, 7, 119n89; as the throne of God, 24; as the Throne of Solomon, 24-30, 59, 90. *See also* Throne of Wisdom

Massiac (Cantal), 206

Maurice, St., reliquary bust given by King Boso, 77, 80-81

Maurs, statue of St. Césaire, 79

Meillers (Allier), 187-88, Reg. 86, Fig. 151

Mende (Lozère), 36, 203, Reg. 110; statue of St. Privatus, 2n11, 14, 39, 41, 79

metal sheathing of statues, 10-15. *See also* repoussé; lead sheathing

Meymac (Corrèze), 206

miracles, 3n2; immunity to fire, 48; discovery by shepherds or bulls, 3n2

mimetic function, *see* images, transcendental role of

mobility, 8, 40, 52

Molompize (Cantal), 160, Reg. 7, Fig. 67

Monastier, statue of St. Chaffre, 14, 67-68, 79, 169, Figs. 16, 17

Monistrol-d'Allier (Haute-Loire), 139, 176, Reg. 46, Figs. 113, 114

Montbolo (Pyrénées-Orientales), 181-82, Reg. 64, Fig. 131

Mont-devant-Sassey (Meuse), 16, 51, 147-48, 151, 193, Reg. 96, Figs. 8, 168, 169

Monteignet (Allier), 144, 185-86, Reg. 79, Fig. 144

Montmorency-Beaufort (Aube), 191, Reg. 91

Montpellier, Bibl. de la Faculté de Médecine, MS H 304, 56n83

Montpeyroux, Château (Puy-de-Dôme), *see* Thiers

Montvianeix (Puy-de-Dôme), statue from, 16-17, 19n38, 22, 136-37, 158, Reg. 3, Figs. 60-63. *See also* Morgan Master

Morgan Madonna, 16-17, 19n38, 136-38, 156-57, Reg. 1, Figs. 54-56, frontispiece; as a type, 16, 138-41, 152, 154, 156-57; related works, 159-62; same artist or workshop, 157-59; stylistic variants, 163-66. *See also* Morgan Master; New York, Metropolitan Museum of Art

Morgan Master, 136-38, 156-58; localization of oeuvre, 158; related styles, 138, 152, 154. *See also* Morgan Madonna

Mosan art, 147n25, 151

mother goddesses, 62, 64-65

Moulins (Allier), 206

Moussages (Cantal), 137-38, 157-58, Reg. 2, Figs. 57-59. *See also* New York, Metropolitan Museum of Art; Morgan Master

Mouziey-Teulet (Tarn), 194, Reg. 99, Fig. 172

Mozat, capitals, 141

Münster, head of St. Paul, 79-80

Nancy, Private Collection: I, 160-61, Reg. 10, Fig. 70; II, 175, Reg. 43, Fig. 108; III-VI, 186-87, Reg. 82-85, Figs. 147-50

Narbonne, crucifix of Theodard, 73, 78, 81

natural form, new interest in, 147

Nevers: Epiphany play, 55; Musée Lapidaire de la Porte du Croux, 192-93, Reg. 95, Fig. 167. *See also* Paris, Bibl. Mazarine, MS 1708

New Haven, Conn., Yale University Gallery of Art, stone sculpture from Angers, Saint-Martin, 150-51, 199-202, Figs. 188a, b

New York, Metropolitan Museum of Art, Throne of Wisdom statues: Dreicer, 173-74, Reg. 38, Fig. 104; Martin, 138, 170-71, Reg. 32, Figs. 95, 96; from Autun (at the Cloisters), 16, 18, 118, 145, 188-90, Reg. 87, Figs. 152, 153. *See also* Morgan Madonna

New York, Private Collection, 206

Nicaea, *see* Council, Oecumenical, Seventh

Nicholas of Verdun, 151

nikopoia iconography, 23, 65

Nogent, "pre-Christian" statue of the Virgin, 62n6. *See also* Guibert of Nogent

Notre-Dame d'Estours, *see* Monistrol d'Allier

oak, 16

Oberpleis, retable, 52, Fig. 10

oblatio, 54

Odeillo (Pyrénées-Orientales), 181, Reg. 61, Fig. 128

offertorium, 53n72, 54

Officium Stellae, *see* Epiphany play

Orcival (Puy-de-Dôme), 13-16, 44-45, 64, 99n17, 138, 168-70, Reg. 31, Figs. 90-94

Ottonian sculpture, style of, 113

Paderborn, Diözesan Museum, Imad Madonna, 15-16, 39-40, 112, 115, 124-29, Figs. 44-46. See also Imad, Bishop of Paderborn

Palmesel, 58; of Ulrich of Augsburg, 58n90, 100

Parentignat (Puy-de-Dôme), 138, 159-60, Reg. 6, Fig. 66

Paris: Bibl. Mazarine, MS 1708, 55n80; Bibl. Nationale, MS gr. 510, 86-87, Fig. 20, MS lat. 384, 57n86, MS lat. 1152, 53n72, MS lat. 1213, 58n87, MS lat. 17558, 77, Figs. 18, 19; Louvre, altar frontal from Carrières-Saint-Denis, 196, Fig. 177, statue of the Throne of Wisdom, 138, 172, Reg. 34, Figs. 98-100; Musée de Cluny, 162, Reg. 14, Fig. 74; Musée des Arts Décoratifs, 178, Reg. 54, Fig. 121; Saint-Germain-des-Prés, 75; Saint-Martin-des-Champs, see Saint-Denis; Synod (825), 71n55, 81

Pavie (Gers), 206

Payerne, image of Mary, 102

Peiresc, Fabri de, see Paris, Bibl. Nationale, MS lat. 17558

Peter Damian, 25

Peter Manlius, 70n52

Philadelphia Museum of Art, 206; I, 179, Reg. 56, Fig. 123; II, 201-02, Reg. 107, Fig. 187

pilgrimage, 95 and passim

Planès (Pyrénées-Orientales), 182, Reg. 65, Fig. 132

Poitiers, abbey of Sainte-Croix, 195, Reg. 100, Fig. 173

polychromy, 19-20

Pompierre (Vosges), tympanum reliefs, 51, 148, 193

Pope Benedict III, 70; Gregory III, 65, 70; Hadrian I, 71n55, 89; Hadrian II, 74-75, 85; Leo III, 70; Paschal I, 70; Paul I, 70n52; Stephen II, 70

portability, 8, 60, 132

Pouilly-en-Auxois (Côte-d'Or), 206

Prats-Balaguer (Pyrénées-Orientales), 181, Reg. 63, Fig. 130

"pre-Christian" statues of the Virgin and Child, 62n6

Presepe (praesepe), 56n84

preservation, 38, 134

Presles-et-Thierry, see Soissons

processions, 40-44 and passim

Prunay-le-Gillon, statuette now at Saint-Germain-en-Laye, 64, Fig. 12

Prunières (Lozère), 180, Reg. 59, Fig. 126

Le Puy, Throne of Wisdom statue from, 2n1, 39, 99n18, 102-05, Fig. 24; "pre-Christian" origin, 62n6; pilgrims, 95; processions, 43; as a reliquary, 36

Pyrénées-Orientales, type of statue, 16, 142-43

Queen of Sheba, 21, 27, 28n67

Quem quaeritis, Easter play, 53n72

Rabanus Maurus, 26n62, 72n55

Ragenarius, Duke, statue of, 111, 75-76, 80, 85

Raleigh, North Carolina Museum of Art, 165-66, Reg. 24, Fig. 84

Raymond of Saint-Gilles, 104-05

Rellinghausen, processions, 43

Redon, Saint-Sauveur, crucifix given by Duke Solomon, 73

regional styles, 134-54

Register, explanation of, 4, 156

Reims (Marne), 206

relic compartment in statue, 37-38; specific examples, passim

relics: used for fund raising, 40n25; within statues of saints, 37; of the Virgin, 31-32, 34-35, 96, 98, 104

reliquaries: as chests, 32; as earliest statues, 31, 76-80; as statuettes in copper and enamel, 37n16. See also Bernard of Angers

Remiremont (Vosges), 206

replicas, 4-5

repoussé technique, 9-10, 12-14, 168, 196; alternation of silver and silver gilt, 168, 196; correspondence between sheath and wood core, 13, 169; use of a bone tool, 13n16. See also Theophilus

retardataire examples, inclusion in Register, 4n3

revetment, see repoussé; metal sheathing of statues; lead sheathing

Rich, Edmund, Archbishop of Canterbury, 47

Ringelheim Crucifix, 78

Riom, Private Collection, see Clermont-Ferrand

Robert, Abbot of Mozat, vision, 10, 96-97

Rocamadour (Lot), 144, 185, Reg. 78, Fig. 143

Rochelambert (Haute-Loire), 162, Reg. 13, Fig. 73

Rodez, Majesty of Mary, 2n1, 42, 99-100; statue of St. Amandus, 42, 79; Synod, 42-43

Rome: Lateran Palace, Triclinium mosaic, 83; Private Collection, 177-78, Reg. 52, Fig. 119; Sta Francesca Romana, icon, 48n58; Sta Maria Maggiore, processions, 42, *praesepe* chapel, 56n84, 70n52

Rouen: Epiphany plays, 56-57, 56n83; Musée Départemental des Antiquités, 161, Reg. 12, Fig. 72. *See also* Montpellier, Bibl. de la Faculté de Médecine; Paris, Bibl. Nationale, MSS lat. 384, 1213

Sablon, Vincent, 21, 62n6, 106n51, 107-08

Saint-Benoît-sur-Loire, 42

Saint-Cirgues (Puy-de-Dôme), *see* Nancy, Private Collection I

Saint-Denis: column statues, 146, 153, Figs. 156, 157; statue from Saint-Martin-des-Champs, Paris, 15-16, 200-01, Reg. 105, Fig. 185

Saint-Flour, *see* Lyon, Musée des Beaux-Arts

Saint-Germain-en-Laye, *see* Prunay-le-Gillon

Saint-Gervazy (Puy-de-Dôme), 160, Reg. 9, Fig. 69

Saint-Laurent-Chabreuges (Haute-Loire), Entremont Chapel, 138, 163, Reg. 17, Fig. 77

St. Louis, Missouri, City Art Museum, 206

Sainte-Marie-des-Chazes (Haute-Loire), 175, Reg. 42

Saint-Martin-de-Lenne (Aveyron), 176, Reg. 48

Saint-Maurice d'Agaune, bust of St. Candidus, 79

Saint-Nectaire (Puy-de-Dôme): bust of St. Baudimus, 79; Throne of Wisdom statue, 162, Reg. 15, Fig. 75

Saint-Pourçain-sur-Sioule (Allier), *see* Tournus

Saint-Rémy-de-Chargnat (Puy-de-Dôme), 138, 163, Reg. 16, Fig. 76; as a type, 162, 163-67

Saint-Riquier: bronzes, 74n77; choir, 87

Saint-Savin (Hautes-Pyrénées), 143, 182-83, Reg. 67, 68, Figs. 134, 135; as a type, 143, 183-84

Saint-Victor-la-Rivière (Puy-de-Dôme), *see* Nancy, Private Collection VI

Saugues (Haute-Loire), 16, 139, 175-76, Reg. 45, Fig. 112; as a type, 142, 175-80

Saulzet-le-Froid (Puy-de-Dôme), 206

Saumur (Maine-et-Loire), 151, 202, Reg. 108, Fig. 189

Schillingskapellen, *see* Frankfurt-am-Main, Liebieghaus

Seat of Wisdom, *see* Throne of Wisdom

Second Nicene Council, *see* Council, Oecumenical, Seventh

sedes sapientiae, 1, 24n57, 26 and *passim. See also* Throne of Wisdom (Seat of Wisdom); Madonna in Majesty

Senlis: portal sculpture, 148-49, 197-200, Fig. 182; style, 149-52, 190, 197-200. *See also* Cambridge, Mass., Fogg Museum of Art

sheathing, *see* lead sheathing; metal sheathing; repoussé technique

Soissons (Aisne), 203, Reg. 109, Fig. 190

Solomon, Duke: statue of, 74-76, 80, 85; crucifix given to Saint-Sauveur, 73

Solomon, King: as archetype of the wise ruler (a "New Solomon"), 89-90; as prefigure of Christ, 27. *See also* Throne of Solomon; Mary as the Throne of Solomon

Song of Songs, 20, 23n55

Souvigny (Allier), 144, 186, Reg. 81, Fig. 146

Spain, statues in, 143nn10-11, 208

Speculum humanae salvationis, 27

statua, 1n1

Stephen II, Bishop of Clermont-Ferrand and Abbot of Conques, 31, 78, 90, 95-99. *See also* Clermont-Ferrand

stone sculptures with Throne of Wisdom iconography, 26, 29n72, 132, 153-54, Figs. 1, 2

Sweden, statues in, 208

Switzerland, statues in, 208

Synod, *see* Arras; Frankfurt; Paris; Rodez. *See also* Council

Taralon, J., study of Conques, St. Foy, 68-69, 81

Targasonne (Pyrénées-Orientales), 184, Reg. 74, Fig. 141

Tanchelm, heretic, 45

Theodoric, equestrian statue of, 73-74

Theodulph of Orleans, 72-73; *Ad Judices*, 73; possible authorship of *Libri Carolini*, 72n60. *See also Libri Carolini*

Theophanu Book Cover, *see* Essen

Theophilus, *De Diversis Artibus*, 12-13, 19n38

Theotokos, 2, 24

Thiers (Puy-de-Dôme), Private Collection, 166, Reg. 26, Fig. 86

Thiofrid, Abbot of Echternach, 12n13

Thoisy-le-Désert (Côte-d'Or), 151n40, 190-91, Reg. 90, Fig. 163

Three Kings play, *see* Epiphany play

throne, 86-90. *See also* Mary as the throne of God

Throne of Solomon: Mary as, 24-30, 59; secular meaning of, 89-90; later iconographic development, 26n64

Throne of Wisdom (Seat of Wisdom), 1n1; crown, 22; iconography, 22-30; international phenomenon, 4; function, 44-45, 60; origins, 6, 61-91; significance, 155 and *passim*

Thuir (Pyrénées-Orientales), 179-80, Reg. 57, Fig. 124

Toulouse, procession, 43-44

Tournus, Notre-Dame-la-Brune, 15-16, 44, 45n48, 51, 138-39, 167-68, Reg. 30, Figs. 6, 89; as a type, 15-16, 138-41, 170-74

Tourzel-Ronzières (Puy-de-Dôme), 174-75, Reg. 41, Fig. 107

transcendental function of art, 61, 84. *See also* images, transcendental role of

trope, 53n72, 54

Turlande (Cantal), 206

1200, as a terminal date, 4

tympana with representations of the Throne of Wisdom, 29, 153-54

Ulrich of Augsburg, *see Palmesel*

Utrecht, statue of the Virgin, 45, 102

Vabres, statue of St. Marius, 79

Valempoulières (Jura), 206

Vassivière, processions, 44n44

veneratio, 72n55

Venice, San Marco, *sedia*, 87-88, 90, Fig. 21

Venus, 46-47, 63, 73

Verdun: Adam Master, 147, 151n38, 193; Nicholas of, *see* Nicholas

Vergheas (Puy-de-Dôme), 174, Reg. 40, Fig. 106

Vernols (Cantal), *see* Clermont-Ferrand, Musée Bargoin II

Vernouillet (Allier), Musée Communal de Bourbon l'Archambault, 186, Reg. 180, Fig. 145

Vézelay, reliquary statue of the Virgin and Child, 2n1, 32-35, 39, 102, 188; date of, 35-36; devotion to, 48; immunity to fire, 33, 35; relics within, 34, 35; textual source for, 33-34, 32n7

Vic (Moselle), 193-94, Reg. 97, Fig. 170

Vierge miraculeuse, 9n2, 103, 167, 179, 185, 189, 194, and *passim*

Vierge noire, 20-22, 160, 172-73, 183-85, 189, 203

Vierge reliquaire, 6, 31, 37, 38

Vievy (Côte-d'Or), 190, Reg. 89, Fig. 162

Virgin, *see* Mary; *sedes sapientiae*; Throne of Wisdom; Madonna in Majesty; *Vierge*; *Virgo*

Virgo paritura, *see* Chartres Cathedral, legend

Visitatio, *see Quem quaeritis*

Walcourt, Notre-Dame de Walcourt, 15, 48, 129-30, Figs. 50, 51

walnut, 16-18

Washington, Private Collection, 164, Reg. 20, Fig. 80

Wessex, King Ine, statues for, 70, 100

William of Malmesbury, 46

wood, 9, 16; prevention of cracking, 16-18; techniques in working, 16-19

Worcester, Mass., Worcester Art Museum, 191, Reg. 92, Fig. 164

Yale University Gallery of Art, *see* New Haven, Conn.

Young, K., study of liturgical drama, 53, 58

Zurich, Private Collection, 165, Reg. 22, Fig. 82; Kunsthaus, 178, Reg. 53, Fig. 120

ILLUSTRATIONS

1. Arezzo, Sta Maria della Pieve, Adoration of the Magi
2. Beaucaire (Gard), Museum, Madonna enthroned as the Throne of Wisdom

3. Clermont-Ferrand (Puy-de-Dôme), Bibl. Municipale, MS 145, fol. 130v, Golden Majesty of Clermont-Ferrand
4. Antwerp, Plantin-Moretus Museum, M.17.4, fol. 15v, Adoration of the Magi

5

6

7

8

5. Clermont-Ferrand (Puy-de-Dôme), Notre-Dame-du-Port, south portal, lintel, Adoration of the Magi
6. Tournus (Saône-et-Loire). Saint-Philibert, *Notre-Dame la Brune* from Saint-Pourçain-sur-Sioule (Allier), Reg. 30

7. Pompierre (Vosges), tympanum, Adoration of the Magi
8. Mont-devant-Sassey (Meuse), Madonna (before restoration), Reg. 96

9

11

12

10

9. Frankfurt-am-Main, Liebieghaus, Madonna from Schillingskapellen
10. Oberpleis, Adoration of the Magi, retable

11. Bernard (Vendée), mother goddess
12. Saint-Germain-en-Laye, Musée des Antiquités Nationales, cast after a lost original from Prunay-le-Gillon (Eure-et-Loir), mother and child

14

13

15

13. Conques (Aveyron), St. Foy
14. Conques (Aveyron), St. Foy, detail of the head
15. Conques (Aveyron), St. Foy, detail

16

17

18

19

16. Le Monastier (Haute-Loire), St. Chaffre
17. Le Monastier (Haute-Loire), St. Chaffre with metal sheath removed
18. Paris, Bibl. Nationale, MS lat. 17558, fol. 28r, drawing by Peiresc of the reliquary head of St. Maurice, 879-887

19. Paris, Bibl. Nationale, MS lat. 17558, fol. 28v, draw-
ing by Peiresc of the reliquary head of St. Maurice, 879-887, with the crown of Hugh of Arles, 926-947

20

21

22

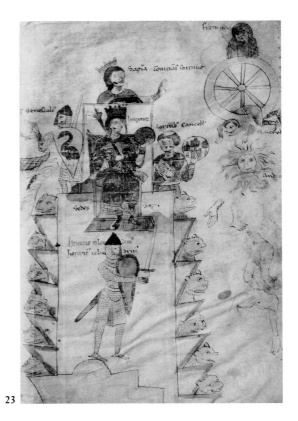

23

20. Paris, Bibl. Nationale, MS gr. 510, fol. 355, *Homilies of Gregory Nazianzus*, 867-886, the Emperor and dignitaries before the throne
21. Venice, San Marco, *Sedia*

22. Aachen, Palace Chapel, Throne of Charlemagne
23. Bern, Bürgerbibliothek, Codex 120, fol. 147, Peter of Eboli, *Liber ad Honorem Augusti*, late twelfth century, Henry VI seated on the *sedes sapientiae*

24. *Notre-Dame du Puy*, engraving from B. Faujas de Saint-Fond, 1778

25. *Notre-Dame de Chartres*, drawing by Chanoine Etienne in 1682

26. *Notre-Dame de Chartres*, seventeenth-century engraving by Leroux

27. *Notre-Dame de Chartres* carried on a litter, engraving of a pilgrim's badge or *signum*

28. Essen, Minster, Golden Madonna

29. Essen, Minster, Golden Madonna

31

30

32

30, 31. Essen, Minster, Golden Madonna
32. Essen, Minster, Golden Madonna, detail of the
underside of the throne

33

34

35

36

33. Essen, Minster Treasury, detail of the First Mathilda Cross, 974-982
34. Cologne, Cathedral, Gero Cross

35. Dublin, Trinity College, *Book of Kells*, Madonna
and Child
36. Essen, Minster Treasury, Theophanu Book Cover,
ca. 1039-1056, detail of the Madonna enthroned

37

38

37, 38. Hildesheim, Cathedral Treasury, Golden Madonna with gold sheath removed

40

41

39. Hildesheim, Cathedral Treasury, Golden Madonna with gold sheath removed; back view showing removable panel

40, 41. Hildesheim, Cathedral Treasury, fragments of the gold sheath of the Madonna

42

44

43

42. Hildesheim, Bronze Doors of Bernward, 1015, detail of the Madonna from the Adoration of the Magi
43. Mainz, Altertumsmuseum, Ivory Madonna
44. Paderborn, Diözesan Museum, Imad Madonna, 1051-1076, the back before recent restoration

45, 46. Paderborn, Diözesan Museum, Imad Madonna, 1051-1076

47a

47b

48

49

47a,b. Essen-Werden, Abbey Church, stone reliefs with
enthroned figures

48. Cologne, Schnütgen Museum, Madonna
49. Frankfurt-am-Main, Liebieghaus, Madonna

50

51

52

53

50, 51. Walcourt, Saint-Materne, *Notre-Dame de Wal-court*

52. Brussels, Musées Royaux d'Art et d'Histoire, Ma-donna from Hermalle-sous-Huy
53. Liège, Musée Diocésain, Madonna from Evegnée

54. New York, Metropolitan Museum of Art, Morgan
Madonna (Gift of J. Pierpont Morgan, 1916), Reg. 1

55. New York, Metropolitan Museum of Art, Morgan
Madonna (Gift of J. Pierpont Morgan, 1916), Reg. 1

56

57

56. New York, Metropolitan Museum of Art, Morgan
Madonna (Gift of J. Pierpont Morgan, 1916), detail of
the head, Reg. 1

57. Moussages (Cantal), Saint-Barthélémy, *Notre-
Dame de Claviers*, detail of the head, Reg. 2

58

59

58, 59. Moussages (Cantal), Saint-Barthélémy, *Notre-
Dame de Claviers*, Reg. 2

60. Private Collection, *Notre-Dame de Montvianeix*,
Reg. 3

62

61

63

61, 63. Private Collection, *Notre-Dame de Montvianeix*, Reg. 3

62. Private Collection, *Notre-Dame de Montvianeix*, detail of the head, Reg. 3

64a

64b

65

66

64. Heume l'Eglise (Puy-de-Dôme), Reg. 4:
a. before restoration; b. after restoration
65. Aubusson (Puy-de-Dôme), *Notre-Dame d'Aubusson*, Reg. 5
66. Parentignat (Puy-de-Dôme), Château de Lastic, Reg. 6

69

70

67. Molompize (Cantal), Vauclair Chapel, *Notre-Dame de Vauclair*, Reg. 7

68. Cologne, Burg Collection (formerly), Reg. 8

69. Saint-Gervazy (Puy-de-Dôme), *Notre-Dame de Saint-Gervazy*, Reg. 9

70. Nancy (Meurthe-et-Moselle), Private Collection I, Reg. 10

71

72

73

74

71. Geneva, Musée d'Art et d'Histoire, Reg. 11

72. Rouen (Seine-Maritime), Musée Départemental des Antiquités de la Seine-Maritime, Reg. 12

73. Rochelambert (Haute-Loire), Château, Reg. 13

74. Paris, Musée de Cluny, Reg. 14

75

76

77

78

75. Saint-Nectaire (Puy-de-Dôme), *Notre-Dame du Mont-Cornadore*, Reg. 15

76. Saint-Rémy-de-Chargnat (Puy-de-Dôme), *Notre-Dame de Saint-Rémy*, before restoration, Reg. 16

77. Saint-Laurent-Chabreuges (Haute-Loire), Entremont Chapel, *Notre-Dame d'Entremont*, Reg. 17

78. Chanaleilles (Haute-Loire), *Notre-Dame du Villeret d'Apchier*, Reg. 18

79

80

81

79. Mailhat, near Lamontgie (Puy-de-Dôme), *Notre-Dame de Mailhat*, Reg. 19

80. Washington, D.C., Collection of Mr. and Mrs. Robert Sargent Shriver, Jr., Reg. 20

81. Geneva, Giraud Collection, Reg. 21

82

83

84

82. Zurich, Bührle Collection, Reg. 22
83. Durham, North Carolina, Duke University Museum, Reg. 23

84. Raleigh, The North Carolina Museum of Art, Reg. 24

85

87

86

88

85. Bredons (Cantal) I, formerly in the church at Albepierre-Bredons, Reg. 25

86. Thiers (Puy-de-Dôme), Private Collection, *Notre-Dame de Montpeyroux*, Reg. 26

87. Chauriat (Puy-de-Dôme), Reg. 27

88. Echlache (Puy-de-Dôme), Reg. 29

89. Tournus (Saône-et-Loire), Saint-Philibert, *Notre-
Dame la Brune* from Saint-Pourçain-sur-Sioule (Allier),
Reg. 30

90

91

90, 91. Orcival (Puy-de-Dôme), *Notre-Dame d'Orcival*, Reg. 31

92

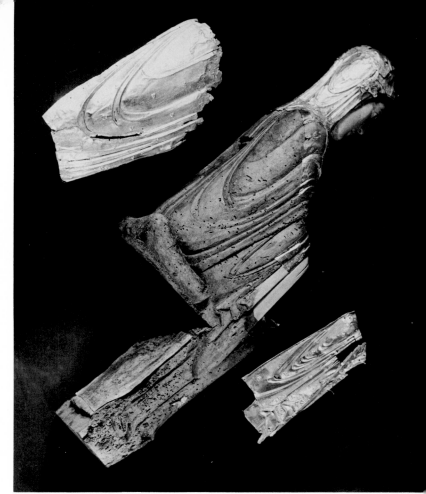

93

92, 93. Orcival (Puy-de-Dôme), *Notre-Dame d'Orcival* during restoration, with metal sheath removed, Reg. 31

94. Orcival (Puy-de-Dôme), *Notre-Dame d'Orcival*, detail, Reg. 31

94

95

95. New York, Metropolitan Museum of Art, loaned by Mr. and Mrs. A. B. Martin (Guennol Collection), Reg. 32

96

96. New York, Metropolitan Museum of Art, loaned by Mr. and Mrs. A. B. Martin (Guennol Collection), detail of the head, Reg. 32

97a

97b

97a,b. Lyon (Rhône), Musée des Beaux-Arts, *Notre-Dame de Saint-Flour*, Reg. 33

98. Paris, Louvre, Reg. 34

99

100

99, 100. Paris, Louvre, Reg. 34

101

102

103

101. Marsat (Puy-de-Dôme), *Notre-Dame de Marsat*, Reg. 35

102. Chalus-Lembron (Puy-de-Dôme), Reg. 36

103. Clermont-Ferrand (Puy-de-Dôme), Musée Bargoin I, Reg. 37

104

105

106

107

108

109

104. New York, Metropolitan Museum of Art (Bequest of Michael Dreicer, 1921), Reg. 38

105. Chassignoles (Haute-Loire), *Notre-Dame de Chassignoles*, Reg. 39

106. Vergheas (Puy-de-Dôme), *Notre-Dame de l'Assomption*, Reg. 40

107. Tourzel-Ronzières (Puy-de-Dôme), *Notre-Dame de Ronzières*, Reg. 41

108. Nancy (Meurthe-et-Moselle), Private Collection II, *Sainte-Marie de Verdun*, Reg. 43

109. Mailhat near Lamontgie (Puy-de-Dôme), Private Collection, *Notre-Dame de Mailhat*, Reg. 44

110

111

112

110. Clermont-Ferrand (Puy-de-Dôme), Notre-Dame-du-Port, south portal, lintel, detail of the Madonna from the Adoration of the Magi

111. Espalion-Perse (Aveyron), Madonna, stone relief
112. Saugues (Haute-Loire), *Notre-Dame de Saugues*, Reg. 45

114

115

113. Monistrol d'Allier (Haute-Loire), Champels Chapel, *Notre-Dame d'Estours*, Reg. 46
114. Monistrol d'Allier (Haute-Loire), Champels Chapel, *Notre-Dame d'Estours*, detail of the head before restoration, Reg. 46
115. La Chomette (Haute-Loire), Reg. 47

116

117

118

119

120

121

116. Bredons (Cantal) II, from Albepierre-Bredons, Reg. 49

117. Cologne, Seligmann Collection (formerly), Reg. 50

118. Clermont-Ferrand (Puy-de-Dôme), Musée Bargoin II, *Notre-Dame de Vernols*, Reg. 51

119. Rome, Private Collection, Reg. 52

120. Zurich, Kunsthaus, Reg. 53

121. Paris, Musée des Arts Décoratifs, Reg. 54

122. Laurie (Cantal), *Notre-Dame de Laurie*, Reg. 55
123. Philadelphia, Museum of Art I, Reg. 56

124

125

126

124. Thuir (Pyrénées-Orientales), *Notre-Dame-de-la Victoire*, Reg. 57
125. Châteauneuf-les-Bains (Puy-de-Dôme), Reg. 58
126. Prunières (Lozère), Reg. 59

128

127

129

127. Corneilla-de-Conflent (Pyrénées-Orientales),
Reg. 60
128. Odeillo (Pyrénées-Orientales), *Notre-Dame de
Font-Romeu*, Reg. 61
129. Err (Pyrénées-Orientales), Reg. 62

130

131

132

133

130. Prats-Balaguer (Pyrénées-Orientales), Reg. 63
131. Montbolo (Pyrénées-Orientales), Reg. 64

132. Planès (Pyrénées-Orientales), *Notre-Dame de Planès*, Reg. 65
133. Cazarilh-Laspènes (Haute-Garonne), Reg. 66

134. Saint-Savin (Hautes-Pyrénées), Museum, Reg. 67

136

137

135

138

135. Saint-Savin (Hautes-Pyrénées), *La Vierge de Castère*, Reg. 68

136. Luz (Hautes-Pyrénées), Saint-Sauveur, Reg. 69

137. Aragnouet (Hautes-Pyrénées), Le Plan Chapel, *Notre-Dame d'Aragnouet*, Reg. 70

138. Hix (Pyrénées-Orientales), Bourg-Madame, *Notre-Dame de la Cerdagne*, Reg. 71

139

141

140

142

143

139. Manosque (Basses-Alpes), *Notre-Dame de Romigier*, Reg. 72

140. Dorres (Pyrénées-Orientales), Reg. 73

141. Targasonne (Pyrénées-Orientales), Reg. 74

142. Frankfurt-am-Main, Private Collection (formerly), Reg. 77

143. Rocamadour (Lot), *Notre-Dame de Rocamadour*, Reg. 78

144

146

145

147

144. Monteignet (Allier), Reg. 79
145. Vernouillet (Allier), Musée Communal de Bourbon l'Archambault, *Notre-Dame de Vernouillet,*
Reg. 80

146. Souvigny (Allier), Saint-Pierre, sacristy, Reg. 81
147. Nancy (Meurthe-et-Moselle), Private Collection
III, Reg. 82

148. Nancy (Meurthe-et-Moselle), Private Collection
IV, Reg. 83
149. Nancy (Meurthe-et-Moselle), Private Collection
V, Reg. 84

150. Nancy (Meurthe-et-Moselle), Private Collection
VI, Reg. 85
151. Meillers (Allier), Reg. 86

152

153

152, 153. New York, Metropolitan Museum of Art, The Cloisters (Purchase 1947), Reg. 87

154

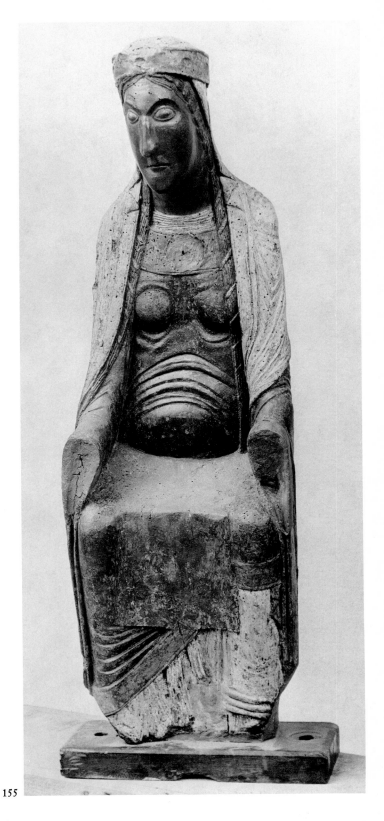

155

154. Dijon (Côte-d'Or), Notre-Dame, *Notre-Dame de Bon Espoir*, engraving after V. Petit, Reg. 88

155. Dijon (Côte-d'Or), Notre-Dame, *Notre-Dame de Bon Espoir*, Reg. 88

156
157
158

159
160
161

156, 157. Saint-Denis (Seine-Saint-Denis, formerly Seine), destroyed sculptures from west facade, drawings by B. Montfaucon
158. Etampes (Yvelines, formerly Seine-et-Oise), south portal, left embrasure, a queen

159-161. Chartres (Eure-et-Loir), Royal Portal:
159. left portal, left embrasure, Old Testament figure; 160. right portal, right embrasure, Old Testament queen; 161. central portal, left embrasure, Old Testament queen

162

163

164

165

162. Vievy (Côte-d'Or), Reg. 89
163. Thoisy-le-Désert (Côte-d'Or), Reg. 90
164. Worcester, Massachusetts, Worcester Art Museum, Reg. 92
165. Collegeville, Minnesota, St. John's Abbey, Reg. 93

168

166

167

169

166. Billy-Chevannes (Nièvre), Reg. 94

167. Nevers (Nièvre), Musée Lapidaire de la Porte du Croux, Reg. 95

168. Mont-devant-Sassey (Meuse), detail, Reg. 96

169. Mont-devant-Sassey (Meuse), Reg. 96

170

172

173

171

170. Vic (Moselle), *Notre-Dame d'Allyn*, Reg. 97
171. Jouhe (Jura), *Notre-Dame de Montroland*, Reg. 98

172. Mouziey-Teulet (Tarn), Reg. 99
173. Poitiers (Vienne), Abbey of Sainte-Croix, *Notre-Dame de Grâce*, Reg. 100

174. Beaulieu (Corrèze), Reg. 101

175

177

176

175. Beaulieu (Corrèze), detail, Reg. 101
176. Beaulieu (Corrèze), Reg. 101
177. Paris, Louvre, retable from Carrières-Saint-Denis

179

178. Cambridge, Massachusetts, Fogg Art Museum (Gift of Friends of the Fogg), Reg. 102

179. Cambridge, Massachusetts, Fogg Art Museum (Gift of Friends of the Fogg), detail of the head, Reg. 102

180

181

182

180, 181. Cambridge, Massachusetts, Fogg Art Museum
(Gift of Friends of the Fogg), Reg. 102
182. Senlis (Oise), Notre-Dame, detail of the tympanum

183

141

184

183. Jouy-en-Josas (Yvelines, formerly Seine-et-Oise),
La Diège, Reg. 103
184. Limay (Yvelines, formerly Seine-et-Oise),
Reg. 104

185

186

187

185. Saint-Denis (Seine-Saint-Denis, formerly Seine),
Notre-Dame de Saint-Denis, from Saint-Martin-des-
Champs, Paris, Reg. 105

186. Baltimore, The Walters Art Gallery, Reg. 106
187. Philadelphia, Museum of Art II, loaned by Raymond Pitcairn, Reg. 107

188a

188b

189

190

188a,b. New Haven, Connecticut, Yale University Art Gallery, stone sculpture of the Madonna and Child from the church of Saint Martin at Angers (Gift of Maitland F. Griggs)

189. Saumur (Maine-et-Loire), *Notre-Dame de Nantilly*, Reg. 108

190. Soissons (Aisne), from Presles-et-Thierry, Reg. 109